The Political Economy of Property Rights reports on comparative research into the transformation of property rights in post-communist countries and China. Two important theoretical questions unify the contributions: What aspects of political systems give credibility to systems of property rights, and what can be learned about large-scale change of economic institutions from the transformation of property rights in post-communist countries? The contributors demonstrate the usefulness of the theoretical and empirical tools of modern political economy for answering these questions. They argue that the credibility of property rights arises from the strategic interaction of political and economic actors, and they apply this perspective and test its implications, using a variety of qualitative and quantitative methods. The empirical evidence forms a basis for testing theories of institutional change. Overall, the volume demonstrates the value of coordinated cross-national research by area specialists sharing a common focus on questions of political economy.

THE POLITICAL ECONOMY OF PROPERTY RIGHTS

POLITICAL ECONOMY OF INSTITUTIONS AND DECISIONS

Editors
James E. Alt, Harvard University
Douglass C. North, Washington University of St. Louis

Other books in the series
Alberto Alesina and Howard Rosenthal, *Partisan Politics, Divided Government and the Economy*
Lee J. Alston, Thrainn Eggertsson, and Douglass C. North, *Empirical Studies in Institutional Change*
James E. Alt and Kenneth Shepsle, eds., *Perspectives on Positive Political Economy*
Jeffrey S. Banks and Eric A. Hanushek, *Modern Political Economy: Old Topics, New Directions*
Yoram Barzel, *Economic Analysis of Property Rights*, Second Edition
Robert Bates, *Beyond the Miracle of the Market: The Political Economy of Agrarian Development in Kenya*
Peter Cowhey and Mathew McCubbins, *Structure and Policy in Japan and the United States*
Gary W. Cox, *The Efficient Secret: The Cabinet and the Development of Political Parties in Victorian England*
Jean Ensminger, *Making a Market: The Institutional Transformation of an African Society*
Murray Horn, *The Political Economy of Public Administration: Institutional Choice in the Public Sector*
Jack Knight, *Institutions and Social Conflict*
Michael Laver and Kenneth Shepsle, *Cabinet Ministers and Parliamentary Government*
Michael Laver and Kenneth Shepsle, *Making and Breaking Governments*
Brian Levy and Pablo T. Spiller, *Regulations, Institutions, and Commitment*
Leif Lewin, *Ideology and Strategy: A Century of Swedish Politics (English Edition)*
Gary Libecap, *Contracting for Property Rights*
Mathew D. McCubbins and Terry Sullivan, eds., *Congress: Structure and Policy*
Gary J. Miller, *Managerial Dilemmas: The Political Economy of Hierarchy*
Douglass C. North, *Institutions, Institutional Change, and Economic Performance*
Elinor Ostrom, *Governing the Commons: The Evolution of Institutions for Collective Action*
J. Mark Ramseyer, *Odd Markets in Japanese History*
J. Mark Ramseyer and Frances Rosenbluth, *The Politics of Oligarchy: Institutional Choice in Imperial Japan*
Jean-Laurent Rosenthal, *The Fruits of Revolution: Property Rights, Litigation, and French Agriculture*
Charles Stewart III, *Budget Reform Politics: The Design of the Appropriations Process in the House of Representatives, 1865–1921*
John Waterbury, *Exposed to Innumerable Delusions: Public Enterprise and State Power in Egypt, India, Mexico, and Turkey*

THE POLITICAL ECONOMY OF PROPERTY RIGHTS

Institutional change and credibility in the reform of centrally planned economies

Edited by

DAVID L. WEIMER

University of Rochester

 CAMBRIDGE
UNIVERSITY PRESS

PUBLISHED BY THE PRESS SYNDICATE OF THE UNIVERSITY OF CAMBRIDGE
The Pitt Building, Trumpington Street, Cambridge CB2 1RP, United Kingdom

CAMBRIDGE UNIVERSITY PRESS
The Edinburgh Building, Cambridge CB2 2RU, United Kingdom
40 West 20th Street, New York, NY 10011-4211, USA
10 Stamford Road, Oakleigh, Melbourne 3166, Australia

First published 1997

Printed in the United States of America

Typeset in Sabon

A catalog record for this book is available from the British Library.

Library of Congress Cataloging-in-Publication Data
The political economy of property rights : institutional change and
credibility in the reform of centrally planned economies / edited by
David L. Weimer.
    p. cm. – (Political economy of institutions and decisions)
Includes indexes.
ISBN 0-521-58101-X (hardback)
1. Property and socialism. 2. Right of property – Communist
countries. 3. Post-communism. I. Weimer, David Leo.
        HX550.P7P67 1997
    333.3'0947 – dc20   96-36258
                                      CIP

ISBN 0-521-58101-X hardback

In memory of William H. Riker –
teacher, scholar, colleague, friend

Contents

List of figures and tables   page ix
List of contributors   xi
Series editors' preface   xiii
Preface   xv

1 The political economy of property rights   1
   David L. Weimer
2 Credible commitment and property rights: The role of
   strategic interaction between political and economic actors   20
   Daniel Diermeier, Joel M. Ericson, Timothy Frye, and Steven
   Lewis
   The political commitment to markets and marketization   43
   Barry R. Weingast
3 Political determinants of the success of economic transition   50
   Nikolai Mikhailov
   Comment on "Political Determinants of the Success of
   Economic Transition"   80
   Adam Przeworski
4 Russian privatization and the limits of credible commitment   84
   Timothy Frye
   Three issues of credible commitment and Russian
   privatization   109
   John M. Litwack
5 Legislative politics and the political economy of property
   rights in post-communist Russia   113
   Brendan Kiernan and Francis X. Bell
   Commitment, coordination, and the demise of the
   post-communist parliament in Russia   139
   Steven S. Smith

Contents

6   Private firms, city government, and arbitration: Enforcing
economic legality in St. Petersburg   150
Joel M. Ericson
Comment on "Private Firms, City Government, and
Arbitration"   179
Anthony Jones

7   Property rights and institutional change in the Czech and
Slovak republics   182
Mariusz Mark Dobek
Comment on "Property Rights and Institutional Change in
the Czech and Slovak Republics"   205
Sharon Wolchik

8   Institutional structures, labor interests, and evolving
privatization bargains in Poland   208
Lorene Allio
Comment on "Institutional Structures, Labor Interests, and
Evolving Privatization Bargains in Poland"   232
Bartlomiej Kaminski

9   Privatization as institutional change in Hungary   239
László Urbán
Comment on "Privatization as Institutional Change in
Hungary"   256
Kálmán Mizsei

10 Marketization and government credibility in Shanghai:
Federalist and local corporatist explanations   259
Steven Lewis
Federalist and local corporatist theories: A comment on an
empirical test   288
Victor Nee

11 Learning about the economy: Property rights and the
collapse of the East German industrial economy   294
Hannes Wittig
Misinformation, insecure property rights, and the collapse of
the East German economy   314
Susanne Lohmann

12 Post-communist privatization as a test of theories of
institutional change   319
*Lorene Allio, Mariusz Mark Dobek, Nikolai Mikhailov, and
David L. Weimer*
Explaining the complexity of institutional change   349
Jack Knight and Douglass C. North

Indexes   355

Figures and tables

FIGURES

Figure 4.1: Voucher prices   *page* 98
Figure 10.1: Shanghai counties, 1992   272

TABLES

Table 2.1: Sequence of actions in one-play investment game   29
Table 3.1: Electoral systems and governments in six former
    communist countries   64
Table 3.2: Explaining the economic performance of post-
    communist countries in 1993   72
Table 3.3: Explaining the predictions of economic growth in
    1994 and 1995   75
Table 3.4: Explaining the economic performance of post-
    communist countries in 1994   77
Table 4.1: Political events and voucher prices   99
Table 5.1: Logit analysis of probability of supporting the creation
    of the presidency   129
Table 5.2: First difference effects of probability of supporting the
    creation of the presidency   130
Table 5.3: Logit analysis of probability of accepting as basis of
    discussion economic reform proposed by Boris Yeltsin   133
Table 6.1: The changing composition of City Arbitration Court
    cases, 1990 to 1993   159
Table 8.1: Strike activity in Poland, 1989 to 1993   215
Table 8.2: Cumulative privatizations via Articles 19, 37, and 5   220
Table 8.3: Liquidation via Article 37: Local versus state as
    founding body, 1990 to 1993   227
Table 10.1: Investment, industrialization, decentralization, and

enterprise competitiveness across suburban counties and
districts of Shanghai Municipality, 1992 — 274
Table 10.2: Foreign investment in Shanghai: Percent of total new
operating enterprises by type of fiscal jurisdiction, 1988–93 — 278
Table 11.1: Chronology of German unification — 307
Table (11c)1: No investment under insecure property rights — 315
Table (11c)2: Some investment possible under insecure property
rights — 316
Table 12.1: Competing theories of institutional change — 321
Table 12.2: Post-communist privatization and theories of
institutional change — 345

Contributors

Lorene Allio, Emory University
Francis X. Bell, University of Rochester
Daniel Diermeier, Stanford University
Mariusz Mark Dobek, Benedictine College
Joel M. Ericson, University of Toronto
Timothy Frye, Columbia University
Anthony Jones, Northeastern University
Bartlomiej Kaminski, University of Maryland
Brendan Kiernan, Monitor Company
Jack Knight, Washington University of St. Louis
Steven Lewis, Washington University of St. Louis
John M. Litwack, Stanford University
Susanne Lohmann, University of California at Los Angeles
Nikolai Mikhailov, University of Rochester
Kálmán Mizsei, Institute for EastWest Studies
Victor Nee, Cornell University
Douglass C. North, Washington University of St. Louis
Adam Przeworski, New York University
Steven S. Smith, University of Minnesota
László Urbán, Budapest University
David L. Weimer, University of Rochester
Barry R. Weingast, Stanford University
Hannes Wittig, McKinsey and Company
Sharon Wolchik, George Washington University

Series editors' preface

The Cambridge Series on the Political Economy of Institutions and Decisions is built around attempts to answer two central questions: How do institutions evolve in response to individual incentives, strategies, and choices? and How do institutions affect the performance of political and economic systems? The scope of the series is comparative and historical rather than international or specifically American, and the focus is positive rather than normative.

The political and economic transformations under way in Eastern Europe, the former Soviet Union, and China provide an ideal "laboratory" for studying change in the institution of property rights. The authors in this volume both extend the theory of the political economy of property rights and apply that theory to analysis of the transformations going on in these transition economies.

This study is the result of a unique experiment by the late Bill Riker (to whom the volume is dedicated) and the editor to assemble a group of political scientists with country specializations, expose them to the methods and theories of political economy, and then engage them in a coordinated field-research project studying questions relevant to understanding the evolution of property rights. Specifically, the authors focus on political and economic factors determining the credibility of the newly created rights to private property and the path of transformation from state ownership to other forms of property holding.

Preface

In the summer of 1990, William H. Riker and I began having conversations about the dramatic political liberalization taking place in Eastern Europe. The emerging political leaders of post-communist countries were professing a desire to accompany political reforms with transformations from socialist to market economies. Our discussions soon focused on the role of property rights in these transformations. We shared several beliefs: Property systems fundamentally affect economic performance; the effectiveness of market economies in achieving economic growth depends on extensive private ownership of the means of production; and private property generally contributes to maintenance of liberal political regimes, directly by creating a basis for opposition to governments and indirectly by contributing to the effectiveness of market economies. But we also had scholarly interests in property rights arising out of our prior research. Riker's arose most immediately from his research on the evolution of property rights to airport landing slots. Mine arose out of my research on U.S. petroleum regulation during the 1970s, which reduced the credibility of property rights in oil markets. It seemed to us that the events unfolding in Eastern Europe, the former Soviet Union, and even China provided an extraordinary "natural experiment" for comparative study on a grand scale of the political economy of property rights.

Yet we feared that compartmentalization of the social sciences might prevent this wonderful research opportunity from being fully exploited. While economists tend to dominate the theoretical side of political economy, they rarely invest in the detailed institutional knowledge that would be necessary to understand deeply the evolution of property rights. Country specialists in political science have exactly the knowledge of language, culture, history, and political institutions that allows them to observe the transformation closely, but they too often earn these capabilities at the expense of more general training in social science methods and theory. Further, investment in acquiring detailed contextual knowledge of one country or a few countries tends to isolate country specialists from one another so that, in the absence of common theoretical questions, empirical work tends not to cumulate comparatively. (Indeed, we quickly discovered what in our naïveté struck us as a surprisingly strong separation between Eastern European and Soviet specialists.)

We decided that we would make our contribution to the scholarly exploitation of the natural experiment by organizing the Comparative Property Rights Project. We would assemble political scientists with country specializations, expose them to the methods and theories of political economy, help them coordinate their empirical research around questions relevant to understanding the evolution of property rights, facilitate their field research, and prepare a volume in which to present their findings. Fortunately, a private foundation saw merit in our proposal and gave us a grant of sufficient size to begin the project. The newly created W. Allen Wallis Institute of Political Economy at the University of Rochester adopted the project as its own and added to our coffers.

In 1991 we began recruiting fellows for the program. We were pleased and reassured to receive applications from more than fifty qualified country specialists. From this field we enlisted four predoctoral fellows, three postdoctoral fellows, and a legal fellow. These fellows, joined by several Rochester graduate students in political science, two precocious undergraduates, and a visiting lawyer from Germany, spent the fall 1992 semester with us in a preparatory seminar. We provided exposure to neoclassical and neoinstitutional economics, especially as applied to property rights; social choice theory, especially as applied to constitutions; and game theory, especially as a basis for the theory of institutions. The fellows took the lead in providing the seminar participants with background on the political transformations in their countries of specialization: Czechoslovakia, China, Hungary, Poland, and Russia.

During the first few months of 1993 we collectively struggled with how to coordinate the fellows' field research. Our initial concern that the economic transformations would not be well documented was allayed by the systematic comparisons of privatization then being assembled by Roman Frydman, Andrzej Rapaczynski, and John S. Earle in a series of books that have since been published by the Central European University Press. So we felt free to move on to more general questions: What political and economic factors determine the credibility of the newly created formal rights to private property? What political and economic factors determine the path of transformation from state ownership to other forms of property holding? The first question derives from one of the most fundamental questions in political economy: How can governments powerful enough to establish rules convince economic actors that they will not arbitrarily change them? The second question falls within the larger debate over the nature of institutional change. These questions, along with a substantive focus on property rights, serve to unify the contributions to this volume.

Shortly after the fellows left to do their field research in the spring of 1993, Bill Riker entered the hospital to be treated for cancer. His death at the end of June was a great blow to me, the fellows, and my colleagues at the University of Rochester. Though not young in years, Bill possessed enormous intellect and energy. As all of us can attest, he had great intellectual enthusiasm that was contagious among those around him.

Bill's death was an especially great personal loss to me. Our association began in his political strategy course when I was an undergraduate. When I returned to Rochester to join the faculty, I found that he had very much more to teach me. He became my mentor and my friend. I miss him very much.

The Comparative Property Rights Project has undoubtedly suffered from his absence. Although I have done my best to bring the project to a successful conclusion, I am certain that Bill's participation in the last stages would have made the final product better.

Many people besides the authors and discussants have contributed to the project. In his capacity as director of the Wallis Institute for Political Economy, Eric Hanushek provided the project with its institutional home. Valerie Bunce, G. Bingham Powell, Jack Knight, John Mueller, and Jeff Burds visited seminars to share their insights, and Randall Calvert, Jeffrey Banks, and Melanie Manion provided valuable insights at various stages of the project. James Alt offered valuable advice on several points. Tamas Fellegi and Lydmilla Kareva, though prevented by circumstance from contributing to the volume, were full members of the project who enriched the seminars, as did Thomas M. Kruessman during his stay. Nikolai Mikhailov, an exceptionally capable and diligent research assistant throughout the project, became an important contributor to this volume. Roger James also did an excellent job as a research assistant. Pamm Ferguson cheerfully took on the extra administrative burden involved in the project and carried it expertly. I thank, in addition to these specific individuals, colleagues in the Political Science Department at the University of Rochester and elsewhere for many informal discussions that enriched the project. I would also like to thank the Faculty of Social Sciences at Lingnan College, Hong Kong, for encouragement and logistical support during preparation of this volume.

1

The political economy of property rights

DAVID L. WEIMER

1.0 INTRODUCTION

Property rights, the relations among people concerning the use of things, lie at the nexus of economics and politics. Property rights systems, which include the rights themselves and the formal and informal institutions that create them, structure economic transactions, including decisions concerning the exchange and accumulation of physical, human, and intellectual capital, and the preservation of natural resources. The state, as maker and enforcer of formal rules, plays a fundamental role in shaping the property rights system. Yet more subtle forces are also at work. Economic change, such as the availability of new technology or major shifts in the relative prices of commodities and assets, often creates pressures for changes in property rights. The property rights system may affect political stability through its impacts on the creation and distribution of wealth. These more or less obvious connections suggest that understanding the institution of property rights is an extremely important project for political economists.

The political and economic transformations under way in the countries of Eastern Europe, the former Soviet Union, and China provide a unique "natural experiment" for studying change in the institution of property rights. More than a score of countries are attempting to move from centrally planned economic systems with extensive state ownership of the means of production to much more decentralized market economies. With the exceptions of perhaps China and the former Yugoslavia, previous attempts by centrally planned economies to achieve substantial economic decentralization largely failed, leading some experienced observers to identify changing the property rights system as an essential element of meaningful reform (Schroeder, 1988; Solinger, 1989; Kornai, 1990; Batt, 1991; Comisso, 1991).

The efforts currently under way, however, are taking place in very differ-

1

ent political circumstances. All these countries except China have abandoned political systems in which communist parties forcibly maintain their "leading role" and have begun to establish democratic institutions. This simultaneous political transformation opens the door for substantial change in economic institutions, though it also complicates the task political economists face in sorting out the various interrelationships among changes in political and economic institutions. Thus it becomes all the more important for political economists to focus initially on a fundamental yet distinctly identifiable institution like property rights.

In this chapter I present a conceptual framework for thinking about the political economy of property rights. First, I consider property rights as an institution, reviewing the theoretical and empirical evidence concerning the system of property rights as an exogenous variable affecting economic and political performance. Second, I consider the emergence of new property rights systems as institutional change. This sets the stage for the chapters presented in this volume, which largely treat the system of property rights as endogenously determined by the interaction of political and economic actors. Finally, I provide a brief overview of the subsequent chapters, indicating how they fit within this framework.

2.0 PROPERTY RIGHTS AS INSTITUTIONS

Institutions are relatively stable sets of widely shared and generally realized expectations about how people will behave in particular social, economic, and political circumstances. Expectations structure behavior by informing individuals about the likely consequences of alternative courses of action. Formal institutions embody expectations in rules sanctioned by the state. Informal institutions embody them in the norms and conventions of various communities. Whereas formal institutions are maintained to some extent by centralized enforcement, informal institutions are maintained by decentralized enforcement alone.

Several aspects of this descriptive definition are worth noting. First, it distinguishes between institutions and organizations (North, 1990; Knight, 1992). Organizations are collective actors, perhaps with their own institutions of internal governance, that make choices subject to broader institutional constraints. The distinction has relevance to theories of institutional change that focus on the role of organized interests as agents of change (Olson, 1982; Knight, 1992; North, 1993). It is important in the chapters in this volume that consider the politics of privatization of state-owned enterprises.

Second, the definition leaves open the question of why the expectations are relatively stable: Why do people conform to the expectations? An emerging rational choice theory of institutions addresses this question directly (Schotter, 1981; Calvert, 1995). It defines an institution as an equilibrium strategy in a repeated game that represents some recurrent social interaction. As such, it avoids recourse to exogenous enforcement as an explanation for why people conform to expectations. It thus provides a useful framework for thinking about constitutional choices that must be enforced endogenously.

Third, laws do not always define institutions. For laws to be defining, people must expect that they will be followed. For example, one may legally own a bicycle left unprotected on a busy street. Yet if one has no expectation that the ownership will be respected by others, the legal ownership is not an institution. An institutional analysis of property rights must go beyond the law itself to the expectations that it engenders.

2.1 Definition of property rights

Property rights are relations among people concerning the use of things (Furubotn and Pejovich, 1972). They specify relations among those who have various rights and those who have duties to honor the rights, as well as the mechanisms that are available for inducing the compliance of duty bearers.

The rights themselves may take complex forms (Barzel, 1989). Consider, for instance, a house on a city lot. The owner of this asset has a right to live in it, but zoning laws may deny her the right to use it to house a business. She may have the right to sell it, but civil rights laws may deny her the right to close the sale to protected classes of people. She may have the right to the income stream generated from renting the house, but she may not have the right to rent it to three or more unrelated adults.

The rights to the ownership of organizations are typically even more complex. For example, a stockholder in a corporation may have the right to a share of its assets and the income it generates, but not the right to interfere with the use of the assets by the chief executive officer without the consent of the owners of a majority of shares. The feasibility and desirability of various distributions of rights in and among organizations depend on the institutions of corporate, contract, bankruptcy, tort, and property law.

When legal institutions are weak or incomplete, property rights are informal. For example, in Peru those wishing to establish housing on state land organize "invasions" to establish informal rights (de Soto, 1989). The invaders recognize each other's rights to the use of specific plots. Although these forms of property have no legal basis, and indeed may involve violation of laws, the government typically refrains from using force to evict the invaders. Eventually, the squatters' de facto rights may be made de jure.

3

Neoclassical economics classifies property by nominal ownership: Private property is owned by a specific individual who controls its use; common property is collectively owned by a defined set of individuals with some governance structure that determines use by individuals within the collectivity; state property is owned in the name of citizens, and its use is determined by an agent of the government; and open access property is owned by no one and available to be used by anyone who can physically gain access to it (Bromley, 1991). It is often analytically useful to classify property systems in terms of these broad categories. Nevertheless, a classification of property rights systems based on their functional characteristics provides a better basis for understanding them as institutions that shape economic behavior.

2.2 Salient characteristics of property rights systems

Four characteristics of property rights systems are especially relevant to economic behavior: clarity of allocation, cost of alienation, security from trespass, and credibility of persistence (Riker and Weimer, 1993, 1995). These characteristics affect the efficiency with which an economy uses its available assets. The credibility of persistence is also important for dynamic efficiency and political stability.

2.2.1 Clarity of allocation. Every economic system allocates rights to commodities and assets in some way. De jure allocation, while typically precise, is rarely complete. De facto patterns of use complete the allocation, sometimes superseding de jure allocations. Allocation by de facto use, however, often involves imprecision that precludes alienation and undercuts security from trespass and credibility of persistence.

Neoclassically based welfare economics assumes a clear and precise allocation of private property rights to all commodities and productive assets as a precondition for the Pareto efficiency of competitive equilibriums within a market economy. Markets fail to achieve Pareto efficiency when private property rights are not clearly defined. In the case of open access to natural resources, the so-called tragedy of the commons, inefficient overconsumption and underinvestment result. In the case of externalities, markets for certain goods, such as freedom from pollution, are missing so that inefficiency results because people do not have a mechanism for revealing their marginal valuations of the goods. The prominent neoclassical solution for correcting the inefficiency caused by externalities is the allocation of private property rights over the good to facilitate its market exchange (Coase, 1960).

Neoinstitutional economics explicitly considers specific structures of property rights and transaction costs (Eggertsson, 1990). A central concern in neoinstitutional economics is the structuring of contracts between principals and agents (Jensen and Meckling, 1976). The costs of writing, monitoring, and enforcing contracts, which depend on legal and social institutions, determine how much discretion the principal should optimally delegate to agents. The introduction of transaction costs greatly complicates welfare comparisons between alternative organizational forms (Bromley, 1989; Murrell, 1991).

Nevertheless, the use of private assets is in general more clearly allocated, and therefore more efficient, than the use of state assets because the principals designing and executing contracts delegating the use of state-owned property have weaker incentives to specialize in monitoring capabilities than do private principals (De Alessi, 1983; Lott, 1987; Vining and Weimer, 1990). A considerable empirical literature supports the assertion that private assets are more efficiently used than state assets (for reviews, see Boardman and Vining, 1989; Vining and Boardman, 1992).

The governance structure of common property determines how clearly it allocates rights to members of the collective. Elinor Ostrom (1990) identifies a number of factors that contribute to long-enduring common property resources: clearly defined borders, congruence between rules and local conditions, representative collective choice arrangements, agents with an incentive to monitor use, the graduated application of sanctions, the availability of conflict-resolution mechanisms, and the recognition of the collective by government authorities. Yet, as she notes, long endurance does not imply that the common property is being used efficiently. For example, Libecap and Johnson (1980) find that grazing on Navajo land is long-enduring but clearly inefficient. Perhaps the most striking evidence on the general inefficiency of common property resources is the dramatic increase in Chinese agricultural output after the shift in the organization of agriculture from the collective farm to the household responsibility system (Lin, 1992).

Socialist economies, with large amounts of state and common property, have less clear allocations of use rights than do market economies and therefore are likely to be less efficient (Moore, 1981; Kornai, 1990). In the post-communist countries, the weakening of the central political and economic planning institutions makes the allocations of use even less clear, providing an explanation for their immediate economic decline (Olson, 1992). Allocations are also muddied by claims against property that was previously expropriated by communist governments. More extensive de jure private ownership improves the clarity of allocation and generally leads to a more efficient use of assets.

2.2.2 Cost of alienation. Efficient responses to changes in technology, the distribution of wealth, and consumer tastes require reallocation of commodities and assets. The less costly it is to alienate property, the more effectively market forces can move commodities and assets to their highest-valued uses. The costs of alienation are likely to be high for transferring de facto use rights. Human history suggests that black markets readily develop for illicit commodities. However, such markets are less likely to develop and work effectively for long-lived and lumpy assets, like land and industrial capital, that cannot be easily broken down into small units suitable for hidden spot transactions. The costs of alienation may render de facto use rights unsuitable as collateral for loans, undercutting the development of capital markets, which in turn hinders the development of effective private markets in housing and other capital goods. Indeed, the difficulty of alienating apartments to which individuals often have strong use rights in many of the post-socialist countries also hinders the development of national labor markets by interfering with residential mobility.

Legal restrictions on the transfer of formal property rights may also impede alienation and lead to inefficiency. In the case of privatized Native American tribal lands in the United States, for instance, restrictions on alienation through both sale and bequest resulted in a fragmentation of farms (McChesney, 1990). Empirical research finds this fragmentation of holdings to be one of the major reasons for relatively low agricultural productivity on reservation lands (Anderson and Lueck, 1992).

Government policies can raise the cost of alienation in numerous ways. Several of the post-communist countries, for example, have placed restrictions on the sale of assets to foreign investors. Price controls, a lingering legacy for selected commodities in many of the post-communist countries, often raise the cost of alienation by pushing exchanges to black markets. Failure to establish and enforce effective contract law obviously raises the costs of alienating property that cannot be transferred through simple spot transactions (Frye, 1995). At the macroeconomic level, the failure to establish a stable currency raises the cost of intertemporal transfers.

In the case of common property, governance structures that are successful in making them long-enduring are also likely to pose high collective action costs for disbanding in favor of a higher valued use. For example, depending on the collective decision rule in place, it might be very costly to get a sufficient majority of common owners of a mountain pasture to agree to sell it for use as a more economically valuable ski resort. The large number and special status of cooperatives in many socialist countries are likely to reduce economic efficiency by slowing the movement of assets to their most valued uses.

2.2.3 Security from trespass. The efficient use of assets depends on their security from trespass. Insecure rights divert resources to defensive, or even predatory, activities that reduce productivity (Baumol, 1990). Both formal and informal institutions affect security from trespass. Criminal and tort law provide varying degrees of deterrence against trespass, depending on the certainty, fairness, and speed of their administration. Security from trespass also depends on social norms regarding respect for person, property, and the rule of law. The effectiveness of these supporting institutions in providing security from trespass affects the efficiency of market exchange.

Self-protection substitutes for effective institutional support for security from trespass. Owners may take a variety of actions to protect vulnerable assets: They may "harden" them with physical security systems; they may guard them with their own vigilance or that of hired guards; they may hide them from easy observation; they may use violence as retaliation against trespassers; or they may simply shed assets that would otherwise be desirable. All these efforts divert resources from consumption and production.

Weak institutional support for security from trespass encourages opportunism by increasing the relative payoffs from illegitimate versus legitimate activity. Theft, extortion, and fraudulent contracting are not only costly in terms of the self-protection they induce, but also because they involve the diversion of the resources of the predators away from productive uses.

Post-communist countries face a number of obstacles in establishing "economic legality" (Litwack, 1991). They lack traditions of independent courts, and they generally have inadequate judicial and enforcement capabilities to achieve security from trespass through formal institutions. Networks of relationships previously developed to exploit black-market opportunities facilitate the development of criminal organizations that seek to corrupt public officials. These problems appear especially serious in the countries of the former Soviet Union, where "mafia" often extort payments from businesses.

2.2.4 Credibility of persistence. Not just currently held property rights, but also the credibility of their persistence, affect efficiency and economic growth. Uncertainty about the persistence of property rights to natural resources encourages their too rapid exploitation and discourages their preservation (Libecap and Wiggins, 1989; Johany, 1979). The greater the perceived risk of losing existing property rights, the less likely the holders of those rights will be to forgo current consumption to accumulate property, thus slowing investment that contributes importantly to economic growth.

Governments play an especially important role in the credibility of the persistence of property rights. As highly decentralized informal institutions are likely to change slowly, the greatest threat to the persistence of property rights comes from changes in government policy.

A number of economic historians have noted the importance of credible property rights, especially in terms of freedom from arbitrary seizures of property by governments, for understanding relative rates of growth in different time periods and regions (North and Thomas, 1973; North, 1981, 1990; Jones, 1981; Rosenberg and Birdzell, 1986). In addition to fostering economic growth through the accumulation of capital, secure property rights facilitate innovation in economic organization. For example, Douglass North attributes the successful economic development of Western Europe over the last five hundred years to the gradual expansion of the scope of credible commitments to support increasingly complex contracting among economic agents (North, 1993: 19).

Recent cross-sectional comparisons of economic growth rates bolster the assessments made by economic historians. In a study of sixty-eight developed and developing countries, Johan Torstensson (1994) finds a strong negative statistical relationship between the rates of growth of per capita gross domestic product and the index of risk of arbitrary governmental seizure of private property developed by Gerald W. Scully and Daniel J. Slottje (1991). In view of the sensitivity of parameter estimates to changes in specification generally found in growth models (Levine and Renelt, 1992), the robustness of the relationship found by Torstensson gives it added credence. Interestingly, the degree of state ownership of property does not have a statistically significant effect on growth rates after controlling for the risk of seizure.

In parallel work, Stephen Knack and Philip Keefer (1995) construct indexes of the security of property rights using information provided by private firms that assess country risk for investors. They find that these indexes are strong predictors of economic growth.

David A. Leblang (1994) also finds a relationship between property rights and economic growth based on a statistical study of 106 countries using the measure of economic freedom developed by Raymond Gastil and Lindsay M. Wright as a proxy for the strength of property rights. Countries with strong property rights systems appear to have growth rates almost twice those of countries with weak property rights systems. Whether a country has a democratic regime does not appear to have an effect on economic growth once its property rights system is taken into account. Indeed, the imperfect correlation between democracy and the security of property rights may help explain why there does not appear to be consistent empirical evidence that democracy contributes to economic growth (Sirowy and Inkeles, 1990; Przeworski and Limongi, 1993).

The political economy of property rights

2.3 Political implications of property rights systems

Historical experience suggests that a decentralized market system with substantial private property is a necessary, though not sufficient, condition for democracy (Lindblom, 1977: ch. 12). What explains this strong empirical relationship between effective private property rights and democracy?

One explanation is that effective private property rights contribute to economic conditions conducive to the preservation of democracy. John Helliwell (1994) finds a positive and robust effect of per capita income on democratic political freedoms. It may be that the redistributive functions of democracy are less divisive in more rapidly growing economies. Thus, by contributing to income growth, effective property rights may help preserve democracy. As there appears to be a positive relationship between wealth and the equality of its distribution (Ward, 1978), economic growth may contribute indirectly to democratic stability as well by reducing the disparity in economic interests. Further, greater equality in the distribution of wealth may result in public policies that are more conducive to economic growth (Alesina and Rodrik, 1994). Specifically with respect to property rights, Gerald Scully (1991) finds that the middle three income quintiles account for a substantially larger fraction of total income in countries with high levels of economic freedom than in those without it. Effective private property rights thus contribute to economic growth and more equal distributions of wealth, which in turn help preserve democracy by lessening the divisiveness of redistributive conflict.

A second explanation recognizes private property rights as generating wealth that can serve as a basis for opposing the concentration of power in the state. Privately held wealth can be used to purchase resources, ranging from newspapers to FAX machines to foreign contacts, that give voice to opponents of the state. It also provides an alternative to state support for social, political, and economic organizations, giving them greater independence and hence increasing their capacity for opposing the state. Thus, decentralized economic resources provide a basis for resisting the concentration of political power that may eventually undermine democratic regimes.

A third explanation for why effective private property rights are a necessary condition for democracy can be found in social choice theory. No social choice rule satisfying minimal conditions of fairness can guarantee a transitive social ordering of alternatives (Arrow, 1963). In the case of unrestricted majority rule voting over alternatives with multiple dimensions, for example, "chaos" results in the sense that, in all but trivial cases

9

of preference patterns, any alternative can be defeated by some other alternative preferred by a majority (Plott, 1967; McKelvey, 1976). The instability of majority rule can be reduced by the introduction of institutional constraints that induce equilibria (Shepsle, 1979). Property rights that have some "constitutional" status in the sense that they are immune from simple majorities serve as such a constraint by reducing the dimensions of routine political choice (Riker and Weimer, 1993; Ordeshook, 1993). Credible property rights thus reduce the risks of democratic instability.

Though these explanations do not speak to the emergence of democracy, they indicate how democratic innovations of whatever origin are more likely to survive in an institutional environment that includes effective private property.

3.0 THE SYSTEM OF PROPERTY RIGHTS AS AN ENDOGENOUS VARIABLE

The preceding discussion considered the implications of particular aspects of the institution of property rights for economic performance and democratic viability. It treated property rights as an exogenous variable within the disciplinary concerns of economists and political scientists. An important task for political economists, however, is to endogenize property rights in the sense of treating them as the result of strategic interaction between economic and political actors. It is an essential task for political economists seeking to understand fundamental economic change in post-communist countries.

3.1 Transformation of property rights as institutional change

A number of theories of institutional change offer conceptual foundations for studying the transformation of property rights in post-communist countries. For our purposes, they can be grouped into three categories: economic, public choice, and distributional theories.

The economic theory sees institutional change as resulting from the realization of opportunities for changes in rules that are Pareto improving (North and Thomas, 1973). Specifically with respect to property rights, Harold Demsetz (1967) and John Umbeck (1981) see new rights emerging through the decentralized cooperation of affected parties to find rules to internalize externalities that become significant because of scarcity resulting from changes in relative prices or technologies. Gary Libecap (1989) extends the economic model by introducing a passive government that provides the framework for bargaining among affected parties. Changes are Pareto improving, but transaction costs may prevent the

10

parties from reaching agreement on rule changes that, if adopted, could be made Pareto improving through accompanying redistribution. Rules that are efficient relative to the status quo may be forgone because transaction costs make the move to the new rules Pareto inefficient. Any changes in rules actually made, however, will increase efficiency.

The public choice theory of institutional change introduces government as a strategic actor pursuing goals such as revenue maximization or electoral success through changes in formal rules (North and Thomas, 1973). The theory of the origins of property rights set out by William Riker and Itai Sened (1991) falls within the public choice theory of institutional change. In addition to the demand for the right occasioned by scarcity, they introduce a government actor who derives a benefit from granting the right. A similar perspective is taken by Fred McChesney (1990) in his study of the changing structure of the ownership of tribal lands by Native Americans. As the driving force in the public choice theory is government, it predicts that changes in property rights follow from changes in government interests.

The distributional theory sees institutional change as the by-product of conflicts among interests seeking distributional gains (Knight, 1992; North, 1993). Bargaining among interested parties establishes rules that have distributional consequences. The rules reflect asymmetries in bargaining power among the participants. Allowing for the possibility of actors using the coercive powers of government, the conflict may result in formal rules that inflict losses on those with weaker bargaining positions. Institutional change can result from a change in either the interests or the resources of the actors.

The distributional theory encompasses the other two theories. The economic theory can be thought of as a special case in which actors are guaranteed payoffs at least as large as under the status quo rules. The public choice theory is the special case in which the government enjoys the superior bargaining position. While the generality of the distributional theory makes it attractive for broadly framing changes in property rights in the post-communist countries, empirically testing it against the other theories with more precise predictions would be a useful contribution to the study of institutional change.

3.2 The problem of credibility

A strong state can use its authority to establish a property rights system characterized by clarity of allocation, low cost alienation, and security from trespass. Yet, a state strong enough to set and implement formal rules that achieve these characteristics may also be strong enough to allow the government in power to change the rules to further its own interests.

11

As economic actors rationally anticipate the possibility of such changes, the property rights system may not be credible to them.

How property rights become credible has claim to being one of the central questions of political economy (North, 1993) and public policy (Rodrik and Zeckhauser, 1988; Blackburn and Christensen, 1989; Levy and Spiller, 1994). It poses a puzzle for theorists: How can states make credible commitments to respect the property rights that they create? The substantive importance of the puzzle to economic growth is obvious.

As previously noted, a number of economic historians have pointed out the importance of credibility of property rights to economic performance (North and Thomas, 1973; North, 1981, 1990; Jones, 1981; Rosenberg and Birdzell, 1986). In recent years, historical research with an explicit focus on the puzzle of credibility has begun to appear (North and Weingast, 1989; Root, 1989). Credible commitments to property rights appear to arise through circumstance or purposeful actions that make it costly for the government to infringe upon the rights. For example, credibility may result from the separation of executive and legislative power (North and Weingast, 1989), the organization of private interests through corporatist arrangements (Root, 1989), and federalism permitting economic competition among governmental units (Weingast, 1993). One might add to the list the fiscal vulnerability of the government to its infringement of rights and informal institutions such as norms concerning the proper exercise of public authority.

Establishing credible property rights is one of the most important tasks facing post-communist governments that seek to foster effective market economies and democratic political institutions. A difficult task for any government, it is all the more difficult for them because of their legacy of institutions with low levels of economic legality and their need to alter radically their formal property rights systems. The observation of their efforts offers a fortuitous opportunity for students of political economy.

4.0 CONTRIBUTIONS TO THIS VOLUME

The chapters in this volume are attempts to further our understanding of the political economy of property rights. With one exception, they treat the property rights system as an endogenous variable to be explained by the interaction of political and economic actors. Although the authors take somewhat different approaches to their subject, all deal to some extent with institutional change or credibility.

In Chapter 2 Daniel Diermeier, Joel Ericson, Timothy Frye, and Steven Lewis lay the conceptual foundations for thinking about credibility. Using a very simple game theoretic model in which a government sets a tax rate after an investor has selected an investment level, they clearly illustrate the problem of credible commitment and suggest a number of ways that political institutions might solve the problem. They also informally sketch out comparative statics indicating the significance of the discount rate of government and the stated tax level for credibility. In his comment Barry Weingast extends the discussion by reviewing the theory of market-preserving federalism and discusses its application to Chinese economic reform.

In Chapter 3 Nikolai Mikhailov provides background on the new post-communist governments. He does not attempt to explain the radical transition from communism to more democratic regimes – perhaps Heresthetics (Riker, 1986) or the theory of "prairie fires" (Kuran, 1989) offer conceptual resources for such a challenging task. Instead, he takes the post-communist political institutions and party systems as exogenous variables for explaining progress in economic reform. In this way he provides comparative background on the post-communist governments dealt with in this volume as a by-product of testing hypotheses about the relationship between political factors and economic reform. In his comment Adam Przeworski notes some of the problems inherent in evaluating the success of pro-market reforms and offers some alternative hypotheses about the characteristics of governments that are likely to promote success.

Chapters 4, 5, and 6 deal with various aspects of the change in property rights in Russia. Timothy Frye considers the politics surrounding the privatization of industry. In particular, he shows how the mass privatization program and the formation of voucher funds made privatization the most credible component of economic reform. This is especially interesting because of the strong opposition involved. In his comment John Litwack considers the various dimensions of credibility and how voucher privatization may have contributed to each of them.

Brendan Kiernan and Francis Bell consider the politics of privatization within the Congress of People's Deputies by focusing on key votes related to the powers of the president to carry out reforms. They find that the extent of small-firm privatization in legislators' districts is an important factor in explaining their votes. They also explore the problems of communication and coordination that make it difficult for the Congress of People's Deputies to make credible commitments. In his comment Steven Smith argues for a broadening of perspective to include players outside of the legislature. He sees lack of capacity for implementation, substantive policy differences, and high-threshold voting rules as alternative explanations for the lack of commitment to a program of reform by the Congress of People's Deputies.

Joel Ericson takes a close look at privatization in St. Petersburg. He explains the incentives and opportunities of local government bodies for infringing on property rights and also documents how the newly independent courts, by increasingly ruling against government agencies, have begun to make rights more credible. In his comment Anthony Jones stresses the importance of informal, as well as formal, institutions as part of the development of property rights in Russia.

Chapters 7, 8, and 9 deal with Czechoslovakia, Poland, and Hungary. Mariusz Dobek compares the privatization experiences of the Czech Republic and Slovakia, noting that greater credibility has been achieved in the Czech Republic, which spread ownership widely through voucher privatization, than in Slovakia, which initially attempted to privatize primarily through direct sales. He emphasizes the importance of the distributional consequences of privatization strategies in democratic regimes. In her comment Sharon Wolchik extends the discussion of the importance of the distributional consequences for understanding differences between the republics in terms of their politics and privatization strategies.

Lorene Allio considers the role of organized labor in Polish privatization. The price of interenterprise debt, a measure of the credibility of the privatization program, reflects political and strike activity by labor. She finds that labor cannot easily play a constructive role within the existing framework of political institutions so that the government's commitment to the privatization of large state enterprises is not fully credible. Bartlomiej Kaminski develops and critiques a number of points raised by Allio. Most broadly, he questions whether the slow rate of privatization of large state-owned enterprises is really significant for overall economic reform.

László Urbán analyzes the politics surrounding Hungarian privatization. He characterizes the selected strategy of privatization by sale as a continuation of the decentralization begun under the communist government that was consistent with both expert opinion and the demands the new government faced in raising foreign exchange to service its debt. Subsequently, however, the first elected government attempted to modify the privatization strategy to increase its electoral support. In his comment Kálmán Mizsei takes a longer view of the Hungarian reform process to add insights on the formation of informal norms that may be impeding the creation of an effective corporate culture.

In Chapter 10 Steven Lewis investigates the credibility of property rights created at the local level in China. In particular, he uses evidence from the region around Shanghai to investigate the federalist and corporatist theories of credibility. He finds the evidence generally consistent with the federalist theory. The evidence is inconsistent with at least the fiscal dependence version of the corporatist theory. In his comment Victor Nee distinguishes between the state-centered and local versions of the corporatist theory as it is applied to China, and he notes that both the local corporatist and federalist theories take account of the incentives facing both political and economic actors.

The political economy of property rights

In Chapter 11 Hannes Wittig considers the puzzle of why the West German government so overestimated the value of East German assets despite information offered by private investors. His explanation is that, because the property rights system did not allow investment in the East during the early stages of unification, investors could not make their statements credible. This suggests an additional aspect of a credible private property right: It facilitates the transmission of information about the value of assets from economic actors to government policy makers. In her comment Susanne Lohmann refines the theory underlying Wittig's hypothesis by showing that the possibility of some investment under insecure property rights could be sufficient to elicit truthful private information about economic conditions.

In the final chapter Lorene Allio, Mariusz Dobek, Nikolai Mikhailov, and I attempt to test the economic, public choice, and distributional theories of institutional change against the privatization experiences in Eastern Europe and the former Soviet Union. We first derive refutable hypotheses from the theories regarding the efficiency, electoral advantages, and distributional consequences of institutional change. We then test the hypotheses with reference to the initiation and termination of informal privatization, worker participation in privatized firms, and the relationship between privatization strategies and corporate control. In their comment, Jack Knight and Douglass North discuss some of the difficulties in formulating critical tests of the theories. They suggest that a more fruitful approach to determining the relative merits of the theories lies in a closer investigation of the conditions under which each of them does the best job in explaining institutional change. They also note that the inability of institutional designers to predict consequences complicates not only their task but also the task of those who wish to explain institutional change.

In summary, the chapters that follow exploit the post-communist "natural experiment" by adopting a common focus on the political economy of property rights. In doing so, they contribute to some extent to our understanding of the central problem governments face in making credible commitments, and of the fundamental social process of institutional change. I hope that they also suggest the potential benefits of more collaborative research in comparative political economy.

REFERENCES

Alesina, Alberto, and Dani Rodrik, "Distributive Politics and Economic Growth," *Quarterly Journal of Economics* 54: 2 (1994), 465–90.
Anderson, Terry L., and Dean Lueck, "Land Tenure and Agricultural Productivity on Indian Reservations," *Journal of Law and Economics* 35: 2 (1992), 427–54.

David L. Weimer

Arrow, Kenneth, *Social Choice and Individual Values*, 2nd ed. (New Haven, CT: Yale University Press, 1963).

Barzel, Yoram, *Economic Analysis of Property Rights* (Cambridge: Cambridge University Press, 1989).

Batt, Judy, *East Central Europe from Reform to Transformation* (London: Royal Institute of International Affairs, 1991).

Baumol, William J., "Entrepreneurship: Productive, Unproductive, and Destructive," *Journal of Political Economy* 89: 5/1 (1990), 893–921.

Blackburn, Keith, and Michael Christensen, "Monetary Policy and Policy Credibility: Theories and Evidence," *Journal of Economic Literature* 27: 1 (1989), 1–45.

Boardman, Anthony E., and Aidan R. Vining, "Ownership and Performance in Competitive Environments: A Comparison of the Performance of Private, Mixed, and State-Owned Enterprises," *Journal of Law and Economics* 32: 1 (1989), 1–33.

Bromley, Daniel, *Environment and the Economy: Property Rights and Public Policy* (Cambridge, MA: Basil Blackwell, 1991).

Economic Interests and Institutions (New York: Basil Blackwell, 1989).

Calvert, Randall L., "The Rational Choice Theory of Social Institutions: Cooperation, Coordination, and Communication," in Jeffrey Banks and Eric Hanushek, editors, *Modern Political Economy: Old Topics, New Directions* (Cambridge: Cambridge University Press, 1995), 216–67.

Coase, Ronald, "The Problem of Social Cost," *Journal of Law and Economics* 3: 1 (1960), 1–44.

Comisso, Ellen, "Property Rights, Liberalism, and the Transition from 'Actually Existing' Socialism," *East European Politics and Societies* 5: 1 (1991), 162–88.

De Alessi, Louis, "Property Rights, Transaction Costs, and X-Efficiency," *American Economic Review* 73: 1 (1983), 64–81.

Demsetz, Harold, "Toward a Theory of Property Rights," *American Economic Review* 57: 2 (1967), 347–59.

de Soto, Hernando, *The Other Path* (New York: Harper & Row, 1989).

Eggertsson, Thrainn, *Economic Behavior and Institutions* (Cambridge: Cambridge University Press, 1990).

Frye, Timothy, "Caveat Emptor: Institutions, Contracts and Commodity Exchanges in Russia," in David L. Weimer, editor, *Institutional Design* (Boston: Kluwer Academic, 1995), 37–62.

Furubotn, Eirik, and Svetozar Pejovich, "Property Rights and Economic Theory: A Survey of Recent Literature," *Journal of Economic Literature* 10: 4 (1972), 1137–62.

Helliwell, John F., "Empirical Linkages Between Democracy and Economic Growth," *British Journal of Political Science* 24: 2 (1994), 225–48.

Jensen, Michael C., and William H. Meckling, "Theory of the Firm: Managerial Behavior, Agency Cost, and Ownership Structure," *Journal of Financial Economics* 3: 4 (1976), 305–60.

Johany, Ali D., "OPEC and the Price of Oil: Cartelization or Alteration of Property Rights?" *Journal of Energy and Development* 5: 1 (1979), 72–80.

Jones, Eric L., *The European Miracle: Environments, Economies, and Geopolitics* (Cambridge: Cambridge University Press, 1981).

Knack, Stephen, and Philip Keefer, "Institutions and Economic Performance: Cross-Country Tests Using Alternative Institutional Measures," *Economics and Politics* 7: 3 (1995), 207–27.

16

Knight, Jack, *Institutions and Social Conflict* (Cambridge: Cambridge University Press, 1992).

Kornai, Janos, "The Affinity Between Ownership Forms and Coordination Mechanisms: The Common Experience of Reform in Socialist Countries," *Journal of Economic Perspectives* 4: 3 (1990), 131–47.

Kuran, Timur, "Sparks and Prairie Fires: A Theory of Unanticipated Political Revolution," *Public Choice* 61: 1 (1989), 47–74.

Leblang, David A., "Property Rights, Democracy and Economic Growth," Thomas Jefferson Program in Public Policy Working Paper No. 27, College of William and Mary (1994).

Levine, Ross, and David Renelt, "A Sensitivity Analysis of Cross-Country Growth Regressions," *American Economic Review* 82: 4 (1992), 942–63.

Levy, Brian, and Pablo T. Spiller, "Institutional Foundations of Regulatory Commitment: A Comparative Analysis of Telecommunications Regulation," *Journal of Law, Economics, and Organization* 10: 2 (1994), 201–46.

Libecap, Gary D., *Contracting for Property Rights* (Cambridge: Cambridge University Press, 1989).

Libecap, Gary D., and Ronald N. Johnson, "Legislating Commons: The Navajo Tribal Council and the Navajo Range," *Economic Inquiry* 28: 1 (1980), 69–86.

Libecap, Gary D., and Steven N. Wiggins, "The Political Economy of Crude Oil Cartelization in the United States: 1933–1972," *Journal of Economic History* 49: 4 (1989), 833–56.

Lin, Justin Yifu, "Rural Reforms and Agricultural Growth in China," *American Economic Review* 82: 1 (1992), 34–51.

Lindblom, Charles E., *Politics and Markets* (New York: Basic Books, 1977).

Litwack, John M., "Legality and Market Reform in Soviet-Type Economies," *Journal of Economic Perspectives* 5: 4 (1991), 77–89.

Lott, John R., Jr., "The Effect of Nontransferable Property Rights on the Efficiency of Political Markets," *Journal of Public Economics* 32: 2 (1987), 231–46.

McChesney, Fred S., "Government as Definer of Property Rights: Indian Lands, Ethnic Externalities, and Bureaucratic Budgets," *Journal of Legal Studies* 19: 2 (1990), 297–335.

McKelvey, Richard D., "Intransitivities in Multi-dimensional Voting Models and Some Implications for Agenda Control," *Journal of Economic Theory* 12: 3 (1976), 472–82.

Moore, John H., "Agency Costs, Technological Change, and Soviet Central Planning," *Journal of Law and Economics* 14: 3 (1981), 189–214.

Murrell, Peter, "Can Neoclassical Economics Underpin the Reform of Centrally Planned Economies?" *Journal of Economic Perspectives* 5: 4 (1991), 59–76.

North, Douglass C., *Structure and Change in Economic History* (New York: W. W. Norton, 1981).

Institutions, Institutional Change and Economic Performance (Cambridge: Cambridge University Press, 1990).

"Institutions and Credible Commitment," *Journal of Institutional and Theoretical Economics* 149: 1 (1993), 11–23.

North, Douglass C., and Robert Paul Thomas, *The Rise of the Western World* (Cambridge: Cambridge University Press, 1973).

North, Douglass C., and Barry R. Weingast, "Constitutions and Credible Commitments: The Evolution of the Institutions of Public Choice in Seventeenth Century England," *Journal of Economic History* 49: 4 (1989), 803–32.

David L. Weimer

Olson, Mancur, *The Rise and Decline of Nations* (New Haven, CT: Yale University Press, 1982).

"The Hidden Path to a Successful Economy," in Christopher Clague and Gordon C. Rausser, editors, *The Emergence of Market Economies in Eastern Europe* (Cambridge, MA: Basil Blackwell, 1992), 55–75.

Ordeshook, Peter, "Some Rules of Constitutional Design," *Social Philosophy and Policy* 10: 2 (1993), 198–232.

Ostrom, Elinor, *Governing the Commons: The Evolution of Institutions for Collective Action* (Cambridge: Cambridge University Press, 1990).

Plott, Charles, "A Notion of Equilibrium and Its Possibility under Majority Rule," *American Economic Review* 57: 4 (1967), 787–806.

Przeworski, Adam, and Fernando Limongi, "Political Regimes and Economic Growth," *Journal of Economic Perspectives* 7: 3 (1993), 1002–1037.

Riker, William H. *The Art of Political Manipulation* (New Haven, CT: Yale University Press, 1986).

Riker, William H., and Itai Sened, "A Political Theory of the Origin of Property Rights: Airport Slots," *American Journal of Political Science* 35: 4 (1991), 951–69.

Riker, William H., and David L. Weimer, "The Economic and Political Liberalization of Socialism: The Fundamental Problem of Property Rights," *Social Philosophy & Policy* 10: 2 (1993), 79–102.

"The Political Economy of Transformation: Liberalization and Property Rights," in Jeffrey S. Banks and Eric A. Hanushek, editors, *Modern Political Economy: Old Topics, New Directions* (Cambridge: Cambridge University Press, 1995), 80–107.

Rodrik, Dani, and Richard Zeckhauser, "The Dilemma of Government Responsiveness," *Journal of Public Policy Analysis and Management* 7: 4 (1988), 601–20.

Root, Hilton, "Tying the King's Hands: Credible Commitments and Royal Fiscal Policy During the Old Regime," *Rationality and Society* 1: 2 (1989), 240–58.

Rosenberg, Nathan, and L. E. Birdzell, Jr., *How the West Grew Rich* (New York: Basic Books, 1986).

Schotter, Andrew, *The Economic Theory of Social Institutions* (Cambridge: Cambridge University Press, 1981).

Schroeder, Gertrude E., "Property Rights and Issues of Economic Reforms in Socialist Countries," *Studies in Comparative Communism* 21: 2 (1988), 175–88.

Scully, Gerald W., "Rights, Equity, and Economic Efficiency," *Public Choice* 68: 1–3 (1991), 195–215.

Scully, Gerald W., and Daniel J. Slottje, "Ranking Economic Liberty Across Countries," *Public Choice* 69: 2 (1991), 121–52.

Shepsle, Kenneth A., "Institutional Arrangements and Equilibrium in Multidimensional Voting Models," *American Journal of Political Science* 23: 1 (1979), 27–59.

Sirowy, Larry, and Alex Inkeles, "The Effects of Democracy on Economic Growth and Inequality: A Review," *Studies in Comparative International Development* 25: 2 (1990), 126–57.

Solinger, Dorothy J., "Capitalist Measures with Chinese Characteristics," *Problems of Communism* 38: 1 (1989), 19–33.

Torstensson, Johan, "Property Rights and Economic Growth: An Empirical Study," *Kyklos* 47: 2 (1994), 231–47.

The political economy of property rights

Umbeck, John R., *A Theory of Property Rights with Application to the California Gold Rush* (Ames, Iowa: Iowa State University Press, 1981).

Vining, Aidan R., and Anthony E. Boardman, "Ownership Versus Competition: Efficiency in Public Enterprise," *Public Choice* 73: 2 (1992), 205–39.

Vining, Aidan R., and David L. Weimer, "Government Supply and Government Failure: A Framework Based on Contestability," *Journal of Public Policy* 10: 1 (1990), 1–22.

Ward, Michael Don, *The Political Economy of Distribution* (New York: Elsevier, 1978).

Weingast, Barry R., "Constitutions as Governance Structures: The Political Foundations of Secure Markets," *Journal of Institutional and Theoretical Economics* 149: 1 (1993), 286–311.

2

Credible commitment and property rights: The role of strategic interaction between political and economic actors

DANIEL DIERMEIER, JOEL M. ERICSON, TIMOTHY FRYE, AND STEVEN LEWIS

(Credible) commitment is not the whole solution to the problems we confront today. But throughout history it is overwhelmingly the most pressing issue.

Douglass North (1993: 14)

1.0 INTRODUCTION

Most observers of economic changes in the post-communist countries and China have emphasized the speed, efficiency, and distributional consequences of reform, but few have addressed the fundamental question of property rights: Do economic and political actors believe that property rights are credible? Unless property rights are credible, reform is unlikely to be effective in promoting economic growth and political stability. Understanding the credibility of property rights, and how it arises, should therefore be of central concern to students of the reform of centrally planned economies.

Property rights systems consist of some combination of formal (legal) and informal institutions.[1] Formal institutions are credible to the extent that people believe that they are not subject to arbitrary change. Absent credible formal institutions, people often create informal institutions that promote many types of economic activity. These informal rules, however, often do not provide as strong an incentive for economic actors to invest their assets in the most socially productive uses. Therefore, the credibility of formal rules established by the government plays an important role in shaping economic activity and promoting economic growth. The government's role in establishing these formal institutions brings politics to the fore of the analysis.

---

[1]Institutions are seen as "the rules of the game in society, or more formally, as the humanly devised constraints that shape human interaction" (North, 1990: 3). In this essay we are interested in the emergence of such rules as equilibrium outcomes of interactions between actors (Eggertsson, 1990; Calvert, 1995).

Credible commitment and property rights

All new governments face a problem in making credible commitments to property rights because they have not yet had an opportunity to establish either a reputation for self-restraint or a demonstrated capacity for implementing policies (Linz, 1978). This problem is especially severe in post-communist countries. The Communist Party that formally ruled in each country expropriated vast amounts of private wealth after assuming power. While in power, ruling communist parties exacerbated the problem to a greater (Poland) or lesser (Hungary) degree by their failure to commit to a long-term economic strategy (Korbonski, 1989).

Moreover, during the transformation of a centrally planned economy (CPE), the government's incentive to tinker with property rights is high for two primary reasons. First, as actors make decisions under great uncertainty, they may wish to change policy as the effects of initial choices become apparent (Litwack, 1991a, 1991b; Riker and Weimer, 1993). The costs of particular policies are difficult to foresee, and the losers may seek institutional change to mitigate their losses. Frequent changes in institutions, however, undermine credibility. Second, the opportunity for arbitrary intervention in the economy by bureaucrats often increases during the transition as the state's monitoring capacity declines (Shleifer and Vishny, 1993; Shleifer, 1994).

Some observers give pride of place to the credibility of changes in property rights. John Litwack identifies credibility as a major problem for CPEs undergoing transformation (Litwack, 1991a, 1991b). Guillermo Calvo and Jacob Frankel focus their attention on the credibility of credit markets as a critical issue in the transformation (Calvo and Frankel, 1991). In a broader, more formal treatment of changes in property rights in the former CPEs, Adam Przeworski devotes great attention to the credibility of policy changes (Przeworski, 1991; Przeworski and Limongi, 1993). He argues that politicians can use economic "shock therapy" as a commitment device to raise the costs of changing course. Przeworski is correct to emphasize the importance of the credibility of changes in property rights, but his reliance on a commitment device – "shock therapy" – may be insufficient to explain the credibility of changes in property rights in many situations. A commitment device may not always be available despite the benefits it could bring to the government and to economic actors. Actors who expect to be affected adversely by a shock therapy program may have the resources to veto such a bridge-burning tactic. Even if a shock therapy program is introduced, it may be curtailed. Actors can sometimes rebuild burned bridges, even if the costs are great. Finally, a government may simply lack the capacity to make credible commitments to sweeping changes in property rights that they pronounce.

Most treatments of credible commitment focus on a commitment device. In this chapter we broaden the concept and present a slightly differ-

21

ent view of credibility and commitment. We treat the credibility of property rights as emerging from the strategic interaction of political and economic actors. On this view, credible property rights are neither granted by governments nor seized by private actors: They emerge as an equilibrium outcome of strategic interaction among relevant actors. Our treatment of credible commitment subsumes the traditional approach and allows us to make predictions about behavior and outcomes when a commitment device is not at hand.

We begin by discussing general conceptions of credibility and commitment and their importance in explaining the stability and mutability of institutions, including property rights. We distinguish between explanations that view credibility as essentially exogenous, in that it comes from the abilities and constraints of actors, and explanations that view credibility as endogenous, in that it emerges from their strategic interaction. Traditional exogenous conceptions of credible commitment provide critical insights into the bargaining that underlies change in many institutions, but they do not provide a useful understanding of the change and maintenance of institutions when commitment devices are not available.

We then address this problem by presenting a very simple model of the interaction of political and economic actors that endogenizes credibility. In this model credibility is a consequence of the stability of individual expectations about future government actions to redefine or violate relevant property rights. These expectations of future government behavior are themselves shaped by the existing structure and behavior of government as well as the government's expectations about the future behavior of economic actors. This model simply, but adequately, captures one of the fundamental problems of change in property rights in countries introducing market-oriented reforms: Given the nature of governmental decision making, are proposed changes in property rights sufficiently credible to encourage and sustain investment in new economic institutions?

This model should be useful in the comparative study of institutions. The treatment of institutions, such as a set of property rights, as equilibrium outcomes in strategic bargaining has proved useful in exploring a variety of institutions including gender relations, common-pool resources, and international relations (Knight, 1992; Ostrom, 1990; Keohane, 1984). In this chapter we hope to contribute to this literature by extending this view of institutions to the study of property rights.

2.0 CREDIBILITY AND COMMITMENT

The terms credibility and commitment provoke considerable debate in the political economy literature. In our usage, credibility refers to *expectactions* about the future actions of strategic actors. If actors believe that

22

their partners in a given endeavor will strategically change the terms of future interactions to their advantage, then they will be reluctant to cooperate now. They will prefer to break off their interaction now to avoid future losses. For example, creditors who expect potential borrowers to default on loans in the future will be loath to lend money to the borrowers today. In forming beliefs about a borrower's future behavior, creditors frequently use past behavior as a cue. Creditors rely on an institution that identifies the degree of credibility of entrepreneurs and borrowers: the credit rating.

But not only individuals can lack credibility. A government that capriciously adjusts its definition and enforcement of property rights may find that it lacks credibility with economic actors. As the newly established communist governments of Russia, China, and Eastern Europe discovered soon after seizing power, governments that nationalize private assets find it hard to stimulate future investment by private actors. The problem of government credibility toward future investment is quite common. Emperors, kings, and modern-day legislatures also face this credibility problem when they nationalize industries, tax income and investment, regulate the money supply, and take other steps to change the distribution and creation of wealth in their societies (Root, 1989).

But what of commitment? Commitment typically refers to *constraints* intended to shape the beliefs of other actors. An actor uses these actions to convince other actors that the costs of failing to abide by the constraints are prohibitive. In other words, it may be rational for an actor to find a means to "tie one's hands" to enhance credibility. The exchange of hostages and the placing of promissory notes in the hands of neutral parties are simple examples of the strategic actions of commitment.[2]

Commitments can be more or less credible depending on the magnitude of the costs imposed on future deviations from the promised action. At one extreme lies the no-cost case. An actor merely announces a "commitment" (so-called cheap talk) that does not cost anything to make and is typically discounted by other actors. For example, as discussed in Chapter 11, West German investors who had information about the true state of the East German economy that was unavailable to the government in 1990 told the leadership in Bonn that the East German economy was in such poor shape that they would invest in the East only if tax rates were very low. As the investors have an incentive to tell the government this regardless of the true state of the East German economy, the Bonn

---

[2]Committing to a course of action can, and often does, produce joint gains by increasing the set of cooperative outcomes. These gains often, but not always, outweigh the losses from a lack of discretion incurred by committing to a particular strategy (Kydland and Prescott, 1977). Actors often make a trade-off between committing to a policy and retaining the flexibility to react to unforeseen circumstances.

government rationally discounted these statements. Rational actors place little credibility in such cost-free announcements.

On the other extreme lie cases in which a strategy physically rules out future action. A general may burn the bridges behind his troops to inform the enemy commander that the threat to defend a current position at any cost is credible. Such credibility, it is hoped, will deter an enemy assault.[3]

2.1 Commitment devices

A common view of credible commitment sees it as resulting from commitment devices that compel actors to abide by a set of rules because it is too costly to violate them. Actors increase the credibility of their actions by reducing their payoff if another course of action is chosen. Kings often demonstrated their commitment to treaties with the Roman Empire by sending family members to Rome who would be killed in the event the king reneged. Japanese warlords demonstrated commitment to the Shogun by establishing households in the capital that were vulnerable to retaliation by the Shogun for disloyalty.

A credible commitment to a course of action can also be demonstrated by creating a probability, but not a certainty, that a feared event will occur. Sometimes known as brinkmanship, this strategy enhances the credibility of a threat because the outcome is left to chance and cannot be altered by any actor. The "Doomsday Machine" in the movie *Dr. Strangelove* is an extreme example of this strategy.

As the state typically has greater potential to change rules opportunistically or engage in arbitrary expropriations than other actors, state actors face a particularly vexing commitment problem. Barry Weingast states the problem succinctly: "A government strong enough to protect property and enforce contracts is also strong enough to confiscate the wealth of its citizens" (Weingast, 1993a: 287). A strong state may be its own worst enemy. One way to mitigate this problem is to rely on an exogenous commitment device that raises the costs of expropriation.

For example, Hilton Root argues that the Old Regime monarchy and corporate societies in France increased the security of property rights by placing limits on arbitrary state interventions in credit markets (Root,

---

[3]There is some semantic confusion about these issues in the literature. Sometimes, especially in the game-theoretic literature, the term "commitment" is only used if the corresponding action is actually binding, e.g., by restricting future feasible sets of actions (Friedman, 1986). According to this usage the term "non-binding commitment" is self-contradictory. Other authors reserve the term "pre-commitment" for these cases (Schelling, 1960). According to our usage "committing yourself to an action in a set of actions A at time t" means imposing some cost $c \in [0, \infty]$ upon your future payoff at t if you choose any action not in A at t. By influencing the incentives to deviate at t, the parameter c may reflect the credibility of such a commitment.

1989). During the Old Regime, the king paid higher rates than private borrowers for loans from individual financiers because he could renege on loans with impunity. To mitigate this problem the king helped individual financiers form corporate bodies that lent to the Crown collectively at rates that were lower than those charged by individual financiers. Corporations borrowed from a wider range of citizens and could mobilize more funds for the king. Most importantly, the king had less incentive to renege on a loan from a corporation than from an individual financier because reneging on a corporation would spark much more political opposition. The corporate bodies could lend at lower rates because the threat of nonpayment was reduced. Paradoxically, by limiting his options, the king increased his ability to borrow.

2.2 Credible commitment: strategic interaction

The focus on commitment devices has offered great insight into a variety of intriguing puzzles, but we believe a slightly different conception of the origins of commitment will offer greater insight into the credibility of property rights. By viewing the credibility of commitment to a set of property rights as a product of strategic interaction among actors rather than solely as a result of a commitment device, we can make predictions in a much broader range of cases, use comparative statics analysis to form hypotheses, and offer a novel way of exploring changes in property rights. In this view, secure property rights are neither granted solely by the state, nor seized by private actors: they emerge as an equilibrium outcome of the interaction of political and economic actors. An equilibrium simply means that no interested party can do better by changing its actions, given the actions of other parties. Thus, we use noncooperative game theory to model strategic interactions instead of the decision-theoretical treatment of commitment devices. We predict only those property rights regimes that can be sustained as Nash equilibria. The occurrence of other outcomes would be inconsistent with our approach.

Some authors have begun to treat credible commitments in a similar fashion. Douglass North and Barry Weingast argue that credible commitment to property rights in England emerged as an equilibrium outcome of bargaining between Parliament, the king, and powerful interest groups in the wake of the Glorious Revolution of 1688 (North and Weingast, 1989). In their view, prior to 1640 the king's arbitrary interventions into financial markets discouraged investment and led to insecure property rights. Frequent royal interventions in the economy sparked revolts that toppled the monarchy and led to parliamentary dominance. Parliamentary supremacy also offered the prospect of unrestrained government intervention to alter property rights; economic actors were reluctant to invest their capital, and growth sputtered. In 1688 the Parliament and the king, recognizing the costs of their interventions in the economy, reached a new constitutional arrangement that allowed for a separation of powers with multiple veto points on important economic legislation. If the king or Parliament transgressed private property rights, then the holders of capital would revolt against the transgressor and install the rival. Moreover, the new constitutional arrangement allowed the courts to review important legislation. Over time, as the popular belief in the strength of checks on arbitrary interventions by the state increased, so did the security of property rights.

Elsewhere, Weingast argues that "market-preserving federalism" established checks and balances on arbitrary changes in property rights (Weingast, 1993a). Competition among local governments, and between local and federal governments, for investment ensures that egregious restrictions on property rights will provoke capital flight and reduce government revenue. Weingast attributes the economic growth of the United States in the nineteenth century in part to the commerce clause of the U.S. Constitution and the majorities in Congress that favored limited federal government from 1787 until the 1930s. In his words this clause and the alliances that backed it "prevented states from regulating interstate markets and from erecting various forms of trade barriers" (Weingast, 1993b: 15). The interaction among states, and between state and federal governments, generated secure property rights without relying on a commitment device.

Strategic interaction does not always generate equilibrium outcomes with pleasing normative qualities. In many cases the state and economic actors may wish to sustain a set of property rights but fail to do so. Since the late 1980s, Russian governments have campaigned intensively for foreign investment, and foreign investors have indicated a willingness to provide capital, but since the government has short time horizons and a history of expropriation, investors have directed their capital elsewhere. In a case such as this, strategic interaction produces an equilibrium that leaves everyone worse off.

3.0 MODELING STRATEGIC INTERACTION

We develop the notion of property rights as institutions by introducing a simple formal model. The model is not intended to capture the full richness of interactions between political and economic actors. Rather, it serves three purposes. First, it demonstrates how property rights can be understood as arising from the strategic interaction of economic and political actors. Second, it suggests a general framework that allows us to generate particular models intended to capture specific political-economic environments. Third, it generates hypotheses that can be subjected to empirical verification.

This approach differs from neoclassical economic approaches to property rights that are rooted in efficiency considerations and offer little insight into the behavior of political actors. It also differs from political science approaches that seek to link regime type to the security of property rights (Alesina and Rodrik, 1992: Przeworski and Limongi, 1993; Olson, 1993). As the results from the latter literature have been ambiguous, two prominent observers noted that "fairly precise differences in the rules for political competition appear to make big differences in the behavior of politicians. As a consequence large differences emerge in the choices of political elites operating within democratic systems" (Bates and Krueger, 1993: 459). Our approach seeks to provide more refined links between political decision making and economic outcomes that operate below the level of regime type.

Game-theoretic analyses of political and economic phenomena emphasize the details of the choice situation the actors face: Do the agents move simultaneously or sequentially? Can they observe each other's moves? Who moves first? Who moves second?[4] Which details are considered relevant is, of course, a decision by the modeler. Only the testing of the generated hypothesis will determine whether a particular model has explanatory power. The advantage of game-theoretic models is that they allow one to study the importance of institutional details in a precise and explicit manner.

The particular form of interaction between the relevant political and economic actors shapes the features of the resulting property rights system. This includes assumptions about the actors' goals and beliefs. Assuming that politicians are primarily interested in holding office typically leads to different predictions about their behavior than assuming that they pursue substantive policy goals. We assume that economic actors will at least partially base their decisions on their expectations concerning the political environment. A potential investor, for instance, will consider potential changes in government or government policy that could lead to changes in tax rates or macroeconomic policy. These political constraints on economic decision making, however, are the consequence of some underlying process: They are the outcome of the strategic interaction of political actors. We emphasize that economic actors – unions, corporations, peak associations – might be players in this political game as well.

---

[4]Prominent examples of the relevance of this distinction include industrial organization (e.g., Stackelberg vs. Cournot competition), bargaining theory (e.g., first-mover advantage in a Stahl-Rubinstein bargaining game), or the role of recognition in government formation and legislative politics (Baron-Ferejohn legislature models). For details of these models, see Fudenberg and Tirole (1991).

We close our political-economic model by assuming that the goals of these political actors are in some sense related to economic outcomes. In some cases the connection to economic outcomes is obvious, as in the case of unions or special-interest groups. In other cases different assumptions about the goals of political actors have been suggested in the literature, and which to use will be a modeling decision.

3.1 A simple model

We keep the analysis transparent by beginning with an extremely simple form of political-economic interaction summarized in Table 2.1. Suppose there is one producer, P, and a government, G. First, the producer can choose to invest at a fixed cost greater than 0, $c > 0$, in which case he receives an amount of revenue, $r > c$. If he chooses not to invest, he receives a payoff of zero. After the producer has decided whether or not to invest, the government sets a tax rate, t, with t being between 0 and 1. The tax rate can be seen as an index of the security of the investor's right to the revenue generated by the investment. Thus the government's income is $t \cdot r$ if the producer invests, and zero otherwise. The producer's profit is $(1 - t)r - c$ with investment, and zero in the case of no investment. Alternatively, one may interpret the government setting t as changing its taxation policy ex post, that is, after investment has occurred. As national investors base their decisions on the expected rate, there is no need to include any announcements by the government before the investment decision is made as long as these announcements (as in our model) do not convey additional information.

We make the standard assumption that the producer wants to maximize profit. Making assumptions about the goals of political actors is less straightforward. State actors have been usefully modeled as maximizing tenure, revenue, efficiency, or autonomy, but observers frequently assume that the behavior of governmental agents is best captured by incorporating both efficiency and distributional concerns. Political actors may primarily want to serve constituents, such as districts, or local and national party organizations, but they are also interested in increasing economic efficiency, even if only to have a bigger pie to distribute. These two goals, however, are typically in conflict. Distributional policies affect economic incentives and thus have to be balanced with concerns of economic performance.

Tax rates highlight this trade-off quite well. Taxes can finance distributional benefits to some groups in society, but taxes also alter the incentives of economic agents to produce and invest, and therefore affect the total amount of benefits that can be distributed. For our argument we only need to assume that the government's preferred tax rate, induced by

Table 2.1. *Sequence of actions in one-play investment game*

---

1. Producer P chooses whether or not to invest with anticipated tax
   rate $t \geq 0$; $r > c > 0$
2. Government G sets tax rate t, $0 \leq t \leq 1$
3. Game ends with payoffs:
   G: $t \cdot r$
   P: $\begin{cases} (1 - t)\, r - c \text{ if investment made} \\ 0 \text{ if investment not made} \end{cases}$

---

political considerations like the desire to be reelected, is high enough that producers would be forced to reduce their economic activity, for example, their investment in capital. We make our model as simple as possible, however, by assuming that governments try to maximize tax income. Their preferred tax rate is 1. This strict assumption is unrealistic, but it can easily be relaxed without altering the logic of the argument. We also simplify the model by using a tax rate as an example for any government policy that alters the net return on investment, such as regulations, tariffs, or fixed exchange rates.

If both actors play the game only once and use rational foresight, then the game has a unique solution.[5] The government sets the tax rate at t = 1, and the producer chooses not to invest. We solve this game by so-called backward induction. Given that the producer has invested, then in order to maximize tax income, the government will take all the producer's revenue by setting the tax rate at 1, t = 1 (remember that the game ends after the government's decision). But then the producer's profit equals −c. So she is better off not investing. Because the producer can anticipate the government's rational expropriation of potential profit − government setting t = 1 − she chooses not to invest.

Note that this outcome is not Pareto efficient, that is, both the government and the producer can be made better off by altering the institutional arrangement. The government would like to choose a tax rate less than 1, t′ < 1, that still provides an incentive for the producer to invest and yields some positive tax revenue. Thus a government in control of the tax rate would like to commit itself to some tax rate less than 1, t′ < 1, but because the government controls tax policy and can change the tax rate at any time, producers anticipate that after investing, the government will expropriate their investment by setting t = 1 and tax away all profits.[6] Both actors would benefit from the government being able to "tie its

[5]Technically speaking, it has a unique subgame-perfect equilibrium.
[6]It turns out that the government's optimal tax rate t* would leave the producer just indifferent between investing and not investing. Thus t* = (r − c)/r.

hands," but because it cannot, the actors are stuck in a mutually bad outcome.

Note that if the government were able to commit itself to some tax rate lower than 1, $t' < 1$, this could be interpreted as a very primitive form of the producer's right to the after-tax revenue, $(1 - t')r$. According to this interpretation, the government respects P's claim to $(1 - t')r$. For this right to be credible, the government must be able to commit itself to respect this right, which it cannot accomplish in a single-play game.

By interpreting this as the nucleus of a property right, we can see how different types of political interaction have different consequences for the credibility of property rights. We consider several kinds of political interaction as stylized illustrations: dictatorial decision making, majority rule, federalism, and interest group bargaining.

3.2 Dictatorial decision making

For a dictatorial decision process we maintain the assumption of a single-actor government. We consider, however, the case in which the government and the producer interact repeatedly. The intuition driving this interaction is that the government has an incentive to build a reputation for respecting producer rights to encourage investment and eventually realize greater tax revenue. A well-known result from game theory, however, shows that no finite number of interactions will suffice to encourage investment in the game we have set out (Selten, 1975).

The reasoning is straightforward. Suppose the actors know that the game will be repeated exactly 100 times. In period 100, the last period, the actors simply face a one-play game. As both actors are aware of this, the outcome will be the same as in the one-play game described above: no investment, no tax revenue. Now consider period 99, the next-to-last period. In this period the actors know that no matter what they do now, in the next period the outcome will be no investment and no tax revenue. But then no actor has an incentive to choose any other action than would be optimal in the single-shot game. After all, no matter what they do, their payoff will be zero in the last round. They might as well maximize their payoff in period 99. But now this reasoning also works for period 98, 97, 96 . . . 1. Thus in every period, beginning with round 1, the single-shot equilibrium is repeated: The producer never invests, and the government receives no taxes.

The key insight from this exercise is that the government will set a tax rate less than 1, $t' < 1$, only if this will maximize expected revenue; and the producer will invest only when he expects his investment to be safe, that is, if he knows that the government has no incentive to expropriate his gains with higher than expected tax rates. Thus economic decisions are based on rational expectations about political behavior. But in a finitely repeated game, the government never has any incentive to set a lower tax. So the producer will never invest.

Of course, this somewhat counterintuitive result occurs because both players know their interactions end at a fixed time, period 100. We can avoid the backward induction logic by considering an infinite interaction.[7] Consider the following game. The producer and the government interact repeatedly, but after each period there is a positive probability "d" that they will also interact in the next period. In general, d is the probability that the game will continue. Consequently, the actors are never sure that they are playing in the last period. The possibility of future interactions may make it worthwhile for the government to build a reputation for respecting investment.

The parameter d has different interpretations in different contexts. If the government is run by a dictator, $(1 - d)$ may capture the probability that he will be overthrown. If the government is seen as a party leader in a political system dominated by disciplined parties, then $(1 - d)$ measures the combined probability of losing the next election – if there are competitive elections between parties – or being replaced by an inner-party rival. In general, then, d represents the probability that an actor will stay in power for the next round. This introduces a form of discounting future payoffs, which could be combined with the standard time preference used in economic models. The particular challenges to political leaders critically depend on the political system. A Communist Party leader faces different challenges than the British Labour Party leader. Our analysis suggests that, to understand the stability of political and economic institutions, one should analyze the particular threats to political actors.

Whether it is worthwhile for the government to forgo the short-term benefits of expropriation (setting $t = 1$) in the first round depends on the equilibrium strategies played. We consider a simple "trigger-style" equilibrium. Consider some tax rate, t' slightly lower than the equilibrium tax rate needed to attract investment, t^*, $t' < t^*$, that is, some tax rate at which it is still worthwhile for the producer to invest. As long as in all previous periods the producer invests and the government chooses a tax rate of t', the producer will continue to invest, and the government will continue to respect the producer's investment by choosing a tax rate of t'. If, however, the government ever defects and expropriates investment by setting the tax rate at 1, $t = 1$, then the producer will never invest again. She will "boycott" the government and invest elsewhere, either abroad or

---

[7]An alternative modeling strategy is the introduction of incomplete information. As this route is technically more demanding than the use of a simple heuristic model warrants, we choose not to discuss it in this chapter. See Kreps et al. (1982) for a discussion.

in the second economy. In turn, if the producer ever fails to invest at a tax rate of t', then the government will set t = 1. For some parameter values t* and d, these punishments for a defection from the equilibrium path are sufficient to induce the government to set t' < t* and thus encourage investment. In other words, we should expect changes in the government's chosen tax rate, the equilibrium tax rate, and continuation probabilities to be reflected in the rate of investment.

To understand the rationale behind this reputation-building mechanism, note first that on this punishment path both players simply repeat the one-play equilibrium: no investment and t = 1. Once the players find themselves on this punishment path, no player has any incentive to deviate. On the punishment path the one-period average payoff is 0 for both players, while on the suggested equilibrium path, the average payoff is t'·r for the government and (1 − t')r − c for the producer. As we assumed that the government's chosen tax rate is just lower than the equilibrium rate needed to attract investment, t' < t*, the producer makes a positive after-tax profit, and the government receives positive revenue.

This suggested play is not a single-shot equilibrium. Actors may have incentives to improve their short-term payoff. If they deviate, however, then the punishments are invoked. An actor will stay on the equilibrium path if the long-term benefits, that is, average discounted payoff on the equilibrium path, exceed the average discounted payoff from current defection and the subsequently invoked punishment. So the producer stays on the equilibrium path if (1 − t')r − c ≥ (1 − d)0 + d·0 = 0, or t' ≤ (r − c)/r = t*, and the government stays on this path if t'·r ≥ (1 − d)r + d·0, or t' ≥ (1 − d).[8]

Note that the constraint on the producer is not binding. As long as the producer is confident that the government will keep the tax rate at t', she will invest. Whether the government can be expected, however, to keep its promise and maintain a tax rate of t' will depend in our model on the parameters t' and d. Only if d and t' are sufficiently large will it be worthwhile to refrain from cheating the producer. The expected political benefits from playing the equilibrium strategy must be sufficiently high. In our simple model these benefits depend only on the equilibrium tax rate and the government's probability of political survival. In a more general model, other parameters are relevant, especially revenue, r.

We can already draw some conclusions from our simple model. If we interpret t' as a decision by the government not to expropriate all the revenue from the producer, and thus as a simple form of property right, then the credibility of this right will depend on the strategic incentives

---

[8]For the right-hand-side payoff note that if the producer does not invest, then the government will set t=1 subsequently. But then there is never an incentive to invest in future periods, which leads to a total, and thus average, payoff of zero. For an introduction to the use of average payoffs, see Myerson (1991).

facing the actors. Let us, for instance, interpret d as the likelihood that the government will survive until the next period. Then the credibility of the property rights will critically depend on this likelihood. If d falls below 1 − t', then the government will no longer honor these property rights and will increase the tax rate. The producer will anticipate this expropriation and will refrain from investing. Property rights are credible only if the expected benefits for the government, that is, tax revenue, are high enough to make it worthwhile to forgo expropriation. In our model this leads to the counterintuitive consequence that if d < 1 − t', then property rights can be made more credible by raising the tax rate. It is worthwhile to consider the logic behind this consequence. By raising the tax rate the expected benefits for the government increase. Thus, it faces higher opportunity costs from cheating the producer, and this makes property rights more secure.

We can easily expand our model by including more than one producer with more than one production level. In fact, instead of focusing on a single investment decision, we can include a variety of players interacting in a market. If trade is part of our economic model, then we have to face the problem of contract enforcement. If enforcement is costly, then governments have a short-term incentive not to punish contract infringements. Again the government is faced with a credibility problem, this time regarding its commitment to enforce contracts. If traders believe that the government is not committed to punishing breaches of contract, then they will be reluctant to trade. A similar problem arises if the costs to the government of collecting taxes is great. If traders believe the government is not credibly committed to punishing tax cheats, then they will refrain from paying taxes. The same logic can therefore be used to model contract enforcement and tax payment and collection as a strategic decision.

For our simple model to have an investment equilibrium, however, all actors have to be able to observe perfectly a defection by the government. Recent developments in the theory of repeated games have relaxed this prohibitively strong assumption (Abreu, Pearce, and Stacchetti, 1986). Even partial or "noisy" observability of defections may be enough.

3.3 Majority rule decision making

In the next model we relax the assumption of a single-actor government and consider the consequences of a stylized majority rule for the credibility of property rights. Suppose the government consists of three actors who live only a finite number of periods, say, three. After an actor "dies" she is replaced by a new actor who again lives for three periods.[9] We

---

[9] A variant of the model can be found in Tabellini (1987).

know from the previous discussion that if any of these three actors were a dictator, then, by backward induction, no tax rate less 1 could be sustained as an equilibrium in a single play of the game.

Now consider the following scenario. Suppose that in the first period there is one "old" actor in his last period, one "middle-aged" actor who has one more period to go, and one "young" actor who just entered the game. Decisions are made by majority rule. We still maintain the assumption that actors want to maximize tax revenue and that producers use a trigger punishment if the governments selects a tax rate higher than t'.[10] An old actor will never vote for any $t' < 1$ because he is playing the last round of a finite interaction.[11] But consider a middle-aged actor. If she votes for $t = 1$, then her payoff in her last period will be 0, because the producer will not invest in that period. If she votes for a lower tax rate, $t' \leq t^*$, then her payoff in the last period will be $t' \cdot r$ provided a majority votes for t' in the last period. This may give her an incentive to vote for a tax rate that respects the producer's investment. So consider the following suggested strategy combination. Old actors will always vote for $t = 1$, middle-aged actors will vote for t' if $2t' \cdot r \geq r + 0$ (or $t' \geq 1/2$) and for $t = 0$ otherwise, and young actors will vote for t' if $3t' \cdot r \leq 1$ (or $t \geq 1/3$). So middle-aged and young actors will vote for t' if their total expected payoff from sticking with t' is higher than the combined payoff of defection and subsequent noninvestment. Note that the constraint on the young actor is not binding if the middle-aged actor already has an incentive to vote for t'. Thus the middle-aged actor determines whether t' can be sustained in equilibrium. The key to this result is that if the chosen tax rate is greater than or equal to $1/2$, $t' \geq 1/2$, then a voter who is currently decisive expects that future generations will keep sustaining the chosen rate, t'. But given this expectation she has no incentive to deviate either. Therefore t', which creates a secure property right, can be sustained in equilibrium: The government continues to respect the producer's property rights, and the producer continues to invest.

This analysis indicates that a democratic decision rule may improve the credibility of property rights and thus economic performance. The credibility of economic institutions, therefore, depends on the expectation that future decisions will be made by majority rule as well. Any uncertainty about future political decision processes will reduce credibility. This result reveals the value of stable political institutions for economic development. The current government's commitment to property rights is credible because the actors expect that future governments will have no incentive to violate property rights either. One of the benefits of constitu-

[10]For a similar model in a (legislative) framework, see Diermeier (1995).

[11]Technically, we assume that voters will never use weakly dominated strategies. Intuitively this means that they will act as if they were pivotal.

tions is that they reduce uncertainty about current and future decision rules and help to coordinate the behavior of political and economic actors (Ordeshook, 1993). The result also reveals the value of the dispersion of political power for secure property rights. A government with the stylized majority rule depicted above should be able to make more credible commitments to property rights than a government with a more dictatorial decision-making process.

In this simple model we assumed that changes in the voting population are both deterministic and anticipated. We could easily introduce continuation probabilities or stochastic changes in the distribution of voters. These changes will typically have different effects on the credibility of t'. Some insights, however, can be gained even from our simple model. First, in some cases a majoritarian decision process can sustain property rights that could not be sustained under dictatorial rule. Second, the distribution of voters matters. If we had three actors of the same "age," then $t' < 1$, and hence secure property rights, could not be sustained, because in some period all actors would be in their last period and a majority would vote for $t = 1$. But because this predatory tax rate would be anticipated by other actors, the commitment to t' "unravels," and all actors are stuck in the inefficient one-period equilibrium. As another example, consider a two-voter model with a weighted majority rule, that is, some voter commands the majority of votes. In some period, however, this voter will be in the last period and therefore vote for $t = 1$. But, then again, the commitment to maintaining a tax rate less than 1, $t' < 1$, collapses. The model thus generates insights into the relationship between different decision-making procedures and the security of property rights that can be tested against empirical observations.

3.4 Federalism and decision making

As a next step one could consider the effects of different degrees of separation of power within the polity.[12] On one extreme lies the dictatorial regime depicted above. Here the credibility of property rights depends on the probability that an *individual* decision maker stays in power. In contrast, in our simple majoritarian system no single individual could unilaterally determine the tax rate, t. By reducing the influence of any indi-

[12]We use the concept of "separation of powers" in a broader sense than a division between legislative, executive, and juridical branches of government. Here separation of powers refers to the inclusiveness of decision rules, i.e., the number of political actors that have to agree in order to change policy. Examples of factors influencing inclusiveness are the quorum needed to change government policy, electoral laws, federalism, and independent judicial review, but also the coalition formation in multiparty systems or interest-group bargaining in neo-corporatist systems.

vidual political actor somewhat, however, we could increase the credibility of property rights because the costs of changing the tax rate increase. Consider the effects of federalism. As noted above, North and Weingast (1989) suggest that the quasi-federalist structure in eighteenth-century Britain was critical in encouraging economic growth.

From these considerations we can see that the underlying political decision process has consequences for the credibility of commitment. Some political systems are unable to encourage investment, because producers know that at some time the government will have an overriding incentive to renege on its promise. But this will be anticipated by the producers who consequently stop investing. This logic suggests a testable hypothesis: Other things equal, governments with dispersed political power are better able to make a credible commitment to property rights than are governments with more concentrated powers.

3.5 Interest groups and decision making

Our interpretation that property rights are the result of the political and economic interaction between strategic actors is especially apparent if the political environment is seen as a bargaining process between relevant interest groups. We may model this interaction as a sequential bargaining process (Rubinstein, 1982). Economic institutions like property rights can then be interpreted as equilibria in a repeated bargaining game. As in the previous models, bargaining outcomes can be sustained by threats to reduce economic activity in the case of reneging.

If property rights are the result of some underlying bargaining process, then the particular features of the property rights arrangement should reflect the asymmetries that characterize the bargaining situation. Typical asymmetries include resources, opportunity costs, or time preference. Changes in the institution can then be traced back to changes in the exogenous bargaining parameters, such as splits in coalitions, unexpected election results, or external trade shocks.

The key insight from these models is that secure property rights are neither granted by the government, nor in any sense "given," but are equilibrium institutions that arise from the strategic interaction of economic and political actors. All actors are sequentially rational in the standard sense of game theory. They anticipate the consequences of their actions and the rational subsequent responses of other actors. Property rights, therefore, are respected only if the relevant agents cannot improve their payoff by violating them. Producers invest because, given their strategy, the government will not violate their rights, while, in turn, the government will respect the rights of economic agents because the opportunity costs of violating property rights are too high. Therefore, in equilibrium, the behavior of political and economic agents is self-enforcing. Given the behavior of economic agents, political actors have no incentives to alter their actions, while economic agents have no incentive to alter their actions under the assumption that the political actors play their equilibrium strategies. So, when will an institution change? Changes will occur due to unexpected shocks to the critical parameters of the model that lead to a different equilibrium. If d, for instance, drops below the threshold needed to sustain investment in repeated play, then only the no-investment equilibrium is possible.

Moreover, the analysis indicates how different forms of political inter-actions influence the credibility of property rights, the choices of rational economic actors, and, hence, the incentives of political actors to violate these rights. There is no a priori reason to expect political or economic institutions to be Pareto efficient. The actors may face the dilemma that everybody would be better off under different political or economic institutions, but these institutions will not be created because they are not self-enforcing.

4.0 EXAMINING PROPERTY RIGHTS IN THE FORMER SOVIET UNION, CHINA, AND EASTERN EUROPE

What implications does this view of the origins of commitment have for the study of property rights in the former Soviet Union, China, and Eastern Europe? First, this model emphasizes the role of political institutions in creating credible property rights and promoting economic growth. Economically efficient reform strategies may not generate the desired result if political institutions are perceived to be too weak to implement them. Reformers must not only "get the prices right," as advised by neoclassical economists, they must also "get the institutions right." Second, the model emphasizes the importance of strategic interaction. Both political and economic actors anticipate the future consequences of their actions and the responses of other actors before deciding on a course of action. Paradoxically, credible constraints on future alterations in the set of property rights can enhance the security of property rights. These constraints can assume a variety of forms. A stable power-sharing arrangement between president and parliament, a competitive party system that punishes frequent changes in property rights, a corporatist agreement that raises the costs of changes in future policies, and even informal rules may reduce the incidence of unpredictable changes in property rights and promote growth and stability.

Our approach, while applicable to all political-economic systems, is especially relevant to the countries under study. In contrast to Western democracies where the basic political institutions are stable and social conflicts are mainly over economic policies and to Latin American countries where, despite radical political changes, economic institutions are rather rigid, the countries of Eastern Europe face the dual tasks of transforming their economic and political institutions simultaneously. From the perspective of political economy this offers a unique opportunity to study the interplay of economic and political actors. An approach that explicitly models this seems to be especially promising in explaining the variance in reform programs adopted by countries that seemingly face similar economic problems.

One example of the logic depicted in our model is the "equilibrium trap" that plagues the interaction of economic and political actors in Russia (Frye, 1995). Given the short time horizons of many Russian political elites, economic actors are reluctant to invest. For example, all retail traders in the Russian economy would be better off if each paid their taxes and allowed the state to enforce contracts. The state has economies of scale and scope and, in theory, can enforce contracts at lower cost than private enforcers and thus charge lower taxes than private enforcers (North and Thomas, 1973). As private traders do not view state enforcement of contracts as credible, they have strong incentives to hire private enforcers. Once a few traders hire private enforcers, they gain a comparative advantage over other traders, and all traders are then compelled to hire private enforcers (Gambetta, 1994). The fees charged by private enforcers tend to be higher than those charged by the state in a competitive political system, and thus traders are made worse off (Olson, 1993). Moreover, the state loses tax revenue because the traders pay fees to private enforcers rather than taxes to the state. As its revenue declines, the state's commitment to enforce contracts becomes less credible, making private enforcement even more attractive. In the absence of a credible commitment by the state to enforce contracts, no actor will have an incentive to deviate from using more expensive private enforcers, and as a result traders and the state will be worse off than under full enforcement by the state. Traders rely on informal institutions, such as social ties, blacklists, and deposits to engage in trade, but these institutions, particularly during a transition, are often quite fragile.

General bargaining agreements, or "pacts" among political actors and relevant interest groups (O'Donnell, Schmitter, and Whitehead, 1986), also highlight the logic of our model and can be tested using comparative statics analysis. Political and economic actors have attempted to create these pacts in Hungary, Germany, and Poland and to a certain extent in Russia. Agreements of this sort will be credible only if every participant in the bargaining can be expected to stick to the agreement. For example, if unions accept wage cuts in exchange for unemployment benefits, then the credibility of their promise will depend on the union's ability to control its members and prevent wildcat strikes. If these promises are not credible, then other actors anticipate that the union leadership will eventually be forced to renege on its agreement and will refuse to accept any general agreement in the first place. The lack of exogenous commitment devices or self-enforcing agreements explains why so many "pacts" unravel during the transition.

A related question concerns the puzzle of why attempts to agree on a social pact fail over a long period and are then suddenly successful. Our model suggests that in this case we should expect a radical change in the parameters of the bargaining environment. For example, political parties may be forced to reassess their beliefs about their degree of support from the voting population.

The German "solidarity pact" of March 1993 between the large national parties, the federal government, and the state governments about the long-term transfer payments and investments in East Germany illustrates this logic. While a conservative-liberal coalition controlled the national government, the Social Democrats controlled the majority of the Länder (states). Due to the federal structure of the German government, both national and state governments must agree on any major economic package. In addition, due to the strong involvement of interest groups in German parties, both unions and business associations are usually represented in the negotiations. During a long bargaining process both the ruling coalition and the opposition tried to position themselves for the upcoming elections in 1994. This strategy presumed that both actors expected to win the next elections if they chose the right bargaining strategy. Both parties, however, had to change their beliefs about the chances of winning after the local elections in Hessen indicated strong support for the parties of the extreme right. This victory created serious doubt in the expectations of both major parties about forming the next government. Within a week the parties agreed upon the "solidarity pact." The stability of this and other pacts, however, depends on the actors' expectations about future electoral returns.

What are the advantages of this altered conception of the origins of commitment to a certain set of property rights? First, it offers insight into a number of puzzles concerning property rights in our countries of study that are overlooked by traditional notions of commitment. Whereas commitment is usually viewed as exogenous to the key strategic interaction, our model incorporates it. We view commitment not as a device or artifact whose existence is fortuitous to the explanation but as the product of ongoing interaction between political and economic actors. Second, the conception of commitment here also allows us to examine a variety of formal and informal institutions that can strengthen commitment to a set of property rights. It does not simply beg the question by asserting that property rights are secure because they are guaranteed in the constitution or because they are economically efficient. Formal rules, such as constitutions or governmental decrees, are insufficient to make a credible commitment to a set of property rights. Our model thus helps reveal the importance of such informal institutions as norms and other internally enforced rules and laws. Third, our model generates hypotheses about the relationship between different processes of political decision making and the security of property rights that can be tested against the evidence in a wide range of cases.

REFERENCES

Abreu, Dilip, David Pearce, and Ennio Stacchetti, "Optimal Cartel Equilibria with Imperfect Monitoring," *Journal of Economic Theory* 39: 1 (1986), 251–69.

Alesina, Alberto, and Dani Rodrik, "Distribution, Political Conflict and Growth: A Simple Theory and Some Empirical Evidence," in Alex Cukierman, Zvi Hercowitz, and Leonardo Leiderman, editors, *Political Economy, Growth, and the Business Cycle* (Cambridge, MA: MIT Press, 1992), pp. 23–50.

Bates, Robert H., and Anne O. Krueger, "Generalizations Arising from the Country Studies," in Robert H. Bates and Anne O. Krueger, editors, *Political and Economic Interactions in Economic Policy Reform* (Cambridge, MA: Basil Blackwell, 1993), pp. 444–72.

Calvert, Randall L., "The Rational Choice Theory of Social Institutions: Cooperation, Coordination, and Communication," in Jeffrey S. Banks and Eric A. Hanushek, editors, *Modern Political Economy* (Cambridge: Cambridge University Press, 1995), pp. 216–67.

Calvo, Guillermo A., and Jacob A. Frankel, "Credit Markets, Credibility and Economic Transformation," *Journal of Economic Perspectives* 5: 4 (1991), 139–48.

Diermeier, Daniel, "Commitment, Deference, and Legislative Institutions," *American Political Science Review* 89: 2 (1995), 344–55.

Eggertsson, Thrainn, *Economic Behavior and Institutions* (Cambridge: Cambridge University Press, 1990).

Friedman, James, *Game Theory with Applications to Economics* (Oxford: Oxford University Press, 1986).

Frye, Timothy, "Caveat Emptor: Institutions, Credible Commitment and Commodity Exchanges in Russia," in David L. Weimer, editor, *Institutional Design* (Boston: Kluwer Academic, 1995), 37–62.

Fudenberg, D., and J. Tirole, *Game Theory* (Cambridge, MA: MIT Press, 1991).

Gambetta, Diego, *The Sicilian Mafia: The Business of Private Protection* (Cambridge: Cambridge University Press, 1994).

Keohane, Robert, *After Hegemony: Cooperation and Discord in the World Political Economy* (Princeton, NJ: Princeton University Press, 1984).

Knight, Jack, *Institutions and Social Conflict* (Cambridge: Cambridge University Press, 1992).

Korbonski, Andrzej, "Politics of Economic Reform in Eastern Europe: The Last Thirty Years," *Soviet Studies* 41: 1 (1989), 1–19.

Kreps, David, Paul Milgrom, John Roberts, and Robert Wilson, "Rational Cooperation in the Finitely-Repeated Prisoners' Dilemma," *Journal of Economic Theory* 27: 2 (1982), 245–52.

Kydland, Finn E., and Edward C. Prescott, "Rules Rather than Discretion: The Inconsistency of Optimal Plans," *Journal of Political Economy* 85: 3 (1977), 473–91.

Linz, Juan, *Breakdown of Democratic Regimes: Crisis, Breakdown and Reequilibriation* (Baltimore: Johns Hopkins University Press, 1978).

Litwack, John, "Legality and Market Reform in Soviet-Type Economies," *Journal of Economic Perspectives* 5: 4 (1991a), 77–89.

"Discretionary Behavior and Soviet Economic Reform," *Soviet Studies* 43: 2 (1991b), 255–79.

Myerson, Roger, *Game Theory: Analysis of Conflict* (Cambridge, MA: Harvard University Press, 1991).

North, Douglass C., *Institutions, Institutional Change, and Economic Performance* (Cambridge: Cambridge University Press, 1990).

"Institutions and Credible Commitment," *Journal of Institutional and Theoretical Economics* 149: 1 (1993), 11–23.

North, Douglass C., and Robert Thomas, *The Rise of the Western World: A New Economic History* (Cambridge: Cambridge University Press, 1973).

North, Douglass C., and Barry Weingast, "Constitutions and Commitment: The Evolution of Institutions Governing Public Choice in Seventeenth Century England," *Journal of Economic History* 59: 4 (1989), 803–33.

O'Donnell, G., P. Schmitter, and J. Whitehead, *Transitions from Authoritarian Rule* (Baltimore: Johns Hopkins University Press, 1986).

Olson, Mancur, "Dictatorship, Democracy, and Development," *American Political Science Review* 87: 3 (1993), 567–76.

Ordeshook, Peter, "Some Rules of Constitutional Design," *Social Philosophy and Policy* 10: 2 (1993), 198–232.

Ostrom, Elinor, *Governing the Commons: The Evolution of Institutions for Collective Action* (Cambridge: Cambridge University Press, 1990).

Przeworski, Adam, *Democracy and the Market* (Cambridge: Cambridge University Press, 1991).

Przeworski, Adam, and Fernando Limongi, "Political Regimes and Economic Growth," *Journal of Economic Perspectives* 7: 3 (1993), 51–71.

Riker, William H., and David L. Weimer, "The Economic and Political Liberalization of Socialism: The Fundamental Problem of Property Rights," *Social Philosophy and Policy* 10: 2 (1993), 79–102.

Root, Hilton, "Tying the King's Hands: Credible Commitments and Royal Fiscal Policy During the Old Regime," *Rationality and Society* 1: 2 (1989), 240–58.

Rubinstein, Ariel, "Perfect Equilibrium in a Bargaining Model," *Econometrica* 50: 1 (1982), 97–109.

Schelling, Thomas, *The Strategy of Conflict* (Cambridge, MA: Harvard University Press, 1960).

Selten, Reinhard, "Reexamination of the Perfectness Concept for Equilibrium Points in Extensive Games," *International Journal of Game Theory* 4: 1 (1975), 25–55.

Shleifer, Andrei, "Establishing Property Rights," *Proceedings of the World Bank Annual Conference on Development Economics* (Washington, DC: World Bank, 1994), 93–117.

Shleifer, Andrei, and Robert Vishny, "Corruption," *Quarterly Journal of Economics* 108: 3 (1993), 599–617.

41

Tabellini, Guido, "Reputational Constraints on Monetary Policy: A Comment," *Carnegie-Rochester Conference Series on Public Policy* 26 (1987), 183–90.

Weingast, Barry, "Constitutions as Governance Structures: The Political Foundations of Secure Markets," *Journal of Institutional and Theoretical Economics* 146: 1 (1993a), 286–311.

"The Political Foundations of Democracy and the Rule of Law," Stanford University (1993b), 1–48.

The political commitment to markets and marketization

BARRY R. WEINGAST

1.0 INTRODUCTION

Confronting the problems of simultaneous economic and political reform in the former socialist countries demonstrates that politics and economics are inextricably linked. Put simply, economic reform and political reform need to be mutually compatible. This proposition is easy to see if we consider the *fundamental political dilemma of an economic system*: Any government strong enough to provide the minimal institutional requirements of markets — for example, a secure system of property rights, an objective judicial system, a stable monetary system — is also strong enough to extract the wealth of its citizens (Weingast, 1995a). To be effective, markets require secure, limited government, implying that marketization is as much a political problem as it is an economic one. As the chapters in this volume attest, designing either political institutions or markets in the former socialist states without considering their interrelationship is folly.

Political economists must confront a central question: What forms of political institutions are compatible with economic institutions that are consistent with effective markets? In the language of modern economics, this requires that markets be the incentive-compatible policy choice of politics. To foster marketization, political institutions must provide a credible commitment to respect limits on governmental behavior required by markets. Unfortunately, we are remarkably ignorant about these processes.

This brings me to the important essay by Daniel Diermeier, Joel Ericson, Timothy Frye, and Steven Lewis defining the essence of the commitment problem.[1] Their logic demonstrates the delicate interaction of politics and economics. They begin with a private investor, or entrepreneur,

[1]See also Levey and Spiller (1994), North (1990, 1993), North and Weingast (1989), Root (1994), Weingast (1995a), and Williamson (1994).

who must decide whether to invest in a project that has positive social returns. At the current tax rate, this project is assumed to be privately profitable. The problem is that the current tax rate alone is not sufficient information for the entrepreneur's calculus: Tomorrow's tax rate, which is chosen only after the investment has occurred, must also be anticipated. The pursuit of other political goals may lead the government to raise tax rates ex post.[2] Entrepreneurs, aware of this political risk to returns on investment, forgo profitable investments. Unless the government can commit to today's low tax rates, the prospects of higher tax rates tomorrow deter socially productive investment. Political risk drives a wedge between the social and private returns from investment, thus deterring the very entrepreneurial activity necessary for successful marketization (North, 1981). When the government can commit to stable tax rates, however, the investment remains privately profitable, and entrepreneurs have an incentive to undertake them.

How does a political system commit to the range of limits on its powers necessary for successful marketization? Unfortunately, we remain remarkably ignorant about this problem.

I use the remainder of this comment to make some brief remarks about one route by which a range of states have, over the last several centuries, committed to the form of limited government necessary to foster markets, a form of government I call *market-preserving federalism*. Elsewhere, I argue that market-preserving federalism provides the political foundation for economic growth during the industrial revolution in eighteenth-century Britain, the rise of the United States to become the richest nation in the world in the nineteenth and early twentieth centuries, and the spectacular economic success of economic reform in modern China (Weingast, 1995a; see also McKinnon, 1994; and Montinola, Qian, and Weingast, 1995).

2.0 MARKET-PRESERVING FEDERALISM

The most fundamental feature of federalism is decentralization. But not all systems of decentralization are federal (Riker, 1964). As a special type of federalism, *market-preserving federalism* requires a specific allocation of authority and responsibility among different levels of government (Weingast, 1995a): (F1) There exists a *hierarchy* of governments with a *delineated scope of authority* (for example, between the national and subnational governments) so that each government is autonomous in its

---

[2]As Diermeier et al. observe, the incentive to increase revenue may arise for a variety of reasons. For example, the government may be responsive to rent-seeking; or, as McKinnon (1995) has observed, it might be a market-oriented government meeting unexpectedly hard times, forcing it to raise more revenue by any means possible.

44

own sphere of authority. (F2) The subnational governments have primary *authority over the economy* within their jurisdictions. (F3) The national government has the authority to police the *common market* and to ensure the mobility of goods and factors across subgovernment jurisdictions. (F4) Revenue sharing among governments is limited, and borrowing by governments is constrained so that all governments face *hard budget constraints*. (F5) The allocation of authority and responsibility has an *institutionalized degree of durability* so that it cannot be altered by the national government either unilaterally or under the pressures from subnational governments.

These conditions define the institutional arrangements of market-preserving federalism. F1 contains the defining characteristic of federalism. Beyond decentralization, the task of preserving market incentives requires that the authority of the national government over markets must somehow be limited. Market-preserving federalism accomplishes this by the addition of conditions F2 through F5.

Condition F2 grants authority over the economy to subnational governments, restricting the national government to public goods such as policing the common market for goods, services, and factors (F3).

Hard budget constraints (F4) are necessary because they directly tie local revenue to local economic prosperity. A local government's financial problems remain its own. This provides important incentives for local officials, for their government's fiscal health is directly related to local economic prosperity. In contrast, easy bailouts from financial problems significantly diminish local government officials' incentives to worry about the consequences of their choices. Without a hard budget constraint on the national government, the latter could use its monetary discretion to get around the constraints on its authority.

Finally, F5 provides for credible commitment to the federal system and thus for limits on the national government's ability to dismantle or alter the system. The condition concerns the self-sustaining nature of federalism and is central to its survival.

As Oliver Williamson (1994) observes, what is critical in the definition of market-preserving federalism is not whether a state calls itself federal – *de jure federalism* – but whether that state satisfied the conditions noted above – *de facto federalism*. Many de jure federalisms are nothing like market-preserving federalism, for example, in Argentina, Brazil, and India. In these cases, conditions F2 and F5, and often F4, fail. The failure of conditions F2 and F5 implies that the political discretion and authority retained by the central government in these systems greatly compromises their market-preserving qualities. Similarly, the decentralization of the former Soviet Union strikingly contrasts with market-preserving federalism. That system granted little political authority to local governments.

As administrative units of the central government, these governments had little autonomous political power over their local economies. The center also carefully controlled factor mobility. All but condition F1 failed in that system. Interestingly, England during the industrial revolution, though not nominally a federal system, satisfied all the conditions (Weingast 1995a).

The economic effects of market-preserving federalism have long been understood by economists (see, e.g., Oates, 1972; Rubinfeld, 1987; Tiebout, 1956), and I will provide only the briefest sketch here. The market-preserving characteristics obtain because of federalism's dual restrictions on governments. The national government is limited in its control over the economy to truly national public goods such as maintaining the common market. Although this government has the greatest potential to interfere with marketization, market-preserving federalism limits its power to do so. Subnational governments have power over their local economies, but they are significantly restricted in their ability to hinder markets.

The common market condition implies an absence of internal trade barriers. In combination with market-preserving federalism's other conditions, this induces competition among lower jurisdictions, greatly limiting the incentives for rent-seeking and market intervention. In the presence of a common market, a jurisdiction that provides a less hospitable economic environment finds that it loses factors of production to their competitors. Market-preserving federalism thus ties local economic prosperity to local political choice, giving political actors the incentives to foster marketization. And precisely these factors can be seen at work in the cases mentioned.

3.0 SELF-ENFORCING MARKET-PRESERVING FEDERALISM

The above outline of the characteristics and effects of market-preserving federalism begs the issue of what maintains this system. If market-preserving federalism fosters marketization, then how does the government commit to it? That is, how is condition F5 satisfied in practice? As William Riker (1964) observed, the fundamental political problem to be solved in any federalism is how to prevent the national government from undoing, destroying, or simply ignoring the restraints on its powers.

In order for the limits on government inherent in the system of federalism to survive, these limits must be self-enforcing on national political officials. Any attempt to violate these limits must be associated with large costs. Maintaining federalism thus requires that the survival of national political officials depends upon their honoring these constraints. The specific mechanisms that generate these costs differ from case to case. Moreover, these are deep questions, requiring careful modeling and investigation. Below I summarize some of the insights discussed elsewhere at greater length.[3]

The basic mechanism can be simply summarized: *All* governments need a sufficient degree of support among the population to survive. Naturally, the minimum level of support necessary for an authoritarian government to survive is typically lower than the majorities necessary for democratic governments. This has important implications. If citizens are unanimous in their views about fundamental rights, then any government seeking to violate those rights risks withdrawal of support and hence its survival. In contrast, when citizens are divided, the government can violate what some citizens view are their fundamental rights because the government retains the support of others. Taken together, these imply that sustaining limited government with universal rules applying to all citizens requires that a consensus develop about the appropriate limits on government. This is one of the central principles generating the relevant costs of violating the constraints of limited government and hence making limited government self-enforcing on sovereigns and political officials.

The People's Republic of China provides an interesting case of evolving market-preserving federalism (Montinola et al., 1995a; Weingast, 1995b). I briefly sketch the broad context here. In Chapter 10 Steven Lewis attempts to test the theory of market-preserving federalism by looking at the distribution of investment across local governments in Shanghai.

Chinese leaders did not set out to create a system of federalism. Instead, their pragmatic approach to the reform of socialism led them to a series of steps that decentralized various powers, including fiscal authority. This decentralization not only created a system of incentives among local governments for preserving their newfound power, but gave them the fiscal resources and muscle to resist efforts by the central government to undo the system (Oi, 1992; Shirk, 1993).

The decentralization of fiscal authority, which provides most provinces and large cities with the residual rights to tax revenue, is fundamental to the process of reform. From the mid-1980s through 1993, most central government taxes were collected by local governments, which then passed along revenue according to agreed-upon formulas. These formulas provided local governments with strong incentives to foster local economic prosperity, for they increased the total resources at their discretion. Not only has this allowed many regions to get rich, but their newfound eco-

---

[3]The approach sketched here is developed in a series of papers that present the model and then several applications. See Weingast (1994, 1995a, 1995b).

nomic and political muscle places them in a position to resist attempts by the central government to undo the system. Indeed, precisely such an attempt was defeated after the Tiananmen Square episode (Shirk, 1993). During a time of their highest political ascendancy in the reform period, the anti-reformers proved unable to roll back or derail reform.

Several other factors raise explicit barriers to undoing the system of reforms. Fiscal considerations have become an important barrier against the anti-reform coalition between anti-reformers in the central government and, say, the interior provinces that remain poor and least affected by the reforms. Not only is the central government significantly constrained at present, but a retrenchment against the reforms would make this worse, for it would generate far larger fiscal commitments for the government.

Another consideration arises from the system of internal guest workers (Solinger, 1995). The huge floating population of migratory workers, largely from the interior and working in the coastal provinces experiencing reform, cannot become citizens of the provinces in which they work. The estimated number of these floaters, between 60 million and 100 million, is phenomenal by Western standards. Because floaters are not citizens, any retrenchment would put these workers' jobs at risk and threaten to send them back to their home provinces, requiring that they be fed and given shelter. In short, any serious retrenchment immediately implies that the floaters would become fiscal liabilities of the anti-reform coalition. Because that coalition is already fiscally constrained, this mechanism requires that the anti-reformers be willing to bear a huge cost to implement their program, one that risks its success. Of course, the potential magnitude of this cost is unclear. Nonetheless, these substantial costs of retrenchment must give pause to anti-reformers.

4.0 CONCLUSION

Reform in the former socialist states must confront the fundamental political dilemma of an economic system. Because marketization requires a form of limited government, all serious efforts at market reform necessarily involve political reform. Unless the political system credibly limits its own authority, marketization will not be effective, despite having the appropriate economic characteristics. Diermeier et al. demonstrate the importance of credible commitments, and how they may arise from interaction between economic and political actors. Market-preserving federalism provides not only a historically significant illustration of how a particular institutional form can structure this interaction to create credible commitment, but one of significant relevance for the economic success of post-socialist China.

REFERENCES

Levy, Brian, and Pablo T. Spiller, "Institutional Foundations of Regulatory Commitment: A Comparative Analysis of Telecommunications Regulation," *Journal of Law, Economics, and Organization* 10: 2 (1994), 201–46.

McKinnon, Ronald, "Market-Preserving Fiscal Federalism in the American Monetary Union," *Spectrum* 68: 3 (1995), 36–45.

Montinola, Gabriella, Yingyi Qian, and Barry R. Weingast, "Federalism, Chinese Style," *World Politics* 48: 1 (1995), 50–81.

North, Douglass C., *Structure and Change in Economic History* (New York: W. W. Norton, 1981).

Institutions, Institutional Change and Economic Performance (Cambridge: Cambridge University Press, 1990).

"Institutions and Credible Commitment," *Journal of Institutional and Theoretical Economics* 149: 1 (1993), 11–23.

North, Douglass C., and Barry R. Weingast, "Constitutions and Credible Commitment: The Evolution of the Institutions of Public Choice in Seventeenth Century England," *Journal of Economic History* 49: 4 (1989), 803–32.

Oates, Wallace, *Fiscal Federalism* (New York: Harcourt Brace Jovanovich, 1972).

Oi, Jean C., "Fiscal Reform and the Economic Foundations of Local State Corporatism in China," *World Politics* 45: 1 (1992), 99–126.

Riker, William H., *Federalism* (Boston: Little, Brown, 1964).

Root, Hilton, *The Fountain of Privilege: Political Foundations of Markets in Old Regime France and England* (Berkeley, CA: University of California Press, 1994).

Rubinfeld, Daniel, "Economics of the Local Public Sector," in Alan J. Auerbach and Martin Feldstein, editors, *Handbook of Public Economics*, Vol. 2 (New York: Elsevier, 1987), 571–646.

Shirk, Susan, *The Political Logic of Economic Reform in China* (Berkeley, CA: University of California Press, 1993).

Solinger, Dorothy J., "China's Urban Transients in the Transition from Socialism and the Collapse of the Communist 'Urban Public Goods Regime,'" *Comparative Politics* 27: 1 (1995), 127–46.

Tiebout, Charles M., "A Pure Theory of Local Expenditure," *Journal of Political Economy* 64: 5 (1956), 416–24.

Weingast, Barry R., "The Political Foundations of Democracy and the Rule of Law," working paper, Hoover Institution, Stanford University (1994).

"The Economic Role of Political Institutions: Market-Preserving Federalism and Economic Growth," *Journal of Law, Economics, and Organization* 11: 1 (1995a), 1–31.

"The Political Foundations of Limited Government: Sovereign Debt in 17th and 18th Century England," working paper, Hoover Institution, Stanford University (1995b).

Williamson, Oliver, "The Institutions and Governance of Economic Development and Reform," working paper, University of California at Berkeley (1994).

3

Political determinants of the success of economic transition

NIKOLAI MIKHAILOV

1.0 INTRODUCTION

All countries in Eastern Europe and the majority of the newly independent states that emerged after the collapse of the Soviet Union are experiencing two radical transitions at the same time: from communist regimes
to democratic political systems and from socialist economies based on
state ownership and central planning to free market economies. These
two processes are interdependent and the failure to achieve progress in
one may have adverse consequences for the other. Successful market
reforms may speed up democratic consolidation, but a failure to sustain
economic policy reforms and a continuous decline in living standards of
the population may endanger the very existence of democracy.

The process of political transformation affects the scale, the speed, and
eventually the success of economic reforms. Which political factors are
most likely to have strong impacts on the process of economic transformation? The recent literature on the determinants of success or failure of
reform efforts in Third World countries suggests one possible explanatory
variable – the existence of a strong and autonomous state (Bates and
Krueger, 1991; Evans, 1992; Kahler, 1990).

It should be noted, however, that distinguishing between strong and
weak states in a post-communist context makes little sense. The fall of
communist rule and the collapse of the system of central planning rendered obsolete the old bureaucratic structures responsible for the management of the economy in every country in the region. All of these
countries now face the task of re-creating effective institutions for regulating the economy.

Instead of searching for differences in state power, I stress the significance of internal cohesion of the governments that direct the process of
economic transformation in the post-communist countries and their ability to maintain parliamentary support. In section 2, I argue that when

50

control over policy making is shared by many political parties in coalition cabinets, or when the governments have a low level of parliamentary support, the likelihood of inefficient economic policy is heightened.

Fragmented coalition cabinets, minority governments, and government instability over time are often the results of parliamentary fragmentation. I discuss the impact of parliamentary fragmentation on the economic performance of post-communist countries in section 3.0.

While parliamentary fragmentation can be partially attributed to the heterogeneity of post-communist societies, the role of the electoral laws, which may promote or discourage fragmentation, should not be underestimated. In sections 3.1 through 3.3, I review the electoral systems that have been recently used in the six countries studied in detail in Chapters 4–9 and 12 (Poland, Hungary, the Czech Republic, Slovakia, Russia, and Ukraine), and I demonstrate that a clear connection between electoral laws and the degree of parliamentary fragmentation exists.

The nature of the economic strategy pursued during the transformation period depends on the preferences of parties or other political forces that control the government. Left-wing parties are usually much more concerned about unemployment than are parties of the Right. They also tend to support a much higher level of state intervention in the economy. The cabinets controlled by the Right place a stronger emphasis on keeping inflation low. Different preferences translate into different policies, which in turn cause substantial variation in economic outcomes. The impact of ideological orientation of the parties in power on economic policies and outcomes is analyzed in section 4.

Section 5 examines whether the progress achieved in implementing market reforms in the four East Central European countries, Russia, and Ukraine through 1993 is consistent with the theoretical propositions that I develop. In sections 5.1–5.3, three of these propositions are subjected to statistical analysis that is based on data from sixteen post-communist countries. In section 5.1, I define the dependent and independent variables. Section 5.2 examines the determinants of inflation, GDP growth rates, and changes in ownership structures of transitional economies in 1993. In section 5.3, I analyze the economic performance of the sixteen post-communist countries in 1994.

2.0 MULTIPARTY CABINETS, MINORITY GOVERNMENTS, AND THE EFFECTIVENESS OF GOVERNMENTAL POLICIES

Market-oriented reforms in Eastern European countries are often endangered by frequent political crises caused by serious disagreements among parties that form coalition governments. Political instability translates into incoherent economic policies that in turn increase the costs of transition. I propose the following hypotheses:

Hypothesis 1. The coherence of economic policies and, eventually, the success of market reforms are inversely related to the number of "effective parties" in government.[1]

Parties that form coalition governments have distinctive constituencies and different political and ideological interests. It is easier for parties to fulfill electoral promises, satisfy the demands of core constituencies, and achieve their programmatic goals if they can get control over those cabinet positions in which their interests are especially strong.

The distribution of ministerial portfolios in multiparty cabinets usually reflects not only the numerical strength of parties in the legislature, but also the different priorities of the coalition members. Once in control of an important ministry, parties possess a considerable degree of autonomy in pursuing their preferred policies.

As a result, collective government often consists of largely autonomous actors, with the prime minister and his party lacking the capacity to implement coherent economic policies. For instance, all parties may agree that inflationary policies should be avoided, but none will accept the proposals that may incur costs upon their core constituencies. The problem is, of course, that if every coalition party succeeds in defending the interests of its constituents, inflationary pressure would never subside (Roubini and Sachs, 1989).

As the number of parties in the coalition increases, it becomes more and more difficult to find acceptable compromises. Deliberations within the government generally will be more time consuming, which may slow down economic reforms.

The politicians often face a trade-off between a more cohesive government and a higher level of parliamentary support for the cabinet. My second hypothesis acknowledges the significance of securing the majority in the legislature for the success of the government's reform efforts by distinguishing between majority and minority governments:

Hypothesis 2. Countries in which minority governments are rare or nonexistent will have a significantly better record of economic performance than will countries in which minority governments are frequent.

---

[1] To measure the effective number of parties that form the cabinet, I use a formula developed by Laakso and Taagepera (1979) that is sensitive not only to the number of parties, but also to their relative sizes. It is calculated on the basis of the parties' numerical strength in the legislature: ENP (effective number of parties) = $1/\Sigma s_i^2$, where s_i is the proportion of seats of the ith party. High values correspond to considerable fragmentation of the cabinet.

The formation of a minority government oftentimes represents an intense legislative conflict. The parties in parliament are deeply divided and cannot agree on a stable coalition capable of proposing and implementing coherent economic policies. In such situations, conflicting parties may agree to appoint a caretaker minority government that is kept in office as long as it remains passive in policy formation (Powell, 1982).

But the lack of reforms can only worsen the recession in post-communist countries. With the old system of central planning destroyed and the new system based on market mechanisms not yet built, the conservation of existing institutions is likely to cause further contraction of the economy.

For a minority government to be effective in implementing market-oriented reforms, it must be able to get the support of at least some parties outside the governing coalition. The most common way to achieve this goal is to offer policy concessions to potential support parties. But in Eastern Europe and Russia, which suffer from a high degree of political polarization and low elite support for compromises with ideological and political opponents, building a legislative majority is a formidable task for minority cabinets.

Finally, minority governments generally stay in office for a much shorter period of time than do single-party majority governments or majority coalitions (Powell, 1982; Strom, 1990; Laver and Schofield, 1990), and they are also subject to the greatest amount of subsequent turnover (Strom, 1990). As a result, one might expect many dramatic changes in policies in countries in which minority governments are frequent. Such changes can only slow down the process of economic transformation.

3.0 ELECTORAL SYSTEMS AND PARLIAMENTARY FRAGMENTATION

Both the effective number of parties in the cabinet and the degree of parliamentary support for the government depend on the fragmentation of the legislature. The greater the number of parties in the legislature, the more difficult it is to create and maintain majorities that are so essential for the passage of legislation necessary for implementing market-oriented reforms. Hence, the following hypothesis:

Hypothesis 3. Economic performance of the former communist countries is inversely related to the fragmentation of their legislatures.

Parliamentary fragmentation in turn may be at least partially explained by the effects of electoral systems adopted in the former communist countries. In the next four sections I review the electoral systems that have been used in East Central Europe, Russia, and Ukraine since 1989. All electoral systems are subdivided into those in which elections were held on a nonparty basis (Poland 1989, Russia 1990, Ukraine 1990), pure proportional representation (Poland 1991), modified proportional representation (Czechoslovakia 1990 and 1992, Poland 1993), and majoritarian and mixed systems (Hungary 1990 and 1994, Russia 1993, Ukraine 1994).

3.1 Elections on a nonparty basis

The reforms started by Gorbachev in the Soviet Union in the second half of the 1980s did not affect all countries of the Soviet bloc in the same way. The leaders of the communist regimes in Poland and Hungary were willing to start or accelerate their own liberalization, whereas their counterparts in Czechoslovakia, East Germany, and Romania did not allow any opposition to emerge.

As part of the program of increasing legitimacy of their regimes, the ruling elites in the Soviet Union, Hungary, and Poland were willing to abandon the practice of uncontested elections and allow several candidates, including representatives of the opposition, to compete first in the local (Hungary 1985, Soviet Union 1987) and then in the national elections (Poland 1989, Soviet Union 1989, Russia, Ukraine, and other republics of the former Soviet Union 1990). These elections, however, were often heavily rigged in the communists' favor and did not allow genuine multi-party competition.

In Poland only one-third of the seats in the lower house of the parliament were freely contested, and even there the Solidarity candidates, like everyone else, had to compete as individuals. The other two-thirds of the seats were filled with the appointed members of the Communist Party and its Popular Front allies.

In Russia and Ukraine, the 1990 elections to the republican Supreme Soviets were also held on a nonparty basis. In practice, this electoral system meant a considerable advantage for the Communist Party of the Soviet Union, which at that time still was the only legal political party in the Soviet Union. In rural areas, in which the opposition forces had not yet established their organizations, the Communist Party leaders were able to ensure victories by the candidates supported by the party apparatus. But even in urban areas, in which the opposition groups were much stronger, the candidates supported by the CPSU still had an advantage over everyone else, having easy access to the media (still under party control) and other resources (Slider, 1990).

Thus, one consequence of nonparty elections was a substantial over-representation of anti-reform political forces in the parliaments of Poland,

Russia, and Ukraine. The communist domination of the Ukrainian Supreme Council (Verkhovna Rada) essentially prevented the possibility of radical market-oriented economic policies in Ukraine. In Russia the anti-reform majority in the legislature mounted an all-out assault against stabilization measures introduced by the Gaidar government and its mass privatization program, nearly succeeding in derailing the country's transition to a market economy.

The other major effect of the nonparty elections was the high level of parliamentary fragmentation. From the beginning, deputies elected in single-member districts as individuals were less bound by party discipline than are legislators in the parliamentary systems of the West. With the splintering of Solidarity and Democratic Russia, and the dissolution of the communist parties, deputies increasingly began to vote on issues according to their own interests, making the task of building stable coalitions necessary for the passage of legislation almost impossible.

Finally, nonparty elections prevented the development of strong parties and party systems. Most parties emerged after the elections and at best had only a few representatives in the parliament. For instance, only 38 out of 421 deputies of the Ukrainian Supreme Council were prepared to admit a party affiliation at the end of 1992 (Wilson and Bilous, 1993). The lack of influence of parties in parliaments and governments translated into minuscule budgets, absence of regular party presses, and low memberships. Without new elections, it was extremely difficult to attract the attention of the voters to individual party identities, and the majority of the public remained ignorant of the parties' programs and activities.

Weakness of political parties helps to explain why factions in the parliaments were small and ill-disciplined and why the governments had so much trouble in creating parliamentary coalitions necessary for the passage of legislation. Moreover, the absence of strong parties left little hope that the next elections would produce less fragmented legislatures.

3.2 Pure proportional representation

In Eastern Europe, an electoral system that closely resembles pure proportional representation was used only once – in the Polish elections in October 1991. The dissolution of the Polish Communist Party and the disintegration of the Solidarity coalition that previously united almost all anti-communist forces left the deputies of the Polish Sejm uncertain about the electoral prospects of the country's numerous political parties. Reflecting this uncertainty, the new electoral law was drafted to ensure that everyone had a fair chance to be represented in the new parliament.

The law adopted in July 1991 had no minimum threshold for representation and combined the elements of the Hare-Niemeyer[2] and Sainte-Lague[3] methods of seat distribution (Webb, 1992), both of which are impartial between large and small parties and tend to yield closely proportional results (Lijphart, 1990). The only deviation from pure proportionality was the distribution of 69 (out of 460) seats from a National List to only those parties that secure at least 5 percent of the national vote or win seats in at least five constituencies.

Polish President Lech Walesa strongly objected to such hyperproportionality, arguing that it would yield a fractionalized parliament incapable of building a stable majority. He vetoed the election bill twice, but both of his vetoes were overridden by a two-thirds parliamentary majority.

The president's predictions turned out to be quite accurate. Twenty-nine different parties won seats in the Sejm, the largest one with less than 14 percent of the seats. Even after several small parties merged with the larger ones, the parliament was still divided into eight to ten factions of roughly similar size (Vinton, 1993). Forming a coherent coalition with the support of a parliamentary majority in such conditions proved to be virtually impossible, and a new election became the only way out of the deadlock.

3.3 Modified proportional representation

Matthew Shugart (1992) lists three major variables that can be manipulated to reduce the degree of proportionality of PR systems: the electoral formula, the minimum threshold, and the size of electoral districts. All of these elements of the electoral system were affected by the new Polish electoral law.

Parties competing in the 1993 parliamentary elections had to obtain at least 5 percent of the popular vote to get representation in the legislature. For multi-party coalitions, the threshold was set at 8 percent. The new law also raised the number of electoral districts from thirty-seven to fifty-two, which again was supposed to benefit large parties and thus reduce the fragmentation of the Sejm. The electoral formula was changed from the

[2]In the Hare-Niemeyer electoral formula, the total number of valid votes is divided by the number of seats in a district to calculate a quota of votes that entitles parties to one seat. Every party gets as many seats as it has quotas of votes. Any unallocated seats are then given to those parties having the largest numbers of unused votes.

[3]In the modified Sainte-Lague formula, seats are awarded sequentially to parties having the highest "average" numbers of votes per seat until all seats are allocated. Each time a party receives a seat, its "average" goes down. The "averages" are calculated according to a formula in which the numerator is the party's total vote and the denominator uses 1.4 as the first divisor and then uses the odd-integer divisor series: 3, 5, 7, and so forth.

combination of Hare-Niemeyer and Sainte Lague methods to d'Hondt formula,[4] which is the least proportional among the highest averages methods and systematically favors the larger parties (Lijphart, 1990).

The combination of all these changes, as well as the higher threshold for sixty-nine bonus seats divided among the largest parties and stringent requirements for parties that wanted to register their regional and national lists, dramatically reduced the fragmentation of the Sejm. Among the fifteen major contenders in September 1993 elections, only six managed to win seats in the parliament. The number of effective parliamentary parties went down from 10.9 in 1991 to 3.9 in 1993. Finally, the problem of creating a government relying on the majority support in the legislature has been solved easily because two post-communist left-wing parties, the Democratic Left Alliance and the Polish Peasant Party, won almost two-thirds of the seats in the Sejm.

3.4 Majoritarian and mixed electoral systems

Two subtypes of majoritarian electoral system are used in elections in Eastern Europe: the plurality, or first-past-the-post method, and the two-ballot majority runoff. The plurality rule for selecting the winner of elections stipulates that elections are held in single-member districts and the winner is the candidate with the most votes. The empirical studies of elections in post–World War II democracies have found that plurality formulae give a greater advantage to large parties over small ones than do PR systems (Rae, 1971; Lijphart, 1994). With few exceptions, Canada and India the most notable ones, plurality rules have led to the formation of stable two-party systems. Other parties, unless their support is heavily concentrated in particular regions of the nation, are denied parliamentary representation or prevented from entry by a combination of "mechanical" and "psychological" effects (Duverger, 1963; Riker, 1982; Lijphart, 1994).[5]

A plurality voting system may seem to be much more conducive to governmental stability in the former communist countries than is proportional representation. Yet one should be extremely cautious in applying

---

[4]The d'Hondt formula is the other of the only two highest-averages methods in actual use for the allocation of seats to parties. The numerator of the formula is the party's total vote, and the denominator uses integers 1, 2, 3, and so on.

[5]By "mechanical effect" Duverger (1963) meant the underrepresentation of small parties resulting from electoral rules that deviate from perfect proportionality. According to Riker (1982, p. 761), "The mechanical effect gives politicians an incentive to abandon parties that win even less than they might be expected to." "Psychological" effect refers to the strong disincentive for voters to choose minor parties because their votes might be "wasted" and even indirectly contribute to the victory of least-liked parties.

the insights from the study of mature democracies to countries in which democracy is just taking root.

Plurality rules have been used for the election of 225 deputies of the Russian State Duma. As this election took place simultaneously with the election based on PR, we have a unique natural experiment which can be used to compare the effects of the two electoral systems.

The plurality formula clearly did not work as it was supposed to in the first genuinely free election in Russia. Eight out of thirteen parties that qualified for the election cleared the 5 percent threshold in elections based on PR. The plurality voting system caused a higher degree of fragmentation: Twelve out of thirteen parties managed to win seats in single member constituencies, as did thirty independent candidates. The effective number of parliamentary parties calculated separately for each of the two systems also demonstrates that PR with the 5 percent threshold reduced the degree of fragmentation much more effectively than did the plurality system.[6]

The other subtype of majoritarian system, the two-ballot majority run-off formula, was used in the 1994 Ukrainian election. With Ukraine's electoral law clearly biased against political parties (Wasylyk, 1994), most parties, with the exception of the communists, failed to achieve significant representation in the parliament. Among 338 seats allocated after the two rounds of elections, 170 went to independent candidates, which makes the Ukrainian legislature the most fragmented one in all Eastern Europe.

The impact of electoral systems on parliamentary fragmentation and, therefore, on the effective number of parties in government and the degree of the government's support in the legislature is strong and predictable. The situation least conducive to the success of market-oriented reforms appears to occur when elections are held on a nonparty basis. After such an election, anti-reformers in the parliament are overrepresented, political parties remain weak or virtually nonexistent, and the legislature is usually so fragmented that the formation of a government with stable majority support becomes an extremely difficult task. Individual deputies have no reason to back unpopular austerity measures, and whatever support the reformers have when they introduce radical market reforms quickly wanes when the social costs of reforms become visible. Therefore, I propose the following hypothesis:

Hypothesis 4.   Countries in which elections are held on a nonparty basis will have worse records of economic performance than countries with other electoral rules.

[6]$N_s = 6.4$ for 225 deputies elected by PR with the 5 percent threshold; $N_s = 8.3$ for 219 deputies who won in single-member districts according to plurality voting.

When a system of pure proportional representation is used for the elections, the degree of parliamentary fragmentation is only slightly lower and the same executive-legislative deadlock is likely to occur.

It is often argued that the best way to create strong two-party systems and stable majority governments is to introduce electoral rules based on plurality voting. The use of such rules in the first free parliamentary elections in Russia, however, shows that the effective thresholds for representation imposed by plurality voting may be relatively low in the early stage of formation of party systems.[7] The two-ballot majority runoff formulae could be even more conducive to the success of small parties and independent candidates.

This short review of electoral rules used in countries of East Central Europe, Russia, and Ukraine suggests that proportional representation systems with electoral formulae, the size of the districts, and the thresholds of representation favoring large parties achieve the best results in reducing parliamentary fragmentation and creating conditions for effective government. The combination of "mechanical" and "psychological" effects eliminates small parties from political competition and strengthens internal discipline within large ones. The formation of strong and stable party systems is likely to follow, which, in turn, improves the chances of successful economic transformation.

4.0 THE IMPACT OF LEFT AND RIGHT PARTY GOVERNMENTS ON THE SUCCESS OF ECONOMIC TRANSFORMATION

Parties, or other political forces that control the government, are the main agents determining the nature of the economic strategy pursued during the transformation period. Parties have different core constituencies, and they have to implement policies favoring these constituencies in order to stay in power.

In developed countries, supporters of Left parties usually have greater exposure to rising unemployment than supporters of Right parties. The latter incur greater losses from inflation than core constituents of Left parties. The proponents of the Partisan Theory of macroeconomic policy suggest that parties promote policies consistent with the interests of their supporters (Hibbs, 1977; Hibbs and Dennis, 1988). In their view, Left governments are more likely than Right governments to pursue expansionary policies designed to yield lower unemployment and extra growth, but often at the price of higher inflation. Governments controlled by the Right, on the other hand, pay much more attention to keeping inflation low.

[7] For a definition of a concept of effective threshold of representation, see Lijphart (1994: 25–9).

In addition, Left and Right parties differ with respect to their preferences concerning the extent of government management of the economy, the degree of public ownership of industry, and the reduction of income inequality. Right-party governments advocate minimum intervention in the economy and rely on private agents to establish the national level of input factors. In countries where public ownership of industries is high, privatization becomes one of the major issues on the government agenda. As private investment is financed by savings, and savings in turn depend on the level of profits, Right governments try to keep taxation low and nondistortionary to avoid reducing private resources.

Governments controlled by the Left, on the other hand, generally support a much higher level of state intervention in the economy. In order to correct both market failures and economic inequalities, the governments allocate physical and human capital, either directly, through state-owned enterprises (SOEs), or through regulatory schemes that alter the investment behavior of private agents.

A second wave of partisan models has concluded that several structural and institutional arrangements place heavy limits on the capacity of parties to affect macroeconomic outcomes according to their political preferences. These models have stressed that partisan effects on inflation, unemployment, and output, although significant in size, are only temporary (Alesina, 1987; Alesina, Cohen, and Roubini, 1992). Increasing international trade lowers the effects of internally engineered expansionary policies, and growing capital mobility across borders entails a corresponding loss of autonomy in macroeconomic policies.

In the post-communist countries, however, the existing economic and institutional arrangements constrain macroeconomic policies to a much lesser degree. Because these countries are still almost unaffected by the growing internationalization of the economy, the parties in power should have a higher, more permanent impact on economic strategies and outcomes.

Right governments have a clear advantage over Left governments in implementing the programs of macroeconomic stabilization and privatization necessary for the radical transformation of the economic system. Simultaneous liberalization of prices and imposition of stringent wage restraints lead to a drastic decline of living standards of blue-collar workers, the core constituency of the Left parties. Cuts in state subsidies to industrial enterprises often cause numerous bankruptcies and high unemployment. Privatization programs also often result in the shedding of excess labor by the new owners.

As a result, Left governments are often unwilling to initiate radical reforms (Ukraine, Belarus), or they may be unwilling to continue reforms initiated by the previous Right governments (Slovakia). But even those

Left governments that appear to be committed to liberal economic policies face an enormous pressure to slow down the process of economic transformation (Poland, Hungary).[8] Therefore, I expect the governments in which Left parties play a leading role to be less successful in implementing market reforms than Right governments, which are less dependent on the support of the disadvantaged social groups and thus can pursue liberal economic policies without the risk of alienating their core constituency. Hence, the following hypothesis:

Hypothesis 5. The longer the Right or Center-Right governments have been in office, the greater will be the progress in transforming the economies of the post-communist countries and the better will be the records of their economic performance.

5.0 THE ROLE OF GOVERNMENTS IN ECONOMIC TRANSITION

The four East Central European countries, Russia, and Ukraine share one important characteristic: in the pre-1989 period, state ownership was far greater than all other forms of ownership combined, often approaching 100 percent of industry. There were important differences in how much the state owned and how the state apparatus managed industrial enterprises, but they paled in comparison to differences between these countries taken as a group and advanced industrialized nations.

The reason why the transformation from command to market economy turned out to be so difficult is clearly related to this peculiar owner-

[8]Despite the seemingly firm support of continuity in economic policies by the leadership of both the Polish Democratic Left Alliance (SLD) and the Hungarian Socialist Party, the future of the reform process in both countries is uncertain.

In the case of Poland, the pressure for a reversal of liberal policies emanates from three major sources. The SLD's coalition partner, the Polish Peasant Party, demands increased subsidies, cheaper credit, and protection from foreign competition for farmers. It also supports increased pensions and public-sector wages, as well as greater expenditures for education, health care, and environmental protection. The OPZZ trade union federation, which controls 61 out of 171 SLD's seats in the Sejm, also opposes many policies advocated by the leadership of the Democratic Left Alliance, most notably the attempts to keep wages in SOEs under control. It is also willing to see the deficit raised so that subsidies to state industry could be restored and social welfare programs expanded (Vinton, 1994). Finally, many of the rank-and-file members of the party and its electorate are disappointed to see the party's shift from moderate opposition to the economic policies of the previous governments during the campaign to unequivocal support for austerity measures in the aftermath of the elections.

Likewise, the Hungarian Socialist Party has to withstand pressure for significant increases in social spending from the trade unions, members of the old nomenklatura within the party, and voters who expect a real change in governmental policies and rapid improvement in living standards.

ship structure. The vast majority of SOEs proved to be incapable of finding adequate responses to the challenges posed by the transition process. In view of the state sector's record, it comes as no surprise that economic results in most countries discussed in this chapter have so far been disappointing.

The governments of the East Central European countries, Russia, and Ukraine now must withstand pressure for bailing out loss-making state firms and simultaneously press ahead with large-scale privatization programs as the only long-term solution to economic problems confronting the transitional economies. In addition, several governments of the post-communist countries need to implement macroeconomic stabilization programs and such structural adjustment measures as trade liberalization or the creation of effective taxation systems (Przeworski, 1991).

How successful the governments of the post-communist countries will be in dealing with these tasks may to a large extent depend on their internal cohesion, ability to control parliamentary majorities, and their placement on the Left-Right continuum based on economic policy preferences. The degree to which governmental power is dispersed across political parties in coalition cabinets and the level of the government's support in the legislature in turn depend on the electoral systems adopted in these countries. Table 3.1 describes the electoral system, the number of effective parties in Parliament and cabinet, the percentage of seats controlled by the governing parties in the legislature, and the ideological orientation of the government for each of the six countries discussed in this chapter.

If one compares the four East Central European countries, Russia, and Ukraine on these political characteristics, then one expects Hungary and the Czech Republic to have the best overall economic performance rating. In both countries the electoral systems discourage proliferation of parties. Both in Hungary and the Czech Republic, Right parties controlled the government for the duration of the transition period through 1993, and the ruling coalitions, which consisted of three or four parties, were clearly dominated by one coalition member – the HDF in Hungary and the ODS in the Czech Republic.

The prospects for successful transition in Poland and Slovakia are predicted to be less favorable. In Poland the four Solidarity governments continuously had to deal with fragmented parliaments, and none of them enjoyed majority support in the Sejm that is necessary for the timely passage of important legislation. After the September 1993 elections, the former Communist Party gained control of economic policy. While committed to the continuation of reforms, the leadership of the Democratic Left Alliance is under tremendous pressure to abandon liberal economic policies and may have to make important concessions to opponents of market reforms to stay in power.

In the newly independent Slovakia, one of the major political obstacles for successful economic transformation is the instability of the party system that is currently undergoing a second realignment since the fall of the communist regime. Another factor is the weakness of the Right parties in Slovakia. The only party that is committed to liberal economic policies, the Christian Democratic Movement, won only 18 of 150 seats in June 1992 parliamentary elections and had to stay in the opposition for almost two years.

The biggest political impediments to economic transformation exist in Russia and Ukraine. In these two countries, anti-reformers always had a numerical superiority in the parliaments, and parties are just emerging as influential political actors. In Russia, however, the final say in the matter of economic policy belongs to the president of the country. For this reason, the opponents of market reforms were never able to capture the key positions in the executive branch. The much greater role of the pro-market reformers in economic policy making, guaranteed by the control of the executive branch by the Russian presidency, explains the differences in speed and scale of reforms in these two countries.

The relative accomplishments of the six countries in building market economies are consistent with the set of hypotheses proposed in the previous sections of this chapter. The Czech Republic, despite the negative growth in its gross domestic product recorded in 1993 (real GDP went up 2.1 percent in 1994), has clearly been the biggest success story among all former communist countries. The country's innovative voucher privatization program transferred almost a thousand medium and large industrial enterprises to private owners. The government's consistent macroeconomic policy led to balanced budgets and significant surpluses in the trade balance. Inflation is low by East European standards (around 20 percent in 1993), and the unemployment rate (3.5 percent) is one of the lowest in all of Europe.

In Hungary, on the other hand, the undeniable successes, like a rebound in industrial production in 1993 or the dynamic increase of direct foreign investments in recent years, were mixed with some troubling developments. The Hungarian budget deficit is the worst in Eastern Europe with the exception of Serbia's. Privatization of large industrial enterprises is very slow, and the preponderance of the state sector in the country's overall economy is still overwhelming. Unemployment has reached 13 percent, the foreign trade deficit exceeded U.S.$3 billion in 1993, and the foreign debt increased to U.S.$29 billion, leaving the country with the highest per capita foreign debt in the region.

Table 3.1. *Electoral systems and governments in six former communist countries*

Country/year of election	Electoral system	NPL	Cabinet/PM	Term in office	NPC	PSL	IO
Hungary 1990	Mixed: 176 seats through plurality voting; 120 seats through PR with 4% threshold; 90 seats through the national list	3.8	Antall (I) Antall (II)–Boross	6/90–2/92 2/92–6/94	1.8 1.7	59.3 55.4	Right Right
Hungary 1994	Mixed: 176 seats through plurality voting; 125 seats through PR with 5% threshold; 85 seats through the national list	2.9	Horn	6/94–present	1.6	72.3	Left
Poland 1989	Election on a nonparty basis	n/a	Mazowiecki Bielecki	9/89–1/91 1/91–12/91	n/a n/a	n/a n/a	Right Right
Poland 1991	PR with no threshold	10.9	Olszewski Suchocka (I) Suchocka (II)	12/91–5/92 6/92–4/93 4/93–11/93	2.7 4.6 3.9	23.5 42.2 38.0	Right Right Right
Poland 1993	PR with 5% threshold	3.9	Pawlak	11/93–present	2.0	65.9	Left
Czechoslovakia 1990	PR with 5% threshold	4.1	Calfa	6/90–6/92	1.8	62.0	Right
Czech Republic 1992	PR with 5% threshold	5.7	Klaus	7/92–present	2.3	52.5	Right

		NPL			NPC	PSL	IO
Slovak Republic 1992	PR with 5% threshold	3.2	Meciar (I)	6/92–3/93	1.4	59.3	Left
			Meciar (I)	3/93–11/93	1	44.0	Left
			Meciar (III)	11/93–3/94	1.4	53.3	Left
			Moravcik	3/94–present	3.6	45.3	Left
Russia 1990	Election on a nonparty basis	n/a	Yeltsin/Gaigar	11/91–12/92	n/a	n/a	Right
			Yeltsin/Chernomyrdin	12/92–present	n/a	n/a	Right
Russia 1993	Mixed: 225 seats through plurality voting; 225 seats through PR with 5% threshold	8.3	Yeltsin/Chernomyrdin	12/92–present	n/a	n/a	Right
Ukraine 1990	Election on a nonparty basis	n/a	Fokin	9/90–9/92	n/a	n/a	Left
			Kuchma	9/92–9/93	n/a	n/a	Left
			Kravchuk/Zvyagilsky	9/93–6/94	n/a	n/a	Left
Ukraine 1994	Two-ballot majority runoff	16.3	Kuchma/Masol	7/94–present	n/a	n/a	Left

Notes:
NPL – effective number of parties in the legislature
NPC – effective number of parties in the cabinet
PSL – percentage of seats in the legislature held by the parties in power
IO – ideological orientation of the government

Sources: Foreign Broadcast Information Service – Daily Report on Eastern Europe, 1992–4; Foreign Broadcast Information Service – Daily Report on Central Eurasia, 1992–4; Keesing's Record of World Events, 1989–94; RFE/RL Research Report, 1992–4; RFE/RL News Briefs, 1993–4.

The contrast between Hungarian and Czech economic performance in 1993 clearly demonstrates the limits of a model built only on the basis of political factors. Political variables identified in previous sections are not the only ones relevant for the success of economic reforms. Other factors, such as the size of the foreign debt or the government's choice of strategy for economic transformation (gradualism versus the "shock therapy" approach), may be important and, therefore, should be considered in the analysis of the transition process.

Poland was the first country in Eastern Europe to experience economic recovery. The country's GDP increased 1 percent in 1992 and almost 4 percent in 1993. But inflation, the budget deficit, and unemployment remain high, and the mass privatization program has not yet started. The dismal performance of the state sector and the government's inability to achieve any significant progress in privatizing large industrial enterprises cloud the prospects for sustained economic growth.

The worsening economic situation in Slovakia, Russia, and Ukraine can be attributed primarily to political factors. Many of the economic problems faced by Slovakia after independence had to do with the discontinuity within the government. The Meciar government rejected the radical reforms that had been engineered by Czechoslovakia's former finance minister Vaclav Klaus, but had no clear program of its own. As a result, virtually no progress was made in arresting the recession of 1990–2, the voucher privatization program was discontinued, and the hopes that foreign investment would increase substantially after independence did not materialize.

In Russia the crisis in executive-legislative relations prevented the reintroduction of fiscal austerity measures. Inflation, while lower than in the previous year, still reached 880 percent in 1993, and the budget deficit remained extremely high. But on the other hand, the government achieved a major success in implementing a mass privatization program that transferred nineteen thousand industrial enterprises to private owners.

By the end of 1993, the economic crisis in Ukraine had reached such proportions as to conjure up images of total economic collapse. Ukraine's weak and divided government resorted to expansionary fiscal and monetary policies that produced hyperinflation and, consequently, a reversion in the second half of 1993 to the techniques of central planning. No progress in privatization has been achieved and 95 percent of industrial assets remain in the hands of the state.

This short review of progress in the transition to market economies in the four East Central European countries, Russia, and Ukraine supports the thesis that effective government is necessary for the success of the market reforms. The evidence presented is, of course, suggestive rather than conclusive, and further analysis is required for a better understanding of interconnectedness between political and economic transitions.

5.1 The impact of political factors on economic performance: Defining the dependent and independent variables

In the next three sections I subject some of the proposed hypotheses to a more rigorous test. It is common to evaluate economic performance of countries by comparing such factors as unemployment, inflation, and GDP growth rates. In the post-communist countries, however, low unemployment may be a poor indicator of successful performance. Rather, it may be a result of a continuing flow of governmental subsidies to inefficient companies and a lack of privatization – two features that characterize nations with no, or very little, progress in creating well-functioning market economies.

In contrast to unemployment, inflation is one of the most important indicators of economic performance for the post-communist countries. Continuing high rates of inflation in several transition economies are the direct result of the failure of stabilization efforts. Inflation, therefore, can be used as a measure of the success or failure of macroeconomic stabilization.[9]

The speed and magnitude of changes in the size of the private sector in the post-communist countries is another indicator of the success or failure of economic reforms. All governments in Eastern Europe and in the newly independent states that emerged after the collapse of the Soviet Union declared their support for rapid privatization and pledged to create favorable environments for the growth of private firms. The actual achievements of these countries in ownership transformation vary enormously, however. To measure the progress of the post-communist nations in creating an ownership structure compatible with market economies, I

[9]I create two dependent variables that measure inflation: One is operationalized as the natural logarithm of average annual consumer price inflation in 1993 (INFLATION93), the other one as the natural logarithm of average annual consumer price inflation in 1994 (INFLATION94). Before the dissolution of the Soviet Union at the end of 1991, no statistical analysis of the economic performance of the post-communist states could have been possible, because of the small number of countries in the sample. In 1992 extremely high rates of inflation in all independent states that emerged after the collapse of the Soviet Union can be largely attributed to the impact of the one-time elimination of the Soviet pricing system. Only in 1993, with the separation of their monetary systems and increasing policy differences, can one include these states in the analysis as independent observations and explain their rates of inflation using the same set of parameters as in the case of the other Eastern European nations.

use the private sector share of GDP at the beginning of 1994 as the second dependent variable.[10]

Although successful implementation of stabilization and privatization programs is often seen as a major precondition for general economic recovery, its short-term effects – such as high interest rates and the reduction or elimination of price supports and subsidies to industries, and the growth of unemployment as a result of restructuring following privatization – may further deepen the transitional recession (Przeworski, 1993). Two other dependent variables that I use in this study – GDP growth rates in 1993 and 1994 (GROWTH93, GROWTH94) – measure the magnitude of this recession.

One should be cautious, however, in drawing inferences from the analysis of data on growth rates in the post-communist countries. In 1993 many of these countries were still in the early stages of the transition process in which some decline in output was inevitable. It would be more interesting to look beyond temporary developments and evaluate the determinants of the future economic growth in the region.

To find which factors increase the likelihood of sustained economic recovery in Eastern Europe and Russia, I use another growth-related dependent variable: the economic performance rating taken from the September 1994 issue of *Euromoney* (RATING). It is based on the judgment of economists from leading banks and financial and economic institutions about the prospects of growth in 1994 and 1995 for more than 160 nations, including all post-communist nations. The rating depends on several factors, such as the current rate of economic growth, monetary stability, current account balance, budget deficit or surplus, unemployment, and structural imbalances.

As the *Euromoney* rating is based on multiple criteria for evaluating the magnitude of the transitional recession and the prospects of recovery, it appears to be a more valid measure of the overall economic performance of post-communist states in 1993 than is the GDP growth rate. The latter not only ignores other aspects of macroeconomic performance and the nonlinear nature of the relationship between policies and economic outcomes (in the case of post-communist countries this relationship is more likely to resemble a J-curve), but it may also be thrown off the mark by an arbitrary time interval imposed on the data. For instance, the near collapse of the Albanian economy in 1992 was followed by the miraculous 11 percent growth in 1993, placing Albania on the top of the list of sixteen countries included in the analysis and far ahead of the second-place Poland. The very low baseline for calculating the growth rate in this

[10]I used private sector shares of GDP estimated by the European Bank for Reconstruction and Development as reported in the *Economist*, December 3–9, 1994, p. 27.

case makes the comparison of Albania with other countries less affected by the crisis in 1992 somewhat misleading.

On the other hand, in contrast to the GDP data, the *Euromoney* rating undoubtedly reflects the preferences of western economists who participated in *Euromoney*'s surveys. The participants in the survey may be biased in favor of the countries that introduced sweeping reforms and may rate them much higher than those nations in which the governments adopted a gradualist approach to economic transformation. It is impossible to estimate the magnitude of the bias before the actual data on performance of the post-communist states in both 1994 and 1995 become available. Therefore, the results of the analysis with the *Euromoney* rating as the dependent variable should be viewed as tentative and highly dependent on the validity of the neoliberal model of economic development.

Among the explanatory variables included in the model, the most important ones for the purposes of this study are the six political variables. Two of them single out those countries that had parliaments elected on a nonparty basis. I create two indicator variables that assume the value of one for countries that had legislatures elected on a nonparty basis at the beginning of 1993 (NONPARTY93) or at the beginning of 1994 (NONPARTY94), and zero otherwise.

To construct the remaining political variables, I first measure the length of the transition period in each of the post-communist countries included in the sample.[11] To operationalize the parliamentary fragmentation variable, I calculate the measure of fragmentation for each legislature elected during the transition period. If there were two or more elections, I multiply the fragmentation measure for each legislature by the number of months between elections, sum up the resulting figures, and divide them by the length of the transition period. The first variable that measures[12] parliamentary fragmentation (FRAGM93) covers the period from the date when the first freely elected government comes to power or the date of independence to the end of 1993. The second variable (FRAGM94) extends the period under examination to the end of 1994.

[11]I choose the day when the new government assumes power after the first free election (semifree in the case of Poland, because the June 1989 election led to the change in regime) as the starting point of the transition period for all Eastern European countries with the exception of Slovenia and Macedonia. In the case of the former republics of the Soviet Union and Yugoslavia, the starting point of the transition period is the date of independence.

[12]I use the inverse of the effective number of parties measure to operationalize the parliamentary fragmentation variable. Without this transformation, treating the members of a legislature elected on a nonparty basis as independents results in extremely high values of the fragmentation variable. The inverse compresses these values toward zero.

The remaining two political variables capture the placement of the governments on the Left-Right continuum. To operationalize them, I single out all Right or Center-Right governments and divide the number of months they were in power by the total length of the transition period.[13] The first variable (RIGHT93) is calculated for the period from the beginning of the transition process to the end of 1993. For the second variable (RIGHT94), this period is extended for an additional twelve months.

Unfortunately, it is not possible to test hypotheses 1 and 2, which link the degree of fragmentation of the government and its level of support in the legislature to success or failure of market reforms. As I discussed earlier, several countries held elections on a nonparty basis. As a result, some of the governments consisted of people who did not belong to any political party. Similarly, the legislatures mostly consisted of deputies without party affiliation. The support of the government by the existing parliamentary factions was rarely stable throughout time, and often the coalition necessary for the passage of legislation had to be created anew on every issue.

Two control variables are included in the model. One, the nation's GDP per capita in 1993 (PCGDP93), is used as a proxy for the level of economic development. My expectation is that the more developed countries would achieve greater progress in fighting rising prices and transforming the ownership structures of their industries, would have a lower decline in GDP, and would have higher economic performance ratings than the less developed ones. The second control variable (LNGDP93) accounts for the size of the economy. It is operationalized as a natural logarithm of the country's GDP in 1993. I expect that countries with large economies would make slower progress in implementing market reforms than countries with smaller economies.

Out of twenty-seven former communist countries, only sixteen are included in the analysis. Countries that had protracted international or civil wars (Armenia, Azerbaijan, Bosnia, Croatia, Georgia, Serbia and Montenegro, and Tajikistan) are excluded because the impact of these wars on the affected economies far outweighed the influence of all other factors. Four countries of Central Asia (Kazakhstan, Kyrgyzstan, Turkmenistan,

---

[13]The operationalization of this variable is based on a combination of historical and spatial criteria. First, all governments in which the successors to the former communist parties were the largest party in the government have been coded as non-Right. Next, this category was expanded by including the governments that were dominated by a non-communist left-of-center party (for example, HZDS in Slovakia, LDS in Slovenia, or the Agrarian Party in Moldova). This last coding decision is obviously less than perfect because one necessarily has to rely on somewhat subjective judgments of country experts.

and Uzbekistan) and Mongolia are also excluded due to the lack of reliable statistical data.

5.2 The impact of political factors on economic performance: Explaining the economic performance of post-communist countries in 1993

Table 3.2 reports the results of ordinary least squares (OLS) regression analyses for 1993.[14] The results presented in the first column strongly support the hypotheses about the relationship between the fragmentation of the legislature and the control of the government by the Right on the one hand, and the government's success in fighting inflation on the other. Both coefficients of interest have the expected sign and are statistically significant at the 1 percent level.[15]

The results from the second regression (Model 2, column 2) demonstrate that the impact of the existence of a parliament elected on a nonparty basis on inflation is also very strong. The coefficient on this indicator variable has the predicted sign and is also statistically significant at the 1 percent level. The substantive interpretation of the results of this regression, which must take account of the logarithmic specification of the dependent variable, is as follows. First, controlling for the impact of the other independent variables, countries in which the legislature was elected on a nonparty basis had a rate of inflation in 1993 almost seven times as high as in those countries that used different electoral rules for choosing the members of their legislatures. Second, again controlling for the effects of the other independent variables, countries in which the Right or Center-Right governments were in power for the duration of the transition process had inflation rates in 1993 less than one-fifth as high as in countries in which parties of the Right were never in power.

Serious inflationary pressure remains a major problem for all post-communist countries. None of these countries has been able to bring yearly inflation rates down to single-digit levels. But although some nations are likely to cross this threshold in the near future, others have not

[14]For legislatures elected on a nonparty basis, the measure of fragmentation assumes very small values because each member of the parliament is treated as an independent. As a result, the two variables that measure the fragmentation of the legislature and the existence of the parliament elected on a nonparty basis are closely correlated (-0.6995). For this reason, I estimate two separate models for each dependent variable. The first model includes the fragmentation of the legislature, the ideological orientation of the governments, and the two control variables. The second model includes the existence of the legislature elected on a nonparty basis, the ideological orientation of the governments, and the two control variables.

[15]It is also worth noting that the regression line fits the data extremely well. The adjusted R^2 for this regression is 0.78, and it is 0.80 for the second model.

71

Table 3.2. Explaining the economic performance of post-communist countries in 1993

	Dependent variables					
	Inflation in 1993 (INFLATION93), %, natural log		Private sector share of GDP (OWNERSHIP), %		Real GDP growth in 1993 (Growth 1993), %	
Independent variables	Model 1	Model 2	Model 1	Model 2	Model 1	Model 2
Level of economic development (PCGDP93), GDP per capita in U.S. dollars	−0.52[a] (0.14)	−0.32[a] (0.12)	−0.73 (1.38)	−1.31 (1.14)	1.16 (1.1)	−0.03 (1.16)
Size of the economy (LNGDP93), natural log of GDP in billion U.S. dollars[c]	0.36[b] (0.15)	0.27[b] (0.15)	−0.4 (1.55)	0.32 (1.45)	0.47 (1.24)	0.58 (1.48)
Fragmentation of the legislature (FRAGM93)	−5.81[a] (1.48)		17.4 (14.99)		34.72[a] (11.97)	
Electoral system based on nonparty elections (NONPARTY93)		1.94[a] (0.44)		−9.08[b] (4.28)		−8.62[b] (4.37)
Right or Center-Right governments (RIGHT93)	−1.8[a] (0.55)	−1.69[a] (0.52)	31.48[a] (4.49)	30.04[a] (5.06)	3.08 (4.49)	3.44 (5.17)
Constant	8.01	5.77	29.15	35.86	−19.13	−5.68
Adjusted R[2]	0.78	0.80	0.71	0.77	0.31	0.11

Note: Standard errors are in parentheses.
[a]Significant at the 1 percent level, one-tailed test.
[b]Significant at the 5 percent level, one-tailed test.
[c]GDP dollar estimates for all countries are derived from purchasing power parity (PPP) calculations rather than from conversions at official currency exchange rate.

yet launched their stabilization programs and are careening toward hyperinflation. As the results of the regression analysis demonstrate, political factors such as the fragmentation of the legislature, the electoral system, and the ideological orientation of the government explain this variation. In countries in which the legislatures are highly fragmented, elections are held on a nonparty basis, or governments are controlled by a post-communist Left, inflation often runs out of the control of policy makers and becomes the number one economic problem.

Two out of three political variables also have a strong impact on the speed of the ownership transformation process in the post-communist countries. The coefficients of the electoral system and ideological orientation of the government variables in the regression with the relative size of the private sector in 1994 as the dependent variable (Model 2, column 4) have the predicted signs, and both of them are statistically significant. The substantive impact of these political factors is large. Keeping the effects of the other independent variables constant, the private sector's share of GDP produced in countries in which the governments were controlled by the Right for the duration of the transition process is 30 percentage points higher than in countries in which the Right was never in power. The presence of a legislature elected on the nonparty basis produces the opposite effect, decreasing the private sector's share of GDP by about 9 percentage points. The impact of parliamentary fragmentation on the ownership structure (Model 1, column 3) is very weak. The relevant coefficient has the predicted sign, but it fails to pass even the least stringent test of statistical significance.

The results of the remaining two regressions, in which the GDP growth rate in 1993 is the dependent variable, are weaker than the findings on the determinants of inflation. Although coefficients on the parliamentary fragmentation (Model 1, column 5) and electoral system (Model 2, column 6) variables have the predicted signs and are statistically significant, the estimated coefficients for the ideological orientation of the governments variable are not significantly different from zero in either regression. The overall fit of the two models is much worse than in the case of the first four regressions.

Taken together, the results of the analysis, especially from the first two and the last two models, present an interesting subject for further investigation. The model performs extremely well in explaining the variation in the success of macroeconomic stabilization, which is, perhaps, the most crucial goal of reforms in the initial stage of the transition. All the factors that are hypothesized to influence economic performance are found to have a strong impact on the rate of inflation in post-communist countries.

The model, however, is far less successful in explaining the current growth rates in transition economies. And since inflation and growth in 1993 are only weakly correlated, no other model that uses the same set of independent variables in analyzing both inflation and growth data is likely to perform much better.

Two conflicting explanations of the weakness of the relationship between inflation and growth can be found in the literature. One, which is consistent with the neoliberal model of economic development, admits that the lack of relationship between the two phenomena or even a positive relationship may exist in the early stage of the transition process. But it also predicts that once macroeconomic stabilization, privatization, and other programs necessary for the functioning of the market economy are completed, those post-communist states that were the first to implement them would also be the first to experience sustained economic growth.

The second explanation challenges the predictions of the neoliberal model and argues that successful stabilization programs may significantly reduce public investment in infrastructure, weaken or eliminate measures to induce private investment, and, due to excessively high interest rates, cause numerous bankruptcies of viable firms (Tanzi, 1989; Przeworski, 1993). According to this point of view, successful stabilization is likely to undermine future growth, and therefore the absence of the positive relationship between the success of stabilization and growth found in 1993 is not transitory.

To investigate the consequences of successful stabilization for future growth I estimated three other regression models with the *Euromoney* economic performance rating as the dependent variable. The results are reported in Table 3.3. The first two of these regressions explain the variation in the prospects of future growth in terms of the three political variables and the two control variables. In contrast to the results of the regressions with GDP growth rate in 1993 as the dependent variable, the coefficients on all political variables have the predicted signs and are statistically significant at at least the 5 percent level.

Another way to look at the same problem is to analyze the impact of both current inflation and growth rates on the *Euromoney* rating. In this regression, the coefficient on the growth rate variable is insignificant, which means that the prospects for future growth are unrelated to 1993 growth rate. In contrast, the inflation rate in 1993 appears to have a very strong negative impact on future growth in transition economies.

If the *Euromoney* rating evaluates the overall economic performance of the post-communist states correctly and is able to predict the post-1993 growth rates in the former communist countries accurately, then one can be confident that future growth in these countries is unrelated to their

Table 3.3. *Explaining the predictions of economic growth in 1994 and 1995*

Independent variables	Dependent variable *Euromoney* rating of economic performance (RATING)		
	Model 1	Model 2	Model 3
Level of economic development (PCGDP93), GDP per capita in U.S. dollars	1.13[a] (0.45)	0.82[b] (0.26)	
Size of the economy (LNGDP93), natural log of GDP in billion U.S. dollars[c]	−0.02 (0.51)	0.4 (0.33)	
Fragmentation of the legislature (FRAGM93)	9.31[a] (4.92)		
Electoral system based on nonparty elections (NONPARTY93)		−5.07[b] (1.19)	
Right or Center-Right governments (RIGHT93)	4.2[a] (1.84)	3.36[b] (1.15)	
Inflation in 1993 (INFLATION93), %, natural log			−2.04[b] (0.49)
GDP growth rate in 1993 (GROWTH93), %			−0.04 (0.11)
Constant	1.53	5.11	20.3
Adjusted R^2	0.55	0.83	0.61

Note: Standard errors are in parentheses.
[a]Significant at the 1 percent level, one-tailed test.
[b]Significant at the 5 percent level, one-tailed test.
[c]GDP dollar estimates for all countries are derived from purchasing power parity (PPP) calculations rather than from conversions at official currency exchange rates.

1993 growth rates. Instead, it is the success of macroeconomic stabilization that determines the prospects of general recovery in the region. In this case the model proposed in this chapter would be fully appropriate not only for explaining the success or failure of stabilization efforts but also for predicting successfully the growth patterns for transitional economies. In the next section I investigate the effects of the political variables on inflation and growth rates of sixteen post-communist countries in 1994. The results of this analysis would give at least a partial answer to the question of which of the two explanations of the relationship between stabilization and growth better explains the processes that take place in transitional economies.

*5.3 The impact of political factors on economic performance:
Explaining the economic performance of post-communist
countries in 1994*

The results from the four OLS regressions with inflation and growth rates
in 1994 as the dependent variables are reported in Table 3.4.[16] The
results provide strong support for all hypotheses tested. In the two regressions with inflation as the dependent variable, all three relevant coefficients are in the predicted direction and are statistically significant at the
1 percent level. More important, the coefficients on all three political
variables have the correct signs and are statistically significant in the
regressions with growth rates in 1994 as the dependent variables. The
most interesting finding is, of course, the positive and significant parameter estimate on the ideological orientation of the government variable
(RIGHT94). Substantively, the size of the coefficient means that the difference in 1994 growth rates between countries in which the governments
were controlled by parties of the Right from the beginning of the transition period and the countries in which parties of the Right had never been
in power exceeds 9 percentage points.

Earlier I discussed two explanations of weak correlation between inflation and growth in 1993 and the lack of relationship between the ideological orientation of the governments variable and GDP growth rates in
1993. These two explanations offered different predictions of how successful the model would be in explaining economic growth in subsequent
years. The tests of hypotheses 3 through 5 based on 1994 data suggest
that the explanation consistent with the neoliberal paradigm is correct,
and that countries that were the first to implement macroeconomic stabilization and large-scale privatization programs were also the first to resume economic growth.

6.0 CONCLUSION

The success of market reforms in the former communist countries depends on several political factors. One of these factors is the internal
cohesion of the governments that direct the transformation process. Frag-

---

[16]The indicator variable that singles out the countries that had parliaments elected
on a nonparty basis is highly correlated not only with the parliamentary fragmentation
variable (−0.5849), but also with the ideological orientation of the governments variable (−0.5122). For this reason, two models in this table include the fragmentation of
the legislature variable (FRAGM94), the ideological orientation of the governments
variable (RIGHT94), and the two control variables. The other two models include
only the electoral system variable (NONPARTY94) and the two control variables.

Table 3.4. *Explaining the economic performance of post-communist countries in 1994*

Independent variables	Inflation in 1994 (INFLATION94), %, natural log		Real GDP growth in 1994 (GROWTH94), %	
	Model 1	Model 2	Model 1	Model 2
Level of economic development (PCGDP93), GDP per capita in U.S. dollars	−0.37[a] (0.14)	−0.31[a] (0.14)	2.28[a] (1.19)	1.34[b] (0.85)
Size of the economy (LNGDP93), natural log of GDP in billion U.S. dollars[d]	0.38[a] (0.16)	0.37[a] (0.18)	−1.75 (1.34)	−1.7[b] (1.07)
Fragmentation of the legislature (FRAGM93)	−4.9[c] (1.78)		44.73[c] (15.06)	
Electoral system based on non-party elections (NONPARTY93)		2.13[c] (0.61)		−19.61[c] (3.64)
Right or Center-Right governments (RIGHT93)	−1.65[c] (0.57)		9.24[a] (4.84)	
Constant	6.3	3.97	−19.48	1.2
Adjusted R^2	0.69	0.57	0.56	0.7

Note: Standard errors are in parentheses.
[a]Significant at the 1 percent level, one-tailed test.
[b]Significant at the 5 percent level, one-tailed test.
[c]Significant at the 10 percent level, one-tailed test.
[d]GDP dollar estimates for all countries are derived from purchasing power parity (PPP) calculations rather than from conversions at official currency exchange rates.

mented coalition cabinets are often plagued by internal struggles among the coalition members and are usually incapable of implementing coherent economic policies.

Another factor is the government's ability to maintain the support of a parliamentary majority. Reforms initiated by minority governments are much more likely to be slowed down or completely blocked by the opposition than are policies supported by the government that controls the majority of seats in the legislature.

Government cohesion and its parliamentary support are in turn determined by the degree of parliamentary fragmentation. Highly fragmented legislatures are incapable of passing legislation necessary for implementing economic reforms, without which the economic crisis in post-communist countries could only deepen.

Another factor that influences the economic performance of the post-communist countries is their electoral systems. In countries in which the parliament is elected on a nonparty basis, the overrepresentation of anti-reformers in the legislature and a high degree of parliamentary fragmentation make the task of rapid transition to a market economy extremely difficult. Other electoral rules, such as pure proportional representation or two-ballot majority run-off systems, may also cause parliamentary fragmentation and thus slow down reforms.

Finally, the ideological orientation of parties in power also affects the scale, the speed, and, eventually, the success of the transition process. Many Left parties in the former communist countries – most notably, the communist parties and their allies in Russia and Ukraine – reject market-oriented economic policies. Other Left parties are committed to continuation of reforms but face strong opposition to this course from their rank-and-file members and the electorate. Governments controlled by the Right, on the other hand, are less constrained by the preferences of their core constituencies in implementing fiscal austerity and privatization programs and thus are more likely to make greater progress in creating well-functioning market economies.

REFERENCES

Alesina, Alberto, "Macroeconomic Policy in a Two-Party System as a Repeated Game," *Quarterly Journal of Economics* 103: 3 (1987), 651–78.

Alesina, Alberto, Gerald Cohen and Nouriel Roubini, "Macroeconomic Policy and Elections in OECD Economies," *Economics and Politics* 4: 1 (1992), 1–30.

Bates, Robert H., and Anne O. Krueger, "Generalizations from the Country Studies," in Robert H. Bates and Anne O. Kruger, editors, *Political and Economic Interactions in Economic Policy Reforms: Evidence from Eight Countries* (Oxford: Blackwell, 1991), 460–72.

Duverger, Maurice, *Political Parties: Their Organization and Activity in the Modern State* (New York: Wiley, 1963).

Evans, Peter, "The State as Problem and Solution: Predation, Embedded Autonomy, and Structural Change," in Stephen Haggard and Robert R. Kaufman, editors, *The Politics of Economic Adjustment: International Constraints, Distributive Conflicts, and the State* (Princeton, NJ: Princeton University Press, 1992), 139–81.

Hibbs, Douglas A., Jr., "Political Parties and Macroeconomic Policy," *American Political Science Review* 71: 4 (1977), 1467–87.

Hibbs, Douglas A., Jr., and Christopher Dennis, "Income Distribution in the United States," *American Political Science Review* 82: 2 (1988), 467–90.

Kahler, Miles, "Orthodoxy and Its Alternatives: Explaining Approaches to Stabilization and Adjustment," in Joan M. Nelson, editor, *Economic Crisis and Policy Choice* (Princeton, NJ: Princeton University Press, 1990), 33–61.

Political determinants of economic transition

Laakso, Markku, and Rein Taagepera, "The 'Effective' Number of Parties: A Measure with Application to West Europe," *Comparative Political Studies* 12: 1 (1979), 3–27.

Laver, Michael, and Norman Schofield, *Multiparty Government: The Politics of Coalition in Europe* (Oxford: Oxford University Press, 1990).

Lijphart, Arend, "The Political Consequences of Electoral Laws, 1945–85," *American Political Science Review* 84: 2 (1990), 481–96.

Electoral Systems and Party Systems: A Study of Twenty-seven Democracies 1945–1990 (Oxford: Oxford University Press, 1994).

Powell, G. Bingham, Jr., *Contemporary Democracies: Participation, Stability, and Violence* (Cambridge, MA: Harvard University Press, 1982).

Przeworski, Adam, *Democracy and the Market: Political and Economic Reforms in Eastern Europe and Latin America* (Cambridge: Cambridge University Press, 1991).

"The Neoliberal Fallacy," *Journal of Democracy* 3: 1 (1993), 45–59.

Rae, Douglas W., *The Political Consequences of Electoral Laws* (New Haven, CT: Yale University Press, 1971).

Riker, William H., "The Two-Party System and Duverger's Law: An Essay on the History of Political Science," *American Political Science Review* 76: 4 (1982), 753–66.

Roubini, Nouriel, and Jeffrey D. Sachs, "Political and Economic Determinants of Budget Deficits in the Industrial Democracies," *European Economic Review* 33: 5 (1989), 903–38.

Shugart, Matthew Soberg, "Electoral Reform in Systems of Proportional Representation," *European Journal of Political Research* 21: 3 (1992), 207–24.

Slider, Darrell, "The Soviet Union," *Electoral Studies* 9: 4 (1990), 295–302.

Strom, Kaare, *Minority Government and Majority Rule* (Cambridge: Cambridge University Press, 1990).

Tanzi, Vito, "Fiscal Policy, Stabilization, and Growth," in Mario Blejer and Ke-Yourg Chu, editors, *Fiscal Policy, Stabilization, and Growth in Developing Countries* (Washington, DC: International Monetary Fund, 1989).

Vinton, Louisa, "Poland's New Election Law: Fewer Parties, Same Impasse?" *RFE/RL Research Report* 2:28 (1993), 7–17.

"Power Shifts in Poland's Ruling Coalition," *RFE/RL Research Report* 3: 11 (1994), 5–14.

Wasylyk, Myron, "Ukraine Approaches Parliamentary Elections," *Ukranian Legal and Economic Bulletin* 2: 1 (1994), 20–4.

Webb, W. L., "The Polish General Election of 1991," *Electoral Studies* 11: 2 (1992), 166–70.

Wilson, Andrew, and Arthur Bilous, "Political Parties in Ukraine," *Europe-Asia Studies* 45: 4 (1993), 693–703.

Comment on "Political Determinants of the Success of Economic Transition"

ADAM PRZEWORSKI

The central thesis of Nikolai Mikhailov's chapter is that cohesive, majority governments with a strong executive and controlled by the Right are more effective than others in pursuing successful economic reforms. This belief is shared by proponents of radical pro-market reforms: A "strong" state is needed to impose and persevere with such reforms. The merit of Mikhailov's analysis is that he identifies those aspects of the "strong" state that he considers important, and he brings to bear systematic evidence to test his hypotheses.

I am not persuaded that the strong-state thesis is true, but before getting to this point there is a prior issue that needs clarification.

How should we go about evaluating the success or failure of pro-market reforms?[1] One way, followed by Joan Nelson (1990) and most of her collaborators, is to define success merely in terms of a continued implementation of reform measures, whatever they may be. This is clearly not a satisfactory criterion, as it assumes that whatever policies are followed are appropriate. Yet we know that reform policies and their sequencing differ from country to country, and that some of these policies are mistaken and some of their sequences generate disaster (Edwards, 1990). The second way to proceed, implicit in most economic literature, is to claim that as long as reforms include stabilization, structural adjustment, and privatization, they are successful. This conception assumes that stability and competition are sufficient to improve welfare – specifically, to generate economic growth. And this assumption is dubious at best for at least two reasons (Przeworski, 1993). First, both stabilization and structural adjustment entail several policies that undermine the conditions for future growth: reduction of aggregate demand, excessive interest rates that make good firms go under together with bad ones, and reduction of public investment in infrastructure. Second, market competition is

---

[1]This discussion is based on Bresser Pereira, Maravall, and Przeworski (1993).

not a sufficient condition for growth: Indeed, in the neoclassical growth model, perfect competition leads to stagnation in the absence of exogenous technical change.

Moreover, evaluation of reforms is particularly difficult given their intertemporal character. While exogenous shocks, most importantly the collapse of Soviet-bloc trade, account for between one-third and one-half of the decline of output in six Eastern European countries (for different estimates, see Bruno, 1993; Rodrik, 1993; Rosati, 1993), the remainder of the decline can be attributed to the reforms themselves. The cumulative decline in gross domestic product between 1989 and 1993 ranged from 12 percent in Poland to 29 percent in Romania (Balcerowicz and Gelb, 1994). Most, although not all (Brada and King, 1992), scholars now agree that pro-market reforms are likely to generate a short-term decline of output, incomes, employment, and investment. But because these immediate effects are currently observed and the ultimate effects are only hypothetical, current experience is a poor source of inferences about the future: As unemployment mounts, real incomes decline and firms go under – are we to conclude that reforms are having effects or that things are simply getting worse? Here is a sample assessment by the IMF (*Survey*, November 29, 1993: 357): "The Baltic countries made substantial progress toward establishing macroeconomic stability. . . . Inflation decelerated rapidly, . . . and real incomes declined. . . . This process was associated with unavoidable losses in output and employment." Is this a description of success or of an accelerating economic crisis?

Clearly, the ultimate criterion of success can only be economic growth with a humane income distribution. Yet, as this is the ostensible, yet distant, goal of reforms, while in the meantime they are costly, trying to measure their success may be simply premature. This seems to me to be the endemic difficulty of the now already immense literature on the political determinants of the success of economic reforms: The dependent variable has not yet fully revealed itself.

Having just sounded this skeptical note, let me join Mikhailov on a limb and summarize my view of the relation between "strong" governments and the success of reforms. My view is much more mixed, and, on balance, I am inclined to believe that "weak" governments may be more successful than "strong" ones. "Strong" governments may be more likely to adopt a radical reform program, but several questions need to be asked: First, is it going to be a good program, from a purely technical economic point of view? Second, will a program adopted by a "strong" government be credible to economic agents? Third, will it be consistently pursued? Clearly, answers to these questions depend to some extent on what we mean by "strong." For example, governments with a "strong" executive, endowed with extensive decree powers, are able to adopt whatever policies they wish. But the very fact that policies are adopted by decree indicates that the government does not enjoy sufficient support to muster a majority. Hence, economic agents will anticipate that such policies are only as stable as the governments that adopt them. The world is full of governments that issue innumerable decrees with little effect on the behavior of economic agents.

Having reviewed the experience of several countries in Latin America, Southern Europe, and Eastern Europe, Bresser Pereira et al. (1993: 208–13) reach the following conclusions: First, consultation may serve to improve the technical quality of reform programs. For example, the Balcerowicz Plan in Poland lowered the protection of the agriculture sector in a clearly excessive way, and the subsequent governments had to beat a way back. Had the Peasant Party participated in the elaboration of the plan, this overshooting would have been avoided. Second, discussion and negotiation may serve to build political support for the particular reform strategy. Such a negotiation is not always possible, as some measures require surprise to be effective. Yet a policy that results from political negotiations may be more credible, precisely because the prospects of continuation of such a policy are greater if it enjoys political support. Decrees are often ineffective because economic agents suspect that the policies are politically unsustainable. Finally, although this is not a subject of Mikhailov's analysis, one must worry about the effects of economic reforms on democracy. A technocratic policy style deprives the political forces of incentives to participate in democratic institutions and may threaten their consolidation.

I emphasized the points of disagreement with Mikhailov's thesis to clarify the issues. Obviously, governments must be able to govern: They cannot merely consult and negotiate. And certainly some of the potential partners will irresponsibly pursue their narrow self-interests to the detriment of the broadly desirable change. But I am repeatedly struck by the paradox that the most ardent advocates of decentralized decision making in the economic sphere are those who vigorously and unabashedly demand centralized political direction over the reform process. If economic agents are so smart in allocating resources, then why should they be so mistrusted as citizens?

To close, let me make a brief comment on the Right–Left dimension that Mikhailov employs in his analysis. I am skeptical of its fundamental importance for two reasons. First, even extreme Left governments are capable of reform. I note that the reform program proposed by the last communist government in Poland, headed by Mieczyslaw Rakowski, was not any less radical than the Balcerowicz Plan, and that Hungarian communists decontrolled 90 percent of prices by 1989. Second, I also see the economic situation, as well as the pressure emanating from the international financial institutions, as much more constraining than does Mikhailov. Hence, I do not think that the Left will pursue much different policies than the Right. They are likely to pay more attention to the public sector, cautiously extend some income protection, and be more open to political negotiations with their opponents. If anything, these will be beneficial corrections of the original programs, but they will be minor in scope and will not undermine continuity on the road to the market.

REFERENCES

Balcerowicz, Leszek, and Alan Gelb, "Macropolicies in Transition to a Market Economy: A Three-Year Perspective," paper presented at the Annual Bank Conference on Development Economics, World Bank, Washington, DC, April 28–9, 1994.

Brada, Josef C., and Arthur E. King, "Is There a J-Curve for the Economic Transition from Socialism to Capitalism?" *Economics of Planninq* 25: 1 (1992), 37–53.

Bresser Pereira, Luiz Carlos, José Maria Maravall, and Adam Przeworski, *Economic Reforms in New Democracies. A Social-Democratic Approach* (Cambridge: Cambridge University Press, 1993).

Bruno, Michael, "Stabilization and Reform in Eastern Europe: Preliminary Evaluation," in Mario I. Blejer, Guillermo A. Calvo, Fabrizio Corcelli, and Alan H. Gelb, editors, *Eastern Europe in Transition: From Recession to Growth?* (Washington, D.C.: World Bank Discussion Paper No. 196, 1993), 12–38.

Edwards, Sebastian, "The Sequencing of Economic Reform: Analytical Issues and Lessons from Latin American Development," *World Economy* 13: 1 (1990), 1–14.

Nelson, Joan M., editor, *Economic Crisis and Policy Choice* (Princeton, NJ: Princeton University Press, 1990).

Przeworski, Adam, "The Neoliberal Fallacy," in Larry Diamond and Marc F. Plattner, editors, *Capitalism, Socialism, and Democracy Revisited* (Baltimore: Johns Hopkins Press, 1993), 39–53.

Rodrik, Dani, "Making Sense of the Soviet Trade Schock in Eastern Europe: A Framework and Some Estimates," in Mario I. Blejer, Guillermo A. Calvo, Fabrizio Corcelli, and Alan H. Gelb, editors, *Eastern Europe in Transition: From Recession to Growth?* (Washington, DC: World Bank Discussion Paper No. 196, 1993), 64–85.

Rosati, Dariusz, "Poland: Glass Half Empty," in Richard Portes, editor, *Economic Transformation in Central Europe: A Progress Report* (London: Centre for Economic Policy Research, 1993), 211–73.

4

Russian privatization and the limits of credible commitment

TIMOTHY FRYE[1]

1.0 INTRODUCTION

Post-communist privatization offers an intriguing opportunity to explore important themes in political economy. The Russian case raises particularly interesting questions. Why, in contrast to many post-communist counterparts, did the Russian government promote a rapid voucher privatization? How did it try to make this program more credible amid great uncertainty? What drove changes in the credibility of the privatization program over time?

First, drawing on recent work in positive political economy, I argue that a political logic drove the choice of privatization strategy in Russia. This literature suggests that insecure incumbents facing a polarized opposition have strong incentives to pursue policies aimed at constraining the options of future governments (Persson and Svensson, 1989; Alesina and Tabellini, 1990). Facing a polarized opposition to rapid reform and ruling with temporary decree powers, the Yeltsin government favored a rapid voucher privatization strategy that it hoped would be difficult for current and future governments to reverse. These political incentives made a rapid voucher privatization that recognized the gains of enterprise managers an attractive strategy.

Second, I argue that the Yeltsin government tried to increase the credibility of its strategy by distributing vouchers to the public. Lacking strong political institutions that make government commitments more credible, Russian reformers tried to use the voucher as a commitment device to reduce two aspects of the credibility problem. The aim of using the voucher was both to signal the government's commitment to a populist, rapid,

[1]I gratefully acknowledge helpful advice from Joel Helman, Eric Reinhardt, Larisa Gorbatova, Rory MacFarquhar, Alison Alter, Letitia Rydjeski, Kira Sanbonmatsu, an anonymous reviewer, and the members of the Property Rights Project. All errors are mine.

large-scale privatization and to raise the political cost of changing the privatization program ex post.

Third, I test the model presented in Chapter 2 by tracing the effect of political events on the credibility of the Russian privatization program as measured by the market price of the voucher.[2] If the fear that privatization would be reversed by political events were great, then we would expect voucher prices to fluctuate with political events that threaten the reformers. The evidence suggests that the voucher played a limited role in increasing the credibility of privatization. Many seemingly important political events had little impact on the voucher price, but the December 1993 elections, and the resignation of Yegor Gaidar in January 1994, substantially affected it. Evidence from the market for vouchers suggests that the political costs of significantly altering privatization were perceived to be too low to withstand these major political shocks. In short, brokers seemed to believe that the government could use vouchers to make it more difficult to reverse privatization, but that the government could also "untie its hands" and change course when these costs were particularly high. The evidence presented here appears generally consistent with the hypotheses generated by the model in Chapter 2, but also suggests that the government's ability to tie its hands is not unlimited.

The argument presented is narrow. Others have addressed the relation of formal privatization to stabilization and corporate governance.[3] I address the analytically prior tactical question of how politicians try to make reforms more credible. I focus on how Russian reformers tried to use the voucher as a signaling and commitment device in an environment of great uncertainty and tremendous interest group pressure.

2.0 CREDIBILITY AND ECONOMIC REFORM

Politicians who introduce reforms face two credibility problems (Rodrik, 1989). First, announced policy changes often provoke skepticism from potential supporters because they cannot tell how serious the government is about implementing them. Governments often have an incentive to pay lip service to reform to attract investment, loans, and political support, but actors outside the government cannot distinguish sincere from dissembling reformers. Lacking this information, potential supporters are reluctant to back reform. A truly reformist government can differentiate itself by send-

[2]This is a "most difficult" case for studying commitment. Vouchers in Russia were worth far less than vouchers in Czechoslovakia.

[3]Frydman and Rapaczynski (1994) offer the most sophisticated analysis of these relationships. Privatization here refers to the transfer of cash flow and control rights to non-state actors (Grossman and Hart, 1986). The cost of exercising rights to enterprise assets remains high.

ing a signal to the public that reveals its intentions. If this signal is seen as costless to make, as are most campaign promises, then the public will be skeptical. If, however, the signal creates a significant cost for the sender, then the government increases the chances that the public will believe its message. For example, a government may devalue the currency beyond reasonable levels to signal commitment to trade reform.

Second, a reformist government faces a credibility problem because its optimal ex post strategy may differ from its optimal ex ante strategy (Kydland and Prescott, 1977; North, 1990; Weingast, 1993). Announced policy may not be believed because the public expects the government to abandon reform in the future. This possibility may lead actors to believe that there is no sense in supporting reforms today, because they will be undone tomorrow. As everyone can foresee this logic, even potential winners may be reluctant to support a policy change, and reform will be stillborn.

Incumbents can mitigate these credibility problems by creating institutions that raise the costs of changing course. If the costs of changing policy are high, then incumbents may convince skeptical potential supporters that they will not deviate from their plans regardless of unforeseen circumstances. Self-imposed constraints can compel incumbents to exercise maximum effort to keep reform on course.

Governments that rule with short time horizons and a polarized opposition face especially severe credibility problems. Short time horizons raise expectations of a change in government leading to a probable change in policy. A polarized opposition with policy preferences far from those of the incumbent exacerbates the commitment problem by increasing the magnitude of expected change in policy that will accompany a new government. Following this logic, governments with short time horizons operating in polarized political systems should favor policies that are difficult for the current and future governments to reverse.[4] Although politicians may choose policies based on electoral, efficiency, revenue, or interest group concerns, the view presented here suggests that incumbents facing severe credibility problems may favor policies that try to constrain current and future governments.

2.1 Credibility and Russian reform

More than in most other post-communist countries, Russian reformers began the transition with a high probability of losing office and a po-

---

[4]The logic of this argument is drawn from the literature on strategic debt (Persson and Svenson, 1989; Alesina and Tabellini, 1990). It argues that a conservative government with a short time horizon may use debt to discourage a liberal successor government from spending on social programs.

larized opposition. Skepticism in the parliament toward reform can be traced to the parliamentary elections of 1990 (Sobyanin, 1994; Andrews, 1994). The parliament elected Boris Yeltsin chairman by a small margin only after several ballots in the summer of 1990. Moreover, Yeltsin lacked a party organization in the parliament, and roll-call votes suggest that the "democrats never had a majority among the deputies in the Congress" (Sobyanin, 1994: 191). Support for rapid reform in the government was often tenuous, and reformers never held a majority within the cabinet.

The basis of Yeltsin's formal authority also raised doubts about his commitment to reform. As discussed in Chapter 5, the parliament expanded the president's power to conduct economic reform by decree in November 1991, but it retained the authority to revoke these powers. Holding vast, but temporary, decree powers, the president had a strong incentive to use these powers quickly while they remained in force.

In addition to facing a high probability of losing office, reformers made policy in a highly polarized political system. Voting records from parliament during 1990–1 suggest the "polarization of the body into two large and stable groups of deputies, which occupy diametrically opposed positions on literally all questions of political principle. These positions have remained virtually unchanged during the two-and-one-half-year life of the Russian Congress" (Sobyanin, 1994: 192). Andrews similarly finds a high degree of polarization among Supreme Soviet deputies on roll-call votes prior to the passage of the State Privatization Program (Andrews, 1994). Others also viewed politics in this period as polarized (Roeder, 1994).

Ruling with short time horizons in a polarized political system, Russian reformers favored a privatization plan that it hoped would constrain the policy options of future governments. These political factors increased the attraction of a rapid voucher privatization that the government believed it would be costly to jettison. Gaining managerial acceptance to rapid formal privatization, however, required great concessions. This political logic drove the strategy of Russian reformers. To better understand the incentives facing Russian reformers and the privatization outcome, I identify the players and their goals.[5]

3.0 BARGAINING FOR PROPERTY RIGHTS IN RUSSIA

3.0.1 The executive. The president and his allies sought to use privatization to reaffirm their reformist credentials and to make privatization

---

[5]Most work on Russian privatization stresses the important role of interest groups, particularly enterprise managers. Yet, politicians faced powerful managerial lobbies in most post-communist countries, but we find great variance in initial privatization strategies. While not ignoring the role of interest groups, this work also stresses the choices made by political actors making decisions amid great uncertainty.

difficult to reverse. They tried to limit state actors from holding shares gained through spontaneous privatization to reduce their ability to roll back reform. They also wanted to create a constituency that would raise the political costs of reversing reform by granting shares to the public and by encouraging the creation of voucher funds. In addition, by privatizing rapidly they hoped to deter any future government from reversing the program. Future tampering with privatization meant taking assets from the de facto and de jure holders of these rights, a costly endeavor for any government.

3.0.2 Ministries. Pro-privatization reformers in the Executive branch had a strong ally in the State Privatization Agency (GKI). Created to oversee privatization, GKI favored the rapid transfer of state assets, individual rather than collective ownership of shares, and tight corporate control (*Izvestiya*, February 28, 1992: 1). Initially cool to the voucher plan, GKI became its leading defender and established an alliance with the voucher funds (Rutgaizer, 1993). GKI's support in the government was tenuous, particularly after Chernomyrdin became prime minister in December 1992. Chernomyrdin once compared (later retracted) GKI's privatization to Stalin's tragic collectivization of agriculture (*Itar-Tass*, April 1, 1993: 1). In response, GKI insulated itself from other ministries and conducted a vast public campaign for mass privatization.

Other ministries opposed the privatization proposal developed by GKI. The Minister of Industry complained that "the policy of GKI is fundamentally incorrect" (*Izvestiya*, September 10, 1992: 2). Sectoral ministries, often transformed into various types of "production associations," were active, if not always successful, lobbyists for sectoral interests (Frydman et al., 1993). In the first six months of 1991, 126 concerns, 54 industrial unions, and 1,500 industrial associations were created in the Soviet Union (Radigin, 1992). Ministries sought to leave shares in holding companies managed in part by ministerial bureaucrats, expand the cross-ownership of shares by enterprises and ministries, and keep enterprises under their purview and out of the privatization program. A few production associations managed to keep many shares under their control, but the collapse of the centrally planned economy undermined most ministries, and many lost use and income rights to enterprise assets.[6]

3.0.3 Private claimants: Managers and workers. By seizing use and income rights to assets prior to formal privatization, industrial managers

---

[6]Local governments held rights to industrial assets, but GKI used proceeds from privatization to buy them off. Resistance to privatization across regions is beyond the scope of this essay.

became the most influential lobby on privatization issues. These rights allowed managers to arbitrage between state and market prices and to strip assets. They also brought managers a privileged political position. Managerial interests were relatively concentrated and minimized the problem of collective action. The Russian Union of Industrialists and Entrepreneurs (RUIE) led the largest managerial lobby and claimed to represent six thousand industrial enterprises (*Nezavisimaya Gazeta*, June 2, 1992: 1). In June 1992 the RUIE, the Democratic Party of Russia, and the Peoples' Party of Russia formed the Civic Union, an alliance that claimed to hold 40 percent of seats in parliament. The RUIE had allies in the government after three pro-industry deputy ministers were appointed in June 1992 and after Chernomyrdin became head of government in December 1992. Vast control rights over enterprises and well-placed allies gave managers a virtual veto over any privatization plan. The diversity of managerial interests makes generalizing about their preferences difficult. In brief, managers split on the rate and scope of privatization, but united against outside ownership and in favor of increased shares for managers.

Workers in Russia also emerged as an important lobby. The peak labor group, the Federation of Independent Trade Unions (FITUR), boasted (very optimistically) of 60 million members. It controlled the State Pension Fund, retained property from the Soviet era, and deducted dues automatically. Workers benefited from their large number of votes, the normative appeal of worker ownership, and their lobby in the parliament. Weak organization, however, limited their influence on policy. FITUR, a successor of a Soviet-era trade union, suffered from weak sectoral coordination, which made mass action difficult.

To offset this weakness, workers and managers formed a brief marriage of convenience against outside ownership. The RUIE formalized this alliance by cofounding Russia's largest trade union paper. This temporary coalition hindered the distribution of shares to outsiders and allowed the better-organized managers to use the workers as a screen for their interests (Gimpelson, 1994).

3.0.4 Non-enterprise employees.   Professionals, private-sector and white-collar employees, pensioners, and others who worked outside of enterprises also claimed a stake in industrial assets. Facing severe collective action problems, these groups had weak representation, but as the base of Yeltsin's support, their claims could not be costlessly dismissed. A complete insider takeover of privatization, as in Ukraine or Belarus, would have brought political damage to Yeltsin's core constituencies. The president wanted to maintain at least the perception that privatization would protect interests outside the industrial sector, because economic reform had brought hardship to many members of his coalition. The loss of these base constituencies could threaten the president's ability to conduct reform, compete with rivals in the parliament, or retain office. Creating broad support for privatization gained political salience as stabilization sputtered in 1992 and 1993. Yeltsin faced the veto of enterprise insiders and the need to maintain at least a veneer of public participation in privatization to satisfy his core supporters.

3.1 The bargaining process

In the fall of 1991 the Russian government prepared plans for privatization as part of a reform package.[7] On December 27, 1991, the Yeltsin government issued "The Fundamental Provisions of Privatization," which proposed a single option of privatization in which workers received 25 percent of nonvoting stock and the managers received 5 percent of voting stock. Remaining shares would be sold at public auction, and the workers' collective could buy 10 percent more shares at a 30 percent discount. The provisions included the sale of assets by auction, limited voting rights for workers, and a ban on the cross-holding of shares.

The Yeltsin government proposed a privatization program based largely on these provisions to the Supreme Soviet in March 1992, where the industrial lobby sought to expand its share of assets, reduce the transferability of shares, and sell assets for cash, rather than vouchers. The parties compromised on a second option that allowed enterprise insiders to buy 51 percent of shares at a closed auction prior to public sale. GKI officials accepted this option, but tried to discourage its use. They raised the price of shares at the closed auction to 1.7 times the January 1992 book value and required immediate payment – the first option allowed a three-year payment plan. They also required a two-thirds majority vote within the enterprise, rather than a simple majority as in the first option. Nevertheless, high inflation allowed insiders to purchase controlling shares at nominal prices and foiled GKI's efforts to limit use of the second option.

The industrial lobby was successful in including a third option for small and medium-sized enterprises that allowed managers and workers each to buy 20 percent of shares if they agreed to restructure. The Supreme Soviet passed the Privatization Program on June 11, 1992.

Not all the demands of enterprise insiders were encoded in the Privatization Program. Reformers ended transferability restrictions that would have kept all shares within the firm. They revoked many long-term leases signed as sweetheart deals between ministerial bureaucrats and enterprise

---

[7]The first Russian Law on Privatization passed on July 3, 1991, but subsequent legislation superseded it.

managers. The reformers kept the voucher as a component of public participation in privatization and included a tight timetable for transferring 70 percent of enterprises to private ownership within two years. Given the perverse incentives of claimants to preprivatized assets, the reformers hoped a less than ideal, but rapid, privatization would cause less political and economic damage than maintaining the status quo.

3.2 Early results of the privatization program

Early results of Russian privatization highlight the program's speed and benefits for enterprise insiders. In contrast to expectations, by July 1, 1994, fourteen thousand medium and large enterprises (70 percent of Russian industry) had been transformed into joint-stock companies. According to GKI, 73 percent of privatized enterprises chose the second option that allowed insiders to buy 51 percent of shares at low prices. Surveys conducted in 1993 by GKI found that on average workers owned 53 percent of the shares in an enterprise, managers 17 percent, outsiders 14 percent, and the state 16 percent (Pistor, 1994). A smaller study of twenty-four enterprises found that workers held slightly less than half of enterprise shares (Bim, 1994).

These figures, however, understate managerial control rights. Managers often find friendly outside investors who retain them in exchange for preferential treatment, gain voting rights of workers' shares, dominate shareholder meetings, and use their informational advantages to frustrate outsiders. They also try to block the registration of shares and to hold auctions in remote regions inaccessible to fund agents (Pistor, 1994). Significant outsider influence on corporate boards is rare, and outsiders' rights are poorly protected (Gorbatova, 1993; Blasi, 1994). Rapid progress in formal privatization has left extremely weak corporate governance in its wake.

Perhaps of more importance to reformers, formal privatization did not stall in Russia as it has in many post-communist countries. Given the starting conditions in Russia and the difficulty of separating the state from ownership in the post-Soviet world, the initial progress of formal privatization in Russia merits attention.

4.0 INCREASING THE CREDIBILITY OF THE PRIVATIZATION PROGRAM

As noted earlier, policy outcomes reached today may be undone by new political circumstances tomorrow. Frequent tinkering with tax, investment, and regulatory policy in response to political change has plagued reform in all post-communist countries. Similarly, many of these countries passed privatization programs only to see progress undermined by frequent changes in the political environment. The difficulty of formally privatizing large-enterprises in Poland and Hungary is striking in this respect.

Most observers, and Russian reformers in particular, feared that hostile interest groups would alter privatization after passage of the Privatization Program. Writing in the winter of 1993 one observer noted, "It is doubtful – to put it no higher – whether the new prime minister [Chernomyrdin] will follow the path of privatization selected by his predecessor" (Major, 1993: 88). As expected, some managers, workers, and bureaucrats tried to make "corrections" ex post. The appointment of pro-industry ministers in June 1992, the fall of the Gaidar government in December 1992, and a poor showing by reformers in parliamentary elections in December 1993 weakened the government's ability to limit these corrections. These shifts in bargaining power lead one to expect changes in the pace and content of privatization.

Anticipating this threat, Russian reformers chose a rapid privatization strategy and used vouchers to try to constrain current and future governments from changing privatization. Privatization vouchers played a central role in this strategy. The design of the voucher program indicates a keen sensitivity to credibility concerns.

First, the voucher program aimed to raise the political costs to the government of changing course.[8] Altering privatization would mean taking small, but tangible, gains from all citizens. Expropriating these benefits would also severely limit the reformers' claim to represent the public interest. Further, by making the voucher tradeable, the Russian government encouraged active rather than passive public participation in the program. Prior to the decision to introduce vouchers, individuals were to receive personal privatization accounts according to a law passed by the Supreme Soviet on May 7, 1991. Privatization accounts had several limitations. They could not be traded and could only be used for buying shares in enterprises. Account holders would benefit from privatization only when the account was traded for a share, and only if the enterprise paid a dividend. Privatization accounts did not permit the creation of investment funds and thus would not create an organized interest group to support privatization. The ability of the current or a future government to annul these accounts at little cost was greater than under a voucher system. Reformers elsewhere in Eastern Europe made their vouchers nontradeable and denominated in points rather than currency, but Russian

[8]Interviews with Andrei Shleifer, advisor to the Russian government, May 5, 1994, and Petr Fillipov, member of Supreme Soviet Committee in charge of privatization, December 20, 1994.

reformers opted for tradeability and ruble denomination out of concerns over the credibility of the program.

Second, by using vouchers, the reformers aimed to expand the role of the reformist GKI in privatization at the expense of ministries that opposed the program. It would also allow the president to bring reformers into decision-making positions by placing them within GKI.

Third, by frontloading and distributing the benefits of privatization widely through vouchers, the reformist government also sought to make future tampering with privatization more difficult. Issuing vouchers complicated the creation of closed joint-stock companies by raising the public expectation that it would have access to shares. Three contributors to the privatization program noted: "Since popular involvement was deemed absolutely necessary for the sustainability of Russian privatization, vouchers were a clear choice" (Boycko, Shleifer, and Vishny, 1995: 83).

Fourth, vouchers also aimed to accelerate privatization. They were distributed in less than four months and hastened the rate of public auctions by increasing demand for shares. The reformers hoped a rapid privatization would increase credibility because once shares are distributed the political costs of expropriating them would dramatically increase.

Fifth, the vouchers offered an immediate benefit that reformers hoped would muffle opposition to a privatization plan that concentrated wealth in the hands of enterprise insiders. GKI opinion polls in the summer of 1993 found broad support for the program (Boycko et al., 1993: 178). Surveys by Lynn Nelson and Irina Kuzes (1994) and by Richard Rose (1993) found that public opinion was not an obstacle to privatization during 1992 and 1993.

Tolerance for privatization in Russia in 1993 contrasts with the unpopularity of the large-enterprise privatization programs in Poland and Hungary. Like Russia, these countries granted vast benefits to enterprise insiders, but unlike Russia, they did not use vouchers, and the public displayed antipathy to their initial programs (Kiss, 1994). In some respects, privatizing heavy industry has proved more difficult in Hungary and Poland than in Russia.

By distributing vouchers and encouraging their concentration in investment funds, the government sought to raise the political costs of altering privatization. The voucher is an inefficient means of distributing assets due to high transaction costs and weak corporate governance, but the government weighed these losses against the political benefits of constraining current and future governments.

Why would economic actors, like some managers, bureaucrats, and workers who had the potential to benefit from future changes in privatization, allow the introduction of a device that could make introducing these changes more difficult? Vouchers allowed enterprise insiders to purchase assets quickly and cheaply, key considerations given the presence of competing claims to assets and limited domestic capital. Vouchers also ensured a degree of popular support for the program. As David Stark notes, insider privatization in Hungary and Poland was derailed, owing in part to equity concerns (Stark, 1992). Finally, uncertainty about the future of reform gave stakeholders an incentive to solidify their gains quickly, rather than risk losing them.

5.0 CREDIBILITY AND VOUCHER PRIVATIZATION

The Yeltsin government introduced voucher privatization by decree on August 14, 1992. Vouchers are a claim against the equity of an enterprise undergoing privatization. Distributed free to all citizens, vouchers had a nominal value of 10,000 rubles (an average monthly salary in November 1992) and could be exchanged for shares in an enterprise, traded for cash, or sold to a voucher investment fund. Like all ruble-denominated assets, vouchers lost much of their value in 1992 and 1993 because of the high rate of inflation.

GKI registered the first voucher fund in late 1992, and by November 29, 1993, 631 funds operated in Russia. Moscow and the Moscow region had the most funds with 143.[9] St. Petersburg and its surrounding region had forty-six funds, and the Sverdlovsk region had twenty-five. By October 1993, 70 percent of all regions had registered at least three funds, and seventy-nine of eighty-eight regions had registered at least one fund (*Reforma*, No. 48, 1993: 2). Large funds also had agents in many regions.

The number of funds was larger than expected, but the market was concentrated. As of April 1994, First Voucher Fund controlled 4,200,000 vouchers, Alpha-Capital had 2,400,000, MN-Fund had 1,450,000, and Lukoil-Fund had 1,168,000. The sixteen largest funds held 71 percent of vouchers placed in funds (GKI Funds Monitoring Unit, interview, December 21, 1993). By the end of voucher privatization in July 1994, the public had invested 139 million of 148 million vouchers in enterprises, thus indicating great public interest in the program (*RFE/RL Daily: Central Eurasian Report*, July 1, 1994: 1).

Wise or fortuitous investment could bring great returns. Shares in the communications giant Rostelekom were issued at 80 U.S. cents, but traded at U.S.$6.50 by August 1994. The vast majority of funds, however, are unlikely to pay significant dividends. Many voucher funds experienced severe financial difficulties and are relatively inactive. Promises to "make your voucher golden" or pay high dividends attracted many investors, but

---

[9]Interview with Galina Shalina, head of the GKI Funds Monitoring Unit, December 21, 1993.

also reduced the credibility of the funds. Few funds paid dividends.[10] As the funds face little monitoring and lack accounting skills, the scope for abuse is great.[11] Using data submitted to GKI, one researcher found that only six of forty account balances did not include gross violations (Gorbatova, 1993).

Several scandals involving organizations that collected vouchers also reduced the credibility of the funds.[12] The outcry accompanying the three major scandals in 1992–3 provoked GKI to compensate deceived voucher holders to keep privatization on track. This rapid response reveals a sensitivity to the political costs of canceling voucher privatization.[13] These political costs are often critical. In one of the few cases of voucher privatization conducted elsewhere, low dividends discredited and stalled a program in British Columbia after high initial public support (Andreff, 1991).

After voucher privatization the number of active funds fell, but during voucher privatization the largest ones were backed by prominent economic organizations that were active in other spheres of the economy. Exporters, banks, industrial groups, and emerging market companies often supported the funds. For example, Alpha-Capital, which is backed by Alpha-Bank, had a declared capital of 30 billion rubles (roughly U.S.$30 million) and dealers in 120 cities. CS First Boston traded more than 16 million vouchers from December 1993 to June 1994 (*Euromoney*, September 1994: 92).

Despite the precarious financial position of many funds, the largest became prominent organizations during voucher privatization, and any group seeking to alter privatization needed to reckon with their interests. More important, the funds had a base of shareholders whose interests needed to be considered by any party that sought to abandon privatization.

---

[10]During voucher privatization, many funds relied on speculation. One fund manager boasted of selling packets of shares in fourteen of fifteen firms at a profit within two weeks. Interview, December 15, 1993.

[11]The Director of the GKI Funds Monitoring Unit noted that of 168 balances submitted in June 1993, only two were in order (interview, December 21, 1993). Given the difficulty of monitoring, it is surprising that more scandals did not occur.

[12]At least sixty funds did not submit their account balance to GKI for quarterly review in the summer of 1993 (*Izvestiya*, September 28, 1993: 2). Instead of removing their licenses, GKI published their names in a national paper. Within a week, thirty funds submitted balances to GKI (*Izvestiya*, October 2, 1993: 1). The accuracy of these balances is open to question, however.

[13]Major scandals involved two unlicensed firms in St. Petersburg (Aramis and Revansh) in December 1992, an unlicensed Moscow firm (Technical Progress) in December 1993, and a large fund claiming to invest in oil and diamonds (Neft-AlmazInvest) in the spring of 1994. GKI compensated voucher holders to restore faith in reform during the initial stage of privatization, October 1992 to January 1994, but did not do so after this period.

6.0 MEASURING THE CREDIBILITY
OF PROPERTY RIGHTS

I have argued that political factors were central to the choice of privatization strategy in Russia. I have also argued that the government used the voucher to try to signal commitment to reform and to raise the political costs of reversing course. One question remains: What drove changes in the credibility of property rights specified in the Privatization Program? In other words, did the public perceive the program as credible?

As implied in the model presented in Chapter 2, we view the credibility of property rights as endogenous to the interaction between political and economic actors: Credible property rights depend on actors' beliefs that other actors will respect their rights. Shifts in the discount rates of relevant actors, particularly the government, affect these beliefs and shape the credibility of property rights. In a political setting, these shifts include elections or votes of no confidence that a government may lose. Rather than losing office, incumbents may appease opponents by altering a reform. If the costs of doing so are low, then these shifts will reduce the credibility of property rights. If, however, political actors raise the costs of changing course, then these shifts will have less impact, and traders can base their decisions on economic factors.

In the Russian case this logic suggests some observations that would be apparent if the voucher were a potent commitment device. If traders believed that the costs to the government of reversing privatization were low, then voucher prices should fluctuate with shifts in the discount rate of government reformers. This discount rate can be interpreted as the probability that the reformers will lose office. If traders believed that the rules for privatization were credible, then voucher prices should be higher (due to a lower risk premium) and should not vary with political shocks. After vouchers are collected by the funds and are widely used in auctions, the political costs of altering the privatization program should be higher. Moreover, economic rather than political events should drive fluctuations in the voucher.

6.1 Credibility of the Russian privatization program

One measure of the credibility of the privatization program is the market price of the voucher. A vice chairman of GKI noted: "The valuation of the voucher is an indicator of how seriously the government regards privatization and market reforms" (*Izvestiya*, August 25, 1992: 2). By February 1993 the voucher market became sufficiently liquid that traders could easily register their perceptions of changes in the political and economic environment on privatization.[14]

Before we consider data from the voucher market, it is worth noting that public participation in Russian privatization was at a high level. While governments in Ukraine, Bulgaria, Romania, and Kazakhstan had difficulty persuading the public to pick up vouchers, more than 97 percent of the Russian population obtained vouchers by the end of privatization.

Three findings emerge from observation of the voucher market. First, voucher prices were extremely low in comparison to similar assets. For example, the implied market value of two giants of Russian industry, Uralmash and Perm Motors, were U.S.$4 million and U.S.$6 million, respectively (Boycko, Shleifer, and Vishny, 1995: 118).

Second, as shown in Figure 4.1, the largest changes in the voucher price were associated with economic rather than political events. Impending auctions of attractive assets in the energy sector in early November 1993 increased the voucher price from U.S.$12.30 to U.S.$22.64 (84 percent) in one day. Large swings in the voucher price were also associated with auctions for valuable assets on June 1, 1993 (40 percent) and March 21–4, 1994 (22 percent). In comparison, the average daily change in the dollar price of the voucher was 4.6 percent.

Third, as indicated in Table 4.1, the voucher seems to have had a positive, but limited, effect on the credibility of the privatization program. Of nine important political events analyzed between January 1993 and June 1994, only two had substantial and significant impacts on the price of the voucher. Massive sales of vouchers following the elections of December 1993 and the resignation of Gaidar in January 1994 suggest that brokers believed that privatization could still be significantly altered even after vouchers had been distributed and auctions had been occurring for one year.[15]

---

[14]Vouchers were traded for rubles and for dollars. I rely more heavily on the dollar rate in my analysis for three reasons. First, dollars represent a relatively constant value over time, and Russian financial institutions (and many individual Russians) who were active in the voucher market often held dollars. Second, the dollar price and the real ruble price for vouchers were highly correlated (0.98), indicating a great deal of cross-trading between dollars, rubles, and vouchers. Third, inflation rates were reported *weekly*, while the *daily* fluctuations of the voucher provide the most interesting information on the credibility of privatization. Much information is lost when deflated ruble prices are averaged for a week. In addition, the difficulty of calculating weekly inflation indexes introduces another source of error. Inflation-adjusted voucher prices produce similar results. As a check, I also cite the exchange rate adjusted price of the voucher.

[15]Regression analysis available from the author supports the findings. A simple time series model suggests that only two of nine seemingly important events – the elections of December 1993 and Gaidar's announcement that he would not join the government in January 1994 – had statistically significant effects on the dollar price of the voucher.

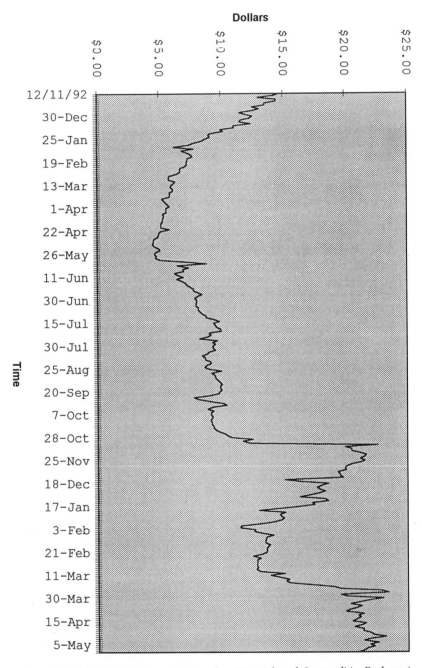

Figure 4.1 Voucher prices (Source: Russian Raw Materials and Commodities Exchange)

Table 4.1. *Political events and voucher prices*

Event	Price ($) t1 (event) t1 + 1 day t1 + 2 day	Percent change	Price (rubles)	Percent change
			Dollars Exchange rate adjusted	
1. Fourth option, 1-14-93	12.40	7.8	5,245	7.8
	11.00	−11.3	4,862	−7.3
	11.04	0.9	4,879	2.9
2. State of emergency, 3-20-93	5.85	−0.7	3,902	−0.6
	5.26	−10.1	3,597	−7.8
	5.40	2.7	3,693	2.7
3. April referendum, 4-25-93	5.17	−11.6	4,110	−10.6
	5.00	−3.3	4,060	−1.2
	4.96	−0.8	4,082	−0.5
4. Parliament blocks program, 7-17-93	9.92	3.4	10,118	3.4
	9.98	−0.6	10,149	0.3
	9.01	−9.7	9,233	−10.3
5. Parliament disbanded, 9-21-93	9.80	−0.6	10,152	−0.7
	9.00	−8.2	9,918	−2.3
	7.76	−13.8	10,080	1.6
6. Crisis ends, 10-4-93	9.31	−10.4	10,085	−11.5
	8.89	−4.5	10,383	−4.3
	9.34	5.1	10,955	5.5
7. Parliamentary elections, 12-12-93	19.60	0.4	24,088	−0.4
	19.80	1.0	24,373	1.2
	15.04	−23.8	18,804	−22.9
8. Gaidar resigns, 1-16-94	17.47	0.9	23,689	−2.5
	16.37	−6.3	22,950	−3.1
	14.56	−11.1	21,898	−4.5
9. Fedorov resigns, 1-21-94	15.13	16.7	23,496	12.7
	14.69	−3.0	22,665	−3.5
	14.79	0.7	22,835	−0.8
Average change[a]	0.53	(4.6)	620	(4.3)
Average change excluding 11-4-93[b]	0.50	(4.3)	582	(4.1)

[a]Average daily price change (and percentage) over the entire period December 11, 1992, to May 17, 1994 (292 trading days).
[b]Average daily price change (and percentage) over the period December 11, 1992, to May 17, 1994, excluding November 4, 1993, which saw an 84 percent price rise in anticipation of the auction of GAZ and energy sector assets.

Some caution is warranted in making inferences from these data, however.[16] First, the data are noisy. This concern is especially prominent during the first four months of trading when the market was thin. Second, the finding that many political events did not have a significant effect on the price of the voucher is a weak one because it confirms a null hypothesis. Third, although many of the events seem to have surprised observers, there is always the possibility that they were anticipated so that prior trading masks their effects.

6.2 Credibility and vouchers: October 1992 to April 1993

Passage of the Privatization Program in the summer of 1992 did not end battles over industrial assets. In the fall some managers and bureaucrats called for greater insider ownership. Arkadii Volskii, a leader of the RUIE, argued that corporatization should be slowed, that the level of state ownership should be changed, and that closed joint-stock companies should be permitted (*Izvestiya*, September 30, 1992: 1). At a meeting with almost the entire government in October, the directors of sixty large enterprises called for leaving 90 percent of shares within companies (*Rossiskaya Gazeta*, October 27, 1992: 1). Several ministers pushed to limit privatization. The Minister of Industry argued that 38 percent of enterprises should remain state-owned, and the energy ministers argued that 70 percent of enterprises under their purview should not undergo privatization (*Biznis M-N*, October 14, 1992: 1).

Within the parliament, factions representing the industrial lobby proposed alternative versions of privatization that favored closed joint-stock companies and holding companies with vast cross-ownership of shares. They also favored selling shares for cash rather than vouchers and reducing the number of unprofitable firms to be privatized (Ellman, 1993). The main programmatic document of the Civic Union called for ending the government's privatization program in favor of creating industrial conglomerates as a new "state-corporate" property form (*Sovetskaya Rossiya*, November 19, 1992: 1). The Supreme Economic Council of the Supreme Soviet offered a similar program that proposed canceling vouchers and giving insiders first claim on ownership. If passed, these steps would have fundamentally changed the Privatization Program.

To counter these plans and to preserve the Privatization Program, the Yeltsin government made the voucher a more attractive investment. It rushed the vouchers into the hands of the public. Voucher distribution

---

[16]No data from before December 11, 1992, are available. As trading volume was low during this period, their inclusion would be questionable. The voucher privatization extended six weeks beyond May 17, 1994, but this period did not include any major political events, so its exclusion from the analysis is unlikely to be important.

began October 1, 1992, and by January 31, 1993, 96 percent of the population had vouchers in their possession (GKI, Annual Report, 1992). The voucher offered an immediate benefit because individuals could trade the voucher for cash. On October 26, 1992, President Yeltsin permitted the use of vouchers to purchase housing and commercial land and increased the amount of state property to be sold for vouchers. A presidential decree issued the same day required that vouchers be used to purchase 80 percent of shares of federal property.

The government also expedited the first auctions to coincide with the opening of the Seventh Congress of People's Deputies, a body known for strong anti-Yeltsin sentiments. Twenty auctions were held in December 1992. The reformers hoped to prevent changes in privatization by bolstering enterprise outsiders who would benefit from voucher privatization and by demonstrating the progress of reform.

The Yeltsin government made several concessions to the industrial lobby during the fall and winter of 1992. Presidential decrees promoted an industrial policy including new subsidies, protection from foreign competition, and increased social spending. Yeltsin allowed parliament to review candidates for the four "power" ministries, Internal Affairs, Foreign Affairs, Defense, and Intelligence. Most significantly, he dismissed the reformer Gaidar in favor of the industrialist Chernomyrdin as head of government.

The market for vouchers reacted swiftly to the change in the government's time horizons because the political costs of reversing privatization were low at this time. Private actors held few vouchers, and the funds were still organizing. Brokers first traded vouchers in small numbers in October 1992 at a rate of roughly U.S.$12 as shown in Table 4.1. Prior to the Seventh Congress of Peoples' Deputies, many expected the Gaidar government to fall under pressure from branch ministries and the industrial lobby. Anticipating this event, voucher prices fell to U.S.$10 in early November. By the end of the month, however, representatives of the president and the industrialists held a flurry of meetings that brought speculation of a rapprochement. On the strength of these meetings, the voucher price rose to almost U.S.$20 on December 3. With Gaidar's removal in early December the voucher price fell by more than U.S.$5 to U.S.$14.70 in less than a week. The voucher price slipped during the early days of the Chernomyrdin government and hovered around U.S.$10 from December to January. Although caution is warranted because the market was very thin during this period, these price data suggest weak credibility for the reform program.

The next challenge to rapid voucher privatization came from labor. In January and February 1993 left-wing Supreme Soviet deputies and some ministerial allies rallied for a "fourth option," privatization that allowed worker collectives to buy 90 percent of enterprise shares at the 1992 book value with a three- to five-year installment plan (*Ekonomika i Zhizn*, No. 1, 1993: 4). According to this plan worker collectives could pay for these shares from retained profits and mortgage on the land under the enterprise, and outsiders could buy the remaining shares on the market.

Pressure from reformers in the government and the holders of vouchers that were threatened by an insider buyout prevented this amendment from reaching a vote in the Supreme Soviet. The government appealed to the 80 percent of the population that would be left out of privatization according to the "fourth option" (*Biznis MN*, February 21, 1993: 4). For example, on December 28, 1992, Yeltsin issued a decree allowing the creation of special banks and voucher funds for military personnel, expanded the number of military factories subject to privatization, and encouraged the Central Bank to conduct an "active credit policy" for defense enterprises. In mid-February the head of GKI met with the Army Reform Group of Supreme Soviet Deputies, the Union of Reserve Officers, and the Union of Armed Forces Veterans to urge them to lobby the parliament to reject the "fourth option." To encourage military support, a GKI official recounted a presidential decree then in preparation that would earmark a portion of state property for officers' vouchers and create a number of closed auctions of military property for officers (*Nezavisimaya Gazeta*, February 18, 1993: 1). These measures increased the stake held by the military, a group that would have been alienated by altering privatization. By rallying groups that would be alienated from an insider buyout, such as teachers, pensioners, doctors, and the military, reformers aimed to raise the political costs of altering the Privatization Program and thereby increase its credibility.

In addition, the "fourth option" received a mixed reception from managers. While many managers saw this option as ensuring insider ownership and continued managerial control of poorly organized workers, other managers, particularly in industries with export potential, began to see the benefits of rapid privatization. This temporary alliance of groups threatened by the fourth option – pro-privatization managers and nonindustrial workers with vouchers – helped to block its adoption.

Despite these efforts to keep privatization on track, the voucher price continued to slide. On January 14, the day the Supreme Soviet announced its decision to discuss the "fourth option," the voucher price fell from U.S.$12.40 to U.S.$11.00. Prices fell in the spring as parliament debated scrapping the privatization program in favor of the "fourth option." The voucher traded between U.S.$4.70 and U.S.$7.00 from February to April.

In the spring of 1993 Yeltsin tried to bolster his declining position by announcing a nonbinding referendum consisting of four questions, including one aimed at measuring public confidence in the government's economic program.[17] In the run-up to the referendum held on April 25, 1993, voucher prices hovered around U.S.$5 as traders expressed pessimism about Yeltsin's chances for victory and the preservation of the privatization program. With Yeltsin's unexpectedly strong showing in the referendum, the discount rate of reformers in the executive dropped because elections in the near term seemed unlikely. Surprisingly, the voucher price did not reflect the changed political situation and declined slightly in May. When some of the first attractive assets came to market in late May, the voucher price increased from U.S.$4.60 on May 19, to U.S.$8.80 on June 2, 1993. In the summer the voucher price hovered around U.S.$9.00. The increase in the voucher price during this period may reveal a market correction, but more likely reveals the importance of economic, rather than political, factors for the voucher market.

6.3 Dogs that didn't bark: May to December 1993

Political instability had little effect on the voucher price in this period. The funds became more active, auctions proceeded apace, and the public showed greater faith in the privatization program despite political turbulence. The market for vouchers became more liquid, easily reaching a volume of U.S.$1 million a day at the larger exchanges. Increased liquidity gives greater confidence in the reliability of the voucher price as an indicator of credibility.

In the summer of 1993 the Supreme Soviet renewed its attack on voucher privatization. On June 17, 1993, the Supreme Soviet's Committee on Economic Reform surprised observers by proposing to suspend Presidential Decree 640, a key document that raised the minimum percentage of vouchers put to market from 20 to 29 percent of all enterprise shares. The committee suggested giving the Council of Ministers, rather than the reformist GKI, the right to distribute property and replace vouchers with privatization accounts. Such a move would have bankrupted the voucher funds.

After reviewing the suggestions of the Committee on Economic Reform, the Supreme Soviet suspended Presidential Decree 640 and removed from GKI the sole right to distribute property, but deputies refrained from introducing privatization accounts. The hesitancy of

---

[17]The referendum asked, "Do you approve of the socioeconomic policies carried out by the president and the government of the Russian Federation since 1992?" Fifty-three percent of voters answered yes.

deputies to cancel voucher privatization indicates a sensitivity to the political costs of such an action.

In a move to remind the deputies of the Supreme Soviet and the government of the number of shareholders whose rights would be impinged by such moves, the voucher funds lobbied the parliament and the government to preserve the Privatization Program. They issued a declaration to rally their shareholders and coordinated their media campaign with representatives of GKI to receive greater exposure. The head of GKI noted, "The interests of tens of millions of people have been squandered in secret for the political gains of the Supreme Soviet and the opposition who back them" (*Izvestiya*, July 22, 1993: 1).

The Supreme Soviet's attempts to derail the Privatization Program fared no better than previous efforts. Yeltsin and the Chernomyrdin government rejected these moves. On July 26, 1993, Yeltsin issued Presidential Decree 1108, repeating the main points of Decree 640, which had been rejected by the parliament, which answered him by annulling this new decree as well. Finally, the government issued a resolution repeating the main points of Presidential Decrees 640 and 1108 that the parliament could not overturn. The market dismissed these attacks as the voucher dipped slightly, but rebounded quickly to roughly U.S.$9.00.

A more serious clash between the president and parliament occurred a month later. After Yeltsin's decision to disband the parliament on September 21, 1993, a two-week stalemate ensued in which deputies ignored executive authority and voted to impeach the president in favor of then vice president Alexander Rutskoi. Among its plans, the parliament intended to end the government's privatization program. Army units loyal to Yeltsin ended the clash by storming the parliament to evict the deputies.

During the crisis traders displayed some optimism toward the preservation of the privatization program despite the uncertainty of the outcome of the crisis. The voucher traded at U.S.$9.80 on September 21 and fell to U.S.$7.76 on September 23 before rebounding to U.S.$9.11 two trading days later. The voucher then held steady and traded at U.S.$9.31 on October 1, the last trading day of the crisis. The exchange rate adjusted voucher price fell by only 2.3 percent on September 23 and also held relatively steady throughout the crisis. A comparison of fluctuations in other indicators of government commitment to reform is instructive. During the crisis traders showed more confidence in the voucher than the ruble or foreign debt. The exchange rate jumped from roughly 1,020 rubles/U.S.$ to more than 1,200 rubles/U.S.$ during the two-week crisis, while the voucher increased in value. The price of Russian foreign debt also fell during the crisis from 37.125 cents per dollar on September 17 to

30.000 per dollar on October 4, only to close at 35.000 per dollar after the fighting.[18]

In the month after this crisis the voucher remained relatively stable, but soared from U.S.$11.70 on November 1 to U.S.$22.64 on November 4, 1993. This jump can be explained in part by increasing confidence in privatization, yet the timing of the change lies in the attractiveness of assets that were for sale at the time. Shares in major oil enterprises and the Gorkii Automotive Factory were coming up for auction.

6.4 The voucher dips and rebounds:
December 1993 to June 1994

The Privatization Program faced its most severe threat following the success of anti-market reform parties in parliamentary elections on December 12, 1993. Running on platforms critical of the government's reforms, the Liberal Democratic Party headed by Vladimir Zhirinovsky, a cosmetically reformed Communist Party, and the Agrarian Party, won 182 of 450 seats in the State Duma, while openly reformist members won only 156. Opposition parties held close to a working majority in the parliament. Despite the strong presidential powers of the new Russian constitution, the parliament may still hinder reform. More important, the strong showing of opposition parties led to the resignation of the two ministers most closely identified with rapid reform, Gaidar and Boris Fedorov, in January 1994. Their resignations not only caused havoc on the foreign exchange and debt markets, they also caused a significant decline in voucher prices.

In the days following these events, the voucher price fell from U.S.$19.60 on December 10 to U.S.$15.08 on December 14. The price dropped again after the resignation of reformist ministers in mid-January. Gaidar ended a month of uncertainty by rejecting an offer to remain in the government causing the voucher to fall from U.S.$17.37 on January 13 to U.S.$12.97 by January 19, a 25 percent drop in dollar terms. The exchange rate adjusted price of the voucher declined during this period more than 12 percent. In this same period, the exchange rate fell from roughly 1,000 rubles/U.S.$ to 1,500 rubles/U.S.$ and would have been much higher but for a U.S.$1 billion intervention by the Central Bank in

---

[18]These indicators are imperfect substitutes, as the prices of rubles, debt, and vouchers are not always driven by the same factors. But at their core, each reflects the government's ability and willingness to continue reform and should react similarly to perceived changes in the government's discount rate. Debt prices were available only from March 1993. Ruble prices are largely determined by Central Bank interventions. Thus the greater fluctuation of the ruble over the voucher is even more surprising.

December. The price of foreign debt also dropped sharply after the December elections and subsequent resignations of reformist ministers. It traded at 54.25 cents per dollar on December 10, and 47 cents per dollar on December 14. The debt price tumbled from 44 to 36 cents per dollar following Gaidar and Fedorov's resignations. Through the first six months of 1994, it traded at roughly 30 cents per dollar.

After the shock of the events of December and January subsided, the voucher price began to rise in March. Unlike the price of foreign debt or the exchange rate, which both continued to slide through the first half of 1994, the voucher price regained all its value and traded at its highest levels. By the middle of March the voucher traded at over U.S.$20 and remained at roughly this level until privatization ended in June 1994.

7.0 CONCLUSION

Final judgments on privatization are premature, but some issues may be explored at this early stage. First, by pursuing rapid privatization, Russian reformers followed a political logic that aimed to constrain current and future governments. Holding vast but temporary power to conduct reform by decree, and facing polarized opposition from most ministries, and managers and workers in many enterprises, President Yeltsin had strong incentives to pursue a strategy of rapid voucher privatization that he hoped would be difficult to reverse.

Second, the reformers tried to use the voucher to signal to their base constituencies that their interests in privatization would not be completely dismissed. The reformers also tried to use the voucher to raise the political costs of reversing privatization. The great benefits to enterprise insiders in the Russian privatization plan, however, limited the impact of the voucher as a signaling and commitment device.

Third, the implications of the model presented in Chapter 2 have generally been borne out. The government's discount rate and its ability to raise the costs of changing course are important determinants of the credibility of property rights. Many exogenous political shocks seemed to have had little effect on voucher prices as brokers dismissed parliamentary attacks on privatization, the surprising results of the April referendum, and the constitutional crisis of September–October 1993. Mass participation in the voucher program seemed to create momentum that made people believe that privatization would continue.

Perhaps more important, the evidence also suggests a recognition that a government's ability to "tie its hands" is not unlimited. Sharp drops in the price of the voucher after the strong showing of anti-reform parties in the December 1993 election and resignations of reformist ministers in January 1994 indicate that confidence in the sustainability of privatization was limited. Brokers seemed to believe that hostile interest groups remained a threat to privatization even after vouchers had been distributed. Thus, even where a government consciously designs a reform program to mitigate credibility problems, it is difficult to erase the fear that reform will not be abandoned.

REFERENCES

Alesina, Alberto, and Guido Tabellini, "A Positive Theory of Fiscal Deficits and Government Debt," *Review of Economic Studies* 57: 3 (1990), 403–14.

Andreff, Wladimir, "Techniques and Experiences of Privatization," mimeo, University of St. Andrews (1991).

Andrews, Josephine, "Legislative Instability: The Dynamics of Agenda Control in the Russian Parliament," mimeo, Harvard University (1994), 1–29.

Bim, Alexander, "Post-privatizatsionnie protsessi," *Voprosii Ekonomiki* 1: 4 (1994), 56–71.

Blasi, Joseph, "Corporate Governance in Russia," paper delivered at the World Bank Conference on Corporate Governance, Washington, DC, December 16–17 (1994).

Boycko, Maxim, and Andrei Shleifer, "Privatizing Russia," *Brookings Papers on Economic Activity*, 2 (1993), 139–81.

Boycko, Maxim, Andrei Shleifer, and Robert W. Vishny, *Privatizing Russia* (Cambridge, MA: MIT Press, 1995).

Ellman, Michael, "The Economic Program of the Civic Union," *RFE/RL Research Report* 2: 11 (1993), 34–45.

Frydman, Roman, and Andrzej Rapaczynski, *Is the State Withering Away?* (Oxford: Oxford University Press, 1994).

Frydman, Roman, Andrzej Rapaczynski, and John S. Earle, *The Privatization Process in Russia, Ukraine, and the Baltics* (New York: Central European University Press, 1993).

Gimpelson, Vladimir, "Why Is There No Mass Unemployment in Russia?" mimeo, Harvard University (1994).

Gorbatova, Larisa, "Voucher Funds," mimeo, Institute of Economics of the Transition Period, Moscow (1993).

Grossman, Sanford, and Oliver Hart, "The Costs and Benefits of Ownership: A Theory of Lateral and Vertical Integration," *Journal of Political Economy* 94: 4 (1986), 691–719.

Kiss, Yudit, "Privatization Paradoxes in East Central Europe," *Eastern European Politics and Societies* 8: 1 (1994), 122–52.

Kydland, Finn E., and Edward C. Prescott, "Rules Rather than Discretion: The Inconsistency of Optimal Plans," *Journal of Political Economy* 85: 3 (1977), 473–91.

Major, Ivan, *Privatization in Eastern Europe* (Brookfield, VT: Elgar, 1993).

Nelson, Lynn, and Irina Kuzes, *Property to the People* (Armonk, NY: M. E. Sharpe Press, 1994).

North, Douglass, *Institutions, Institutional Change, and Economic Performance* (Cambridge: Cambridge University Press, 1990).

Persson, Torsten, and Lars E. O. Svensson, "Why a Stubborn Conservative Would Run a Deficit: Policy with Time-Inconsistent Preferences," *Quarterly Journal of Economics* 104: 2 (1989), 325–45.

Pistor, Katarina, "Corporate Governance in Russia: An Empirical Study," in Michael Mcfaul and Tova Perlmutter, editors, *Privatization, Conversion, and Enterprise Reform in Russia* (Stanford, CA.: CSIA, 1994), 69–84.

Radigin, A. D., "Spontannaia Privatizatsiia," *Problemy Prognozirovaniia* 5: 1 (1992), 18–28.

Rodrik, Dani, "Promises, Promises: Credible Policy Reform via Signalling," *Economic Journal* 99: 6 (1989), 756–72.

Roeder, Philip, "Varieties of Post-Soviet Authoritarian Rule," *Post-Soviet Affairs*, 10: 1 (1994), 61–101.

Rose, Richard, "The Russian Response to Privatization," *RFE/RL Research Report* 2: 47 (1993), 50–5.

Rutgaizer, Vladimir, "Privatizatsiia v Rossii: dvizhenie 'na oshup,'" *Voprosii Ekonomiki* 1: 10 (1993), 26–36.

Sobyanin, Alexander, "Political Cleavages Among Russian Deputies," in Thomas Remington, editor, *Parliaments in Transition*, (Boulder, CO: Westview Press, 1994), pp. 181–203.

Stark, David, "Path Dependence and Privatization Strategies in East Central Europe," *Eastern European Politics and Societies* 6: 1 (1992), 17–54.

Weingast, Barry, "Constitutions as Governance Structures: The Political Foundations of Secure Markets," *Journal of Institutional and Theoretical Economics* 146: 1 (1993), 283–311.

Three issues of credible commitment and Russian privatization

JOHN M. LITWACK

In the fall of 1991, a newspaper reporter interviewed Yegor Gaidar about his primary objectives as the new acting prime minister of Russia. Gaidar responded prophetically that the best-case scenario was one in which he would be removed from power in roughly one year as the most unpopular man in Russia. But by that time, the policies of the past year would have set Russia firmly and irreversibly on the road to building a market economy. That was the mind-set of the group that suddenly came to power by the grace of Boris Yeltsin after the Russian revolution of August 1991. They sought to exploit an unusual and temporary window of opportunity to initiate "shock therapeutic" reform for ensuring the destiny of Russia against inevitably strong and growing political opposition.

Timothy Frye explores one component of this strategy for rapid economic transition: rapid mass privatization. He traces in an insightful and detailed way how privatization on paper and in practice evolved in Russia in response to various political, economic, and social pressures between 1991 and 1994. His chapter follows the original plans of the GKI and executive government, which were quite favorable to outside ownership, through the political and economic factors that led the Yeltsin-Gaidar-Chubias team essentially to sacrifice this objective in the interests of privatizing quickly, to the broad-based voucher privatization program that accompanied an otherwise insider-based process. Frye also gives an interesting summary of how changes in political variables and stability may have affected the value of the voucher during this time in Russia.

Conceptually, Frye concerns himself with the question of credibility in the state's plans for privatization. For privatization to succeed and positively affect economic incentives, the property rights that it creates must be perceived as credible by the population. Here I think that it is useful to distinguish between at least three different issues that are related to this question, all of which Frye touches to one degree or another in his chapter: (1) credibility in the creation and defense of property rights by the

109

state, (2) credible commitment to a distribution of property rights implied by a specific privatization program, and (3) credible commitment that privatization itself will proceed quickly and not be abandoned or reversed.

It should be noted that issue 1 is given much less attention in the chapter than issue 2 or 3. In addition to a transfer of residual control rights, a credible creation and defense of property rights implies a fiscal system that is consistent with making owners residual claimants of income generated from the use of property. This is something that still does not really exist in Russia. Frye indicates early in his chapter that he is not really addressing this set of issues. These are also issues for which Frye's argument about vouchers as a commitment device would not apply. But, for the applied section of the chapter, it should be noted that these factors also represent primary determinants of the market value of formal ownership shares and, by implication, vouchers. One would expect the real value of the voucher to be very sensitive to fiscal and monetary variables as well as to the status of the more specific privatization program. The value of productive assets reflects expectations about income streams that can be generated by their use.

Turning to issue 2, did the state intend the voucher as a commitment mechanism for generating a specific distribution of property rights from privatization, and, if so, has the voucher served such a purpose? This is a rather complicated question. Frye contends that the voucher issue allowed the state to commit to a distribution of assets that was more favorable to the general population relative to insiders than would otherwise be possible. There are several respects in which I believe he may be correct. First, given that the general population has little money to buy productive assets, some sort of broad-based giveaway program, such as the distribution of vouchers, was the only feasible alternative for rapid privatization other than a completely insider-based program. The fact that individuals held these vouchers granted a propaganda tool for the executive government to claim that everyone is participating and receiving a share. Perhaps more seriously, it provided somewhat of a political base for favoring policies that support the value of vouchers, the most important of which could shift the distribution of property in favor of outsiders. For example, after the issue of vouchers in 1992, the executive government altered the privatization program in 1993 in such a way that a larger share of state property had to be sold for vouchers. Finally, it could be argued that the presence of vouchers has facilitated the ability of at least a few new "voucher funds," mostly in conjunction with banks, to take an active interest in the ownership and control of some firms.

Frye himself acknowledges that there were serious limitations in the use of vouchers as a mechanism to affect the distribution of property in

110

privatization. Frye states that their use as a commitment device was "limited by the dominant role of enterprise insiders in privatization" and that this use would have been greater otherwise. If we limit attention here to the issue of commitment to a particular distribution of property, I would conceptualize this point a bit differently. Despite a major effort by the executive government to favor outsiders in the early stages of privatization, the broad-based voucher issue failed to prevent actual privatization from becoming insider-based. From this point of view, whether the state intended the voucher issue to be a commitment device for distribution or not, it essentially failed at that purpose.

The key point here is that vouchers themselves are not a commitment of fixed value. They have a price that fluctuates on the open market. In this respect, vouchers can lead to a variety of distributions of property between voucher holders and others: The smaller the share of the pie that voucher holders obtain, the lower will be the market price of the voucher. My own belief is that the major political battles for distribution in privatization were not significantly affected by the presence of vouchers. As Frye clearly documents in the chapter, the price of vouchers adjusted in a passive way to reflect the outcomes of these battles. Incidentally, in this light, the paradox raised in the chapter as to why the voucher increased in real value in the second half of 1993, despite a growing economic crisis and a maximum of political instability, can be readily explained. Before the referendum in the spring of 1993, power in the central government was very divided between the executive branch and an increasingly assertive parliament. The consensus in parliament was relatively much less favorable to privatization and particularly to outsider-based privatization. The defeat of parliament in the referendum gave rise to expectations that a greater amount of property would actually be received by holders of vouchers. Despite the noise that parliament continued to make after the referendum, the relative power of the president had become much greater, so great, in fact, that he succeeded in disbanding parliament with the support of the military only six months later. But if the executive had wanted to make the voucher issue an effective commitment device for distribution, it would have had to commit itself to interventionist policies aimed at keeping the value of a fixed number of vouchers above some target level. If such a commitment could be implemented, then it would have real distributional consequences.

This leaves issue 3. Can the use of vouchers be thought of as a commitment device to ensure that privatization itself will be carried out quickly and not abandoned or reversed? It may not be obvious at first why rapid privatization, accompanied by vouchers, should be any more credible than rapid privatization that gives everything away to insiders. Yet, it is here where I think that the strongest argument in support of vouchers as a commitment device can actually be made. If the state had simply tried to give away its assets quickly to insiders, without even tipping its hat to the general population, then public outcry might have been strong. This outcry could have become a rallying point for political and social groups opposed to the government. When talk of rapid privatization began, Russian newspapers were full of articles that condemned insider give-aways as an unfair gift to those who happen to be lucky enough to work with valuable state assets. Strong opposition due to distribution questions could have had the effect of paralyzing the privatization process alto-gether. In Poland and Hungary, where vouchers were not used, ambitious privatization plans on paper have been either abandoned or implemented very slowly, as opposed to the voucher-based mass privatization cases of the Czech Republic and Russia. Although a virtual consensus exists in the former countries that privatization should take place, debates on distribu-tional questions have bogged down the entire process. It may be that the primary benefit of the use of vouchers is that it actually allowed the state to proceed with rapid privatization while the battles concerning distribu-tion were still being fought.

Now that the formal privatization process is coming to a close in Russia, we await changes that will transform formal privatization into operational property rights. Currently, privatized and non-privatized en-terprises work under essentially the same circumstances and have the access to the same sorts of funding. Ironically, because of the decision of the government not to give any special favorable treatment to state-owned enterprises, privatized enterprises may have even softer budget constraints than non-privatized enterprises in Russia today.

5

Legislative politics and the political economy of property rights in post-communist Russia

BRENDAN KIERNAN AND FRANCIS X. BELL

1.0 INTRODUCTION

An effective property rights regime based on private ownership of productive resources requires a credible commitment by the state to nonarbitrary enforcement of rights and nonconfiscatory taxes. The dilemma of just how to establish such a regime – and how to make any commitments appear credible in an environment of political, social, and economic upheaval – has plagued the newly democratized countries of Eastern and Central Europe from their inception. This chapter examines how the dilemma was faced in one of these countries as it explores the opening phase of the legislative politics of property rights in Russia. From April 1990 through October 1993, a period that spans both the birth and the death of the Russian Congress of People's Deputies (CPD), Boris Yeltsin and the members of the CPD struggled to create a new system of property rights. Three questions define the distinct phases of the struggle: Why did the Russian legislators create a strong presidency? Why did they go farther, granting to the president extraordinary reform powers? Finally, after having granted those powers, why did they engage in what would ultimately become a bloody battle to take them back?

Each of these three questions has implications for the establishment of a credible commitment to property rights reform. Without such a stable and credible commitment to private property, post-communist economies are likely to stagnate. Because many legislators in the Russian CPD were engaged in a battle to build political futures for themselves, it would have been natural to question the credibility of their commitment in view of the temptation to secure short-run gains at the expense of the longer term economic future. Moreover, modern states are often founded on a division of legislative and executive power. Effective economic reform requires that these legislatures credibly commit to private property.

Before investigating the credibility of property rights reforms made by

113

the Russian CPD, it is necessary to ask which method of analysis is likely to lead us toward a more complete understanding of the processes undertaken in that body. Although this chapter suggests that deputies revolted against the political implications of the social pains of economic reforms, it is in some sense trivial to say that the CPD blocked economic change, and that deputies built coalitions to fight against private ownership of land and other productive resources. The more interesting questions include: When, and how, representatives, individually and collectively, can make credible commitments to fundamental economic change that threatens to alter radically the political status quo.

2.0 RATIONAL CHOICE AND THE POLITICAL ECONOMY OF PROPERTY RIGHTS

Applying the fundamental axioms of rational choice to the Russian CPD, we consider deputies as rational actors who are interested in maximizing their own utilities along a spectrum of possible goals that is little different from that identified by Richard Fenno (1973) and others who study the politics of mature Western legislatures. Although it is important to make this distinction, the analysis in this chapter goes beyond the fundamentals to use theories of institutions developed by Randall Calvert (1995).

Calvert argues that whereas institutions shape the incentive structures faced by political actors, institutions themselves are better viewed as equilibrium outcomes of repeated noncooperative games.[1] From this perspective, secure and stable property rights systems based on private ownership are only possible as an equilibrium outcome of the political game played by the Russian deputies.

Some positive theories consider political institutions as constraints to action, rules binding both winners and losers. Kenneth Shepsle (1979), for example, argues that structure and procedure combine with preference to produce outcomes, and that it would be desirable to explain social outcomes not only in terms of preferences and optimization but also on the basis of institutional features. One problem with this view has been pointed out by William Riker (1980): There are no guarantees that the institutional constraints are stable. The study of legislative politics provides a clear example. Legislators unhappy with institutionally influenced outcomes, so-called structurally induced equilibria, are more likely

[1]The particular equilibria that we are most interested in explaining in post-Soviet Russia are the achievement of a stable and credible commitment to property rights and the creation of the institutional basis of state power. While these equilibria can be thought of as the Pareto-optimal solutions to the noncooperative game observed between Yeltsin and the Russian CPD, it should not be forgotten that there were other equilibria that could have been, and in fact were, achieved.

to vote to change or eliminate institutional rules and procedures than to alter their preferences. When viewed in this manner, institutions cannot be used to explain political outcomes.

Calvert (1995: 288) places the stability problem at the heart of a new theoretical approach in an attempt to create appropriate tools to analyze institutional formation, maintenance, and change. He represents institutions simultaneously as "rules of the game" that structure action and constrain behavior so as to elicit cooperation, and as guidelines that *could* be violated by one or all individuals under adverse circumstances. Addressing the question of stability, he argues that institutional rules (including such legislative examples as procedural rules, committee or party structure, and leadership arrangements) should be viewed as though they were equilibrium outcomes in a formal game.[2]

2.1 Calvert's model and post-Soviet politics

Interpretations of post-Soviet institutional choice that use Calvert's tools must specify the parameters of the game, including (1) a problem or opportunity posed by nature, (2) relevant players, their interests, and potential payoffs, and (3) relevant fixed institutional structures. Only then can existing or potential equilibria be discussed.

To summarize the argument presented in greater detail later, this chapter defines, at a general level, the "opportunity or problem posed by nature" as choosing policies to create an effective government; elements of this general problem have evolved over time. The set of relevant players consists primarily of deputies elected in the spring of 1990 to the new Russian Congress of People's Deputies. Two fixed procedural elements of most post-Soviet systems, described in greater detail below, are especially important elements of the constitutional game in Russia: (1) supreme authority is vested in the legislative branch, where deputies have the right to amend the constitution through a two-thirds majority, and (2) the assemblies are run on a non-party basis with little fractional or bloc

[2]It must be stressed at this point that we are not trying to set up a straw man by choosing Calvert's framework to explain the achievement of equilibrium outcomes in the search for stable institutional settings in post-Soviet Russia. We recognize that there may be more than one way to interpret the events and phenomena in which we are interested in this paper. Indeed, the institutionalism of evolutionary economics provides one possible alternative method of explanation, detailing as it does the modification of institutional structures as a process of problem solving "accomplished by revamping the problematic elements of prevailing institutions to bring them into congruity with what the expanding fund of reliable knowledge indicates is feasible and desirable" (Tool, 1990: 167). We do believe, however, owing to the massive amount of structural change that rocked the institutions of post-Soviet Russia, and the rapid rate at which such change was accomplished, that an explanation that uses the language of game theory is best suited to analyzing the phenomena at hand.

discipline.[3] While stable constitutional systems embody the "equilibria" of the game, constitutional amendments give deputies an opportunity to change the rules. Thus, these institutions are self-enforcing in the truest sense of the word.

3.0 THE POLITICAL ECONOMY
OF CONSTITUTIONAL CHOICE

In the sections that follow we briefly discuss how each of the three principal elements of Calvert's model applies to post-Soviet politics in Russia. What was the problem posed by nature? Who comprised the set of relevant actors and what were their interests? What were the relevant fixed institutions? The ensuing discussion offers preliminary interpretations of how these three factors influenced deputies' constitutional choices. More complete interpretations await empirical analysis of deputorial behavior, policy proposals, and district characteristics.

3.1 The problem

The challenge faced by political actors in the post-Soviet world is *not*, following Linz (1994), finding a stable way to share or exercise power, but rather *creating*, both politically and economically, the institutional basis of state power. This challenge is a legacy of the Soviet era: *Perestroika* and *demokratizatsiia* were attempts made by Gorbachev and the Communist Party to deal with a problem that had become increasingly clear in the latter years of the Brezhnev era, the so-called period of stagnation. Deprived of the economic levers of a market economy, the party could no longer play the "leading and guiding role" mandated in the Soviet constitution.

Perestroika careened out of control when local elites co-opted the institutional forms of legislative power and refused to cooperate with Moscow on questions of economic reform. After the coup attempt, union republic political elites – specifically Supreme Soviet deputies and their elected leadership – were left empty-handed yet faced the same problem that had

[3]Indeed, party discipline as it exists in most West European parliaments, wherein most divisions are expected to fall along party lines, was almost never observed in the early sessions of the Russian CPD. Although a distinct bimodal distribution of opinion among Russian deputies has been identified (notably by Alexander Sobyanin [1994]), political parties as such did not exist in the legislature. Thomas Remington et al. (1994: 162) make the point clearly: "Parties did not select candidates or fund their campaigns. Members of the CPSU could be found on both the left and the right; the party itself lacked a coherent ideological position. . . . Therefore, though 86 percent of the winners were party members, party membership as such at the time of the election had relatively little effect on deputy voting behavior once deputies were elected."

116

threatened Gorbachev in 1985: How to go about re-creating the basis of state power.[4] Without a competent state, political elites could do little to pursue individual interests. The general issue was one of coordination: Which of a range of acceptable economic and political policies should be implemented?

3.2 The players

The relevant actors in the Russian constitutional game are the deputies elected to the union republic legislatures in 1990. In Russia itself, 1,068 deputies (including, at the time, Boris Yeltsin) were elected, 900 in territorial, single-member districts of roughly equal size and 168 in national-territorial districts created to account for Russia's federal nature. These elections were officially conducted on a non-party basis; nonetheless, the Communist apparatus at the local level often controlled the contests to produce what they considered to be acceptable outcomes. Despite the pressure so exerted, approximately one-third of the elected deputies entered the CPD reform-minded; banding together, they created the legislative bloc, Democratic Russia. A second bloc, the Communists of Russia, united conservative communists and also made up approximately one-third of the CPD's membership. A broad group of deputies between the two ideological extremes shifted from one side to the other, creating a situation in which "legislative success went to those who could capture the middle ground" (Remington et al., 1994: 165).

Although our analysis assumes that deputies act on self-interest, we also assume that they must pursue these interests while resolving the common problems of empowering the state. Indeed, the potential anarchy and disintegration of *not* re-creating the state immediately following the dissolution of the union was a frightening prospect. The need to satisfy both of these criteria can be seen as a product of the same interests held by legislators elsewhere in the world, including (1) a desire for reelection (voters demand performance), (2) the attempt to produce "good" public policy from an ideological point of view (authoritarian non-market attempts to reempower the state would compete with democratic market-oriented solutions to the problem), and (3) the desire to increase their own power in the legislature or build a political career,

---

[4]Before the collapse of the Soviet Union in December 1991, the Russian government worked "as an organ of political opposition, not having real power. Eighty percent of [Russia's] economic potential was directly subordinated to the Union cabinet" (N. Garifullina, "Pereiti Rubikon," *Sovetskaia Rossiia*, October 15, 1991: 2). As late as two months after the coup attempt, little had been done to make the Russian Cabinet of Ministers an efficient political tool. Uncertainty over the fate of the union held these institutions in a state of suspended animation.

either through higher elective office or through a move into the executive branch.

Such assumptions of rational self-interest suggest that differential regional effects of various economic policies would sharply influence the potential payoffs of different types of policy for individual deputies. While some deputies may seek rewards outside the legislature – most commonly appointment to a position in the government or elsewhere in the executive – this analysis assumes that deputies' payoffs correlate roughly with the effects of reform on their own districts. Thus, the social costs and consequent pain of economic reform lowers expected future payoffs for most deputies.

3.3 The fixed institutions

Two fixed institutional features played important roles in the politics of constitutional choice in Russia. First, the Russian CPD claimed supreme authority and had the right to resolve any constitutional question. Deputies could amend the constitution by a two-thirds majority.[5] Not afraid to use this power, they enacted more than three hundred constitutional amendments between June 1990 and October 1992.

The institutional legacy of the Soviet era in Russia was particularly important in placing limits on player interaction; it is the source of the second relevant fixed institution. An understanding of the incentives facing deputies requires knowledge of both their electoral history and the institutional structures of the Russian legislature: Electoral and legislative politics are tightly linked. In 1917 Lenin and the Bolsheviks took power in the name of a revolutionary system of self-government councils, the soviets of people's deputies. For seventy years, however, the soviets served as little more than the rubber stamps for a party that administered a centralized economy. Gorbachev's *demokratizatsiia*, the heart of *perestroika*, was designed to revitalize the soviets, not create democratic market government in any Western sense. In 1990 Russia returned a Congress of People's Deputies, which chose a republican Supreme Soviet,

[5]One commentator pointed out the problem behind the conflict in Russia: "A paradoxical thing has happened: the very organ which elevated the democratic, civilized norm of the separation of powers into the principle of state order and which in development of this power constituted the presidential power subsequently, as if recovering from democratic fever, began to win back and redistribute powers in its own favor. . . . If a legislator . . . arrogates the right to adopt the constitution, then he quite naturally stands above the fundamental law. . . . In a rule of law state the legislator cannot do anything, while this is precisely the claim our Congress of People's Deputies and Supreme Soviet continually parades: Anything we decide is lawful. Hence their confidence in their right to endlessly change and improve already adopted laws, adopt laws contradicting the constitution, and redistribute constitutional powers, changing the balance of power" (*Rossiiskie Vesti*, January 4, 1993: 2).

not a parliament. The election was conducted on a nonparty basis and under the banner of Gorbachev's *demokratizatsiia*. Despite bitter ideological battles, little party or fractional discipline developed in the legislature to limit the freedom of deputies to behave as they wished.

4.0 EQUILIBRIUMS IN THE RUSSIAN CPD: SIGNPOSTS ALONG A DIFFICULT ROAD

Some of the consequences of the manner in which these three factors interact can be explored by examining the brief, but tempestuous, existence of the Russian CPD. In March 1990 Russian citizens elected a new Congress of People's Deputies, constitutionally the highest organ of state power. Though empowered to adopt and amend the country's constitution and otherwise consider matters of constitutional significance, the CPD was intended to meet infrequently and so elected a working legislature, the Supreme Soviet, from among its members. As a maneuver designed to ensure Russian sovereignty in the face of Gorbachev's effort to cement the various pieces of the Union into a single, lasting republic, the existence of a Russian presidency was first approved by referendum, then created by the CPD. Boris Yeltsin was elected to fill that office in June 1991. In an attempt to create a system of checks and balances, the CPD gave Yeltsin presidential powers that forced him to deal with the Supreme Soviet on equal footing: The assembly could recall presidential decrees, could override his veto, and had to give its consent for Yeltsin's nominee to the position of prime minister. The Congress reserved for itself the role of final arbiter in all constitutional matters. It appeared as though a foundation had been laid upon which government institutions might be built.[6]

The statement of sovereignty in the face of Gorbachev's bid to ensure the future of the Soviet Union can be seen as the first attempt on the part of the players at finding some sort of equilibrium. Unfortunately, their effort died virtually stillborn as the attempted coup in August 1991 radically altered the political status quo. Russian legislators, and their newly elected president, justifiably feared for both the continued existence of their independent and sovereign nation and their continued existence as legislators within it. At a hastily summoned session of the CPD (the fifth), Yeltsin asked for, and was granted, additional powers to deal with the situation. He suspended the activities of, and eventually banned, the Communist Party. In a further step he issued a series of decrees to fight the continued strength of Communist Party apparatchiks at the local level.

---

[6]For a more complete recounting of these events, see Kiernan (1993).

It was during this emergency session in November 1991 that Yeltsin, taking advantage of his high level of personal popularity, asked the CPD for the power to take steps to reform the economy. The CPD granted him this power along with many others: the rights to appoint ministers without approval by the Supreme Soviet, to restructure the government and ministries, and, most important, to issue presidential decrees that would fundamentally transform the Russian economy. Signing an order that appointed him prime minister in November 1991, Yeltsin and a team of liberal economists began implementing a program of economic shock therapy by presidential decree in January 1992.

This formal ceding of additional power to an already strong president, then, was the second attempt at finding an equilibrium solution to the problem that faced them, but it was an attempt that would meet with only limited success. While Yeltsin proceeded with his effort to create the political and economic bases of state power, legislators continued to be of the opinion that they should be on equal footing with Yeltsin; there was not separation of powers as much as a general sharing of the same powers. Uncomfortable with the notion that Yeltsin might become a dictator, tensions between the legislative and executive branches began to mount.

As he became concerned about his ability to pass legislation through the CPD, Yeltsin appealed directly to the masses to support his reforms, often threatening deputies that he would turn to the people through a referendum if they refused to go along with his plans. He declared that he was "counting on the trust and understanding of the citizens of Russia" because he had "in the most critical moments . . . turned to [the people] for support and always received it" (*Sovetskaia Rossiia,* October 29, 1991: 2). Noting that Yeltsin faced "the completely natural temptation of political popularity," Gennadii Burbulis, a top political advisor, declared that deputies should "sober up and finally realize that they are dealing with a president for whom more Russian citizens voted than for [the entire CPD] together" ("Minoe pole vlasti," *Izvestiia,* October 20, 1991: 1). Yeltsin's popularity was a product, at least in part, of the Russian tradition of "the lure of the strong hand."[7] The Russian people looked to Yeltsin almost as a savior, sharing an almost religious expectation of a good life under a popularly elected president. The success of the reform movement would depend in large measure on the ability to transform such mass expectations into a well-balanced, concrete program of actions.

The conflict between Yeltsin and the deputies, simmering since Novem-

7See Steele (1994), chapter 11.

ber 1991 when they clashed over the State Bank, first threatened to reach unmanageable proportions at the April 1992 session (the sixth) of the CPD. At the same time that the pain of shock therapy was first starting to settle in, Yeltsin asked the deputies to ratify a draft constitution that would have created a strong presidential republic. Preparing for the session, Ruslan Khasbulatov (then the chairman of the Supreme Soviet) had argued that Yeltsin and the executive branch should "renounce unnecessary powers that they did not know how to use" ("R Khasbulatov schitaet, chto prezident i pravitel'stvo Rossii ne umieiut pol'zovatsia dopoluitel'nymi polnomochiiami," *Izvestiia*, March 19, 1992: 2). He called for returning to the Supreme Soviet the right to confirm ministerial appointments and suggested that the CPD should pass public judgment on the performance of ministers. He argued that the Supreme Soviet should defend average citizens, who had turned out to be the victims of reform. At the session, Yeltsin failed to get the constitution he wanted but escaped more serious damage through a tactical retreat. Primarily, this involved bringing experienced industrial managers into the government.

After the sixth session, Yeltsin declared that any attempt to disband the Congress was a political dead end; nonetheless, a few days later he suggested that a constitution could be passed by referendum, and that this constitution would have no place within it for the CPD. Starting from this base level of mistrust, the seventh session in December 1992, called to confirm the expiration of the special presidential powers the CPD had ratified a year earlier, led to a deepening of the rift between the two sides. When the deputies refused to consider Yeltsin's pleas for more time, he threatened once again to turn to the people for their support in a referendum directed against the CPD. Thanks to a deal brokered by Valerii Zorkin, chairman of the Constitutional Court, Yeltsin sacrificed his candidate for prime minister but was allowed to keep his extraordinary powers until April 1993, when a compromise referendum would be held to allow the people to decide on the appropriate balance of legislative and executive powers in a draft of a new constitution.

This attempt on the part of the CPD to take back the power it had previously ceded, and the concomitant struggle between the executive and legislative branches, is the third attempt at achieving equilibrium. The question that remains to be answered, then, is *why*. Why did the CPD cede so much power to Boris Yeltsin and then attempt to take it back? We believe that the key to solving this puzzle lies in moving the analytical focus from the institutional level to the individual level. Sticking with an exogenous view of institutions as constraints to action incorrectly emphasizes "institutional rivalry" at the expense of the individual political decisions that, when summed, define presidents' relationships with legislatures.[8]

4.1 External leadership: The response to weak fractions

Calvert (1995) demonstrates that noncooperative equilibriums are more probable as the outcomes of collective choices when communication is difficult. In the Russian case, institutional pathologies based on "soviet-style" government blocked certain types of coordination and communication that would have allowed the legislature to more readily reach decisions on reform. Although strong parties organize legislatures, making their work effective, parties faced tremendous developmental problems in the Russian CPD. Sergei Filatov, formerly deputy chairman of the Russian Supreme Soviet, complained that it was unable to follow its agenda, because deputies routinely ignored the standing rules and were undisciplined, and that attendance was poor.[9] In addition, the Russian CPD was without well-developed party or committee systems, without established control over the federal budget, and without a credible electoral system. Absent these institutional features, deputies could not reliably coordinate their actions. In sum, the internal structures of the Russian CPD hindered communication and – when combined with the sort of strong ideological disagreement that characterized both executive-legislative relations and the debate within the legislature over the future course of economic reform – did not allow for the creation of credible political agreements among deputies.

This coordination problem, already bad, was made worse by the non-institutionalized character of the CPD. The uncertainty that typically results from such a situation can serve as both a stimulus and an obstacle to change. Studies of the early years of the U.S. Congress, for example, suggest that attempts to overcome uncertainty played a positive role in the evolution of the institution, especially its party system (Aldrich, 1995). On the other hand, uncertainty can be an obstacle to such evolu-

[8]Shugart and Carey (1992) provide tremendous insight into the dynamics of this "institutional rivalry," including the effects of institutional design and electoral rules. By concentrating on a different level of detail we feel that it is possible to gain some understanding as to how and why these institutions, as equilibriums, were not achieved in post-Soviet Russia.

[9]This final condition was especially troubling when one considers the rules concerning the passage of legislation that mandated the approval of an absolute majority of elected deputies and not merely those present and voting. Constitutional amendments required two-thirds of those elected. The effect was to make absentees and abstentions de facto no votes.

tion (Sened, 1990). When actors have a limited notion of how and why a system works, when new incentive structures are not yet developed or completely apprehended, there is a great deal of room for growth, change, and, perhaps most important – as well as most appropriate to the Russian CPD – bitter political conflict. More than one iteration of interconnected electoral and legislative games may be needed before legislators are able to comprehend fully the complex system of interacting forces that they are in the process of creating.

Although the Russian CPD did not have the time to produce a developed party system, this is not to say that deputies existed in a state of chaotic disorganization. Remington, Smith, and Kiewiet (1993) show that two powerful sets of deputies had managed to coalesce early on and remained viable through six congressional sessions. Although both these groups were large enough, in and of themselves, to veto constitutional amendments on any issue, they were neither large nor coherent enough to ensure that deputies within them would be able to achieve their most desired outcomes. The need to capture the middle ground, composed of independent deputies and smaller fractions, necessitated compromise; this made the tasks of coordination and party building more difficult as the rules regarding the passage of legislation allowed deputies dissatisfied with a compromise to vote against it simply by abstaining or not showing up.

Faced with the popular demand for reform, deputies realized that they could not wait for multiple iterations to play out to enable such coordination and cooperation. Feeling a growing electoral pressure, understanding the drawbacks of their system, and recognizing the need for a coordinator to design and implement reforms, deputies granted Yeltsin extraordinary powers in an effort to address the problem of creating an effective Russian government after the coup. Unable to discipline themselves, they created a force outside the CPD and Supreme Soviet rather than looking within it.

Although fractions developed some of the characteristics of a party system, and demonstrated the potential eventually to overcome the coordination problem that plagued the CPD and allow for a cooperative equilibrium solution, time was not on their side. In order to overcome the coordination problem of choosing an appropriate reform strategy deputies granted the president special powers.

When the pain of economic reform became too great, deputies were able to find at least one issue on which coordination *was* possible. As both they and voters faced the increasingly painful results of Yeltsin's economic program, the potential payoffs changed. Over time "nearly 200 deputies changed their political positions from the democratic wing to the communist wing" (Remington et al., 1994: 174).[10] Where they had seen imposing odds against being able to develop such a program of reforms on their own, they found little difficulty in agreeing to strip Yeltsin of his extra powers. However, institutions give tactical and strategic advantages to those who control them. By fully exercising his presidential powers to decree economic reform, Yeltsin manipulated payoffs and created a new set of interests. His commitment to economic reform created a set of deputies in the early congresses who, independent of their fractional associations, were unwilling to see the reform clock turned back, economically or politically. Thus, he was able to avoid impeachment by a handful of votes.

Most of the members of this set were to be found in the democratic wing, but there were others from across the political spectrum who simply could not turn away from the potential payoffs of continued economic reform. Regina Smyth (1990) suggests that economic issues based on regional differences played an influential role in the development of the legislature. If this is true, *then the impact of economic reform on a deputy's willingness to support Yeltsin (or at least not oppose him) should vary according to the expected impact that his policies have on that deputy's region.* If a region does well, or is expected to do well, under Yeltsin's "shock therapy" economic reforms, then an examination of key roll-call votes by deputies from that region should indicate that they are likely to be more supportive of Yeltsin regardless of their political affiliation. Such a pattern of support should be especially evident in light of the fact that fractions served in the capacity of proto-parties, at best, and were inefficient as coordinating mechanisms.[11] In the sections that follow we will take a closer look at this aspect of rational self-interest at the individual level.

4.2 The creation of the presidency

The political landscape in the Soviet Union in the spring of 1991 can best be described as being in a state of disarray. The central feature of Gorbachev's policy of *perestroika* had been an effort to reempower soviets at

[10]The process by which this shifting occurred was actually twofold. While some deputies in the democratic camp found it impossible to support further such a painful process as Yeltsin's shock therapy and actually shifted their allegiances, the replacement of deputies drawn into the executive branch also played a role. Remington et al. (1994) note that more than one hundred deputies, many of them from the democratic wing, moved on in this way, thereby weakening the democratic position.

[11]The weakness of fractions in this regard was such that Alexander Sobyanin (1994: 202) made the observation that "the independent position of deputies who were elected as individuals has made parliament politically ill-organized, unpredictable, and unstable."

all levels in an attempt to breathe life into the slogan "all power to the soviets." Unwilling to stride foresquare along a path of full-bore popular sovereignty that could only be expressed through democratic elections and representative government, and unable to allow the depredations of Communist Party rule to persist, Gorbachev fell back on revitalizing the system from the ground up as a third option.

One of the more direct consequences of Gorbachev's desire to use a strategy of reform communism to realize the creation of a socialist legal state was the devolution of power to the lower soviets, particularly the republic soviets. He repeatedly took the position that "it is very important that each . . . soviet . . . be occupied with its own tasks, fulfilling the functions given to it by law and the party statute" (Gorbachev, 1987: 19). The most direct manner of accomplishing this clearly lies in "using all the constitutional abilities of the all-union and union republic Supreme Soviets, and the local soviets, to increase their role and responsibility before the electorate" (Gorbachev, 1988: 414).

Even as such reform was implemented, elections to local and republic soviets were being carried out in an environment that, though not enthusiastically encouraging and embracing electoral competition between communist and noncommunist candidates, to a large extent tolerated it. In the 1990 elections to the Russian CPD only 3 percent (33 of 1,068) of districts posted candidates who ran unopposed. As a result of this electoral competition, many districts returned deputies who were willing to perform the role envisioned by Gorbachev.

Yet Gorbachev's efforts at reform did not go unchallenged by reactionary forces. At the federal level the revitalization of local and republic soviets, involving as it did the shifting of power and authority away from the center, was looked on with disfavor by more than a few *apparatchiki*. Communist hardliners became convinced that Gorbachev's reforms would not merely result in a retooling of the communist system but in its eventual collapse. Marshaling their resources, these opponents of such sweeping change were able to block much of what Gorbachev wanted to accomplish. As a result, no middle road between continued central command by the Communist Party and the shift to a democratic system of government could be found.

Unable to maintain intact the coalition of groups that had supported his reform efforts, Gorbachev was forced to seek a compromise solution with his opponents rather than press his advantage and demand that the reform effort continue to be carried out.[12] In the end, the reform-minded

[12]Gorbachev later admitted, "I should have taken advantage of the stability and popular consensus that existed in the first stage of *perestroika*, and moved more swiftly toward a market economy" (*Guardian*, December 28, 1991: 1).

deputies who had been elected into the Russian CPD grew disenchanted with federal institutions; many made the decision to try and make a difference at their own level.

A period ensued that has been called "the war of the parliaments" and "the war of the laws." Most of the union republics, Russia among them, declared their sovereignty and began to challenge the authority of the all-union Supreme Soviet, refusing to enforce federal laws in favor of their own. When, on May 29, 1990, Boris Yeltsin was elected chairman of the Russian Supreme Soviet, a move that was followed almost immediately by the successful vote on the declaration of Russian sovereignty, the Soviet Union, for all intents and purposes, ceased to exist.

The war of the laws had continued for more than a year when Gorbachev, unable to hold the union together by decrees, which were opposed by republican Supreme Soviets who refused to enforce them, decided to turn to the people. A referendum was held on March 17, 1991, that Gorbachev hoped would relegitimize the authority of the Soviet Union. And yet, though nearly 77 percent of those who voted supported the idea of a "renewed federation of equal sovereign republics," Gorbachev was unable to claim a victory because of the addition of a second question concerning the existence of a directly elected president in the Russian referendum. Fully 70 percent of those who voted in Russia supported the creation of such a position.

The third (emergency) session of the Russian CPD was originally called by conservative deputies in an attempt to remove Yeltsin from office, but in a shrewd maneuver the chairman was able to delay the opening of the session until after the referendum vote. At the opening of the session Gorbachev ordered a ban against marches and demonstrations, sending fifty thousand Interior Ministry troops into Moscow, nominally at the request of conservative deputies, in an effort to enforce it, but his crude attempt at intimidation backfired. Nearly 250,000 people turned out into the streets in defiance of the ban and the troops in a show of support for Yeltsin.

It was during this session that the Russian presidency was created. Faced with an example of the lengths to which conservative forces would go to secure the union, deputies were left to find the means to prevent the encroachment of the center into affairs that were thought to be more appropriately handled by Russians. The need, then, was to establish an organ that could both stand against the center and pursue the agenda of reform that was vital to the continued survival of the nation. Boris Yeltsin had consistently advanced the notion that this could be satisfied only through the creation of a Russian presidency. Now, after nearly a year in which the Supreme Soviet had shown itself to be unable to reliably follow a clear strategy of reform, the people had also spoken, through the referendum, in favor of creating such a position. Faced with the new prospect of electoral pressure, and with the army's presence threatening Russia's existence as a sovereign and independent state, the deputies who had convened to remove Yeltsin instead gave in to him, setting the date for the first presidential elections even before constitutional amendments had been passed creating the office.

It is through viewing the deputies as individually rational actors that their reasons for creating this post can best be understood. In an atmosphere in which changing the rules of the game (through constitutional amendment) had become commonplace, and in which there was little bloc or fractional discipline, deputies could not credibly commit to a process of reform.[13] Although most agreed that some manner of reform was necessary, there was disagreement, sometimes intense, concerning both the areas that should be the focus of that reform and the pace at which it should advance.

Such disagreements likely could have been worked out through multiple iterations of the interconnected electoral and legislative games that would have resulted in both a party system and the election of deputies who better understood the complexities of the legislative arena from which they operated. Unfortunately, such multiple iterations require the investment of a great deal of time, which was one commodity Russian legislators felt they did not possess. Although there were two reasons for this – the pressure exerted by the popular demand for reform and the danger of losing their sovereignty (and their ability to reform) due to the encroachment of conservative all-union forces – it is more likely that the latter of the two was the true motivating force behind the creation of the presidency at a time when Yeltsin faced the very real threat of being removed from power.

We have argued that fractions in the CPD were inefficient as coordinating mechanisms, allowing deputies the freedom to behave (and vote) as they wished across the full range of issues. Due to the exogenous nature of the danger posed by union encroachment, it is unlikely that blocs or fractions served as the mechanism that influenced deputies' votes. Some factor other than allegiance to these fractions is needed to help explain why deputies would pursue the creation of the presidency as an equilibrium solution to the problem of creating an institutional basis of state power.

[13]One of the clearest examples of this inability to make a credible commitment came during the second session of the Russian CPD. Eager to satisfy the electorate's desire for reform, motions were passed that allowed for the recognition of private ownership of land and that established an agricultural program for the rebirth of the Russian village. Later in the session conservative deputies were able to engineer the passage of a measure that considerably weakened the property bill, making it virtually toothless.

Following Smyth (1990), we use data gathered to gauge the progress of small-enterprise privatization to determine whether a link exists between regional differences in the payoff a politician could expect from economic reform and the likelihood that he or she would support Yeltsin. As the most widely known and popular figure in national politics at the time, Yeltsin was the most likely choice to fill the office of the president when it was created. As his position on economic reform was well known, and included advocacy of rapid privatization, particularly of small enterprises, a vote for the creation of the presidency was a de facto vote for Yeltsin's brand of economic reform. Where there were large numbers of small enterprises the expected payoffs resulting from the creation of the presidency would be high. Consequently, deputies from such districts should have been more willing to vote for the creation of the presidency than those from areas in which there were few small enterprises.

We tested this hypothesis with a logistic regression model of the roll-call vote on the creation of the presidency. The dependent variable is a deputy's up or down vote on whether to ratify a draft decree mandating the creation of the presidency, with a 0 indicating a "nay" vote and a 1 indicating a "yea" vote.[14]

The independent variables, described more fully in the appendix, include whether or not a deputy was affiliated with the Communist Party prior to the election of March 1990 (Former Party), level of education attained (Education), age (Year of Birth), the position on reform of the fraction he had become affiliated with since the election (Fraction), and the number of small enterprises in the deputy's region (Number of Enterprises).

The results of our analysis are presented in Table 5.1. The coefficients that obtain for the first four explanatory variables (Former Party, Education, Year of Birth, and Fraction) indicate a good fit with existing theory: A deputy was more likely to support Yeltsin and the creation of the presidency if he (1) had not been a member of the Communist Party prior to the election of March 1990, (2) was younger, and (3) was a member of

[14]There were five categories into which a deputy could be placed concerning his taken position (or lack thereof) on a given division: (1) yea, (2) nay, (3) abstain, (4) absent, or (5) registered but did not vote. For purposes of our analysis all those who did not vote "yea" are assumed to have cast a nay vote because an absolute majority of elected deputies must vote yea before a measure is passed. Although there were doubtless those deputies who refrained from voting, either by abstaining or arranging to be absent, who wanted to vote nay but could not because there was an expectation on the part of constituents or the leaders of nascent political parties that they should vote yea, there were doubtless many more who refrained from voting not to act strategically but simply because they had not formulated an opinion on the issue at hand (and thus abstained) or were simply unable to vote because they missed either that division or the entire session. Assuming that all such abstention or absence was partaken strategically allows us to take the most conservative possible position.

Table 5.1. *Logit analysis of probability of supporting the creation of the presidency*

Explanatory variable	Parameter variable	Standard error	t-statistic
Constant	−77.64	16.65	−4.64
Former party	−0.66	0.19	−3.51
Education	0.07	0.27	0.24
Year of birth	0.04	0.009	4.74
Fraction	−0.16	0.02	−7.35
Thousands of enterprises	0.21	0.07	2.99

Log-likelihood = −662.51
Number of observations = 1,056

one of the more reform-oriented fractions. Although the *intelligentsia* are believed to have been among Yeltsin's strongest supporters, the coefficient on the Education variable does not carry the expected sign and fails to meet conventional levels of statistical significance.

The final explanatory variable in the model, Number of Enterprises, is included so we can test our own hypothesis: As the number of small enterprises in a deputy's district increases, the deputy will be more likely to support Yeltsin because of the expected benefits of rapid privatization of those enterprises. The parameter estimate is both positively signed and statistically significant, indicating that the number of small enterprises does have an impact on the probability a deputy supported Yeltsin.[15]

The nonlinear nature of the logit model means that the effect on the dependent variable of a one-unit change in a given independent variable is not equal to that variable's corresponding regression coefficient. In order to convey substantive impact, we report first differences. The first differences reveal how much of a change in the probability that a deputy will support Yeltsin and the creation of the presidency we will observe given a specified change in one independent variable, holding all other variables constant at their means.

To provide a better feel for the changes in probability that can be expected, we have calculated first differences at two different points: first, for a change in the independent variables from 25 percent below to 25 percent above the mean; second, for a change from the minimum to the

[15] A likelihood ratio test of the full model against a restricted model with the Number of Enterprises variable removed provided further evidence of the usefulness of including this variable in the model. The log-likelihood for the restricted model was −667.15, therefore R = 2[−662.51 −(−667.15)] = 9.28. With a χ^2 distribution with one degree of freedom we are able to reject the null hypothesis that the parameter estimate on Number of Enterprises is equal to zero.

Table 5.2. *First difference effects of probability of supporting the creation of the presidency*

(1)	(2)	(3)	(4)	(5)	(6)
		Change in		Change in	
		variable	First	variable	First
Variable	Estimate	(from, to)	difference	(from, to)	difference
Constant	−77.64				
Former party	−0.66	(0, 1)	−0.125	(0, 1)	−0.125
Education	0.07	(0, 1)	0.012	(0, 1)	0.012
Year of birth	0.04	(1938, 1949)	0.075	(1917, 1969)	0.348
Fraction	−0.16	(5, 9)	−0.104	(1, 12)	−0.302
Thousands of enterprises	0.21	(0.9, 1.5)	0.02	(0, 4.65)	0.185

maximum value of each variable.[16] The results in Table 5.2 indicate that the coefficients obtained from the logit regression have substantive significance as well as statistical significance. The figures in column 4 reveal that the probability of supporting Yeltsin and the creation of the presidency increases by 0.075 for a 42-year-old deputy as compared to one 53 years old, by 0.104 for a deputy with no fractional affiliation as compared to a member of the fraction Fatherland, and by 0.02 for a deputy from a region that had 1,500 small enterprises as compared to one from a region with only 900. The probability that a deputy would vote in favor of the creation of the presidency, and thereby demonstrate his or her support for Yeltsin, increases greatly if we consider the impact of changing these variables from their lower to their upper extremes, as column 6 shows. The probability of supporting Yeltsin in this way increases by 0.348 when we compare the youngest deputy to the oldest, by 0.302 when we compare the most democratic-reform minded to the most entrenched conservative hard-liners, and by 0.185 when we compare those from regions with the greatest number of small enterprises to those from regions with none.

[16]Note that in each case the first differences reported for the indicator variables Former Party and Education are for a change from 0 to 1. As these variables take on only these two values it would be meaningless to report how much a change from 25 percent below to 25 percent above their means would affect the probability of supporting Yeltsin and the creation of the presidency since values in this range would never be observed. The interpretation of their first differences, reported in Table 5.2, is relatively straightforward: A deputy who had not formerly been a member of the Communist Party was 12.5 percent more likely to support Yeltsin, whereas one who had experienced higher education was 1.2 percent more likely to do so.

Two other roll-call votes from the third session concerning the creation of the presidency (the first asking deputies to include the question of the presidency on the agenda and the second asking them to schedule the presidential election for the spring of 1991) were also subjected to logit analysis, with similar results. It appears as though the Russian presidency was clearly the creation of individually rational actors attempting to find an equilibrium solution based, at least in part, on the expected payoffs that would likely emerge as a result of that solution.

4.3 Strengthening the president's hand

Having established, in the position of the presidency, the means by which they believed a commitment to economic and political reform could be made while at the same time allowing them to pursue their individual interests, the members of the Russian CPD seemed to have fashioned at least a foundation on which they could build the institutional structures that would make their commitments credible and lasting. The creation of the presidency was merely the first in what would have to be a long series of institutional adjustments before the Russians would have a fully functioning system of checks and balances between the executive and legislative branches of government. In creating a presidency, the deputies in many respects created an institution that paralleled their own. Many of the powers that were to be wielded by the president were the same as powers already held – and not relinquished – by the legislature. By sharing these powers the deputies were in fact declaring that the office of the president was intended to be the coordinating mechanism through which the final solution to the problem at hand would be attained; unable to reach a cooperative settlement as to how best to use them, and therefore unable to use them, deputies placed them in the hands of someone who was certain to put them to use.

Once Yeltsin had secured the presidency he moved to distance himself from the democratic movement that had been his base of support. Although his motives for doing so appeared well founded at the time – setting himself up as a free agent willing to work both sides of the political fence – it was a move that turned out to be a grave tactical error. As chairman of the Supreme Soviet, Yeltsin had acted as a lightning rod, galvanizing both democratic and conservative forces. He had been, in effect, the focusing agent for an emerging Left-Right dimension that offered a firm foundation for the development of an effective party system. By first vacating his chairmanship and then failing to tend to his political base, Yeltsin removed himself as a source of influence in legislative development.

Whereas debate in the first four sessions of the Russian CPD had been

131

focused by Yeltsin along this Left-Right dimension – particularly by his calls for political and economic reform and the creation of a presidency – after he vacated the chairmanship to assume the mantle of president and moved to cement his position by issuing a series of presidential decrees, the focus of debate shifted to the desirability of having a strong central executive. Although there was support among deputies for a strong president, there were many who felt that such a move would preclude the legislature from becoming an effective and important branch of the government. The waters were muddied even further because the issue managed to split factions on both sides of the Left-Right dimension during the fifth session of the CPD (as demonstrated by the insightful work of Remington et al. 1994), which made consensus building and cooperation on issues of economic and political reform all but impossible.

It was during a break in this fifth session that conservative forces staged their coup attempt against Gorbachev in a final effort to hold the union together on their terms. When the coup failed, what remained of the central government began to crumble, leaving the republics to pick up the pieces. Much of the economic management that had been the responsibility of the union became Boris Yeltsin's responsibility, and he began to call on the CPD to give him additional powers to pursue a program of radical economic reform.

Although there was a substantial bloc of deputies who opposed either a strong presidency or radical reform, or both, they still lacked any means, such as an effective party system, through which they could have brokered a series of legislative trade-offs and achieved a cooperative equilibrium. Faced with inheriting an economic and political infrastructure that had resulted in the collapse of the Soviet Union, the deputies realized that reform of some sort was needed. They also realized that they could not make a credible commitment to reform so long as the rules of the game remained in a state of flux. Deputies granted Yeltsin's request for extraordinary powers to reform, not because they desired a strong presidency, and not because they wanted private property or endorsed what became known as shock therapy. They granted him the powers because they feared that without some type of reform effort underway their very future as deputies may have been short-lived.

Just as Remington et al. (1994) have shown that the rise of a presidential power dimension in the fifth session of the Russian CPD served to diminish the significance of the Left-Right dimension, we find that on issues that deal with strengthening the president's hand, levels of support for Yeltsin were no longer related to the distribution of small enterprises. When a roll-call vote on accepting as the basis of discussion a draft on the legal basis of economic reform that had been proposed by Boris Yeltsin is modeled with a logistic regression, we find that the parameter estimate on

Table 5.3. *Logit analysis of probability of accepting as basis of
discussion economic reform proposed by Boris Yeltsin*

Explanatory variable	Parameter estimate	Standard error	t-statistic
Constant	26.65	16.54	1.66
Former party	0.32	0.18	1.74
Education	−0.75	0.31	−2.40
Year of birth	−0.01	0.01	−1.60
Fraction	0.01	0.02	0.38
Thousands of enterprises	0.03	0.07	1.66

Log-likelihood = −649.82
Number of observations = 1,056.

the number of small enterprises is no longer statistically significant. Indeed, as the results in Table 5.3 show, the model has lost much of its
explanatory power; even the variable accounting for fractional affiliation
fails to achieve statistical significance.

Clearly, the coup attempt radically altered the political status quo.
When it came to creating the presidency, deputies were able to estimate
the potential payoffs of their decisions and choose accordingly. Later, but
as early as the fifth session, with the waters muddied by the collapse of the
central government and the subsumption of the center's economic and
power bases by the executive branch, the potential payoffs all appeared to
be in terms of what would happen if the process of reform did not
proceed, and soon. Deputies realized that, in the short term at least, it
mattered little what the future economic impact would be in their areas if
they were not able to stay around long enough to do something about it,
one way or the other.

4.4 Tying the president's hands

Yeltsin wasted little time in exercising the powers ceded to him by the
Russian CPD. In a matter of a few days he named himself to the position
of prime minister, declared the Council of Ministers to be the Russian
government, and issued a series of decrees that began the process of
radical economic reform that came to be known as "shock therapy."
Prices were liberalized, social spending was cut dramatically, taxes were
increased, and a privatization plan was put forward. By the time the sixth
session of the CPD convened in April 1992 the consequences of this
program of financial austerity had become painfully clear. Deputies who

133

had, only five months before, granted Yeltsin extraordinary powers began to turn against him and attempted to rein him in.

While legislatures have historically helped to "tie the king's hands" (see, for example, North and Weingast, 1989) circumstances in Russia prevented the CPD from fulfilling that role. The economic system had collapsed under its own weight and was in dire need of reform, but deputies, who had no sure mechanism in place for coordinating legislative trade-offs and who operated in a legislative arena that was in a near-constant state of flux, were incapable of producing a coherent reform program that all deputies (or at least an absolute majority of deputies) were willing to commit to. Faced with the undesirable option of further collapse, they created an agent outside the legislative arena and granted him extraordinary powers, freeing his hands rather than tying them.

Yet, instead of improving, economic conditions worsened. Unable to accept the harsh social and economic – and, potentially, the political – ramifications of Yeltsin's shock therapy program, deputies made an attempt to tie his hands. At the sixth session of Congress, deputies failed to adopt a new constitution, restricted the purchase and sale of land, and placed even stricter controls on the progress of the reform effort, thereby underscoring their inability to make a credible commitment to reform. Subsequent sessions of the CPD were characterized by legislative-executive institutional deadlock. Although compromises were achieved in both the sixth and seventh sessions, they did not prove to be enduring as the CPD began to assume a more obstructionist role.

Popular support for Yeltsin throughout this period, though it did wane somewhat, remained high despite the hardships the people had to endure as a result of his policies. As late as April 1993, in a referendum put to the people, 58.7 percent of those who voted expressed confidence in Yeltsin, and 53 percent approved of the socioeconomic policies carried out by him and his government since 1992. In contrast, fully 67 percent of voters called for early elections of deputies to the CPD.

For all intents and purposes the attempts by the CPD to tie the president's hands came too late. In ceding to the president such extraordinary powers as the right to pursue economic reform by decree, deputies had sent a clear signal that they were unable to do so on their own initiative. When the effects of radical reform began to become clear, deputies began to block the exercise of these powers and, eventually, moved to strip them from the president. And yet they attempted this without first having demonstrated that they themselves could effectively pursue the process of reform.

Yeltsin responded to the Congress's attempts accordingly. Unwilling to sacrifice the progress that had been made toward establishing a market economy, and following as it did an effort on the part of the CPD to impeach him, the results of the April 1993 referendum gave Yeltsin much of the justification he needed to declare the Congress and Supreme Soviet dissolved and call for new elections.

5.0 CONCLUSION

Constitutions and the property rights systems that they help define can be seen as solutions agreed upon by players (deputies), addressing a common problem (the creation of an effective government), whose existence will help them pursue their own interests (from reelection, to political power, to good public policy). Constitutional choice in Russia was heavily influenced by the institutional inheritance from the old communist system, particularly the crippling formula of "all power to the soviets" that was embodied in the failure to create a legislative party system. Under such conditions, the coordination offered by presidential leadership was desirable for deputies anxious to appear as if they were working productively.

This chapter highlights an important dilemma of constitutional choice and political development. If one gives too much power in the drafting process to entrenched interests, they will write the constitution to their own advantage. As Douglass North (1990) has shown, institutions, including both economic and political rules of exchange, produce welfare gains or losses. When incentives or constraints are not oriented to economic growth, institutions can lead to long-term stagnation even while politicians enjoy the fruits of their leading role.[17]

Calvert's framework helps us understand how the problems of reform politics in Russia shifted over time. In early 1991, deputies faced the problem of seizing power from the Soviet Union. They created a presidency to help achieve this end. In late 1991, in a post-coup atmosphere hostile to soviet-style government and open to change, deputies gave Boris Yeltsin the power to reform by decree. Unable to elect a chairman to take Yeltsin's place only three months earlier, and faced with public calls for disbanding the Soviet era legislature, deputies feared gridlock. With no developed party system, no electoral mechanisms, and an underdeveloped committee structure, the CPD was unable to commit to a reform agenda because deputies could not make credible commitments.

In the end, however, even the constitutional amendments passed by the Congress could not serve as a credible commitment: They were good only as long as a qualified majority supported them. As the painful results of

---

[17]"Specific institutional constraints dictate the margins at which organizations operate and hence make intelligible the interplay between the rules of the game and the behavior of the actors. . . . Third World countries are poor because the institutional constraints define a set of payoffs to political/economic activity that do not encourage productive activity" (North, 1990: 110).

reform became apparent and gridlock settled in, the deputies faced a different problem: keeping their jobs. The removal of Yegor Gaidar as premier in the fall of 1992 served notice to Yeltsin that the CPD would eventually take back all the powers it had given him, ending perhaps with his impeachment, or the possible elimination altogether of the presidency. The referendum in the spring of 1993 presented Yeltsin with an opportunity to resolve the longstanding executive-legislative conflict. The final bloody outcome, tanks firing on the White House, was the result.

APPENDIX

The variables used in the logistic regression models are as follows:

Former Party is a dichotomous variable that is used to indicate whether a deputy was a member of the Communist Party (1) or not (0) prior to the republican legislative elections of March 1990. We expect to see that a deputy who was a member of the Communist Party would be less inclined to support the creation of the presidency.

The variable *Education* is also a dichotomous variable measuring the level of education attained, defined as being either higher (1) or less (0). The expectation is that deputies with a higher level of education should have been more likely to support the motion.

Age in the present model is measured by *Year of Birth* and is intended to capture the notion that older deputies should have been more inclined to favor a restoration of the communist regime in some form whereas younger deputies should have been more likely to favor the creation of the presidency and Yeltsin's program of political and economic reform.

The variable *Fraction* uses the ratings created by Alexander Sobyanin (1994) to list fractions within the Russian CPD on a numeric scale that increases from those most likely to embrace a rapid shift toward democratic change and market reform (Radical Democrats and Democratic Russia) to those most likely to oppose it (Russia and the communists). The twelve fractions we have identified, and their associated ordinal ranking, are:

1. Radical Democrats
2. Democratic Russia
3. Left Center/Cooperation
4. Workers' Union
5. Deputies Outside Factions
6. Sovereignty and Equality
7. Change (New Politics)
8. Industrial Union
9. Fatherland

136

10. Agrarian Union
11. Russia
12. Communists

As a deputy moves upward along this ordinal scale, the probability that he will support the creation of the presidency should decrease.

Finally, the variable *Number of Enterprises* simply measures the number of small enterprises, in thousands, in the region the deputy represents in the CPD, as has previously been mentioned. It should be noted at this point that this variable is not district specific, but is only region specific and is a number that, in many cases, is likely an aggregate of several districts. Our expectation is that if such a district-specific number of small enterprises could be produced, it would enable us to produce a more accurate estimate of the impact of this explanatory variable on the probability of supporting the creation of the presidency, but that our finding would remain substantively unchanged.

REFERENCES

Aldrich, John H., *Why Parties? The Origin and Transformation of Party Politics in America* (Chicago: University of Chicago Press, 1995).

Calvert, Randall, "The Rational Choice Theory of Social Institutions: Cooperation, Coordination, and Communication," in Jeffrey S. Banks and Eric A. Hanushek, editors, *Modern Political Economy: Old Topics, New Directions* (Cambridge: Cambridge University Press, 1995), pp. 216–67.

Fenno, Richard F., *Congressmen in Committees* (Boston: Little, Brown, 1973).

Gorbachev, M. S., *Izbraannye rechi i stati 3* (Moscow: Politicheskaia literatura, 1987).

Kiernan, Brendan, *The End of Soviet Politics: Elections, Legislatures, and the Demise of the Communist Party* (Boulder, CO: Westview Press, 1993).

Linz, Juan, "Presidentialism or Parliamentarism: Does It Make a Difference?" in Juan Linz and Arturo Valenzuela, editors, *The Failure of Presidential Government* (Baltimore: Johns Hopkins University Press, 1994), pp. 3–87.

North, Douglass C., *Institutions, Institutional Change, and Economic Performance* (Cambridge: Cambridge University Press, 1990).

North, Douglass C., and Barry R. Weingast, "Constitutions and Credible Commitments: The Evolution of the Institutions of Public Choice in Seventeenth Century England," *Journal of Economic History* 59: 4 (1989), 803–32.

Remington, Thomas F., Steven S. Smith, and D. Roderick Kiewiet, "Voting Alignments in the Russian Congress of Peoples Deputies," mimeo, Emory University (1993).

Remington, Thomas F., Steven S. Smith, D. Roderick Kiewiet, and Moshe Haspel, "Transitional Institutions and Parliamentary Alignments in Russia, 1990–1993," in Thomas F. Remington, editor, *Parliaments in Transition* (Boulder, CO: Westview Press, 1994), pp. 159–80.

Riker, William H., "Implications from the Disequilibrium of Majority Rule for the Study of Institutions," *American Political Science Review* 74: 2 (1980), 432–46.

Sened, Itai, *A Political Theory of Rights*, Ph.D. dissertation, University of Rochester (1990).

Shepsle, Kenneth A., "Institutional Equilibrium and Equilibrium in Multidimensional Voting Models," *American Journal of Political Science* 23: 1 (1979), 27–59.

Shugart, Matthew Soberg, and John M. Carey, *Presidents and Assemblies: Constitutional Design and Electoral Dynamics* (Cambridge: Cambridge University Press, 1992).

Smyth, Regina A., "Ideological vs. Regional Cleavages: Do the Radicals Control the RSFSR Parliament?" *Journal of Soviet Nationalities* 1: 3 (1990), 112–57.

Sobyanin, Alexander, "Political Cleavages Among the Russian Deputies," in Thomas F. Remington, editor, *Parliaments in Transition* (Boulder, CO: Westview Press, 1994), 181–203.

Steele, Jonathan, *Eternal Russia: Yeltsin, Gorbachev, and the Mirage of Democracy* (Cambridge, MA: Harvard University Press, 1994).

Tool, Marc R., "An Institutionalist View of the Evolution of Economic Systems," in Kurt Dopfer and Karl-F. Raible, editors, *The Evolution of Economic Systems* (New York: St. Martin's Press, 1990), pp. 165–74.

Commitment, coordination, and the demise of the post-communist parliament in Russia

STEVEN S. SMITH

1.0 INTRODUCTION

The 1989–93 transition period in Russia presents a difficult challenge to theorists. Fairly open elections were held in 1989 and 1990 for new union-level and republic parliamentary bodies. An empire dissolved, and a new state emerged in the form of the Russian Federation. Within Russia, new parliamentary institutions were created in 1990 and a new presidency was created in 1991. Extraordinary powers were granted to the president in late 1991, but a struggle between the president and parliament over the use and retraction of those powers soon followed. Both the president and parliamentary leaders sought to gain control over policy, the administrative apparatus, and regional authorities through the few means at their disposal. Efforts to craft and implement a new constitution by constitutional means ended in stalemate between the president and parliament and led to the dissolution of parliament by force in late 1993. Explaining what happened, or failed to happen, has become a small industry among social scientists with diverse theoretical perspectives and empirical interests.

The Russian Congress of People's Deputies (CPD), the legislative body elected for the first time in 1990, is a central part of the story. Something happened to the reform forces in the CPD between the elections of 1990 and the dissolution of the parliament by presidential decree in the 1993. At first, the deputies identified with the cause of reform mustered majorities to elect Yeltsin chairman of the parliament and supported his move, even after he made clear his commitment to radical economic reform, to create a presidency. But by 1993 majorities were stacked against Yeltsin, who had been elected Russia's first president in 1991. The result was deadlock between the president and the parliament over basic questions of economic and political reform. The deadlock was broken when Yeltsin dissolved the parliament by decree, enforced the decree by sending troops

139

to the parliament building, quashed a violent uprising, and imprisoned the leaders of the resistance, CPD Speaker Ruslan Khasbulatov and Vice President Alexander Rutskoi. At this writing, the new parliament, the Federal Assembly, and the new constitution implemented in December 1993 have survived for eighteen months, and new elections are going forward as scheduled.

In the preceding chapter, Brendan Kiernan and Frank Bell explained the behavior of the CPD as an effort by its self-interested members to construct an "effective" or "competent" state. As Kiernan and Bell note, critical junctures in the short life of the CPD were the declaration of Russian sovereignty and the creation of a presidency, the extension of extraordinary powers to the president, and the battle over the use and retraction of president's powers. These decisions, they argue, reflected the "institutional pathologies" – coordination and communication problems – of the CPD. The coordination and communication problems prevented the development of credible commitments by CPD deputies to the political and economic reforms essential to creating a stable regime of institutions and property rights. The coordination and communication problems, in turn, were a by-product of the underdeveloped party and committee systems of the CPD.

The Kiernan-Bell analysis is grounded in the "credible commitment" framework and provides an opportunity for me to make some observations about the application of that framework to the early stages of economic and political reform in Russia. Theory in this area is predicated on a simple proposition: There is nothing automatic or inevitable about the emergence of the stable political institutions that are essential to reducing the uncertainty and transaction costs that serve as obstacles to the move to private property and the growth of complex markets. Unfortunately, it is difficult to gain credible commitments to a set of rules or institutions from players who might gain advantage (power, wealth) from reneging on agreements to live by those rules. Therefore, the process of developing enforceable rules – of creating institutional arrangements that are treated as binding by the players – is critical to understanding policy and economic change. As Douglass North (1993: 13) observed, "Property rights are specified and enforced by politics and without an in depth understanding of the way politics evolve it is not possible to understand the way property rights evolve." The Kiernan-Bell analysis of the evolving politics of the Russian CPD during the 1990–3 period is in the spirit of this framework.

In this comment I use the Kiernan-Bell analysis to illustrate the difficulty of translating an abstract theoretical framework into an explanation for a specific set of events. As Kiernan and Bell indicate, a viable account of the CPD's success or failure must define the players and the initial rules of the game. In addition, and perhaps most important, "credible commitment" must be given some operational definition. Each of these issues is considerably more problematic than the discussion in the Kiernan-Bell analysis suggests.

2.0 THE PLAYERS

Discontinuity and uncertainty marked the identity and institutional position of key players during the 1989–93 period in the former Soviet Union. A set of players – Gorbachev, the union-level CPD, Supreme Soviet, and ministers, and, of course, the Communist Party of the Soviet Union (CPSU) – were supplanted by a different mix of players once the Soviet Union dissolved in late 1991 and republic governments became national governments. To be sure, many important players remained in place – the military-industrial nomenklatura, the army and the police, the central bank, the governments of the provincial and ethnic "autonomous" regions, the rural kolkhozes, and others. In North's terminology, these players constituted the organizations that, along with the Russian political elite, would compete to shape institutional arrangements and control public policy. After the demise of the union, these players began to focus on Russian government to a degree that would have been pointless previously.

These changes represented a radical transformation of the political landscape. Russian legislators, who in 1990 were comparable to American state legislators in their governing experience, found themselves at the center of an impending national disaster after the dissolution of the union. The centralized Russian economy had lost its CPSU leadership and coordinating ministries. Responsibility for, as well as the likely actions of, the army and security forces was in doubt. Nuclear warheads located in new states were still armed and targeted. It was left to these legislators, along with their president, to prevent an international calamity.

If we are interested in explaining the success or failure of efforts to adopt and sustain economic reforms during the period, or even to account for the rapid changes in Russia's political institutions, then the full range of players must be taken into account. Even an explanation of the behavior of any one set of these players, such as the deputies of the Russian CPD, requires an account of the behavior of the other key players whose behavior is likely to have affected the strategies of the deputies. For example, the resistance of regional authorities to reform policies emanating from Moscow is essential to understanding the reformers' commitment to a strong presidency. Unfortunately, no reliable account of the goals and strategies of the full range of players is available.

Understandably, therefore, Kiernan and Bell pursue a narrower subject, the behavior of Russian parliamentarians at several critical junctures in the brief life of the CPD, and limit their commentary on the behavior of other players to that which seems most directly connected to deputies' calculations at those times. They give the delimitation of the subject some foundation in their observation that under the old Russian constitution the CPD was the sole arbiter of policy and constitutional arrangements. Focusing on the rulemakers when trying to account for changes in the rules appears to make sense.

And yet, the fact that key players pursued (and others contemplated) extra-constitutional strategies calls into question such a formulation. Yeltsin's extra-constitutional moves against the CPD in 1992 and 1993 can be understood as a response to his estimate that the CPD would never support the kind of economic and political reforms that he favored. If leading opposition deputies anticipated Yeltsin's calculations, some of them would have been expected to give up on parliament and others would have been expected to pursue extra-constitutional strategies of their own, and some of them did so. The resulting mistrust, involving players well beyond the deputies of the CPD, surely shaped the behavior of deputies in ways that extend beyond the coordination problems of the CPD.

3.0 THE INITIAL RULES OF THE GAME

Two features of the political game are treated as fixed by Kiernan and Bell: the sole authority of the CPD to amend the constitution and the nonpartisan basis for CPD decision making. Both claims are critical, but both are arguable. The weakness of the first claim suggests an alternative explanation for the CPD's difficulties; the weakness of the second claim directly undermines the coordination explanation for the lack of credible commitment by the CPD to a reform process.

The Russian CPD was indeed the supreme governmental authority with the final word on legislation and constitutional amendments. But much like the American Continental Congress, the Russian CPD's ability to implement its legislation was extremely limited. In theory, the CPD's ability to implement policy rested on the hierarchy of soviets within Russia, a hierarchy that gave the CPD's presidium an executive function of directing the actions of local soviets and those officials whom the local soviets, in theory, controlled. These connections were not viable. In practice, implementation depended upon the compliance of a large bureaucracy, whose loyalty was initially to union ministries, and provincial officials, many of whose governments claimed substantial autonomy from the White House. By and large, CPD legislation in 1992 and 1993 lacked credibility in the absence of local officials' willingness to enforce it. The unviable soviet system contributed to the creation of the presidency and Yeltsin's effort to build a system of appointed regional administrators (known as governors) and presidential representatives in the regions as a substitute system of central governance. In short, as everyone realized, the CPD's actual influence did not match its formal authority, as everyone realized.

The weakness of the CPD's influence over the implementation of policy stands as a reasonable alternative to Kiernan and Bell's coordination explanation for the CPD's behavior. Perhaps it was not the CPD's commitment and coordination problems that were motivating its members to create and empower the Russian presidency – a credible commitment may not have mattered much. Rather, for both Yeltsin and his eventual parliamentary opponents, the inability of the CPD and the soviet system to effect change of any kind, whatever the status of the CPD's coordinating mechanisms, may have produced the institutional choices of the CPD.

As Kiernan and Bell observe, the 1990 elections were not conducted on a partisan basis, and the new parliament was not organized under party-based leadership. But three features of the new parliament go under-emphasized in the Kiernan-Bell account of the 1990–3 parliamentary insitutions. First, the policy-making activities of the parliament were conducted by the members of the Supreme Soviet, the 252-member body selected from among the members of the CPD. This inner parliament was empowered to adopt laws and other acts, as Kiernan (1993) has reported, and met on a full-time basis. Due in part to the assertiveness and organization of the reformers following the 1990 elections, Yeltsin supporters were able to gain seats in the Supreme Soviet somewhat disproportionate to their numbers in the CPD. For the most part, the Supreme Soviet's policy choices went unchallenged by the CPD. The Supreme Soviet's size, which was much smaller than most national legislatures, and full-time character facilitated communication among deputies to a degree that surely was impossible in the larger CPD.

Second, the CPD and Supreme Soviet inherited from the communist-era Supreme Soviet a leadership structure in the form of a presidium (Remington, Smith, and Davidheiser, 1992). The presidium – comprised of a chairman, deputy chairs, and the chairs of Supreme Soviet commissions and committees (thirty-five members in all) – served as an executive committee for both the Supreme Soviet and CPD. It was first chaired by Yeltsin and then by his chief deputy, Khasbulatov, both of whom were ambitious politicians. The presidium and the highly centralized staff directed by the chairman represented a strong mechanism for communication and coordination of the legislative process. The process of developing legislation, directing the activity of committees, considering alternatives, and building majorities was closely supervised by the presidium, which met weekly to oversee the flow of legislative business.

Third, proto-parties developed in the Supreme Soviet and CPD, and a Council of Factions formed as a body of faction leaders that provided some party-based consultation with the leadership of the presidium. To be sure, membership in factions was voluntary, and factions were not in a position to demand disciplined behavior from their members. Nevertheless, factions met with some frequency, faction leaders consulted with each other, and eventually (in the Sixth Congress) three large blocs of factions were formally organized (see Remington, Smith, Kiewiet, and Haspel, 1993). The blocs were not especially cohesive but were clearly structured along ideological lines and represented the coordinating activity of faction leaders.

These features of the transitional parliament do not mean that coordination problems were in fact surmounted. They only suggest that communication and coordination problems were not as severe as they might have been in a new, large, and nonpartisan legislature. They also indicate that efforts were made to coordinate the behavior of like-minded legislators. Furthermore, they suggest that making the case that weak coordination undermined credible commitment by the CPD requires a more detailed account of the legislative process than is provided in the Kiernan-Bell analysis.

Going beyond the two institutional features emphasized by Kiernan and Bell, the decision rule imposed by the old constitution – that questions be decided by a majority of elected deputies (as opposed to a majority of those voting) – may deserve more emphasis (on this rule, see Myagkov and Kiewiet, 1995). The sharply polarized corps of deputies (Remington et al., 1993), with neither the right- or left-wing blocs owning a majority, combined with absenteeism to make the threshold an impediment to any action by the CPD and, although to a lesser extent, by the Supreme Soviet. The threshold for a constitutional amendment – a two-thirds majority of elected deputies – meant that only changes that did not disadvantage one bloc or the other could be adopted. The decision rules, in short, appeared to be stacked against positive action by the legislative bodies of the transitional era.

The decision rules and polarized alignments, we can hypothesize, would discourage policy leadership and innovation within parliament. If so, the decision rule may have been a barrier to credible commitments on the part of the CPD. But this account of the obstacles to credible commitments is very different from one that emphasizes problems of communication and coordination among deputies. Instead, it emphasizes rules that were initially adopted as a part of a package of reforms designed to emulate the Union Congress and the party congress rules on which its rules were based (Myagkov and Kiewiet, 1995). The inherited rules combined with an alignment of preferences uncommon in the communist era to incapacitate the new parliament. This is a researchable alternative to the coordination thesis.

4.0 CREDIBLE COMMITMENT

Perhaps the most difficult aspect of applying the credible-commitment framework is the identification of a credible commitment independent of the subsequent behavior that it produces. The task involves the identification of a commitment on the part of the relevant player(s) and an assessment of the credibility that other players attach to that commitment. It is not enough that a decision was made or that some genuine commitment was demonstrated. The claim that other players find the commitment to be credible is equally important. Further complicating matters is the fact that the required degree of credibility is not fixed, but rather varies with the expected payoffs to the players of the alternative strategies they might pursue. Thus, the task of the empirical analyst – demonstrating that the necessary credibility was present or absent in a particular historical context – is a very slippery business. In most contexts, demonstrating that credibility, rather than the nature of the commitment or other factors, lies behind the timing of institutional changes is incredibly difficult.

Time and learning introduce additional complications. Credibility is a matter of reputation and acquired over time, sometimes over very long periods of time. Moreover, stabilizing regimes of policy and institutions is a matter of innovation and learning, which take time as well. Elinor Ostrom (1990) is most explicit in arguing that a credible commitment and a matrix of institutions and policies develop quite incrementally and interactively. If time is so critical, then we might not expect to see adaptive institutions even when the matrix of interests clearly dictates a new set of institutions (as far as the analyst can see). The requisite innovations and learning may not have occurred yet. And if rational adaptation takes time, then changing conditions may prevent a rational adaptation from being realized. Periods of rapid change in basic political or economic conditions may not be well suited to rational adaptation.

According to Kiernan and Bell, deputies of the CPD were unable to credibly commit to a process of reform. In their view, deputies lacked party organization and leadership or, alternatively, the time to develop nonpartisan structures within the CPD that could provide the means to coordinate the process of preference aggregation, bargaining, and enforcement of legislative agreements. This institutional handicap made it difficult for deputies to maintain a commitment to a set of institutional arrangements and policies. So handicapped, the argument goes, deputies

145

deferred to Yeltsin in creating a presidency and yielding emergency powers to him. Perhaps, Kiernan and Bell suggest, more time – more iterations of elections and parliaments – would have produced the coordinating mechanisms that would have allowed the CPD to create a stable policy and institutional regime. They suggest, in concluding, that the violent end of the CPD was due to its inability to credibly commit to reform.

But there is an alternative explanation, about which Kiernan and Bell offer a hint in section 4.1, where they note that "though most [deputies] agreed that some manner of reform was necessary, there was disagreement, sometimes intense, concerning both the areas that should be the focus of that reform and the pace at which it should advance." If so, then the problem may have been more the nature of deputies' policy commitments – a deep policy cleavage – than the credibility of commitments. Kiernan and Bell provide no argument that party leadership or some other effective coordinating mechanism imposed would have produced a different pattern of decisions about institutions and economic reform. Indeed, the opposition of a majority of deputies to radical reform may have been quite credible once the common enemy of the Gorbachev administration evaporated. Reformers' certainty about balance of views in the CPD probably contributed to the deadlock between the reformers entrenched in the presidential administration and their opponents in the Congress.

To be sure, the deadlock was not a stable arrangement, given the players' willingness to pursue extra-constitutional means for achieving their goals. By late 1992, no one inside or outside the CPD could have much confidence that the constitutional framework or existing presidential decrees and statutes on privatization, land, and the development of capital markets would remain in place for long. But the coordination and communication problems internal to the CPD may have been a small part of the problem. It is unlikely that even the most creative mind could have devised a mix of policy and institutional arrangements that satisfied the CPD majority and provided institutional stability. If so, then perhaps the absence of stronger coordinating mechanisms (if that is a fair characterization) reflected the low probability that an investment in them would have payoffs for the parliamentary majority.

5.0 CONCLUDING OBSERVATIONS

The fate of the CPD and Supreme Soviet during 1990–3 remains a puzzle. Kiernan and Bell have added another viable candidate to a growing list of possible explanations for the CPD's eventual lack of commitment to a program of reform. I have suggested several alternative explanations that are not necessarily incompatible with the coordination thesis: high-threshold decision rules, the CPD's limited ability to see that policy was implemented, and, most important, the gulf between the CPD and Yeltsin over the substance of policy. I also have suggested that coordination mechanisms existed with the CPD that at least call into question the view that the CPD's lack of commitment to reform was caused by deputies' inability to communicate and coordinate their own strategies.

I began by noting the analytical challenge posed by the brief history of the Russian Congress of People's Deputies. I conclude by noting several types of change that occurred during the 1990–3 period that make the challenge particularly difficult. These sources of change reflect the special volatility of politics in newly democratized or democratizing systems and affect most forms of theorizing about the process of democratization.

5.1 New issues

A rapidly changing issue space makes it very difficult for the analyst to evaluate changes in policy alignments. And the flow of issues during 1990–3 was stunning. Russia created a separation-of-powers system and elected a president, the Soviet Union dissolved and the burdens of state-hood shifted to the Russian government, hundreds of thousands of refugees poured into Russia from neighboring republics, economic conditions deteriorated, private businessmen amassed fortunes through arbitrage, organized crime burgeoned, and regional governments began to ignore the central government. With so many new and highly salient issues of concern to the deputies, it was nearly inevitable that new voting alignments would emerge. And new voting alignments, whatever else was changing, surely contributed to distancing the CPD from the president.

5.2 Changing preferences

Even more challenging are changes in the underlying preferences of the players. Most social science analysis assumes that players' preferences are fixed over a policy space. Alignments may vary from dimension to dimension, but the alignment on any single dimension usually is not too variable within a single parliament or congress. Legislators' preferences, of course, are products of multiple influences beyond their personal beliefs – demands from legislators' party or home constituencies, the political and material incentives that are controlled by others, and so on. A change in the balance of forces in legislators' environment may change the behavior of at least some legislators and alter voting alignments.

As Kiernan and Bell recognize, preferences appear to have changed on a fairly large scale in the CPD. Deteriorating economic conditions might

147

have produced the change in preferences about policy alternatives. So might the mobilization of industrial and social interests against economic reform. And changing preferences might have reflected the influence of the chairman Khasbulatov, who had ambitions of his own and controlled many sources of leverage over deputies – committee assignments, paid jobs in the Supreme Soviet, and perquisites of office such as Moscow apartments, cars, and trips abroad (Remington, 1993).

5.3 Changing players

A final complication in the case of the Russian CPD is significant change in the composition of the legislature. Swings in stance on the presidency may have been caused by a high rate of attrition among reform-oriented deputies. In fact, more than a hundred deputies took positions working for President Yeltsin, in his administration, or as his representatives in the regions or appointed chiefs of regional administration. They were obliged to give up any full-time paid positions that they may have held in the parliament, but could remain deputies and thus vote in the congresses. Some deputies, however, did choose to stop taking active part in the congresses. At the Ninth Congress, with 1,033 duly elected deputies eligible to participate, only 781 registered for the opening session. Since passage of a law required a minimum of 517 votes, nonattendance could complicate the legislative process. And the nonparticipating were disproportionately reformers.

More generally, rapid changes in the composition of the electorate, the interest-group community, party system, and other components of the polity alter the identity of the players who may influence the strategies of others. The disintegration of an empire adds additional sources of change to the class of relevant players. Strategies must not only account for the behavior of other known players but also anticipate the entry or exit of other players from the political game. Changing the game in this way introduces sources of uncertainty that are quite foreign to more stable polities.

Plainly, these sources of change outline a sizable research agenda for students of democratization and other forms of political change.

REFERENCES

Kiernan, Brendan, *The End of the Soviet Era* (Boulder, CO: Westview Press, 1993).

Myagkov, Mikhail, and D. Roderick Kiewiet, "Czar Rule in the Russian Congress of People's Deputies?" paper presented at the annual meeting of the Midwest Political Science Association, Chicago, April 14–16 (1995).

North, Douglass C., "Institutions and Credible Commitment," *Journal of Institutional and Theoretical Economics* 149: 1 (1993), 11–23.

Ostrom, Elinor, *Governing the Commons: The Evolution of Institutions for Collective Action* (Cambridge: Cambridge University Press, 1990).

Remington, Thomas F., "Menage à Trois: The End of Soviet Parliamentarism," paper presented to the annual meeting of the AAASS, Honolulu, November (1993).

Remington, Thomas F., Steven S. Smith, and Evelyn Davidheiser, "The Early Legislative Process in the Russian Supreme Soviet," paper presented at the annual meeting of the Southern Political Science Association, Atlanta, November 1–2 (1992).

Remington, Thomas F., Steven S. Smith, D. Roderick Kiewiet, and Moshe Haspel, "Transitional Institutions and Parliamentary Alignments in Russia, 1990–1993," in Thomas F. Remington, editor, *Parliaments in Transition* (Boulder, CO: Westview Press, 1994), 159–80.

6

Private firms, city government, and arbitration: Enforcing economic legality in St. Petersburg

JOEL M. ERICSON

1.0 INTRODUCTION

Boris Yeltsin's government signaled a strong federal commitment to private property rights when it came to power after the Soviet Union's collapse. The new federal government's legislation, and greater municipal and regional autonomy, elicited a huge wave of locally conducted privatizations.[1] Yeltsin's legislative and administrative reforms did not, however, guarantee that credible commitments to private property rights would emerge when his policies were implemented. City and regional agencies empowered by federal legislation to dispense property rights frequently contested ownership *after* an enterprise was privatized or leased to a private firm. The investments Russia needs for economic growth and political stability were discouraged as private firms experienced costly regulations from local government. Indeed, the question arises of whether local government can ever credibly commit to property rights.

This chapter argues that city government can credibly commit to private property rights when private firms believe that they can sue and prevail over city agencies in Arbitration Court (Arbitrazhni Sud). As this chapter illustrates, when St. Petersburg's Arbitration Court began refereeing the interaction between private firms and local government, reasonably credible commitment to property rights emerged.

In developed market economies, independent courts enable federal governments and local agencies to make credible commitments to private firms (North and Weingast, 1989). Ownership rights and contracts are known to be enforceable ex ante. Russian economic reforms, however, often fail because they are implemented in circumstances that lack clearly specified and consistent patterns of interaction between local government

[1] By July 1993, 2,220 retail shops, 857 restaurants and cafes, and 1,565 service firms were privatized in St. Petersburg (*Ekho*, July 14, 1993, 8).

agencies and private firms. For example, taxes are abruptly changed, leases are unexpectedly invalidated, or ownership of equipment is suddenly contested.

In this chapter, I consider how St. Petersburg's Arbitration Court enables city agencies to commit credibly to property rights by defining and limiting the city's capacity to regulate, distribute, and confiscate property. Arbitration enables government to commit credibly to property rights whenever case rulings define the limits of government regulation. When the court prevents executive agencies from confiscating property rights from private firms, it incrementally increases the credibility of the city's commitment to stable property rights.

Specific examples of the Arbitration Court's cases are cited throughout the chapter to illustrate statistical evidence. Quantitative and qualitative evidence demonstrates that private firms are increasingly suing *and* increasingly winning the cases they bring to arbitration against public agencies and state firms. Firms gain a credible right to property when they can sue city agencies with the expectation of fair treatment. When private firms successfully sue state firms or city agencies in court, the right becomes credible. Moreover, as such rulings accumulate, the institutional framework changes incrementally to "tie the hands" of local government agencies and discourage future attempts to confiscate property (Root, 1989).

The remainder of this chapter focuses on interaction between local government agencies and private investors that the St. Petersburg Arbitration Court referees. The chapter is organized as follows.

First, a differentiation is made between informal and formal property rights to show how credible commitments are more likely to occur when rights are formal. A discussion follows of how the Soviet command economy's legacy of informal property rights impedes economic legality and why the courts are vital to the formalization of property rights and market reform.

Second, I discuss the arbitration of disputes between private enterprises and local government agencies. I show that the tendency of executive organs to rescind property rights is increasingly being restrained by an arbitration court that has undergone significant internal restructuring. Unlike its Soviet predecessor, Gosarbitrazh (State Arbitration Court), the reorganized Arbitration Court is largely independent from local executive power.

Third, I discuss the legalization and registration of private firms starting with cooperative enterprises in the Gorbachev era. Cooperatives re-registered into closed partnerships and joint-stock companies in 1991 and 1992 as part of Yeltsin's reforms, and in response to the expected collapse of the Soviet Union. Numerous property rights issues surround-

151

ing leasing and the host of informal rights left over from the Soviet period were passed on in transition to the Russian Federation with its substantially changed legal system.

Fourth, I consider the leasing of commercial real estate to private firms. Leases are often insecure because they were arranged informally or improperly. City agencies, like the district- and city-level Committees for Management of State Property, actively invalidate leases. By increasing rents and taxes or transferring the ownership of firms entirely, city agencies can undermine the credibility of the property rights they dispense and administer. Moreover, the structure of St. Petersburg's city government reduces the credibility of private property rights for investors because, as a myriad of district-level (*raion*) agencies dispense property rights, they muddle the formalizing efforts of central coordinating agencies. These agencies are ill-equipped to manage rapid changes in ownership or the registration of informal properties to comply with legal codes. They often defect from central city regulation to arrange informal contracts with private firms.

Fifth, I consider taxation. The uneven and arbitrary enforcement of tax laws by St. Petersburg's tax inspectorate negatively affects the credibility of city government's commitment to property rights. Tax breaks promised to the Gorbachev era's cooperative firms are rescinded as those firms reregister into partnerships and joint-stock companies to conform to Russian Federation laws.

2.0 INFORMAL AND FORMAL PROPERTY RIGHTS

Without a codified system of centrally registered ownership rights, market exchanges in Russia tend to gravitate toward informality. Informal agreements only require the consent of the exchangers rather than permission from a potentially confiscatory state agency. Thus, informal agreements are meant to avoid, at least partially, the executive enforcement of formal laws on registration and taxation. Informal exchanges are usually self-enforcing and, when they reoccur over time, they may become important to the overall functioning and performance of an economy.

The Soviet economy as it developed under the leadership of the Communist Party exemplifies the importance of informal transactions in an economy that was ostensibly centrally controlled. Black markets for consumer goods and gray markets for factor inputs were institutionalized within and outside the context of central planning and became vital to the overall functioning of the Soviet economic system. Although "illicit trades undercut the ideology, rationale, and laws of [the Soviet Union's] planned economy, they became so obviously indispensable that they were often tacitly countenanced by higher officials" (Olson, 1992: 62).

Private firms, city government, and arbitration

Without informal (illegal) exchange, the Soviet economy would never have operated as well as it did. Yet, informal exchanges, generally based on personal connections and secrecy, lacked legal safeguards. Parties to an illegal exchange could not seek court protection when their deals went sour or when their profits were confiscated. They were thus vulnerable to rent-seeking by city agencies, especially when the formal structure of the command economy has virtually collapsed.[2]

The informal property rights created by illicit exchanges are very uncertain without an unbroken chain of party officials to countenance them. Although informal exchanges are often costly to negotiate and to enforce, moving them to the legal arena attracts the attention of city agencies that may attempt to invalidate leases, raise taxes, or question the ownership of equipment. Absent protection from these risks, open and impersonal market transactions are unlikely to replace secretive and intensely personal exchanges.

This is a critical point for understanding why Soviet-type economies stagnated in the late 1970s and 1980s. Economies stagnate when informal exchange predominates because the basis of informal exchange is knowledge about one's trading partner. The basis for formal exchange is knowing that if contracts are violated, they can be enforced in an independent court of law. Moving from one set of institutions to another requires that the state be composed of institutions with separation of judicial from executive and legislative powers. Because Soviet-type polities were dominated by single parties, this sort of development was not possible.

The formalization of property rights through the arbitration of disputes promotes economic growth because it stabilizes the expectations that property owners have about the actions of city agencies. More important, arbitration enables credible commitments to property rights to arise endogenously. The credibility is based on the information embodied in the exchange itself, rather than from the perceived strengths of the exchangers. When rights arise endogenously, their credibility can be judged more easily than when they depend upon the asymmetrical political strengths of government agencies and private firms.

In contrast, if firms operate in an uncertain institutional environment, with few rules that can be considered known, tested, and trustworthy, then owners will rely heavily on personal connections, using "informal transactions" to achieve economic goals (Ben-Porath, 1980). If contracts cannot be effectively enforced through the legal system, then transactions are likely to involve informal exchanges between people who have alter-

[2]Eggertsson (1990: 279) defines rent-seeking as "attempts by individuals to increase their personal wealth while at the same time making a negative contribution to the net wealth of their community."

native enforcement mechanisms at their disposal. Such mechanisms can include personal ties developed during the days of Soviet communism to facilitate a firm's successful operation in a centrally organized economic system. In today's Russia, such ties can be useful for gaining special tax privileges or access to property rights from city officials who, in the old system, oversaw planned exchanges.

The persistence of informal ties impedes market development because fixed capital and credit are monopolized and because informal ties lead to opportunistic behavior that ignores economic legality. Groups that enjoy greater bargaining power often monitor informally based transactions to gain rents. Such interventionist behavior characterized successful economic strategies in the institutional context of command administration and economic planning. Yet, absent formal specification of their allowable scope, such interventions in the informal transactions of private firms act to prevent the development of formal activities by these firms (Litwack, 1991; Shlapentokh, 1989).

The dilemma for Soviet reformers was always to find ways to provide managers with the incentives needed to increase planned production. Although permitting private ownership was anathema to the idea of a communist-guided centrally planned economy, providing incentives to managers was viewed as legitimate. Changing incentives, however, involved changes in the de facto rights managers exercised over the assets of their state enterprises. But, as these were effectively use rights rather than ownership rights, managers did not have a strong incentive to maximize the value of the assets they controlled. Seen in this light, the complete failure of reform attempts in the 1960s and the partial failure of reform attempts in the 1980s can be attributed to the inability of Soviet planners to extend stable property rights to state enterprise managers (Birman, 1978; Moore, 1981).

Russia's reformers want market demands to replace administrative commands as production incentives. Yet, property rights must be stable if free prices are to structure exchange. The dilemma for government is how to commit credibly to private property when it must be restrained from the interventionist behavior for which it is renowned. A major difficulty is that the tasks of administering commercial real estate and collecting tax revenues falls upon a variety of local government agencies. Set up precisely to convey the center's commands to the erstwhile state-owned enterprises (SOEs), these agencies have proved unwilling to replace arbitrary interventions with consistent administrative services to firms. Inevitably, government regulation creates winners and losers. From the perspective of a private firm, it matters little whether regulation is on behalf of a CPSU-dominated state or for democratically elected legislatures, mayors, and presidents.

Private firms, city government, and arbitration

Effective implementation of reforms by local agencies is further complicated by the overlapping jurisdictions these agencies have over the establishment of property rights. As Boris Yeltsin (FBIS, 1993: 13) recently complained:

I could cite hundreds of examples when the administration of a town or oblast forbids something, while the local soviet permits exactly the same thing, or vice versa. One body allots a plot of land to its owner, while another body allots the same plot of land to someone else. This is taking place in Moscow and throughout the whole of Russia. The longer this goes on, the greater the confusion which eventually works to the detriment of citizen and state. It not only increasingly holds back, but literally ruins all the reforms and leads to the squandering of Russia's wealth and our national prosperity.

An even greater problem is that city agencies compete with one another to influence the distribution of property rights between firms so as to gain access to rents from the firms. City administrators once interested in diverting resources from planned production to extract rents are today no less interested in extracting rents from private firms.

Such activities served a positive function when production was centrally planned because meeting planned targets often required discretionary behavior to divert labor and inputs in unplanned ways. However, discretionary administrative behavior is anathema to the stable property rights that market production requires. Indeed, as John Litwack (1991: 77) wrote two years before the start of the Russian Federation's reforms: "Without legality, a shift away from central planning toward market allocation may very likely lead to economic decline, inflationary pressures, and a polarization in income distribution, which, in turn could unleash political reaction against the reform process in general."

Economic legality depends upon consistent implementation of noncontradictory laws by government agencies through uniform enforcement so that owners believe their property rights are stable (Demsetz, 1967). If laws are enforced in a discretionary manner by public agencies as they were in the Soviet Union's planned economy, then the ensuing loss of credibility for private property rights will impede the development of trade based on impersonal and stable exchange, and instead reinforce the intricate web of personal relationships used to coordinate exchanges in the absence of legality.

Without legal safeguards guaranteed by an independent court system, most entrepreneurs consider it too risky to venture beyond the realm of informal property rights. They consider it easier to pay a city official's bribe than to subject themselves to the possibility of frequent checks by tax authorities, district agencies, or the mayor's office. Thus, property rights for small private firms in St. Petersburg remain largely informal for two reasons. First, until recently government lacked the capacity to trans-

155

mit credible information pertaining to tax collection and lease agreements. Second, government agencies were not always willing to recognize the validity of arbitration procedures and the independence of arbitration courts.

The incapacity to transmit credible information to investors arises in part from the sheer size and complexity of local government, which makes administration of privatization policies and tax collection very complicated. Moreover, the mass of informally deeded commercial real estate left over from the Soviet period undermines government promises to respect property rights. Lacking legal safeguards, such leases offer government agencies an easy opportunity for extracting rents. The personnel of such agencies are adept (they are often lawyers) at finding legal inconsistencies and other invalid aspects of informally (or incompetently) arranged leases. Moreover, informal leases are often based on undervalued estimates of a property's worth and stated in nominal prices that have lost value through inflation. City officials are tempted to change these lease agreements ex post.

Signaling commitment to investors is problematic for local government because the simultaneous existence of informal and formal property rights presents numerous opportunities for confiscation. Until institutional arrangements arise that raise the cost of reneging on contracts, local government cannot commit itself completely to private property. Independent arbitration courts constrain this confiscatory tendency of executive power when private firms sue the government and prevail. The arbitration process distributes rights more impartially than do officials with rent-seeking interests. It also offers a bridge from informality to formality that avoids the gauntlet of competing city agencies. Accordingly, arbitration potentially offers a stronger political foundation for free market development.

3.0 ARBITRATION AND THE ESTABLISHMENT OF AN INDEPENDENT JUDICIARY

Economic reforms that extended property rights to producers in the Soviet Union were rendered ineffective whenever unchecked executive power confiscated the very wealth that the reforms created. Soviet reformers recognized that independent arbitration courts were needed to make reforms that granted producers clearer and more credible property rights. Yet, Gosarbitrazh remained an organ of government power highly susceptible to executive influence until the end of 1991 when new laws called for an independent court to protect property rights and limit executive power.

To the detriment of their own credibility for protecting private property rights, the executive agencies of the new Russian Federation sometimes exhibit the tendency of their Soviet predecessors as they attempt to keep arbitration of contractual disputes within the jurisdiction of executive power. For example, on October 21, 1991, St. Petersburg's "reform"-oriented mayor, Anatolii Sobchak, signed a directive that stated that the city's district courts and arbitration courts (then Gosarbitrazh) should be directly subordinated to the Judiciary Committee of the Mayor's Office.

The mayor's directive instigated an organized response from St. Petersburg's judges. Meeting on November 18, 1991, to discuss the mayor's actions, they unanimously voted that the directive was illegal.

Federal support for the judges' decision soon followed: City Arbitration Courts were ordered by the Federal Arbitration Court to be withdrawn from the purview of the mayor's Judicial Committee. At a subsequent meeting on March 20, 1992, the St. Petersburg city judges pointed out that the mayor had not even fulfilled Boris Yeltsin's presidential decree: Former CPSU buildings were to be granted to the courts. According to the judges, the expansion of their institutional capacity was absolutely necessary to create an independent judiciary in St. Petersburg and to "defend itself from the influence of local powers." The court's functions were expanded by the Law on Private Property and Enterprises, by the Law on Entrepreneurial Activity, and by Yeltsin's decree of February 25, 1992, on "Ministries of the Russian Federation," which recognized the need for more office and courtroom space and ordered the widening of the court's functions (Konstantinov, 1992).

The independence of St. Petersburg's courts found further support by the year's end with the promulgation of the Laws on Arbitration Courts, Arbitration Procedure, and Status of Judges. These laws formed the basis for the transformation of the formerly executive body, Gosarbitrazh, to its current status of Arbitration Court, an institution designed to be independent from executive influence. The Law on the Status of Judges explicitly stated that judges were to be chosen with lifetime tenure by the Russian parliament and paid out of the federal budget.

Thus, despite Anatolii Sobchak's efforts, a vital step toward creating an institution capable of protecting private property rights from arbitrary executive confiscation occurred in December 1991 when the State Arbitration Court, Gosarbitrazh, was transformed into the Arbitration Court. The change in the court's status and its operating procedures occurred as part of the promulgation of the Laws on Property and the Law on Enterprises and Entrepreneurship.

The fundamental purpose of Gosarbitrazh had been to settle disputes occurring within branches of the command economy. Gosarbitrazh, subordinate to the executive branch, considered cases mostly in terms of whether contracts were being completed according to planned specifica-

157

tions. The explicit consideration of property rights that were to arise with the emergence of new property forms such as cooperatives, and later stock companies and partnerships, posed difficulties for a court traditionally subordinate to the executive.

As new laws concerning property were promulgated and laws governing the court's role in the economy changed, the arbitration court stopped being subordinate to the executive branches of government. According to the Arbitration Court's vice president:

Previously, the court functioned as an executive body, acting to inform enterprise managers about laws governing contracting between state firms, but now we don't have that function because we're not an executive body anymore. Now we consider claims against the state and must thus be separate from it to be impartial. The main thing is that those three laws that were adopted really make the court pay attention to the functioning of a market economy. They represent economic justice now. So their position is quite sensitive as they arbitrate between state and non-state industries and non-profit organizations.[3]

Since 1992 when the Law on Entrepreneurship and Entrepreneurial Activity was put into practice, the court has changed significantly in its ability to hear cases that involve various property forms. Until that time, all cases involving cooperative enterprises were presided over by only one judge.[4] Cases took up to two years to be resolved. Now the court is required to take no longer than three months to resolve cases, has three judges sitting on every case, and rules in favor of private enterprises more often than it did when only one judge presided over all cases involving cooperatives, the only nonstate enterprise legally active prior to the Law on Enterprises and Entrepreneurial Activity. Moreover, the number of judges has been increased from twenty-one to forty in an effort to increase the court's capacity to hear cases.

Table 6.1 presents a random sample of cases involving private enterprises heard, on the one hand by Gosarbitrazh in 1990 and 1991, and on the other by the City Arbitration Court of St. Petersburg in 1993. The comparison shows how the composition of cases changed between 1991 and 1993. By 1993 cooperatives, joint-stock companies, and partnerships were suing state enterprises and government agencies more often than they were being sued by such enterprises and agencies. Moreover, private enterprises were winning suits brought against state firms and city agencies more often.

Although Table 6.1 does not show a dramatic decline over time in the percentage won by city agencies and state firms that sue private firms, it shows a decline in both the absolute number of such cases and their

---

[3]Interview with Ludmila A. Batalova, vice president, St. Petersburg Arbitration Court, August 10, 1993.
[4]This judge was dismissed from the arbitration court for reasons unknown to me.

Table 6.1. *The changing composition of City Arbitration Court cases, 1990 to 1993*

Type	1990		1991		1993	
	Total number of cases/percent overall	Number of cases plaintiff wins/percent overall	Total number of cases/percent overall	Number of cases plaintiff wins/percent overall	Total number of cases/percent overall	Number of cases plaintiff wins/percent overall
Private firm sues private firm	24/7.5	23/95.8	16/6.4	15/93.0	51/18.3	49/96.0
Private firm sues state firm or city agency	27/8.5	20/74.0	34/13.6	31/91.0	151/54.1	147/97.3
State firm or city agency sues private firm	269/84.0	259/96.2	200/80.0	186/93.0	77/27.6	70/90.9

Notes: All cases for 1990 and 1991 appeared in Gosarbitrazh. All cases for 1993 appeared in the City Arbitration Court. Data randomly collected in St. Petersburg Arbitration Court thanks to the cooperation of the court's vice president, Ludmila Alexandrovna Batalova. Unfortunately, data for 1992 were not made available to this researcher.

percentage of the total caseload. The table also shows a dramatic increase in the number and percentages of cases brought against city agencies and state firms by private firms. This reflects an increase in the court's capacity to hear cases, legal changes pertaining to private ownership, and, perhaps, the belief by private firms that they can win such cases. Moreover, the percentage of these cases won by the plaintiff shows a fairly large increase over previous (Gosarbitrazh) years, which reflects changes in the law and, perhaps, the court's independence from executive power. The activities of the arbitration court are receiving much coverage from the local and national press. *Kommersant Daily* and *Delovoye Obozreniya* are, respectively, the most influential national and local business papers in St. Petersburg. Both papers devote regular columns to the court's activities, especially when private firms win important cases against the government.

The fair enforcement of contracts through the courts contributes to the credibility of property rights by transmitting a signal to rights holders that the transfer of their rights according to established rules will be respected. In St. Petersburg it is the Arbitration Court that ensures that parties to a potential agreement have ex ante the "right to be sued" before writing a contract: "If suit does arise, the 'right' seems a liability in retrospect; beforehand it was a prerequisite to doing business" (Schelling, 1960: 43).

Arbitration by an independent court helps ensure that government will meet its commitments. If individuals expect the courts to rule in their favor when the government impinges upon formal property rights, and if it is costly for the government to defy the courts, then property rights are more credible because it is less tempting for the government to impinge upon the rights. Furthermore, as will be illustrated below, in situations of ambiguous rights, the Arbitration Court contributes to the definition of property rights through its rulings.

The contribution to credibility is likely to be especially great when contracts between individuals and government are enforced in favor of individuals, particularly whenever rights deemed "informal" by a government agency are ruled "formal" by the court's overruling of the city agency's claim. In short, the City Arbitration Court is beginning to clarify property rights so those rights can be fairly and consistently enforced.

To illustrate the substantive implications of the changes shown in Table 6.1, the following sections provide examples of how the court prevented St. Petersburg's Tax Inspectorate, Committee for the Management of State Property (KUGI), and Property Fund from confiscating property from private firms.

4.0 LEGALIZATION AND REGISTRATION
OF PRIVATE FIRMS

The first important steps toward the decentralization of state property in Russia occurred as part of Mikhail Gorbachev's attempt to restructure the Soviet Union's planned economic system. Although the explicit intent of Gorbachev's "perestroika" was to allow for the free operation of a small-scale private sector and the less restricted operation of SOEs, implicit in perestroika's decentralization of property rights was an admission that Soviet laws no longer reflected the reality of "informal" activities by Soviet citizens. In effect, those activities had already usurped many of the powers central authorities once used to control virtually all aspects of economic life.

Gorbachev publicly complained about the extensive moonlighting activities of Soviet citizens, which he saw as assuming ever larger shares of resources officially intended for state-controlled production. Personal garden plots had long been an important supplier of fresh produce to the cities. Depending on one's point of view, such informal forms of private property were regularly praised or lamented as being more productive than communal and state farms (Grossman, 1977). Consumer goods were increasingly being produced in underground factories. Managers of state firms diverted production to gray and black markets to gain higher profits for themselves and to facilitate the meeting of plan targets by avoiding complete dependence on the state's supply system and its bottlenecks (Ericson, 1984; Grossman, 1979; Litwack, 1991; Shlapentokh, 1989).

With the promulgation of Laws on Cooperatives and State Enterprises in 1988, private firms in the Soviet Union attained the legal right to use and profit from state-owned property. The Law on State Enterprises explicitly stated that cooperatives could be formed as subsidiaries of state enterprises and that they would not be responsible for meeting plan targets. According to Anthony Jones and William Moscoff (1991: 10), the incentives embodied by the new laws promoted a noticeable reaction from state enterprises: "[Ninety] percent of the businesses that opened during the early months of the cooperative movement were individual labor activities, but after 1988 when the Law on cooperatives was passed, the size of cooperatives began to increase because many state enterprises were converted to the cooperative form."

The new laws allowed the formation of cooperatives to be used by state managers as a means to remove parts of their state enterprises from the auspices of central state management (Johnson and Kroll, 1991). Consequently, the development of cooperative enterprises became markedly different from the small-scale economic activity that characterized their operation before the promulgation of the new laws.

Most significantly, as a new property form, cooperatives made avoidance of the ministries' price and wage controls legal and, with the statutory sanction, made for fundamental changes in the firm's contracts with all levels of government. It was a step toward market exchange in a state-run economy in which planned exchanges among all firms had been formerly enshrined in law that gave no legal protection to firms operating outside of the formal plan.

The creation of new property forms and the explicit legalization of contracts between state and private firms provided opportunities to transfer money from restricted accounts that could not be used for wages to accounts that were not so restricted. Converting ministerially controlled enterprises to cooperative production raised many questions about taxation and prices (*Moscow News*, 1989a, 1989b). Inevitably, the redistribution of wealth caused by the growth of cooperatives and their incorporation as a property form within state enterprises initiated numerous conflicts with local and ministerial officials.

District-level officials were charged with the responsibility of registering and monitoring (taxing) the commercial activities of the newly developing private firms. However, information about the behavior of firms and the officials who administered their activities was rarely centralized and made observable to elected officials in the city council or the mayor's office. With so much room for interpretation, district officials discovered that they had a wide range of tools at their disposal to pressure cooperatives to comply with their opinions on how privatization should proceed ("Vse Dlia Kooperativa," 1989).

Cooperatives learned to avoid excessive monitoring of their activities. By registering in one district, but operating in another, they could avoid tax inspections by inconveniencing district tax inspectors and obscuring their whereabouts to city-wide taxation agencies. Informal agreements to form private firms within state-owned factories enabled state-controlled equipment and workers to produce for private gain and avoid inspection altogether (Rutman, 1993).

The arrangements cooperatives made to register and operate as private firms were complicated by the unsettled nature of their fledgling property rights. Whereas they may have acquired newfound incentives to produce and profit from their private legal status, much of the fixed capital they used remained in the control of city agencies, and in the ownership of the state. This divergence between property rights to income and property rights to fixed capital and real estate gave city agents the opportunity to make ad hoc adjustments to leasing and supply contracts to compensate for inflation or the discovery that a firm's value was greater than originally supposed.

Accordingly, the Law on State Enterprises (1991) recognized that private firms would require legal protection, and the jurisdiction of Gosarbitrazh, the State Arbitration Court, was expanded to include disputes between enterprises and their superior agencies (Article 9). Specifically, the law empowered Gosarbitrazh to invalidate the acts of the enterprises' superior agencies if they exceeded their authority or issued decisions in violation of the law. Hence, the new enterprise law attempted to protect the property rights of cooperatives by establishing legal safeguards for them against arbitrary bureaucratic interference or the discretionary behavior of local officials. The property rights and liability rules were introduced into the traditional Soviet planning system so that cooperatives could be created and allowed to grow. Indeed, managers implemented cooperative policies to reorganize their firms and increase profits. However, cooperatives were doomed to failure because their existence conflicted with the interests of central and local authorities inclined to favor the continuation of state-controlled production and because they were not protected by a court independent from executive power (Kroll, 1989: 30).

Although it was becoming evident in the 1980s that cooperatives were seen by leaders and managers as a way to improve the stagnating Soviet economy, there was also a continuation of the almost total dependence on SOEs that had characterized the Soviet period since the abandonment of the New Economic Policy in the 1920s. More often than not, this meant strong political pressure from ministries for State Arbitration Courts (Gosarbitrazh) to rule in favor of SOEs when there was a conflict of interest with cooperatives. Thus, the experiences of cooperatives operating in a primarily state-controlled economy demonstrated the essential need for a third party to enforce property rights because the interests of government agents remained too embedded in the functioning of the state economy and too prone to opportunistic behavior for them to administer private property forms fairly.

Despite the promulgation of legislation defining the role that cooperatives were to play within the Soviet Union's SOEs, an informal movement to lease enterprises in their entirety started to take hold in 1989–90 and began to supersede cooperatives as a move toward privatization. The institution of the leasing enterprise arose before either the Law on Property and the Law on Enterprises and Entrepreneurship were promulgated in 1991 and, thus, lacked the legal safeguards needed to make it a formally recognized property right.

The leasing collectives' property consisted of each partner's share of the profits. More important, de facto ownership of all or part of the leased capital (usually equipment, not the premises) was gained by the collective through amortization payments set out in the initial lease.

Leasing turned out to be an important preliminary step toward privatization, but because it was an informal step, lacking as it did any legislated specification of private property rights, it left a great deal of space for interpretation and disagreement. Moreover, it left a Soviet legacy of informal property rights that St. Petersburg's officials have had to adjust to correspond to the laws, local codes, and procedures of the new republic.

Leasing collectives were, according to the vice president of the St. Petersburg Arbitration Court, "legally amorphous" – without any juridical structure whatsoever. In the following statement she outlines some of the problems inherent in such an informal property form:

The collectives leasing state property misunderstood that as soon as they leased the equipment or factory from a ministry, they could drop out of ministerial guardianship. They did not understand that they only rented the equipment or property of some kind and did not have the legal right to actually alienate it. The government did not understand that while the lessee only rented out equipment or property, the state did not have the right to dictate how it was to be used. The law on privatization appeared later than the lease-to-own arrangements which were the first primitive steps toward privatization. Leasing was the first step toward denationalization and toward privatization because an entire enterprise could be pulled out of the state economy. If you leased an enterprise to own and paid taxes you could do whatever you wanted, but when the law on enterprises was passed and inflation began, it was unprofitable to sell formerly state run companies [to the collectives] for the money promised under the lease-to-own terms.[5]

Thus, the leasing agreements made in the Soviet era present the current St. Petersburg's city administration with a tricky commitment problem inherited from the Soviet era: Although St. Petersburg's mayor and city council may generally wish to demonstrate their commitment to property rights and honor lease agreements inherited from the Soviet period, this leaves no room for renegotiation of contracts to compensate for near hyperinflation. So, if leasing enterprises pay according to contract, but without an ex post reestimation of property values to account for inflation, then they will be receiving property nearly free of charge. The result has been a major problem for the privatization process as leases are invalidated and renegotiated by city agencies or sometimes turned over to different ownership altogether.

The fundamental Law on Enterprises and Entrepreneurship and the Law on Property were promulgated in 1991. These laws not only increased the legal base from which private firms could draw support, they also set in motion a major restructuring of the system of arbitration

[5]Batalava interview.

courts both internally and in their relationship to structures of executive power. The new laws enable the court to better protect the property rights of private enterprises (Kutlimatov, 1993).

The Law on Enterprises and Entrepreneurship described all forms of property that could legally exist in the Russian Federation, property that ranged from state enterprises to partnerships, joint-stock companies, and joint ventures. Although the law did not mention cooperatives explicitly, it implied that cooperatives were included because partners have stakes in cooperatives in the same way they would in any company formed under the heading of partnership or joint-stock company. These laws were promulgated at the beginning of 1991, but they required legislative acts (*Postanovlenie o vvedenii v destviye*) pertaining to their implementation, especially regarding the reform of the State Arbitration Court (Gosarbitrazh), before they could become operative. Yet, the law on implementation was only promulgated on December 27, 1991, nearly a year after the Law on Enterprises and Entrepreneurship and the Law on Property were passed. So there was a rush to register property formally during the nearly twelve months before the law was actually implemented by labor collectives worried that their current informal status would not pass muster in the Russian Federation.

Thus, the Law on Cooperatives, inherited from the Soviet era, became valid insofar as it did not contradict the Law on Enterprises and Entrepreneurship as put forth by the acts specifying the implementation of the latter law. The act for implementing the Law on Enterprises and Entrepreneurship directed all companies to make their registration papers correspond to the law by reregistering. Accordingly, many cooperatives reregistered into partnerships and joint-stock companies. The numbers of remaining cooperatives dwindled significantly.

As mentioned above, complications arose concerning the property rights of enterprises leased or sold before the laws were passed. A primary complication was the activity of the Mayor's Committee for the Management of State Property (KUGI). The KUGI was active in overturning many of the leases that the enterprises contracted with district agencies, budget organizations, and other enterprises. The city property fund and tax inspectorate were also active in examining the records of reregistered firms.

As cooperatives usually held leases for equipment but not real estate, the KUGI enjoyed considerable leverage in breaking leases. For example, one case currently being heard in Arbitration Court concerns the restaurant collective in the Hotel October which leased-to-own the equipment in the hotel's restaurant, but did not lease (to its legal disadvantage) the real estate upon which it was located. Thus, the KUGI has been trying to expel the collective, which now owns the equipment but not the property where it operates.

According to the Law on Enterprises and Entrepreneurship, if the leasing collective had paid for all the equipment on the premises, then the KUGI would be obligated to sign a leasing agreement with the collective for the premises itself. Yet, in the case of the restaurant and the Hotel October, the premises belongs to the hotel based on the law's Complete Economic Authority clause. So, under such ambiguous circumstances, the Arbitration Court must decide who has the legal right to the restaurant.

Although this case remains unresolved, the court regularly rules in favor of leaseholders against government agencies attempting to invalidate their leases. The court's rulings have not only protected the property rights of the individual firms involved, they have also established limits upon the jurisdictions of local agencies and in so doing have further stabilized property rights. The sections below on leasing and taxing will discuss the effect of the court's actions in more detail.

5.0 LEASING

Privatization of municipal shops, restaurants, services, offices, and nonresidential buildings began in 1991, although, for nonresidential premises and the land they occupied, only a long-term property lease was originally possible. Leaseholders could be chosen via a process of auction, tender, or noncommercial competition. It was generally the workers' collective of an enterprise, however, that took the lease and, notably, without going through the auction process. Workers' collectives usually bought their enterprises with the help of a "sponsor" who uses the labor collective as a front to avoid the auction's paperwork and higher prices.

In the first nine months of 1992, 530 enterprises were privatized. Only about 35 percent of these were sold through auction or trade competitions, because "sponsored" labor collectives were much more favorably positioned to buy the property (*Chas Pik*, 1993).

Whenever the suspicions of privatization agencies are aroused regarding the legality of ownership transfer, sales can be invalidated. Numerous disputes have been brought to arbitration courts concerning the rights of labor collectives to buy their equipment and workplaces.

A major point of contention in disputes surrounding ownership transfer is whether the labor collectives voting to buy out their workplaces were represented by quorums. Privatization agencies regularly invalidate worker buyouts whenever quorums are not present. Such buyouts are often part of the "sponsored" process that privatization authorities are trying to avoid.

Private firms, city government, and arbitration

In "The Labor Collective plus a Bag of Money Equals . . . ?" one of St. Petersburg's most prominent newspapers, *Chas Pik,* described how underground entrepreneurs and former members of the nomenklatura were buying factories under the guise of worker buyouts. In these cases, the "quorum" consisted of several members of management with the labor collective nowhere to be seen. Whereas the invalidation of such sales by privatization agencies can be an effective measure to prevent illegal ownership transfers, privatization agencies are sometimes mistaken about the presence of quorums. It is the Arbitration Court's responsibility to sort out the claims of privatization agencies and workers' collectives when this happens.

For example, the personnel of State Store No. 123 decided to form the partnership Lite in order to buy out their store. On February 24, 1992, Lite won the right to buy the store in open auction. Nevertheless, the officers of the St. Petersburg City Council's Property Fund refused to sign the final agreement to sell the store; they stated that the agreement, which gave the collective a 30 percent special discount and one year to buy the store (a privilege granted to all workers' collectives), was invalid because all of the store's personnel did not attend the meeting that voted in favor of buying out State Store 123. Lite sued the Property Fund in City Arbitration Court, and the court, acknowledging that a quorum was present at the meeting, ruled in favor of the plaintiff (*Commersant Daily,* September 3, 1993).

The general thrust of the Laws on Enterprises and Entrepreneurship and Municipal Property decentralized the ownership of most commercial and residential real estate and some land to local authorities. Nevertheless, the formation of commercial real estate markets and market prices in St. Petersburg is restricted by competing agencies and contradictory procedures. Because commercial real estate is arguably St. Petersburg's most valuable asset, uncertainty about its ownership prevents development in "the Venice of the North." Private ownership would unleash huge amounts of collateral (historic buildings) to gain investment capital. Yet, competition between the executive and legislative branches for control of real estate clouds the investment calculation for would-be lenders, raises the chances that corruption will be part of the process, and causes investors to distrust the acts of city authorities all the more (Gendler, 1993).

The use of land resources and commercial real estate is determined for potential investors by the actions of either the mayor or the city council. Potential investors using the procedure specified by the mayor's office must directly contact each of several departments in the mayor's office to receive information about their intended investment and informal guarantees of the city's cooperation. While this may seem inconvenient, it allows for considerable leeway in forming a lease agreement and, in fact, does not preclude the free use of the real estate intended for development.

If, on the other hand, investors follow the procedure specified by the city council, they must file a claim with the Investment-Tender Commission (ITC). The ITC consists of representatives from the city council and its property fund and various committees from the mayor's office. Ultimately, claims filed with the ITC lead to competitions such as auctions where the claimants bid for the chance to develop a piece of real estate.

In addition to the procedural "clash" between the mayor's office and the city council in St. Petersburg, legislation regarding leasing rules is not very specific, and methods of property valuation are not based on market criteria.[6] Subleasing, for example, has only recently been legalized. Nevertheless, local authorities continue to operate under the assumption that if they give leases to municipal property, the leaseholder cannot sell any of the rights set out in the lease. An even greater problem surrounds the recalculation of rental rates to account for inflation. Property continues to be evaluated in St. Petersburg according to procedures used in the days of central planning. The initial cost and year of construction bear more weight than anything else in determining the "value" of a piece of property. Moreover, the City of St. Petersburg has yet to develop a system for the collection of real estate and land information. The Mayor's Committee for Economic Development is currently developing systems of surveying procedures in cooperation with Swedish and Canadian cadastral agencies (Limonov, 1993).

Although leasing is the favored way for private firms to gain access to factory, retail, and office space in St. Petersburg, there remains a great deal of confusion regarding formal title to commercial real estate. The uncertainty of lease agreements is a key source of concern for entrepreneurs. Precisely because title to the property they lease is questionable, the risk of investing in renovation and other improvements to their properties is too high to be undertaken. Property rights are yet to be embodied in a city register that maps the extent, value, and ownership of real estate. This prevents leaseholders from being confident that their leases will be protected from confiscation by city authorities seeking to formalize property or who are abusing their powers by fraudulently extracting additional rents.

The absence of developed real estate markets makes the valuation of property difficult. Consequently, informal leasing is the most popular way for local agencies to dispense commercial real estate because it passes the

---

6 The Russian parliament initiated the reform of the real estate market with a number of important legislative acts. These acts include the Law on Ownership (January 1991), the Land Code (April 1991), the Land Reform Law (June 1991), and the Law on Payments for Land (October 1991).

measurement costs on to the leaseholder. When property values change to the renter's advantage, usually because of inflation, city agencies can adjust the terms of the lease without fear of judicial repercussion. Thus, informally arranged leases make leaseholders even more vulnerable to confiscation whenever changes in the values of their property become evident to city agencies. They do not provide real security for tenants.

Commercial real estate is generally rented for terms of fifteen years or more from state enterprises, government bodies, or public institutions. When space is obtained from a state enterprise, it is usually leased to individuals who worked in the enterprise before it was registered as a private firm.

A general lack of standardized business procedures for leasing property, changing laws, and an unstable federal constitution cause entrepreneurs to rely heavily on personal connections and bribes to accomplish business objectives. Even when entrepreneurs think that they have a formal lease, city agencies can point to minor violations in the lease contract that invalidate the lease altogether.

Whereas "informal" means can do much to facilitate acquisition of leases, the consequent dearth of "formally" documented leasing agreements that comply with the regulations of St. Petersburg's KUGI leaves many entrepreneurs anxious about the security of their leases and unwilling to invest in their buildings or expand their businesses in other ways.[7]

In June 1993 the KUGI carried out an inspection of leases concluded in Oktyaberskii raion. The inspection illustrates the generally informal nature of leasing agreements in St. Petersburg and the consequent insecure property rights they embody.

The commission inspected 1,411 leasing agreements comprising 91 percent of those presented for inspection. The result of their analysis showed that practically all of the contracts were concluded with violations. These violations consisted largely of improper formation of the leasing contracts, unapproved reregistrations of contracts, and improper calculation of rents. In many cases district commissions assigned to formulate lease agreements leased properties restricted to certain uses. The leaseholders, however, were not informed by the district agencies that they had restricted leases. Moreover, several serious violations were revealed in the compiling of protocols that were registered without the necessary data on the lessor, the type and term of lease, and the size of the premises. In 1,189 cases (76.5 percent) there was no reference to the mayor's directives prohibiting the arbitrary specification of leasing terms.

[7]In the survey of firms conducted by the mayor's Committee for Economic Development, most firms voiced concerns that their lease agreements would be renegotiated or overturned altogether in favor of higher paying tenants.

Some leasing agreements were prolonged without any legal basis (157, or 10 percent). In forty leasing agreements (2.5 percent) the size of the premises did not correspond with that specified in the leasing agreement. Many agreements simply lacked sufficient documentation (465, or 28 percent).

In the course of inspection, the commission discovered a host of hidden subleases, use of premises without a formal leasing contract, or unilateral changes in the designated use of the property. In 93 percent of the inspected leasing agreements the calculation of rent did not correspond with the method of calculation approved by the city council. Random inspection of twenty-three leasing agreements showed that the loss of rental payment incurred by incorrect calculation methods was 1,180,000 rubles (*Ekho*, August 8, 1993: 6).

Contracts with organizations such as schools, hospitals, and institutes that are funded by the Russian Federation budget were almost always incomplete and were especially prone to high levels of informal contracting. The clash between two mayoral committees, the KUGI and the Health Committee, over the ownership rights to Mental Hospital Five provides a comical illustration of how uncertain property rights limits or, as in this case, prevents innovation of corporate forms and investments in growth.

The dispute centers around the ownership of one of the hospital's wards and dates back to December 1991, when a commercial company, Sigma-Valtex Corporation, was invited by the hospital's director to reconstruct old wards, build new ones, and provide the hospital with equipment. As a part of the agreement the hospital would also receive U.S.$10,000 from Sigma-Valtex, and, ostensibly, a 30 percent share in Medus, a company that would be established by Sigma-Valtex in partnership with the hospital. In return, Sigma-Valtex would get an unused hospital building that had lain empty for a year.

Twenty-two months later the hospital's officers, after reading the contract's fine print, realized that it would actually receive only a 12 percent share in the new company, so they retracted the offer to Sigma-Valtex and posted guards around the originally promised building to prevent its seizure by the KUGI, which gave the building to Sigma-Valtex, claiming that the hospital, which did not own the building in the first place, never had the right to give it away. Only the KUGI has the right to make such promises.

The hospital sent a letter to the city council's property committee in May 1992, saying that it intended to use the building for its own purposes. It started reconstruction work even though the partnership with Sigma-Valtex had already been registered, and the building's ownership was thus officially transferred to Medus.

Medus, not deterred by the guards it met when trying to occupy the building, convinced the property committee to issue an order saying it could take possession of the building. St. Petersburg's mayor, Anatoly Sobchak, supporting his property committee's decision, ordered the head of the city health committee to give the structure over to Medus. At the same time, the City Soviet, often a source of laws contradictory to the mayor's decrees, issued an order saying that the building should remain in the hospital's control. To make the fight over ownership more complex and ironic, even while the argument proceeds the mayor's health committee continues to invest in the hospital building's renovation (15.4 million rubles of state money), in contradiction to their orders from the mayor and despite the likelihood that Medus will eventually take possession, (Borisova, 1993).

As another example, consider the case of Farm. In July 1991 the personnel of four cafeterias in Kirovskii raion created the joint-stock company Farm to lease the premises where they worked from Kirovskii raion's Public Catering Association. The St. Petersburg KUGI filed a complaint in response to the formation of Farm arguing that the lease was not valid because, according to a directive of the Presidium of the Leningrad City Soviet from August 4, 1990, only the Main Department of Property (GUI) of the Leningrad Executive Committee (the KUGI's predecessor) had the right to rent out the premises in question. The St. Petersburg City Arbitration Court ruled in favor of Farm; it stated that the 1990 legislation did not specify the exclusive power of the GUI to rent out the properties (*Commersant Daily,* September 3, 1993).

As a measure to further restrict local agencies from overturning lease agreements, the Russian Federation's Higher Arbitration Court ruled on September 3, 1993, that the KUGI has no right to claim that lease agreements are invalid if the KUGI itself did not participate in concluding the lease under question. This ruling was important because it prevented the KUGI from declaring invalid any leases concluded before the KUGI was formed in 1992. Moreover, it was an important example of the independence from executive power that the Arbitration Court is establishing in general because, without the special instructions from Higher Arbitration Court, the St. Petersburg Arbitration Court would have had to rule in favor of the KUGI and in correspondence with the following Presidential orders: "On the Regulation of Leases" and "The Basis of Leasing Legislation in the Russian Federation."

For example, the KUGI tried to establish in St. Petersburg's Arbitration Court that the lease concluded in June 1990 between "Soyuzpechat" and the Kuibeshevskii raion administration to rent a newspaper kiosk on Litenii Prospect for five years was invalid because it was not being used as designated in the leasing agreement. Until September 3, 1993, the KUGI's complaint against Soyuzpechat would have been upheld in Arbitration Court because it corresponded with the president's orders, but thanks to

171

the Higher Arbitration Court's memorandum and its precedent over executive orders, St. Petersburg Arbitration Court was able to rule that the KUGI had no right to file a claim against the defendant.

6.0 TAXATION

An important element in building a reputation that enhances local government's credibility to protect property rights is its capacity to collect taxes fairly and efficiently. Yet a major problem of the reform period has been the inability of the leadership to legalize new forms of property rights and trade while at the same time preventing opportunistic behavior of local agents empowered to tax and administer private firms (Litwack, 1991).

A tax system consistent with credible property rights has at least two characteristics. First, it has the capability to detect tax evaders. Second, it restrains its agents from arbitrarily confiscating the wealth of firms that honestly declare their profits. These circumstances enable firms and executive agencies to signal commitment to one another about property rights. Based on each other's signals of commitment, producers and executive agencies incrementally build credibility for property rights.

Signaling credible commitment in St. Petersburg is complicated by several factors that contribute to an extremely inconsistent interaction between private firms and tax authorities. First, firms must pay a great number of specific taxes. Second, the tax inspectorate has a low capacity to monitor firms. Together these factors foster rampant tax evasion, arbitrary confiscations of profits, and distrust between tax payers and tax collectors.

Local government in St. Petersburg retains its Soviet-style complexity. There are twenty-five different registration organs in St. Petersburg administered by the various district administrations, the office of the mayor, and the Committee for International Trade. Information about registration and taxation from these various points may or may not be collected in one place. The loopholes created by administrative overlaps weaken the long-term security of property rights because conflicting rules and procedures prevent a central registration of ownership subject to formal rules and privy to legal protections.

For example, although all registration information must be given to the City Tax Inspectorate, businessmen may avoid scrutiny by registering their enterprises in a residential area, despite having their offices downtown. According to Andre Krasnovskii, an officer of St. Petersburg's Economic Security Service (a department of the KGB), it is possible to avoid tax inspection altogether by registering and working in different districts or by opening an account in the bank without the requisite stamp from the City Tax Inspectorate.

172

Private firms, city government, and arbitration

Monitoring firms is further complicated by an absence of rules regarding the naming of the firms themselves. Different firms may use the exact same name for their respective businesses in St. Petersburg. There are numerous cases in which as many as ten firms have the same name (Rutman, 1993). Not having formal property rights in the name of the firms itself hinders honest firms wishing to build reputations for lawful business practices. Unfortunately, it also enables Russia's many dishonest firms to swindle the gullible of everything from their apartments to their vouchers.

Keeping up-to-date on Russia's tax code is practically impossible, not only because there are so many different taxes that are frequently revised, but also because the revisions are sometimes done secretly so that they appear without warning.

Although the basic VAT rate was reduced from 28 to 20 percent on January 1, 1993, and the exchange rate used for mandatory foreign exchange surrender was improved, the failure to change tax rates for progressive taxes in response to Russia's near hyperinflation has meant that taxes have actually increased in real terms.

While there are about twenty-five different taxes, any one firm may be liable for only half this number. Tax collectors tend to favor some firms over others in response to their own personal preferences, susceptibility to bribes, and fear of violent repercussions from criminal elements in the ranks of St. Petersburg's entrepreneurs. For example, Alexander Tambovtsev, a tax inspector for the Central Office of the St. Petersburg Tax Inspectorate, heads a special group that collects taxes from the city kiosks. He and his small team of colleagues, all protected by armed guards, collect more taxes than all of the district tax collectors combined. He attributes the difference in success rate to the fear that most district tax collectors (usually women) harbor from mafia threats. They are simply afraid to inspect most of St. Petersburg's mushrooming number of kiosks, a sector of the economy renowned for its ties to mafia groups.

Tax policies are poorly implemented and are not uniformly applied. While Tambovtev's team can assume some of the tax collection burden of district-level inspectors, they remain understaffed and must resort to crude inspection strategies because information about private firms either does not exist or is not locatable in a centrally organized source. While traveling with Tambovtsev's team on its inspections, I observed the method used to inspect firms, the time it took to do an inspection, and the opportunities available to inspectors to accept bribes. Inspections were carried out by one tax inspector and one armed guard initially under the guise of customers. They carry out a simple transaction to see if the kiosk's cashier records the transaction on a cash machine and gives a receipt. If the cashier does not fulfill these requirements, the inspectors reveal their identities and levy fines for the infractions. I was required to remain in the team's vans while pairs of inspectors and guards approached private kiosks and shops. Thus, it is not possible to report the nature of conversations concerning violations. Nevertheless, although the inspection procedure was simple, the inspections I observed in two days of traveling with Tambovstev's team each took over an hour. Such a time period was more than sufficient for the inspectors' official duties, but it may have been needed for gifts (coffee, cigarettes, alcohol) to be given or serious bribe taking to occur.

In addition to major taxes like the VAT, firms may pay the following taxes: a land tax (1.5 percent of land value), a real estate tax (2.5 percent of building value), a local police tax (1 percent of wages), an advertising tax (5 percent of advertising costs), an inventory tax (1 percent of the value of the inventory), a public transport tax (the minimum monthly wage times the number of employees), a road tax (0.4 percent of sales), and a car-ownership tax (1.5 percent of the car's value) (*Ekonomika i Zhizn*, 1992, 1993; *Nalogi i Biznes*, 1992, 1993).

St. Petersburg's arbitration court has heard numerous cases involving private firms against the city's tax inspectorate. These firms were ordered to pay taxes by the tax inspectorate because they reregistered into new property forms to comply with Russian Federation laws. According to the tax inspectorate, these firms had no right to the tax privileges granted to them as cooperatives once they had reregistered into new property forms.

For example, the cooperative Iskra registered in Kirovskii raion on October 19, 1988, and began business on December 1, 1989. As a construction cooperative, Iskra was granted special privileges from the president of the Supreme Soviet whose ruling on August 2, 1989, released all construction cooperatives from paying taxes from July 1, 1989, to October 1, 1991.

Iskra was one of the many cooperatives that, in 1991–92, reregistered into various new property forms such as partnerships and joint stock companies because, as cooperatives, they were not explicitly recognized as legal entities in Russian Federation law. Although Iskra had been given a special tax break as a cooperative, when it reregistered as the joint-stock company Pet-sin in October 1991, the tax inspectorate in Kirovskii raion, saying the privileges no longer applied because Pet-sin was no longer a cooperative, tried to confiscate all profits kept under the special tax privileges for cooperatives.

The tax inspectorate filed suit in the city Arbitration Court against Pet-sin on November 24, 1992, for 1,027,633 rubles in back taxes for the district's budget. The St. Petersburg Arbitration Court ruled on December 21, 1992, that the tax authorities did not have the right to confiscate these profits.[8]

7.0 CONCLUSION

Private property rights cannot be effective if government agents arbitrarily interfere in market transactions. If some exchanges are allowed, but others are arbitrarily curtailed as government agents collect taxes, form contracts, and oversee the privatization of state enterprises, then information is transmitted that undermines the government's commitment to protect property rights and causes firms to rely on informal transactions to accomplish business objectives.

Municipal agencies, deliberately and haphazardly, regulate leases and taxes. The power to choose winners and losers damages credibility when city agencies act to invalidate leases to make room for more favored patrons. This signals that the state is not constrained from confiscating property and that conditions such as inflation or rent-seeking encourage it to seek more favorable lease agreements or sales.

The local agencies that regulate property and taxes, the KUGI and the tax inspectorate, ostensibly favor formalization of property laws and tax procedures but implement policy inefficiently and, often, illegally. Their regulation inflicts losses on private entrepreneurs as they create, register, and operate their businesses. This affects the city government's credible commitment even when the regulations have very popular consequences. For even when the intent and implementation of government regulation aims to make privatization equitable or to prevent criminals from controlling enterprises, it can create losers out of firms that markets would otherwise have rewarded.

Increased paperwork and more bureaucratic red tape are costly, but controllable, transactions only for firms that profit beyond the new margin that the regulations create. Moreover, the increased opportunity for corruption among city agencies that new regulations impose on entrepreneurs can only create winners out of those who were supposed to lose, because they can afford (by definition of being a successful organized criminal) to pay the necessary bribes and fees. Honest businesses, actual or would-be, have the additional tax or registration burdens (and bribes, the price set by the market of rich organized criminal competitors) to pay.

The intended and unintended effects of government regulations and their uneven implementation create losers out of the winners that markets were

[8]Records of the St. Petersburg City Arbitration Court, Delo #858, November 24, 1992.

175

meant to create. Arbitration gives such losers a second chance. When the court rewards losers for suing city agencies, formal institutions begin to signal that the state is credibly committed to private property rights because it shows exactly both the nature of those property rights and that local government is constrained from confiscating them. When property is clearly defined, it is harder for the state to confiscate it. When property is hard to take, it is more likely to be used productively.

Local government's credible commitment to free market exchange and secure property rights requires institutions that restrain its capacity to confiscate wealth and, thus, reduce the economic uncertainty that all prospective and actual private firms face when choosing between continued reliance on informal transactions or risking formal transactions in the hope that they will bring increased profits to the firm.

This chapter demonstrates the independence of the Arbitration Court of St. Petersburg, Russia, by showing how the court restrained government agencies from confiscating the property rights of private firms. Agencies of city government in St. Petersburg, such as the KUGI, Property Fund, and Tax Inspectorate, have all demonstrated inclinations to confiscate property rights (often in response to high inflation) that would not have been restrained if the City Arbitration Court had not undergone restructuring to become a body independent of the executive.

Credible commitments to property rights rarely emerge when the structure of local governance overlaps and conflicts. Ambiguous jurisdictions allow city agencies to confiscate property rights from firms by invalidating their leases, changing tax laws abruptly, or reneging on other agreements. However, when St. Petersburg's Arbitration Court is involved, the commitments of city officials to property rights are made more credible. Private firms learn that they have legal protections when their rights are challenged. Moreover, ambiguities of ownership diminish because the jurisdictions of local agencies dispensing property rights are defined by the court's rulings.

Unlike its predecessor, Gosarbitrazh (State Arbitration Court), St. Petersburg's recently reformed Arbitration Court now enforces tax laws and the city's contracts with private businesses without being directly constrained by the interests of state-owned firms or city agencies. This gives future contracts more credibility for private firms because they know there is a higher probability that they can successfully sue state-owned firms and city agencies. The court prevents a situation in which SOEs and city agencies have a consistent advantage. Furthermore, the Arbitration Court's participation codifies rules and procedures embodying property rights. Thus, the instruments of exchange become more universally attainable, standardized, and centrally registered. This lends further credibility to property rights (de Soto, 1993; Barzel, 1989).

Private firms, city government, and arbitration

A credible commitment to private property rights and attendant development of multilateral impersonal trade will not obtain if economic legality is not also present. Soviet attempts to implement market incentive mechanisms failed precisely because there was no economic legality. So too will current Russian reforms if Arbitration Courts do not continue their activities, which help define property rights and lend credibility to government promises to respect rights.

REFERENCES

Barzel, Yoram, *Economic Analyses of Property Rights* (Cambridge: Cambridge University Press, 1989).

Ben-Porath, Yoram, "The F-Connection: Families, Friends and Firms and the Organization of Exchange," *Population and Development Review* 6: 1 (1980), 1–30.

Birman, Igor, "From the Achieved Level," *Soviet Studies* 30: 2 (1978), 153–78.

Borisova, Yevgenya, "Mental Hospital in Bitter Struggle," *St. Petersburg Press*, September 14–20 (1993), 1–3.

Chas Pik, "kollektiv + 'Denezshni Meshok'=?" 28: 177 (1993), 6.

Demsetz, Harold, "Toward a Theory of Property Rights," *American Economic Review* 57: 2 (1967), 347–59.

de Soto, Hernando, "The Missing Ingredient," *The Economist*, September 11 (1993), 8–12.

Eggertsson, Thrainn, *Economic Behavior and Institutions* (Cambridge: Cambridge University Press, 1990).

Ekho, August 8 (1993), 6.

Ekonomika i Zhizn 15 (1992), 4.
2 (1993), 13.

Ericson, Richard, "The 'Second Economy' and Resource Allocation under Central Planning," *Journal of Comparative Economics* 8: 1, (1984), 1–24.

FBIS-SOV, *Central Eurasian Daily Report*, February 19 (1993), 13.

Gendler, Leonid, "Interaction Between Investors and City Authorities," *Saint Petersburg Report* 1: 1 (1993), 25–7.

Grossman, Gregory, "The Second Economy in the USSR," *Problems of Communism* 26: 5 (1977), 25–40.

"Notes on the Illegal Private Economy and Corruption," in *Soviet Economy in a Time of Change*, Vol. 1, Joint Economic Committee, U.S. Congress (Washington, DC: U.S. Government Printing Office, 1979).

Johnson, Simon, and Heidi Kroll, "Managerial Strategies for Spontaneous Privatization," *Soviet Economy* 7: 4 (1991), 281–316.

Jones, Anthony, and William Moscoff, *Koops: The Rebirth of Entrepreneurship in the Soviet Union* (Bloomington, IN: Indiana University Press, 1991).

Konstantinov, Andrei, "Komu Podchinitsya 'Tretya Vlast' Peterburga?" *Smena*, November 2 (1992), 2.

Kroll, Heidi, "Property Rights and the Soviet Enterprise: Evidence from the Law of Contract," *Journal of Comparative Economics* 13: 1 (1989), 115–33.

Kutlimatov, Vladimir, "Arbitrazhnii Sud Idyet," *Vechernii Peterburg*, September 3 (1993), 1.

Limonov, Leonid, "Organizatsiya Rinka i Nedvizshomosti: Registratsiona Sis-

177

tema Otsenka Nedvishomisti, Printsipi Zemelnoi Politiki," working paper, International Centre for Social and Economic Research (1993).

Litwack, John M., "Legality and Market Reform in Soviet-Type Economies," *Journal of Economic Perspectives* 5: 4 (1991), 77–89.

Moore, John H., "Agency Costs, Technological Change, and Soviet Central Planning," *Journal of Law and Economics* 23: 3 (1981), 189–214.

Nalogi i Biznes, Buliten Gosudarstvenii Nalogovoi Inspektsii po Sankt Peterburg, November 1992, April 1993, Nos. 11, 16.

North, Douglass C., and Barry Weingast, "Constitutions and Commitment: The Evolution of Institutions Governing Public Choice in 17th Century England," *Journal of Economic History* 59: 4 (1989), 803–33.

Olson, Mancur, "The Hidden Path to a Successful Economy," in Christopher Clague and Gordon C. Rausser, editors, *The Emergence of Market Economies in Eastern Europe* (Cambridge, MA: Basil Blackwell, 1992), 55–75.

"Problem? Market Relations Between an Executive Committee and Cooperatives," *Moscow News,* March 25 (1989a), 13.

"Profile with Sausage in the Background," *Moscow News,* February 5 (1989b), 6.

Root, Hilton, "Tying the King's Hands: Credible Commitments and Royal Fiscal Policy During the Old Regime," *Rationality and Society* 1: 2 (1989), 240–58.

Rutman, Mikhail, "'Roga i Kopita' Nalogov Ne Platyat," *Vechernii Peterburg,* June 7 (1993), 1.

Schelling, Thomas, *The Strategy of Conflict* (Cambridge, MA: Harvard University Press, 1960).

Shlapentokh, Vladimir, *Public and Private Life of the Soviet People* (Oxford: Oxford University Press, 1989).

"Vse Dlia Kooperativa," *Izvestia,* March 20 (1988).

Whole St. Petersburg Business Directory, The (St. Petersburg, 1993).

Comment on "Private Firms, City Government, and Arbitration"

ANTHONY JONES

Future historians are likely to see the last decade of the twentieth century as a global turning point, not only because of the reconfiguration of international power relations but also because of the collapse of state-owned economies. For those of us still living in this period, it is difficult to grasp the complexity of the process at work, and we are still trying to identify the variables that are likely to be decisive in determining the outcome. It is already clear that there is no single path to an economy based on private ownership, nor is there any guarantee that a particular society will succeed in making the transition. It also seems clear at the moment that there will be a variety of forms that future economies will take, with different mixtures of state and private ownership, and with different rules for the use of property. The main reason for this belief is the importance of the historical context within which the changes are occurring, for the societies are embarking on the privatization of property from very different starting points.

Arguably the most uncertain of the current changeovers is taking place in Russia, a society that had no well-developed system of private ownership in the past on which to build, and in which the culture of communism was organically closer to the earlier society than was the case for most of the former socialist nations. Russians, for instance, have found it more difficult to privatize land than has been the case in Eastern Europe, and the first years of private enterprise have been very hard.

Joel Ericson's account of how the arbitration court in St. Petersburg has functioned to help institutionalize property rights shows how difficult the whole process has been. What makes this case study of special interest is the fact that St. Petersburg has one of the most pro–private property and enterprise climates in Russia. By the end of 1994, 72 percent of the city's economy was located in the private sector (as compared to about 2 percent in 1990), and 70 percent of the city's enterprises had been privatized.

Yet protections for private property were difficult to achieve, and even now they are not fully in place.

While I am in agreement with the general analysis provided by Ericson, there are a few points on which an alternative perspective may be needed. For example, he clearly shows the importance of the arbitration court in establishing property rights, but it is too early to know if the court is truly an independent body. True, the court no longer routinely supports the state against plaintiffs, but the statistics show that it is now almost impossible for a plaintiff to lose in St. Petersburg. If the court can swing so quickly to one side, it can just as easily swing back. The issue is not just who wins, but whether or not legal, universalistic principles are being applied. As in so many other areas, it would appear likely that political concerns are at work rather than an adherence to the law.

Yet this raises the question of whether or not the law is the answer to the current uncertainty over property rights. Ericson follows an approach that is commonplace in the West, namely, to view legal protection as paramount. But in the context of the transition from communism, this may not be either as possible or as necessary as it seems from the Western view. In the Russian context, informal ties may be the only way in which people are able to function as if they were secure in their property rights, since the environment is so unstable. In short, in the transition period the informal ties are functional. We saw this in the early days of privatization, when deals were made that had no basis in law, but without which changes in economic behavior would not have been possible. It is true that foreign companies will not be eager to operate in a country that cannot guarantee the sanctity of property, but this has not so far been of sufficient concern to Russian officials to cause them to enforce the necessary laws.

Even in the presence of legal guarantees, however, Russia's problems will not be easy to solve. Moreover, laws are only important to the extent to which the environment can protect the laws themselves. The solution to property rights in Russia cannot be only legal, but must be political and cultural as well. The continuing political instability at the nation's center, unresolved conflicts between the center and local areas, the struggle for property going on among the old elite, and conflict between the old and new elite, all make it unlikely that legal safeguards will be respected, at least for the foreseeable future. In addition, there is very little cultural support for private property rights. Throughout Russian and Soviet history, there has been a distrust of property rights, as well as antipathy toward those who had more than others. There is some evidence that this is changing, but it will be a very slow process. This means, among other things, that politicians will gain no particular advantage among the general electorate by running on a platform of support for property rights. Also, local officials can expect no praise from their population for vigorously defending property, save, of course, from those who have property in immediate need of protection.

Likewise, the arbitrary behavior of tax officials and others is also likely to continue, thus perpetuating the instability of the environment. This will be less from a desire to restrict property (although this is certainly the case sometimes), than from the need to raise revenue in a time of economic confusion and crisis.

In sum, as long as the situation remains unstable in Russia, property rights will remain tenuous, regardless of how much progress is made in the legal sphere. Only stability, appropriate laws, and respect for the law, will guarantee property the status it enjoys in long-established democracies. In the meantime, it is likely that there will be more and more informal arrangements to provide a kind of ersatz protection. This may not fit Western models, and it may not fully suit the needs of foreign businesses, but it may be the only way in the short run that Russia can move toward an effective system of property rights.

7

Property rights and institutional change in the Czech and Slovak republics

MARIUSZ MARK DOBEK

1.0 DYNAMICS OF INSTITUTIONAL CHANGE

In this chapter I consider privatization in the Czech Republic and Slovakia as cases of institutional change. Although I present details of privatization in the two republics, I do not emphasize the idiosyncrasies of the transformation of property rights in the two countries. Instead, the emphasis is on making generalizations about the issues of both privatization and the dynamics of institutional change. The term *property rights* is understood here as an *institution*, that is, a set of stable and widely shared expectations about how economic, political, and social actors will constrain their behavior in some specified circumstances with regard to property.[1] Therefore, by analyzing the process of privatization – the transfer of property rights from the state to private actors – I am able to draw conclusions not merely about the dynamics of this particular process but also about institutional change in general.

A number of theories of institutional change have been presented, including those in the literature on social choice. For example, some authors have argued that institutional change is a process driven by resource asymmetries and the desire for distributional gains.[2] I adopt this line of reasoning here, as it is compatible not only with my view of politics but also with a well-established school of thought in political science that points to material incentives as the driving force of politics. When advancing such an argument in the context of a competitive political system, however, I qualify it by recognizing that democracy by its nature requires accommodation and compromise. It is rarely possible for one actor to secure durable gains without accommodating interests of other major actors. This argument in regard to privatization was borne out by my

[1] I would like to acknowledge the influence of ideas presented by Daniel Diermeier, Joel Ericson, Timothy Frye, and Steve Lewis in Chapter 2 on my conceptualization of property rights as an institution.
[2] See, for example, Knight (1992) and North (1993).

earlier analysis of privatization in Great Britain (Dobek, 1993). Therefore, I assume that in a democratic system of government any institution (in this case, property rights) has to be *credible* to major economic, political, and social actors in order to perform its role of constraining behavior. Credibility here means the existence of shared expectations about stability of future actions among strategic actors.

With regard to property rights, I further assume that credibility of this institution cannot be established by an act of commitment by any single actor, including the government. Instead, it is a product of strategic interactions of major interest groups, who have to share expectations about constraints regarding behavior toward property rights by committing themselves to the observance of those constraints. The commitment is strong and durable if major political actors benefit materially from a particular equilibrium of property rights.

This reasoning allows me to hypothesize about the dynamics of property rights as institutional change. Movement from one equilibrium of property rights to another equilibrium is guided not merely by the drive to maximize distributional gains but also by the need to secure stability of those gains (their credibility). The latter is accomplished, in a competitive political system, through a gradual bargaining process that ultimately leads to accommodation and recognition of mutual gains by major actors. The movement to a new equilibrium is initiated when credibility of the old constraints collapses because a sufficient number of important actors either withdraw their commitment or die off. The new equilibrium is not reached until major actors (as determined by assets such as organizational strength, size, expertise, and information) are accommodated in the new distribution and subsequently committed to a new set of constraints. The greater the number of major actors who derive distributional gains from a particular privatization plan, the greater is the expected stability of the property rights.

Although the focus of this study is on the dynamics of property rights in two post-communist countries, the Czech Republic and Slovakia, it has to be understood that property rights are one of the many institutions undergoing changes in the former communist countries. Therefore, the credibility of the emerging system of property rights is closely related to the credibility of other economic and political institutions. As democracy, market exchange, and private property reinforce one another, their respective credibilities are also bound to interact.

2.0 PREPARATION FOR PRIVATIZATION IN CZECHOSLOVAKIA

At the beginning of 1990, when the communist government collapsed in Czechoslovakia, about 86 percent of their economy was state-owned, some 10 percent was under collective ownership, and only 4 percent was privately owned. Thus, at the outset of the process of privatization there was a virtual absence of private ownership of the means of production in both republics. In preparation for privatization, a series of laws was passed in each republic (the Czech and Slovak republics remained federated until January 1993) that abolished the state's legal monopoly on economic activity in April 1990. Among other things, private business entities and operations were legalized with no restrictions on size or profits, and the state's monopoly of foreign trade was removed.[3] Foreign investment up to 100 percent of the company's holdings was permitted, even though foreigners could not buy real estate for private use.

On January 1, 1991, prices were liberalized, and the Czechoslovak currency, the koruna (Kcs), became internally convertible. In the "Scenario for Economic Reform" adopted in September 1990, the major directions of economic reforms in Czechoslovakia were identified. Some of the industries, such as heavy industry and steel production, which were overdeveloped and lacked markets for their products, were to be reduced in size. Economically inefficient, technologically outdated, and environmentally unacceptable enterprises were to be forced either to reform or to liquidate. A shift from production to services was envisioned as creating new jobs for the newly unemployed.

The reform program, although economically desirable, has presented a difficult political task. Only a minority of state enterprises were profitable and equipped with relatively modern technology and used efficient management methods. This necessitated significant reductions in the size, if not complete closures, of a large number of state-owned enterprises (SOEs). Relocation of the labor force and significant unemployment were to be expected. Some of the early estimates envisioned standard-of-living rates declining by 10 to 20 percent and unemployment rising from 2 to 6 percent (Martin, 1991: 9). Those estimates were overoptimistic, however, because as early as September 1992 the unemployment rate in the Czech Republic reached 2.65 percent and in the Slovak Republic 10.6 percent. The estimates for 1994 predicted even higher unemployment rates of 5.7 percent for the Czech Republic and 18 percent for Slovakia.[4]

One would be justified in expecting that the governments of both republics would face increasing difficulties in carrying out pro-market reforms, because they were predicted to have a negative impact in their initial stage (e.g., growing unemployment) on the already deteriorating economic situation. In this context, providing material benefits for major

[3]Still, state monopoly was preserved for economic activity involving "strategic interests" or national defense (Martin, 1991).

[4]See *Hospodarskie noviny,* September 15, 1992, and *The Economist Intelligence Unit Country Report: Czech Republic and Slovakia* (1993: 10, 32).

political actors in post-communist societies becomes a crucial factor in the attempt to create stable private property rights.

3.0 WEAK ORGANIZATIONS AND PRIVATIZATION

The period immediately following the establishment of a non-communist government in Czechoslovakia in early 1990 was characterized by a relative absence of strong political parties, trade unions, and other organizations characteristic of a democratic civic society.

Initially, there were the two broad anti-communist movements, the Civic Forum in the Czech lands and the Public against Violence in Slovakia. The two groups cooperated briefly by forming a winning coalition in the first post-communist parliamentary election of June 1990. Not only did this collaboration not last long, but the two groups shortly thereafter disintegrated, torn by internal divisions. The Civic Forum split along ideological and public policy lines in the spring of 1991 into the conservative Civic Democratic Party, led by Vaclav Klaus, then finance minister in the federal government, and the Civic Movement, more centrist in its orientation with social-democratic leanings and led by Foreign Minister Jiri Dienstbier. The Public against Violence divided, in March 1991, over the issue of federation into the Movement for a Democratic Slovakia, headed by Vladimir Meciar and dominated by Slovak nationalists and separatists, and the Christian Democratic Movement, which favored federation with the Czechs.

Forty parties, out of close to one hundred that were registered, campaigned in the second post-communist elections to the federal and republic parliaments in June 1992. Of those, twelve won seats in the Federal Assembly, eight parties were represented in the Czech parliament, and five entered the Slovak parliament (see the appendix to this chapter).[5]

A striking feature of the June 1992 elections was the defeat of many prominent dissidents who played key roles in the "velvet revolution" of 1989.[6] This development may be ascribed to their inexperience in electoral politics. After all, the elections of June 1990 were largely a one-sided referendum against the totalitarian system in which the heroes of the anti-communist opposition did not even have to define their policy agendas. This first idyllic affair with democracy did not prepare them to run in the 1992 elections. In addition to being more competitive, the

[5]A total of 85 percent of the eligible voters in the Czech Republic and 84.2 percent in the Slovak Republic participated in the elections.

[6]Some of those were Marian Calfa, former federal prime minister, Jiri Dienstbier, former federal foreign minister, Petr Miller, former minister of social affairs, Lubos Dobrovsky, former minister of defense, and many others. The most prominent among the defeated post-communist political elite was President Vaclav Havel, whose chances for reelection were eliminated by the results of the parliamentary elections.

second free elections were conducted in the much more somber atmosphere of June 1992. Post-revolutionary euphoria vanished as the country faced not only a bleak economic situation but also a possible territorial breakup. The popular perception developed that the old idols, after their departure to the country's capital, Prague, had become totally engulfed in endless grandiose debates about future structural arrangements for the country and had lost contact with the day-to-day concerns of their local constituencies to whom, after all, they owed their positions.

By the time of the June 1992 elections, the party system was almost totally divided into two separate Czech and Slovak parts, reflecting the different attitudes and concerns of elites and constituencies in both republics. Only six out of the forty parties participating in the elections had country-wide networks and ran campaigns in both republics. Yet, because these parties were primarily Czech-based, they failed to elect a single candidate in Slovakia.

The vast majority of all parties in both republics supported the general principles of a market economy, a competitive political system, and civil liberties. Their differences were most pronounced in their recommended solutions to the pressing economic problems and the recommended pace of pro-market reforms. Hence, the traditional labels of "Right" and "Left" came to be defined mostly in economic terms: "Right" indicating support for a speedy transition to a market economy with minimum state intervention and "Left" denoting a position favoring gradual transition with continuing significant involvement by the state in the economy and an extensive welfare system. The parties of the political Right looked to countries like the United States under the Republican Party or Great Britain under the Conservative Party as their models; those on the Left were more inclined to look toward countries with strong social-democratic traditions, like Sweden or Germany.

In the Czech Republic, Vaclav Klaus and his Civic Democratic Party, the winner of the 1992 elections (see the appendix to this chapter), became the leading supporters of radical reforms. Klaus, as the Federal Minister of Finance, was among the key architects of the federal privatization program. He has consistently insisted on an extensive and rapid transformation of the property structure despite criticism from leftist parties and trade unions that stressed the social and economic problems stemming from such a policy.

In Slovakia, as indicated by public opinion polls, more voters than in the Czech Republic were willing to support leftist parties that advocated gradual economic reforms, including privatization (Wolchik, 1991: 123). After the June 1992 elections (see the appendix to this chapter), the "leftist" attitude, favoring slow privatization, became dominant among the key political parties in the parliament, including the ruling Movement for an Independent Slovakia led by Vladimir Meciar. The adoption of such a position by the government was influenced by Meciar's own ideas about privatizing. In addition, his rhetoric about a more cautious approach to economic reforms appeared, at least initially, to have some appeal among those who were growing uneasy about the more rapid pace of decline of the Slovak economy (especially in terms of unemployment and inflation) than of the Czech economy.

In the situation described, characterized by a relative organizational weakness and extreme proliferation of organized interests, the ruling parties in both republics initially had much leeway to give expression to their ideological preferences in government programs, including privatization. At the same time, those parties, like any political party in a competitive system, had to be concerned with the impact its policies will have on future elections. Proliferation and weakness of political actors, however, poses a great difficulty in terms of constituency building. These qualities make it hard to assess the relative strength of potential political friends and foes and therefore to craft public policies to maximize electoral payoffs.

Under such circumstances, a "mass" privatization program aimed at the general public rather than at selected smaller groups of constituents may be appealing. A government that distributes assets widely may quickly gain popular support. Especially if the public has been led to believe for decades that it was the sole owner of "public property." As a result, a common expectation in post-communist societies has been that, if privatization is to be conducted, each citizen is entitled to receive his or her share of public assets. Thus, regardless of its economic merits and liabilities, mass privatization has emerged as one of the major policies that may facilitate legitimization of a new system of property rights.

The federal government of Czechoslovakia developed such a mass privatization program, called "voucher privatization," for large enterprises. One of the chief authors of the program was Vaclav Klaus, then the federal minister of finance and subsequently the Czech prime minister after the breakup of the federation. The "voucher privatization," as is subsequently described, constituted a compromise between giving the shares of privatized companies to their workers and distributing them to all adult citizens.

4.0 PRIVATIZATION PROGRAMS IN CZECHOSLOVAKIA

The voucher privatization program enacted before the dissolution of the federation to privatize large enterprises has been the single largest vehicle to redistribute property rights in the formerly state-owned economies of Czechoslovakia. In addition, there have been a number of other schemes adopted that have facilitated privatization of other types of property. Although my primary focus is on the voucher program, it is pertinent to discuss all the major pieces of legislation to gain a fuller understanding of the emerging systems of property rights in both republics.

4.1 Restitution of commercial property

In October 1990 the so-called Restitution Law made possible the return of some seventy thousand pieces of small property (agricultural land excluded), primarily stores, workshops, and apartment houses that were confiscated by the communist government in the period from 1955 to 1961.[7] The former owners, or their heirs, had to claim the property before April 1991. In cases in which the property was irreversibly altered by improvements or use, financial compensation was to be offered rather than restitution in kind.

In February 1991 the so-called Law on Extrajudicial Rehabilitation addressed the issue of the property nationalized in industry after 1948 (i.e., from the date of the communist takeover). The issue proved very contentious, and different proposals were offered in the Federal Assembly. The major points of disagreement were on the beneficiaries of the law (the inclusion or exclusion of emigrés, political parties, churches, and large prewar corporations) and the form of compensation (financial compensation or restitution in kind were proposed as alternative methods).[8]

The first round of debate on the law ended with an impasse on February 5, as no proposal had enough votes to be adopted. Nevertheless, on February 21, a compromise was reached, and the final draft of the law was passed. As a rule, restitution was to be through the return of property. Financial compensation (in the form of privatization vouchers) was to be an exception in cases in which improvements on the property were made and the beneficiaries did not want to repay the costs. The law favored individual voters residing in the country – excluded from the beneficiaries were all corporate owners (e.g., political parties and churches) and emigrés not residing in Czechoslovakia. All claims had to be made by the end of September 1991 to be considered. The law was expected to affect in the long run public property in Czechoslovakia valued at some 300 billion koruna, or about U.S.\$11 billion (*RFE/RL Report on Eastern Europe*, March 15, 1991: 13).

---

[7]Foreigners and Czech and Slovak emigrés were eligible to participate in this program.

[8]The Slovak government opposed the idea of compensation via property. Instead, it supported a scheme in which the previous owner would receive government bonds (*RFE/RL Report on Eastern Europe*, March 15, 1991: 13).

4.2 Restitution of land

Restoration of agricultural property proved to be another contentious issue in the process of privatization in Czechoslovakia. On May 21, 1991, the Federal Assembly adopted the Law on the Revision of Ownership Relations to Land and Other Agricultural Property. This legislation applied to only 34 percent of agricultural land in both republics – the number of eligible beneficiaries was estimated at 3.5 million (*RFE/RL Report on Eastern Europe*, July 19, 1991: 10). The deadline of December 31, 1992, was established for the original owners to state their claims. This deadline was subsequently extended by one year (i.e., to December 31, 1993). To provide swift enforcement of the law, a bill specifying penalties for physical and legal persons that failed to return land to previous owners was adopted in December 1992.

The limited character of the legislation dealing with restitution of land stemmed from the fact that it restricted the size of reclaimed property to 150 hectares (about 370 acres). Also, it gave preference to small land-owners. Those owners of agricultural property nationalized between February 25, 1948, and January 1, 1990, whose holdings exceeded the prescribed size could not benefit from the law. Also excluded from participation were foreign citizens (mainly Germans formerly living in the Czech Republic and Hungarians formerly living in the Slovak Republic, but also millions of Czech and Slovak emigrés in the United States).[9]

Two competing drafts of the law were considered for adoption. The federal government proposed only limited restoration (along the lines of the law that was ultimately adopted). This was justified by the claim that breaking up the existing large state-owned and collective farms and returning them to the original owners would compromise the "efficiency of agricultural production" and leave the country without sufficient production of food. The argument was dubious, as most of the cooperatives and state farms were at that time insolvent (the total debt amounted in 1991 to 35 billion koruna or about U.S.$1.2 billion).

A competing draft of the law, prepared by the Christian-Democratic Union/People's Party (forty seats in the parliament), proposed a complete return to the pre-1948 ownership structure in agriculture. The government's draft was accused of paying "tribute to the former regime [because] it discriminated against the [former] land owners and allowed cooperative members to decide about the property" (*RFE/RL Report on Eastern Europe*, July 19, 1991: 11). The law that was finally adopted, though presented by the government as a compromise between competing views on the subject, allowed for the preservation of most of those

[9]In fact, after adoption of the law, fifteen members of the U.S. Congress sent a protest letter to President George Bush and President Vaclav Havel.

farms. A major factor contributing to this outcome was the relatively large size of the constituency that relied on collective and state farms for employment – amounting to about 11 percent of the total workforce in each republic – and the general lack of alternative employment opportunities for them. The adopted legislation has arguably provided a greater potential for generating credibility for the new ownership structure of land than did the version giving preference to prewar owners and foreigners over current employees of state farms. The latter have not only been in possession of the land, but they also constitute a large group of the electorate whose jobs and welfare are at stake.

Separate pieces of legislation were to regulate the issue of the restitution of land to owners of properties larger than 150 hectares and corporate owners (i.e., mainly churches and religious communities). In October 1993 a bill on restitution of land and property confiscated by the communist government from churches and religious organizations was enacted in Slovakia. In its original version, the law envisioned return of property without any compensation to its current owners. Only cooperative farms and trading companies were exempted from returning confiscated property without compensation. This clause was vetoed by President Michal Kovac, who extended the benefit of refunding the purchase price to private persons. The modified version of the law was adopted by parliament on October 27, 1993, and came into effect on January 1, 1994 (*Economist Intellegence Unit Country Report: Slovakia,* 1994: 33).

4.3 *"Small privatization"*

In October 1990 the Federal Assembly adopted legislation regulating socalled small privatization, that is, plans to sell to private owners more than one hundred thousand small SOEs engaged in trade, commerce, and service that were not subject to the restitution law. The property involved was valued originally at 200 billion koruna (about U.S.$7 billion at the time). The employee buyout scheme envisioned in the original project of the law prepared by the government was rejected. Under this plan employees would have up to five years to complete payments. Instead, a bill was adopted that opened small privatization to the entire population by also making it available to nonemployees. According to the law, disposal of the property was to take the form of auctions open to any potential buyer and with no preferential treatment to any single category of private citizens.

The only exception was found in a number of provisions that gave privileged treatment to Czech and Slovak citizens (and thus legal voters) who resided in the country over foreigners, as well as over corporate entities, foreign or domestic. Most important, only citizens could participate in the first round of auctions. The Czech and Slovak Ministries of Administration and Privatization of State Property were authorized to compile lists of privatized property and determine the call prices. Those prices were to be set on the basis of guidelines issued by the Ministries of Finance in the respective republics. Bids of not less than 50 percent of the price set by the government were accepted. The second round, which involved all enterprises that were not sold in the first round, was open to foreigners. However, if there were no foreign participants, then property could be sold for as little as 20 percent of the original price. Corporate buyers were excluded from participation altogether. In cases in which the privatized enterprise was located on a property that it did not own, or was the subject of restitution, the new owner was guaranteed a two-year lease by the state. Subsequently, it was up to the owner of the property to negotiate a new lease.

In January 1991 the implementation of the program of "small privatization" began. By January 1992 more than twenty-one thousand enterprises in the Czech Republic and more than eight thousand in Slovakia were auctioned off for some U.S.$350 million (Machacek, 1992: 55). From the outset, the greatest controversy associated with the program was the origin of the money that was used to purchase privatized property by successful bidders. The popular press as well as left-of-center parties repeatedly implied that "dirty money" and foreign capital were involved on a large scale (*RFE/RL Report on Eastern Europe*, October 18, 1991: 2). As foreign bidders were legally excluded from the first round of auctions, it was claimed that they frequently used Czech and Slovak citizens as frontmen to obtain ownership of the most lucrative property being auctioned off. This way, it was argued, they were able not only to evade the law but also to buy privatized property for lower prices than they might have had to pay if the auctions were opened legally to foreign investors.

Another charge considered "dirty money" to be the alleged fortunes accumulated illegally by the former nomenklatura, black marketeers, and criminals. It was argued that the amounts paid for some of the privatized enterprises (e.g., the widely publicized case of U.S.$11 million paid for a small brewery in Slovakia) could not have been earned legally under the communist regime. Ultimately, the issue was used deftly by the left-of-center parties (most prominently by the Civic Movement), which, in an attempt to slow down the pace of privatization, pushed for the adoption of an amendment in September 1991 that required all future bidders to document the origins of the funds used in auctions.[10] Opposition to the

---

[10]Pavel Rychetsky, one of the leaders of the Civic Movement and deputy prime minister at that time, publicly explained that he was prompted to support the amend-

amendment by Vaclav Klaus and his Civic Democratic Party proved unsuccessful. Klaus argued that this measure would not accomplish its stated purpose of preventing foreigners and black marketeers from participation in auctions but instead would slow down the pace of privatization and politicize it. Also, he maintained that whatever the origin of the money, it would ultimately help to reform the Czechoslovak economy. Klaus claimed that money used in privatization should be considered earned legally unless proved otherwise in a court of law. It seemed, however, that Klaus did not wish to oppose the amendment too strongly because he realized that the issue of "dirty" money – very sensitive with the public – could be used against his party in the June 1992 elections by his opponents from the Left as well as the Right (e.g., the extreme nationalists from the Republican Party).

Other problems with small privatization included false bidding, which was not penalized until November 1991. This method was employed by groups of extortionists who blackmailed the potential buyers by driving the prices extremely high unless they were paid off, and by managers of the privatized companies who "bought" their companies at auctions and subsequently refused to pay. The latter never intended to purchase the enterprises but merely to stall the process. Also, restitution of commercial property to pre-communist owners significantly slowed down the process of small privatization, especially in the case of SOEs located on the property that was the subject of restitution (Machacek, 1992: 55).

5.0 "LARGE PRIVATIZATION"

The largest privatization program, and therefore the most important one for the new equilibrium of property rights in both republics, was concerned with large SOEs. The law delineating the program was adopted in February 1991.[11] It was to affect some three thousand state-owned companies valued at 300 billion koruna (some U.S.\$10.7 billion). Privatization was to be conducted in three stages. First, large companies and state monopolies were to be broken up into smaller units. Subsequently, all large enterprises were to be transformed into 100 percent state-owned joint-stock companies. Finally, those companies were to be sold to do-

ment by the information the government received about foreign criminal organizations laundering money in the privatization process in Czechoslovakia. He gave examples of property in Prague purchased allegedly by "Arab clans" and property in Karlove Vary (a famous spa) bought by the "Georgian mafia" (Radio Czechoslovakia, as quoted in *RFE/RL Report on Eastern Europe*, October 18, 1991: 3).

[11]My discussion of the law is based on *Act of February 26, 1991, On the Conditions of Transfer of State Property to Other Persons*, with commentary by Frantisek Faldyna (Prague: Czechoslovak Chamber of Commerce and Industry, 1991).

mestic and foreign investors.[12] Privatization of large companies was to be carried out by a variety of means, including direct sale, public auction, public tender, and a voucher plan.[13]

Privatization was to be administered by a number of specialized state agencies. The minister of administration and privatization in each republic was to draw up a list of enterprises to be privatized. The minister of finance was to prepare a "privatization proposal" for each sale determining the number of shares, their prices, the portion of shares reserved for free distribution in a voucher scheme, and a privatization schedule. Each enterprise slated for privatization was to prepare a proposal regarding the sale and include information about the current condition of the enterprise, its prospects, potential buyers that expressed interest in purchasing it, and the attitude of the employees toward the sale. The final decision, however, was to be made by the government. For example, the law explicitly states that the trade unions should be merely "kept informed" about the privatization plans.

Special funds were created on the federal and republic levels to conduct the sales by public auctions or contracts (the Federal and the Czech and Slovak Republic National Property Funds). Their members were nominated by the respective governments and approved by their parliaments. Among their responsibilities was the management of the profits from privatization that were to go toward paying the debts of privatized companies and to cover the costs of privatization itself.

5.1 The voucher plan (kuponova privatizace)

From 40 to 80 percent of the capital or stock of each large company was to be reserved for free distribution among Czechoslovak citizens over the age of eighteen. Each participant of the voucher plan was to receive, upon registration (at a fee of some U.S.$35), a voucher booklet worth one thousand investment points (additional vouchers could be issued in the

---

[12]Unlike the law on "small privatization," according to which foreigners were not eligible to participate in the first round of sales, there were no limits on their participation in the sales conducted in "large privatization." This outcome was reported to be influenced by the experience with the implementation of "small privatization." The exclusive participation of domestic buyers resulted in what were seen as relatively low prices. At the same time, some foreigners used "intermediaries" with Czechoslovak citizenship to purchase enterprises at bargain prices. Learning from this episode, the Czechoslovak legislators decided to adopt more realistic legislation that would at least guarantee the highest possible income from privatization (*RFE/RL Report on Eastern Europe*, March 15, 1991: 14).

[13]Ministry of Administration and Privatization of National Property of the Czech Republic, as quoted in *RFE/RL Research Report* 1: 17, April 24, 1992: 39.

future).[14] Eventually, from November 1991 to March 1992, some 8.5 million people registered for voucher booklets (out of about 11.5 million of those eligible). The vouchers could be exchanged for shares of privatized companies.[15] Those shares could be eventually traded on the stock market that was created in 1991. However, the vouchers themselves were not transferable.[16] Prices of shares were to be expressed in investment points and offered for sale (i.e., in exchange for vouchers) in "privatization rounds." Each privatization round was to consist of four stages (Section 16, *Decree on the Disbursement and Usage of Investment Vouchers*):

1. The announcement of the rate of shares (i.e., the number of shares offered for a hundred investment points)
2. The ordering of shares by eligible citizens
3. The collection and evaluation of orders
4. The publication of results of the privatization round

In a case of oversubscription, not exceeding 25 percent of the total offer, the minister of finance could decide that orders from investment funds were to be only partially satisfied (Section 24). If an offer were oversubscribed by more than 25 percent, then it was to be canceled and followed by a new offer with new higher prices (Section 25). In a case where the demand would be below the supply of shares, all orders were to be satisfied, and the rest of the shares were to be offered in as many future rounds at progressively lower prices as required to sell all the shares.

Instead of determining the orders themselves, owners of the vouchers could "entrust an investment privatization fund" with this task (Section 17). Upon transferring their investment points to a privatization fund, the investors themselves were to receive shares of this fund in the value corresponding to the basic capital thus increased. All shares purchased by the fund were to be used toward expansion of the basic capital of the fund. No fund was to own more than 10 percent of the total equity of a single joint-stock company. All funds had to be registered with the Ministry of Finance in the respective republics (a minimum basic capital of 1 million koruna, or U.S.$36,000, was required). By February 1992, 437 funds were approved and registered – 296 in the Czech Republic and 170 in the

[14]The registration deadline was originally set for January 31, 1992, and subsequently extended to February 29.

[15]The total public assets to be privatized in the voucher plan were reported to be estimated at 260 billion koruna (over U.S.$9 billion). Some commentators considered this valuation to be overstated because of recession and poor financial conditions of the majority of Czechoslovak enterprises (*RFE/RL Research Report*, April 14, 1992: 39–41).

[16]Despite this provision, millions of investment vouchers were reported "missing" from state agencies by early 1992 (*RFL/RL Research Report*, January 31, 1992: 50).

Slovak Republic (*RFE/RL Research Report,* April 24, 1992: 39). They were set up by domestic and foreign individuals and corporate entities (e.g., banks). The government itself was not involved in setting up the funds, but state-owned joint-stock companies were permitted to create their own funds (e.g., state-owned banks). There was no limit on the participation of foreign capital in the funds.

On February 17, 1992, a "zero privatization round" was conducted in which about 8.5 million holders of privatization vouchers were able to place their vouchers in the funds (*RFE/RL Research Report,* February 28, 1992: 44). Ultimately, about 75 percent of them did so.[17] The "zero round" established the size of investment funds for the foreseeable future, as they have the character of "closed" funds; that is, the size of their original capital cannot be changed.

The funds were not subject to comprehensive regulation. Only sporadic references can be found in various legal acts (e.g., the Law on Intermediaries and the Investment Funds Act). This left many issues related to the functioning of the funds unregulated. For example, the maximum size of a single fund was not formally limited. The most successful funds adopted aggressive marketing tactics to attract investors. Among the first who used those tactics was the Harvard Investment Fund, established by a 28-year-old Czech emigré, Viktor Kozeny, a Harvard graduate.[18] Kozeny's fund promised its investors a tenfold return on their initial investment in the voucher booklet (i.e., the U.S.$35 registration fee) should they decide to sell it to the fund after the required one-year waiting period (*New York Times,* March 6, 1992: A6). In fact, it was reported that some clients signed contracts in return for cash to transfer their investment in a year's time to their funds (*Polityka,* May 2, 1992: 12). After the first wave of voucher privatization, the Harvard Investment Fund controlled the third largest portfolio, with 638 million investment points, representing some 7.5 percent of total investable points (*PlanEcon Report,* 1993a: 2). But the domestic financial institutions have quickly caught up with the Harvard Investment Fund's marketing tactics. The Czech Savings Bank (IPF Ceska sporitelna), which ultimately accumulated the greatest portfolio of privatization vouchers, estimated at 790 million to 950 million investment points, offered loans against invested points to all of its potential investors. Some 75 percent of those who invested their points in the Czech

[17]According to Iri Svitka from the Czechoslovak Federal Ministry of Finance (*Polityka,* May 2, 1992: 12).

[18]In a May 1992 interview for the Polish weekly *Polityka,* Viktor Kozeny, founder of the Harvard Capital and Consulting Company, claimed that he and Prime Minister Klaus "have agreed" that his fund should not control more then 20 percent of the privatization vouchers. However, in a separate interview for the same weekly, Iri Svitka, Klaus's advisor, rejected this claim (*Polityka,* May 2, 1992: 12).

Savings Bank's investment fund took the 10,000 koruna loans, an amount equal to some one-third of their investment's book value (*Plan-Econ Report*, 1993a: 1). The success of the bank has been also attributed to what was advertised as their "conservative business strategy" of not lending money to state-owned companies! This is a quite remarkable testimony to the trust in private ownership and the lack of confidence in public companies among citizens of countries with still predominantly state-owned economies.

5.2 First wave of large-scale privatization

The large-scale privatization was to be conducted in two "waves." The first privatization wave was conducted from January to December 1992. By the end of November 1991, the managers of enterprises slated for privatization were required to submit proposals specifying the methods they wanted used to privatize their companies (e.g., 20 percent of shares for employee and management buyout, 40 percent for foreign investors, and 40 percent for the voucher plan). By the end of December 1991, the Ministry of Administration and Privatization of National Property in each republic was to review the proposals and prepare the final plan for the first privatization wave by the end of December 1991. Proposals for the second wave of privatization were to be submitted by May 31, 1992, and the wave was to commence in the fall of 1993.

By October 1991 a serious conflict arose in the Czech Republic between the Ministry of Administration and Privatization of National Property, headed by Tomas Jezek, and the Federal Ministry of Finance, led by Vaclav Klaus. The February 1991 law on privatization of large enterprises left the agencies in charge of privatization with wide discretion as to the extent to which particular privatization techniques were to be utilized (e.g., the voucher plan was to apply to anywhere from 40 to 80 percent of the property of a privatized company). It became apparent that the Ministry of Privatization, under Jezek, favored limiting the voucher method to a minimum, whereas the Federal Ministry of Finance, under Klaus, wanted the maximum use of this option. Klaus and his advisers launched a campaign of criticizing Jezek's ministry, which ranged from offering the "needed technical advice" to outright condemnation for what they saw as "sabotaging" of the voucher plan.

Klaus and his supporters claimed that by privatizing most of the large companies under a voucher system the process of privatization would be accelerated, the property prevented from falling into the hands of foreign owners, and public control over the process maintained. Also, they asserted that the Ministry of Privatization would become entangled in the complex process of evaluating, and eventually executing, complicated proposals in which many different methods of privatization were patched together as opposed to ones in which the voucher method would be dominant. The latter, they argued, would be easier to evaluate and implement. Finally, blunt accusations of bribe-taking and pilfering of state property were leveled against officials from the Ministry of Privatization. It was alleged that their hostility to the voucher plan indicated that they succumbed to management (occasionally referred to as the "mafia" or the "old communist structures") and foreign investors at the expense of the general public.[19]

Jezek's ministry, and his defenders, responded with their own claims and accusations. Klaus and other officials from the Federal Ministry of Finance were criticized for allegedly taking a macroeconomic approach to privatization that did not consider individual problems being experienced by the privatized companies. For example, it was argued that many of the public companies would go bankrupt if they were privatized by using the voucher scheme predominantly. The example of the Skoda Car Company, which entered into joint-venture with Volkswagen, was given to support the claim that reputable foreign investors could save many of the failing Czech companies from bankruptcy (*RFE/RL Report on Eastern Europe*, October 4, 1991: 6). As early as August 1991, the Czech Ministry of Privatization published a list of more than fifty large companies that either formed joint ventures with foreign investors or were bought by them, partially or in their entirety. Among those enterprises were some of the most reputable and largest public companies, many with a monopoly position in the Czech market (*Molda fronta dnes*, December 23, 1992: 6). As discussed below, the final results of voucher privatization were more reflective of the views of Klaus's group.

It took five rounds to conclude the first wave of privatization, as some stocks were oversubscribed, whereas others did not attract enough buyers. Finally, in December 1992 it was announced that 93 percent of the stocks slated for this wave was sold (278 million out of 299 million available shares). The remaining stocks were temporarily transferred to the republics' Foundations of National Property for later sale. Shares valued at some U.S.$6.8 billion were distributed in the first wave of voucher privatization among some 8.5 million adults (some 5.9 million in the Czech Republic and 2.6 million in the Slovak Republic).

The first privatization wave was conducted simultaneously in both republics with Czech and Slovak citizens entitled to acquire stock of companies based in either republic. Ultimately, Czech investors acquired 7.9

[19]For example, Dusan Triska, Klaus's deputy, was quoted as warning the Czech Ministry of Privatization against the danger of selling public companies at nominal prices to management, which could immediately resell them to foreign investors for profit (*RFE/RL Report on Eastern Europe*, October 4, 1991: 7–8).

percent of stock of Slovak companies (representing a book value of 6.3 billion koruna), and Slovak investors acquired 11.1 percent of Czech-based companies (a book value of 22 billion koruna).[20]

6.0 PROPERTY TRANSFER BY DIFFERENT PRIVATIZATION TECHNIQUES AFTER THE DISSOLUTION OF CZECHOSLOVAKIA

6.1 *The Czech Republic*

The government of the Czech Republic, led by Klaus's Civic Democratic Party since its formation in June 1992, has repeatedly expressed its commitment to using vouchers as the dominant mode of distribution of privatized property. This has also been consistent with its policy of favoring domestic ownership over foreign ownership, even when the former has much less capital and expertise. Shortly after the first wave of voucher privatization was completed, the preparations for the second wave began. The second wave was launched in the Czech Republic in October 1993 and entailed shares in some eight hundred companies with a nominal book value of 130 billion koruna, equivalent at that time to some U.S.$4.5 billion. This amount represented a smaller volume of shares as compared to the first wave of voucher privatization valued at some 199 billion koruna, or U.S.$6.8 billion (*PlanEcon Report*, 1993c: 29).

By mid-1993 the process of privatization in the Czech Republic had evolved to include a wide spectrum of beneficiaries. A compromise had emerged between the Ministry of Privatization, supporting the managers and workers in privatized companies who were pushing for privileged treatment in the redistribution of property rights, and the Klaus group, pressing for free distribution of shares to the entire society. Some 88 percent of the book value of privatized companies has been transformed into joint-stock companies or will be in the near future. The remaining 12 percent of the value of privatized property has been disposed of as follows: Direct sales accounted for some 4 percent (52 percent of which was sold to domestic and 48 percent to foreign investors), restitution claims amounted to some 3 percent, employee shares totaled another 3 percent, and the remaining 2 percent was sold through intermediaries (*PlanEcon Report*, 1993c: 25).

As for the 88 percent of the book value of privatized companies that was transformed into joint-stock companies, the majority of shares (62.1 percent) have been distributed for free in voucher privatization to the general public, some shares were held temporarily by the Czech National

[20]*Mloda fronta dnes*, December 23, 1992: 6.

Property Fund (15.2 percent), some shares were transferred for free to municipalities, villages, and health and pension plans (11.6 percent), some shares were given as restitution claims to prewar private owners (3.4 percent), additional shares were given to employees (2.6 percent), and a number of shares were sold to domestic and foreign investors (3.5 percent) (*PlanEcon Report*, 1993c: 26). The figure of 62 percent of shares distributed to the public for free constituted a compromise between the original positions of the Ministry of Privatization (arguing for 40 percent) and the Klaus supporters (arguing for 80 percent).

It is true, as some have argued, that in terms of the *number* of privatized units accounting for different methods of privatization, the three main methods – direct sale, cost-free transfer, and transformation into joint-stock companies and their subsequent disposal mainly through voucher privatization – have been used equally often.[21] When evaluated in terms of the book value of property, however, voucher privatization, accounting for 62.1 percent of all privatized property, swamps direct sales (6.6 percent), public tender (2.8 percent), cost-free tender (2.3 percent), and auction (0.3 percent) (*PlanEcon Report*, 1993c: 27).

6.2 Slovakia

Until the dissolution of the federation in January 1993, the voucher privatization campaign initiated by the federal government was also conducted in Slovakia. Thus, as in the Czech Republic, many persons benefited. Voucher privatization was until 1993 the main privatization method, accounting for more than 88 percent of the book value of privatized property, and only less than 12 percent was privatized by other techniques (*PlanEcon Report*, 1993b: 21–2).

This situation, however, changed during 1993 under the government of Prime Minister Vladimir Meciar. After the completion of the first privatization wave, Meciar announced that voucher privatization would be discontinued in his republic after the dissolution of the federation. Meciar explained this decision by saying that other forms of privatization, especially direct sales, were considered by his government to be more advantageous, mainly in terms of generating financial resources for the state.

The pronounced rationale was that voucher privatization did not generate any income for the state and did not provide any capital for the enterprises, because the shares were distributed free of charge. Also, it

---

[21]The numbers of privatized units by method as of May 1993 were 1,359 units by direct sale, 1,352 by cost-free transfer, and 1,327 by joint-stock company and subsequent voucher privatization (*PlanCon Report*, 1993c: 26).

excluded foreign investors from participation until the trading of distributed shares was to begin.[22]

To justify his decision, Meciar also alluded to the fears of a sizable part of the public apprehensive of high unemployment rates and inflation commonly ascribed to the initially rapid pace of privatization. He did so even though it was not the principle of voucher privatization but rather its fast pace that seems to have worried many Slovaks. Unlike Klaus in the Czech Republic, who constantly preached the virtues of a rapid privatization policy and the establishment of a market economy, Meciar kept promising his weary constituency a smooth transition, which he called a "middle path between communism and capitalism."[23] He claimed that by slowing the pace of privatization it would be possible to save more jobs and keep inflation in check.

The issue of privatization ultimately became one of the main reasons for the collapse of the Meciar government in early 1994. Most important of all, by discontinuing voucher privatization, Meciar gave up the chance to reach the broad Slovak constituencies and generate their support for his party, as well as for a new system of property rights, through the distribution of material benefits.

The abandonment of the voucher program led to a virtual halt in privatization in Slovakia in 1993 and the first few months of 1994, despite Meciar's claims about his determination to continue the restructuring of property rights. While rejecting the Czech-designed privatization program, Meciar did not have a coherent policy to replace it. It became painfully obvious to an increasing number of his onetime supporters that his rhetoric about the "middle path" was a disguise for the lack of a clear vision of revitalizing the Slovak economy.[24] As popular support for Meciar's party was eroding (support for his party declined in public opinion polls from 60 percent in mid-1992 to 14 percent in December 1993), there was also mounting criticism and defection within its ranks. At the end of 1993 increasing efforts were mounted within Meciar's own party to remove him from power. Also, the coalition partner in govern-

[22]According to Prague CTK, December 27, 1992, as quoted in *FBIS-EEU*, December 29, 1992: 28.

[23]Some have argued that the Slovak economy was significantly less developed and less efficient than the Czech economy at the time of the collapse of the communist government. Therefore, it has been suggested that different privatization strategies should be used in both republics. Available statistical data show, however, that, as a result of a regional redistribution policy conducted by the communist government of Czechoslovakia, the Slovak Republic achieved a roughly equal economic parity per capita in major economic indicators with the Czech Republic at the eve of the breakup (Capek and Sazama, 1993: 216).

[24]Prominent in the criticism was a report released by a group called MESA 10, which consisted of independent economists who accused the Meciar government of a failure to develop a clear stabilization and privatization strategy.

ment, the Slovak National Party (SNP), was growing critical of Meciar. For example, SNP leader Ludovir Cernak was outspokenly unhappy about the lack of progress in privatization, and he described a series of public debates on privatization organized by Meciar in the fall of 1993 as mere "political theater" (*Economist Intelligence Unit Country Report: Slovakia*, 1994).

It was under these circumstances that Meciar attempted a series of direct sales to individual investors. These sales led to a scandal and became one of the major factors triggering the downfall of his government in March 1994. In mid-February the government sold thirteen companies to investors who were alleged to be Meciar's cronies. (Meciar was personally responsible for the sales because he retained for himself the portfolios of the privatization minister and the chairman of the Slovak National Property Fund.) On March 9, 1994, President Michal Kovac delivered a state of the nation address that severely criticized Prime Minister Meciar for the "ethics and the style of his politics." In particular, Kovac claimed that Meciar personally told him that he wanted to design the privatization program in a way to ensure financial benefits for his Movement for Democratic Slovakia (*Republika*, March 10, 1994). Kovac's speech, in addition, unified and motivated growing opposition to Meciar's government in the parliament that culminated in a no-confidence vote on March 14, 1994.

Because of the prominence of the issue of privatization in the downfall of the Meciar government, the new government of Jozef Moravcik announced immediately after its formation in April 1994 that it would resume the voucher privatization abandoned by Meciar. Hence, its second wave, modeled after the Czech program, was launched. An investigation was also initiated into the sales of the thirteen companies conducted by the Meciar government in February 1994.

7.0 CONCLUSION

Privatization is still an ongoing and evolving process in the two republics that have emerged from the dissolution of the former Czechoslovakia. Nevertheless, some tentative conclusion about this process and its political and economic consequences can be reached. First, different approaches to privatization are likely to lead to different equilibria in property rights. The mass privatization model, as exemplified by the voucher program in the Czech Republic, is likely to create a large group of property owners and to enjoy a high level of popular legitimacy. This will be accomplished if mechanisms aimed at preserving the initial broad distribution of property owners created by voucher privatization are implemented. This could take, for example, the form of a high capital-gains tax discouraging sale of property and thus stabilizing the emerging equilibrium of property rights.[25] Also, the mass privatization model is congenial to the development and maintenance of an inclusive and highly competitive political system.

It should be noted that some authors have criticized the Czech government for spreading the ownership rights too thinly throughout the entire society. This approach was claimed to be a consequence of the difficulty of overcoming "the 'socialist' thinking of the past (under communism, everybody was a fictitious shareholder in 'national' property so why not just turn fictitious shareholders into actual shareholders" (*PlanEcon Report*, 1993c: 29). This policy was said to be "naive" and "flawed." This was allegedly because "while the Czech model would be functional in a developed and smoothly functioning market environment with [an] ample supply [of] entrepreneurial talent, the Czech economic reformers appear to have forgotten that before they can achieve a functioning 'shareholder-managed economy,' they need an 'entrepreneur-managed economy'" (*PlanEcon Report*, 1993c: 29). This line of criticism, seemingly logical and valid, commits a fallacy of assuming that the Czech government could have alone created a viable system of property rights. As I have argued in this chapter, the latter cannot be accomplished single-handedly in a truly competitive political system. Commitments of major political actors that have stakes in the emerging system of property rights are required, if a set of stable and widely shared expectations about constraints with regard to property is to materialize and endure. In the former Czechoslovakia, where almost all property was state-owned and, therefore, legally belonged to the whole society, interests of all citizens (and voters) are at stake and have to be taken into account. This is the case even more in circumstances in which organizations characteristic of mature competitive political systems are still relatively weak, and thus a broad spectrum of citizens has to be involved to provide legitimacy for the emerging equilibrium of property rights. The post-communist state can no longer impose a system of property rights on its citizens as the latter became empowered with real voting rights and the ability to organize and articulate their interests.

The example of Slovakia illustrates the difficulty of legitimizing a new system of property rights when an attempt is made to limit the number of property owners for either political or economic reasons. After the completion of the first wave of privatization and the collapse of the federation, the Meciar government changed its privatization strategy to rely on direct capital sales, ostensibly for economic reasons. This policy faltered and

---

[25]Admittedly, this kind of stabilizing measure may come with a price of reduced economic efficiency.

greatly contributed to the demise of the Meciar government, as a very small group of its direct beneficiaries, mainly Meciar's supporters and foreign investors (lured by tax holidays and tax breaks), failed to generate legitimacy for the new distribution of property rights. One could imagine that in a noncompetitive political system, a "coerced" system of property rights could have been sought with elite ownership under an authoritarian government. But the competitive political system that has already taken root in Slovakia has rejected Meciar's change in privatization: The general public, deprived of immediate benefits from privatization in the form of free shares, exerted pressure on politicians to reactivate voucher privatization; politicians in parliament brought down the Meciar government with a no-confidence vote; and the new government immediately attempted to create a more stable new equilibrium by broadening the scope of beneficiaries through voucher privatization.

Finally, an interesting ambivalence among the general public in its attitude to the voucher program has manifested itself in both republics: Although people want to acquire ownership rights through the free shares, at the same time they are afraid of the possible increase in unemployment and inflation rates that may be caused by such a program. In the case of Slovakia and the Czech Republic, the desire for immediate and certain material benefits has overcome the anxiety of the future and uncertain negative consequences that might follow.

APPENDIX: THE JUNE 1992 PARLIAMENTARY ELECTIONS IN CZECHOSLOVAKIA

Election results in the Czech Republic (rounded percentages)

Party	House of the People percent/ seats	House of Nations percent/ seats	National Council percent/ seats
Civic Democratic Party/Christian Democratic Party	34/48	33/37	28/76
Leftist Bloc (Communists)	14/19	14/15	14/35
Czechoslovak Social Democracy	8/10	7/6	7/16
Republican Party	7/8	6/6	6/14
Christian Democratic Union	6/7	6/6	6/15
Liberal Social Union	6/7	6/5	7/16
Civic Democratic Alliance	—/—	—/—	6/14
Association for Moravia and Silesia	—/—	—/—	6/14

Source: CSTK (the Czechoslovak Press Agency), quoted in Pehe (1992: 29).

Election results in the Slovak Republic (rounded percentages)

Party	House of the People percent/ seats	House of Nations percent/ seats	National Council percent/ seats
Movement for a Democratic Slovakia	34/24	34/33	37/74
Party of the Democratic Left (Communists)	14/10	14/13	15/29
Slovak National Party	9/6	9/9	8/15
Christian Democratic Movement	9/6	9/8	9/18
Coexistence/Hungarian Christian Democratic Movement	—/—	—/—	7/14
Coexistence/Hungarian Christian Democratic Movement/Hungarian People's Party	7/5	7/7	—/—
Social Democratic Party in Slovakia	—/—	6/5	—/—

Source: CSTK, quoted in Pehe (1992: 29).

REFERENCES

Capek, Ales, and Gerald W. Sazama, "Czech and Slovak Economic Relations," *Europa-Asia Studies* 45: 2 (1993), 211–35.

Dobek, Mariusz Mark, *The Political Logic of Privatization: Lessons from Great Britain and Poland* (Westport, CT: Praeger, 1993).

Economist Intelligence Unit Country Report: Czech Republic and Slovakia, 4th quarter (1993).

Economist Intelligence Unit Country Report: Slovakia, 1st quarter (1994).

Knight, Jack, *Institutions and Social Conflict* (Cambridge: Cambridge University Press, 1992).

Machacek, Jan, "Privatization: More Than an Economic Goal," *East European Reporter,* January–February (1992), 55.

Martin, Peter, "Privatization: A Balance Sheet," *Report on Eastern Europe,* February 1 (1991), 7–9.

North, Douglass C., "Institutions and Credible Commitment," *Journal of Institutional and Theoretical Economics* 149: 1 (1993), 11–23.

Pehe, Jiri, "Czechoslovakia's Political Balance Sheet, 1990 to 1992," *RFE/RL Research Report* 1: 25 (1992), 24–31.

PlanEcon Report, XIX:3–4, February (1993a).
    XIX:13–14, April (1993b).
    XIX:26–27, July (1993c).

Wolchik, Sharon L., *Czechoslovakia in Transition* (London: Pinter Publishers, 1991).

Comment on "Property Rights and Institutional Change in the Czech and Slovak Republics"

SHARON WOLCHIK

The institution of a new system of property rights is, as Mariusz Dobek notes, of great import for any society. As Dobek rightly argues, decisions to privatize economic assets in particular ways are ultimately political decisions that create winners and losers in the society in which they take place. As such, they are influenced in important ways by political as well as by economic factors.

Dobek's essay deftly traces many of the political factors that shaped the decision to adopt voucher privatization in Czechoslovakia after the collapse of communism in 1989. It also highlights the important differences that existed in the views of Czech and Slovak leaders on privatization.

Several additional aspects of the immediate post-communist situation bear emphasis. In the former Czechoslovakia and its successors, the Czech Republic and Slovakia, the reinstitution of a market economy was an especially dramatic change. As in the case of other policies adopted by the country's non-communist leaders after 1989, the process of re-establishing the legal and institutional basis for private ownership and other elements of a market economy was also influenced profoundly by the differing conditions and perspectives of the country's two largest ethnic groups, the Czechs and the Slovaks.

In contrast to the situation in Poland, where agriculture was largely in private hands after 1956, and a sizeable private sector existed during the communist era in trade and services, or in Hungary, where communist leaders introduced significant elements of the market between 1968 and the end of communist rule, in Czechoslovakia there was almost no private sector to speak of prior to 1989. Nationalization of industry, which began during the period of modified pluralism after World War II between 1945 and 1948, was extended to the rest of the economy after the communist takeover of February 1948 and resulted in the elimination of almost all private enterprise in the industrial and service sectors. The country's communist leaders also pursued collectivization aggressively.

205

As a result, the social structure in Czechoslovakia came to differ markedly from that of other developed European countries at similar stages of industrialization. The proportion of capitalists or private owners of industry dwindled to less than 1 percent by the early 1960s and remained at that level throughout the communist period. Most of the property that remained in private hands consisted of very small agricultural holdings.

The importance of this factor for the privatization strategy chosen by the leadership in 1991 is implicit in Dobek's argument. But it bears being made explicit. In large part because its economy was so tightly controlled and property was kept nearly exclusively in state or collective hands, Czechoslovakia avoided the so-called spontaneous privatization of economic assets that occurred in Poland and Hungary in the waning days of communist rule. Under Klaus, the leadership approved a variety of mechanisms to transfer ownership from state to individual hands; these included auctions and foreign investment, as well as the voucher program. As Meciar's actions in Slovakia after June 1992 demonstrate, it is possible for political leaders to choose to forgo the advantages presented by the lack of an entrenched group of former bureaucrats turned entrepreneurs and managers turned owners. One can also argue, as many of Klaus's critics have, that voucher privatization merely postpones the problem of transformation of the economy. However, Klaus and his supporters clearly perceived the political advantages of giving a large portion of the electorate a personal stake in the continuation of economic reforms. And, in contrast to leaders in Poland and Hungary, they did not face sustained opposition to such a move by entrenched interests that would have benefited from emphasis on more traditional methods.

As the results of the June 1992 elections and the eventual breakup of the Czechoslovak Federation illustrate, support for the strategy of a rapid transition to the market depended in large part on the extent to which individuals' living standards deteriorated. In the Czech Republic, where unemployment remained under 3 percent and where many members of the population benefited from the boom in foreign investment and expansion of the private sector, such support was relatively easy to obtain. In Slovakia, on the other hand, where unemployment levels reached 13 percent, and where many more families felt the hardships that economic changes created, public opinion toward the privatization of enterprises, particularly large enterprises, was far less favorable.

Dobek argues that the premature demise of Meciar's government in March 1994 in part reflected his failure to legitimize the alternate program of privatization he proposed. Unfortunately, the results of the September–October 1994 elections, in which Meciar, who explicitly promised to reverse the renewed mass privatization program and return to more "traditional" methods, won the largest proportion of the popular vote, do not bear out this conclusion. Rather, they indicate that attitudes toward privatization are just one of many factors that influence citizens' voting decisions. While many Slovaks appreciated the efforts of the coalition government that replaced Meciar in March to restart the voucher privatization program, their support for such efforts was not strong enough to overcome the other considerations that determined their vote. As in June 1992, one of the most important of these is the perceived well-being of individuals and families.

Developments in Slovakia in 1994 are instructive because they illustrate the importance of linking attitudes concerning property rights not only to the interests of particular groups, but to elite choices and strategies as well. Dobek is right in raising the issue of how a system of property rights can be legitimated in conditions of mass democracy. But as the Slovak experience and those of many other post-communist states demonstrate, it is unfortunately true that a "coerced" system of property rights that gives preferences to certain elements of the elite can indeed be implemented even in a competitive political system, particularly if both the elite and significant elements of the population are ambivalent about the whole project of privatization.

To a large degree, then, it is the Czech exception, and the willingness of the leadership to rely on mass privatization, that needs to be explained. As Dobek cogently argues, both economic and political factors contributed to this choice. The leadership group around Klaus, and Klaus in particular, must be credited with having the political vision to take advantage of the favorable conditions that existed for relying on a mass privatization program as one element in their privatization strategy. These included, in addition to those that Dobek discusses and those outlined earlier in these comments, a population that was generally supportive of privatization and willing to tolerate the short-term decline in their standards of living that the move to the market entailed. They also included the fact that relatively small numbers of individuals lost their jobs. The real test of the legitimacy of the strategy for creating a new system of property relations in the Czech Republic, then, may be yet to come.

8

Institutional structures, labor interests, and evolving privatization bargains in Poland

LORENE ALLIO[1]

1.0 INTRODUCTION

In 1989 organized labor played a crucial role in the political and economic sea change that occurred in Poland. The Solidarity movement was instrumental in the "roundtable" discussions leading to elections and the first post-communist government. This Solidarity government initiated radical reform designed to move the centrally planned economy toward the market. It was only after the course of economic change had been set that the irony of this became clear: Although Solidarity was a labor union as well as a political movement, it redirected the road of Polish politics to run directly through labor's garden.[2] Five years later, privatization had transformed the economic landscape in Poland to a remarkable degree. Privatization in small and medium-sized businesses had progressed at a rapid rate. Yet, the unique institutional position and resultant bargaining strength of labor in post–centrally planned Poland make the privatization of the large industries much more problematic. The process of large enterprise privatization does not facilitate the constructive exercise of this strength. Consequently, I argue that the government's commitment to large enterprise privatization is not fully credible.

Privatization represents an attempt to shift fundamentally the system of property rights from one dominated by public ownership to one dominated by private ownership. It results in a complex interaction of social, political, and economic forces contesting the distribution of costs and

---

[1] I thank the Institute for the Study of World Politics for its support and the Gdansk Institute for Market Economics for its hospitality during the period of this research. The content of this chapter, its opinions and errors are, of course, entirely my own responsibility.

[2] Of course, this is not to say even metaphorically that Polish enterprises were "gardens" even though many did provide swimming pools, vacation homes, and child care. The metaphor is Voltairian in that individuals "tend their gardens," a process from which they derive personal peace of mind and sense of place.

benefits of ownership transformation. This interaction is structured by a variety of institutions that were established both prior to and after 1989 and that have evolved as the result of repeated bargaining in the period that followed. Credible commitment to privatization in the sphere of small and medium-sized state-owned enterprises has resulted from the deployment and revision of institutions that reflect the social-institutional bases of power and that allow for the shifting of property rights in a manner assumed to be beneficial to those who hold this power. The failures of privatization are most apparent in the inertia of large industry privatization. Ironically, this results, in no small part, from the lack of strategic opportunities for labor at the (large) enterprise level, despite its overwhelming power in large industries. By strategic opportunities I mean the ability to choose an option from a range of alternatives with an eye to desirable distributional consequences.

The role of already existing and emerging institutional structures has been crucial in creating this impasse. In view of the state of Polish institutions at the point of political transition and the power these institutions conferred on various groups in society (labor in particular), the Polish government could not privatize unilaterally. It had to allow for negotiation with labor and other groups. The importance of bargaining and negotiation in the transformation of the system of property rights is emphasized by the fact that the most successful portions of the Polish privatization program have been those that involved strategic behavior on the part of the firm. Moreover, those portions of the economy in which the success has been least are ones in which the institutional structures limit the firm-level opportunities for strategic behavior with regard to restructuring and transformation.

2.0 PROPERTY RIGHTS AND BARGAINING STRUCTURES

Property rights are among the most important institutions that structure bargains. Theoretically, property rights have three aspects that together can be considered a property rights "bundle": (1) the right to use an asset, that is, to elect for specific goods any use from an unprohibited class of uses; (2) the right to earn income from an asset and contract over the terms with other individuals; and (3) the right to transfer ownership rights permanently to another party (Eggertsson, 1990).

Indeed, when we "unbundle" (Campbell, 1991) the property rights, we find that various aspects of property rights can be held by different entities; rights can be dispersed. They can be dispersed via functional divisions between categories of rights, or via principal-agent relationships. The variety of possible bundles of property rights, of possible principles and agents, means that the distribution of costs and benefits of moving to a new system of rights, including from public to private ownership, can be extremely complex and varied. Reality is, as always, much sloppier than theory.

As property rights are much more complex as institutional bundles than is first apparent, so too is the environment of related institutions. Surrounding institutions, in addition to property rights, also structure the bargain over privatization. For example, the structure of institutions related to finance can play an important role: Historical debt portfolios, interfirm debts, and access to capital inhibit "selection" (Stiglitz, 1991: 15) and distort the distribution of opportunities for successful transformation. Institutions such as labor codes and regulations governing business collusion can lend bargaining strength to various groups and attenuate the ability of others to exercise property rights.

The complexity of these systems is reflected in distributions of costs, benefits, and interests among groups that are equally complex. Changes in important institutional structures like property rights have distributional impacts that give rise to bargaining among social groups. This bargaining is structured by formal and informal institutions prevailing in the political and economic context. The fundamental object of these bargains is the creation and allocation of power and wealth. Although the specific approach to, and valuation of, these objectives varies with the players, questions of distribution remain at the heart of the game. In the current Polish context, the struggle over wealth and power is being played out in the movement from a centrally planned economy to a market economy; the game revolves around who will pay the costs of this movement and who will receive its benefits.

Bargaining over costs and benefits of economic reform usually takes place on more than one level. In his article on the logic of two-level games, Robert Putnam (1988) emphasizes that bargainers often occupy seats at more than one table. Indeed, bargaining is an interactive and multidimensional process, and a negotiator at one level may have to think of the processes occurring at other levels. As is made obvious in Putnam's work, in matters of economic reform there are often negotiations going on at the level of international financial relations, as well as at the national policy level.

In the case of Polish privatization, it is additionally important to emphasize that enterprise-level bargains influence the other two levels. At the enterprise level, decisions are made as to restructuring of day-to-day operations, and this in turn conditions both the feasibility and the necessity, and to some degree the costs and benefits, of privatization. At the level of the firm, fundamental reorganizations are occurring that affect corporate governance and the role of management and labor in a changing economic environment.

Evolving privatization bargains in Poland

Indeed, three bargaining levels are important to this discussion of privatization in the Polish economy: the international-level bargain, the national-level bargain, and the enterprise-level bargain.

2.1 International-level bargaining

International-level bargaining occurs between the government and international financial institutions over the terms of financial agreements. These terms often include the establishment of macroeconomic goals and policies directly affecting the domestic political economy. It is in the context of the international-level bargain, which in the Polish case includes the stabilization program, that economic reform and privatization take place.

Several international institutions have been active in structuring the Polish reform. The European Bank for Reconstruction and Development (EBRD), the International Finance Corporation (IFC), the World Bank, and the International Monetary Fund (IMF) are among the many organizations providing technical advice and capital to Polish reformers. Of these the IMF is the most important as it plays the role of the "gatekeeper" to further finance: Agreement with the IMF is an important precondition to the receipt of funds from other organizations and to the reduction of Poland's international debt with the London and Paris clubs (Dell, 1983; Biersteker, 1993).

In the post-communist context, IMF programs have had a relative degree of flexibility. They have tolerated departures from the macroeconomic orthodoxy seen in their relations with many governments of the developing world. This is not to say that the IMF has abandoned such orthodoxy all together; the IMF *has* supported decreased budget deficits in times when social programs were being slashed, subjecting Poland to conditionality – requiring it to undergo financial review and to maintain agreed upon budgetary and other economic policy targets – in orthodox form. Undeniably, the regular missions of the IMF negotiating and renegotiating letters of intent, and the suspension of agreement at critical moments for politics and the economy, have influenced the decisions made by Polish governments.

It is impossible and would be erroneous to say that the privatization program has been a result of international bargaining. Yet, there is evidence of direct and indirect influence of international financial organizations on the adoption and implementation of Polish privatization. Indirectly, institutions like the IMF and the World Bank influence economic reform by favoring privatization in their technical advice and in their country programs. More directly, the international financial institutions fund specific privatization programs as well as the restructuring of indus-

211

tries and institutions that facilitate continued privatization. For example, the financing of bank restructuring and reform, the restructuring of the coal mining sector, and the mass privatization program's National Investment Funds are some of the international financial institutions' undertakings directly influencing the implementation of privatization efforts.

2.2 National-level bargaining

At the level of the national bargain, policy decisions involve government, political parties, national-level unions, and other peak organizations. The national level is the primary level for consideration of the privatization program because it is the fulcrum of interrelationships among bargains taking place at the other levels. It is the locus of policy making that structures formal institutions via legislation, and this is the focus of negotiations among national-level peak organizations and political coalitions.

It is at the national level that programs for privatization, affecting all regions and sectors, are made. National-level government actors fear loss of office from voters who have been directly or indirectly affected by the distributional outcomes from privatization. They have the power to influence and implement policy, but face the difficulty of trying to balance the interests of contending social groups with the overall goal of facilitating growth in the Polish economy. In a system in which parties are new and changing rapidly, there is little party loyalty among constituencies. As a result, legislators respond a great deal to the shifting demands of various groups, sometimes even to the point of opposing their own programs and voting out their own governments.

2.3 Enterprise-level bargaining

Micro-bargaining takes place at the level of the state-owned enterprise, among trade unions, workers councils, managers, local-government bodies, and the Ministry of Ownership Transformation. The varieties of structures that the micro-bargain may take are numerous in accordance with such factors as the size of the state-owned enterprise, its sector, and its profitability. The greater the variety of options available, the more likely that there will be a good "fit" for a particular entity's privatization. When the right to initiate privatization and to choose among privatization options, that is, to exercise strategic initiative, has been decentralized to the level of the firm, the result has been a great deal of privatization activity. When this right has been denied, the result has often been conflict articulated at the national level by peak organizations such as labor unions or employers' organizations.

The players in all three bargaining games struggle over property rights to state-owned enterprises (SOEs).[3] They do this according to particular interests and particular strengths. The interests created by the complexity and particularity of property rights structures in Poland are partly due to history; institutions tend to have some continuity through time.[4] The Polish institutions continue to reflect the legacy of the pre-1989 political economy. In 1989 the removal of the Communist Party from power meant that reform programs of the 1980s, which had been adopted but never allowed to function, were given a new lease on economic life. Reforms like the 1981 Law on State Enterprises granted a great degree of self-governance to SOEs but were largely not implemented (Kaminski, 1992) because of the political stranglehold of the communist government.[5] With the collapse of the Communist Party in 1989, the institutional structure came to fit better the intention of the 1980s reforms with a good deal of control lying in the hands of workers' councils (Levitas, 1992; Poznanski, 1993). Following from the reforms of the 1980s, component rights to use, alienation, and profits that make up a property rights bundle would be divided between a government entity, the workers' councils, and enterprise managers. The location of the claims of governments to property rights in state-owned enterprises varied from firm to firm as rights to "profit" were given to the founding body, generally at the level of either the voivod (local) or ministry (national).

The rights to control were distributed between managers and workers' councils. Specifically, the workers' councils had the right to dismiss managers and to participate to a degree in firm-level decisions. This gave labor a certain degree of power in determining the course of a particular firm's reform and the disposition of its profits into investment and wages. These rights, though important, fell short of full "ownership" because they were nontransferable.

Yet the rights conferred to labor via the workers' councils are only a part of the story of labor's strength in Poland. The legacy of Solidarity has helped to maintain labor's theoretically privileged position defined under State Socialism, so that it has become an intrinsic part of the new political economy (Ost, 1992). Labor law grants a good deal of preference to labor

---

[3]The relevant groups participating in these bargains are numerous and complex. For example, the parliament after October 1990 with its thirty parties was certainly not a unitary actor. Labor with the numerous factions in Solidarity and their conflict with OPZZ can hardly be considered a unified entity. Yet, for the sake of this discussion, assume that they are unified because, indeed, certain generalizations can be made about these agglomerations of specific factions.

[4]Even though a dramatic shift toward new economic structures was made in 1989, the persistence of institutional structures from the prior period limited both the means and the extent to which the government could alter those structures. This corresponds to the "institutional path dependence" described by Douglass North (1991).

[5]Specifically, I refer to the Law on State Enterprises of September 23, 1981.

and provides institutional guarantees of its strength. Indeed, in the post-communist period labor law has been strengthened in its favor. The current labor code formalizes requirements that SOEs pay the salaries of union organizers and provide them office space and sometimes telephone and facsimile reimbursement. The privileged institutional position of labor unions is guaranteed by law and strengthened by its institutionalization in the social milieu. Strike activity in Poland has been extremely high in the post–centrally planned period (see Table 8.1) and the influence of labor far outstrips the influence of capital in the formal and informal political arenas.

Managers were left in a weakened position relative to labor as a result of the property rights changes of 1989. Although they were actively given a greater degree of operational independence with regard to the state bureaucracy and their firms, at the same time their rights to exercise control were severely attenuated. This did not mean that the reforming and restructuring activity of managers was completely constrained by relations with workers' councils: This ability varied from firm to firm, and in some cases the relationship worked to ensure that actively reforming, rather than passive, managers maintained their positions (Dabrowski et al., 1993). Nevertheless, the reduction of the labor force in overstaffed SOEs and alignment of production costs with receivables remain highly politicized by the institutional structures of labor relations.

Moreover, it was the managers who were left to deal with the most intractable problems presented by a changing economic system. For example, historical debt portfolios often endangered otherwise healthy firms. The dramatic rise in interest rates after the implementation of the Balcerowicz Plan created seemingly insoluble debt situations, often for firms that had borrowed in order to undertake restructuring, albeit with bad timing. Markets and distribution networks were disrupted early in the post-communist period, and managers were forced to adjust while taking on new tasks, such as marketing and quality control, that were not emphasized in the reform-socialist system of the 1980s.

Another group to be considered is government (parliament, president, the politically appointed staffs of ministries) who have, as mentioned above, the interest of staying in office.

Local government officials may have interests different from those of officials at the national level. For example, provincial officials may find liquidating or reducing employment levels in a local SOE to be particularly burdensome. Their network of relationships with business and labor may also give them insights and perspective on particular industries that puts them at odds with the national-level government and ministries. Indeed, in some of the most affected regions, such as the textile center of Lodz and the mining center of Katowice, local government has been

Evolving privatization bargains in Poland

Table 8.1. *Strike activity in Poland, 1989 to 1993*

Year	Number of strikes	Number of workers	Number of days lost
1989	894	304,700	602,000
1990	250	115,687	159,016
1991	305	221,547	517,647
1992	6,351	752,473	2,360,392
1993	7,443	383,222	580,429

Source: Glówny Urzad Statystyczny, Warsaw.

granted special powers in the privatization process in order both to accelerate the conclusion of deals moving toward a market economy and to redress local social costs arising from it.

In view of the institutions shaping the move toward a market system and the interest and power of various social groups, the most intractable problem in the Polish economy since 1989 has been whether and how to privatize the largest state enterprises. It is crucial to note that the inflexibility of many of these giants leaves them poorly prepared to flourish in a competitive market environment. From an economic perspective, the anachronistic and unhealthy condition of many suggests the appropriateness of their closure, but the number of workers dependent on these state-owned enterprises for livelihood, the strong institutional position of labor, and the huge state investments that these enterprises represent work against their closure.

Because the distribution of costs and benefits of shifting property rights of the large SOEs differ from those of small and medium-sized SOEs, the structure of the bargain differs. Organized labor operating in large SOEs is able to muster thousands in their struggles with government. It is more difficult for union members in small and medium SOEs employing five hundred or fewer to do so. Consequently, the enterprise-level game in the case of the largest SOEs seems to end up with government unable to privatize and labor unable to act as an agent of reform.

Indeed, the privatization of the largest SOEs, or at least their future property rights status, seems to be a key to conditions for long-term stability and rationalization at the macroeconomic level. These firms present their own particular problems for a state no longer focused on controlling the economy from the center. For these SOEs seem to be able to dodge the hard choices between profitability and bankruptcy. They are able to exploit their political muscle because they are huge employers and represent enormous public investments. As these factories are often the

215

largest employers in their regions, closing them involves considerable human suffering. Lack of a sufficiently developed low-cost housing stock and a dearth of job retraining programs leaves the future looking very bleak for these workers were they to lose their jobs.

The mass privatization option is capable of addressing only part of this problem, because it covers only the healthiest of the large firms. The majority of the largest and least healthy firms will remain publicly owned. The ability of some companies to avoid restructuring and the inability of others to find conditions for restructuring stall privatization and cost the state treasury large sums to cover their losses.

3.0 THE DEVELOPMENT OF BARGAINING/PRIVATIZATION INSTITUTIONS

I shall now review major government policy cycles from the perspective of institutional structures and bargaining that takes place within them. In order to discuss the interaction that has taken place given these structures, I divide the post-communist period into four phases: (1) the first year under Mazowiecki, (2) the Bielecki and Olszewski governments, (3) the Suchocka government, and (4) the Pawlak government.[6] Because descriptions of privatization reform programs are prolific in the literature (Mroz, 1991; Stark, 1992, among others), this history will place less emphasis on programmatic details and more emphasis on how evolution in the policy and process of privatization has meant a shift in credible bargaining structures.

3.1 The Mazowiecki government and the Balcerowicz Plan

The Balcerowicz Plan was the first major bargain regarding the restructuring of the economy. It aimed at a macroeconomic stabilization of the economy and movement of firms toward market behavior. The plan was not a privatization plan per se, but implicit in it were the assumptions that firms would start responding to market forces and be financially accountable, and the economy should be opened to trade and investment. This initial framework for the restructuring of property rights resulted from national-level bargaining mostly among technocrats and the various parties in parliament.

On one hand, this initial "enabling" bargain was not directly influenced by firm-level opinion; there was not much of an articulated trans-

---

[6]Because research for this chapter was done in early 1994, only the initial months of the Pawlak government are considered.

formation structure to which firms could respond.[7] On the other hand, this bargain was influenced greatly by relations with external organizations. The commitment of international governments and agencies to the creation of a substantial stabilization fund for Poland provided assurances as to favorable conditions for "shock treatment," thus strengthening the position of the program's proponents. These external relationships were to condition future government options. The need to maintain an IMF agreement as a condition for writing down the international debt and for access to international finances was to limit, though not necessarily dictate, the domestic options of future governments. Thus, it would greatly influence any future bargains with regard to privatization of the Polish economy.

The original strategy was to implement the Balcerowicz Plan to stabilize the monetary system rapidly. Privatization, it was assumed, could follow at a speedy clip once the macroeconomic environment was set. In January 1990 the plan was implemented; prices were liberalized, currency was made internally convertible, and credit was tightened. In the first year of the stabilization, the plan's architects waited with a glow of neoclassical expectation about them for the invisible hand of the market to do its work in creating private property rights.

A general privatization program that was passed in July 1990 emphasized "capital-based" direct sale as a method of privatization.[8] Although other options, liquidation and mass privatization, were mentioned in the program, they were only discussed briefly with the emphasis lying clearly on capital privatization. However, two things soon became apparent. First, the stabilization alone did not provide sufficient incentive for SOEs to restructure. Second, sufficient investment was not available to move privatization along via the direct sale of SOEs alone.

Indeed, within the first year the accomplishments of the Balcerowicz Program in halting hyper-inflation were auspicious, but this element of stability was hardly enough to bring in investors when the atmosphere was imbued with institutional, financial, and political uncertainties. The contraction of production that followed the stabilization, and the unravel-

[7]Indeed, this was one of the reasons that Jeffrey Sachs and the World Bank had for advocating quick movement to a system of private property: It would preempt the emergence of political opposition.

[8]Under commercialization, companies are transformed into joint-stock companies owned by the state treasury. The treasury then undertakes several methods of transferring ownership rights in corporations to private individuals. Under this approach the workers' councils are largely dissolved, but one-third of the seats on boards of directors are allocated to employee representatives. The other two-thirds of the boards of the new companies consist of representatives of the state treasury who can be drawn from many areas: institutional investors, employees or managers of other enterprises, private businesspersons, and so on.

ing of Council for Mutual Economic Assistance (CMEA) markets at the same time, made conditions particularly difficult for the restructuring of industry. Probably more important for purposes of this discussion, the contraction and initial restructuring of the economy began to make clear exactly what the game entailed for players at the micro-level.

In the period when privatization policy was emerging, strike activity was endemic in Poland. Usually the strike activity addressed the government as owner rather than the management of the particular firm or sector. Government was seen as the main player at the micro-level as its policies interfered directly with production decisions. For example, the *popiwek,* or wage control tax, limited wage rises in a time when prices were being liberalized and continued afterward. Firms were encumbered with a variety of taxes, and attempts by management to be granted recognition as independent "employers" were fraught with difficulty. It began to be clear to management that government would not relinquish influence in day-to-day firm operations. It became clear to labor that standards of living were not to be spared in the move toward a new economy. Through this time, the culture of organized labor remained strong despite the schizophrenic nature of Solidarity (as government and labor representative). Nevertheless, many workers changed to other unions. For example, the OPZZ, the communist union before 1989, grew rapidly as a result of defections from Solidarity.

Despite the conflict within and between labor organizations, institutional structures continued to give labor a good deal of de facto power. The structure of unions and the privilege the unions were accorded by socialist labor law guaranteed their continued financial health even as their members suffered financial difficulties. The pride of place accorded to labor in the legal codes was not lost in the political transition.[9]

Unions were not necessarily opposed to privatization via commercialization and capital sale. Using a sample of fifty state-owned enterprises Dabrowski, Federowicz, and Levitas (1992: 33) found that initially there was "much hope" in regard to commercialization on the part of both management and labor. The structure of commercialization bargains seemed advantageous as workers could gain wages with reduced taxation, management could gain independence, and the Ministry of Ownership Transformation (MOT) would find investors. Even with this favorable opinion, the alternative method of liquidation began to move forward, though with less publicity than was received by the more theo-

---

[9]Indeed, it was strengthened as the transition progressed, for example, on May 23, 1991, with the Ustawa 234, "o zwiazkach zawodowych and Ustawa 236, . . . o rozwiazywaniu sporow zbiorowych" ("Law on Labor Unions and Law on Collective Bargaining") (*Dziennik Ustaw,* June 26, 1991).

retically idealized form of single-investor privatization for small and medium-sized (fewer than five hundred employees) SOEs.

The two forms of liquidation, Article 19 for reasons of poor financial condition and Article 37 as a means of privatization, are quite distinct. Liquidation under Article 19 is really bankruptcy. Firms liquidated in this manner are usually in dire financial condition. The liquidation usually involves selling off property and thus a transfer of assets to private ownership so that the enterprise as such ceases to exist.

Liquidation under Article 37 is quite different and can involve strategic behavior at the firm level. The firms that choose to liquidate under Article 37 are usually in a healthy financial condition, and they usually liquidate in order to form a labor-owned enterprise (in about 80 percent of the cases). Because the initial move toward liquidation can be taken by the founding body (a branch ministry or a voivod government) or by the enterprise itself (workers' council), it takes place in a decentralized bargaining structure allowing for labor initiative and with ownership incentives for labor that can exceed those of other privatization pathways. The whole process of liquidation for privatization is negotiated between the founding body and the enterprise workers' council. Negotiation under Article 37 often remains at the local level though all agreements are subject to approval by the Ministry of Ownership Transformation.

These institutional structures articulated early in the transformation established a course for privatization. The privatization act set out various structures for achieving the goal of privatization, each with its related sets of costs and benefits. The government created these structures as policy, but it was the strength of various groups and the distribution of costs and benefits produced by these structures that determined whether the various privatization methods were ultimately pursued.

3.2 The Bielecki and Olszewski governments

After the election of an extremely fragmented parliament in the fall of 1990, legislative work on privatization seemed to move in fits and starts. Through the administrations of Krzystof Bielecki and Jan Olszewski the implementation of the privatization program remained little changed though there was a growing awareness that the laissez-faire approach of the previous year would not move the process forward rapidly.

During this time liquidation as a means for healthy firms to privatize gained significant ground. By the end of Bielecki's term as prime minister the number of projects approved exceeded three hundred. This method continued to grow during the Olszewski government, encompassing more than five hundred mostly small and medium-sized enterprises by the time the Suchocka government was formed. (See Table 8.2.)

Table 8.2. *Cumulative privatizations via Articles 19, 37, and 5*

Government	Date	Article 19		Article 37		Article 5	
		All SOEs	Large SOEs[a]	All SOEs	Large SOEs[a]	All SOEs	Large SOEs[a]
Bielecki	6-30-91	173	28	170	32	162	121
	8-31-91	283	39	273	50	183	138
	9-30-91	370	50	297	57	214	163
	11-30-91	470	58	353	69	233	176
Olszewski	12-31-91	534	64	416	82	244	184
	1-31-92	562	65	441	84	259	192
	2-29-92	589	66	466	89	268	198
	3-31-92	635	67	488	96	273	203
	4-31-92	661	69	508	100	279	208
	5-31-92	690	69	527	104	284	212
Suchocka	6-30-92	707	70	542	107	286	214
	8-31-92	757	72	611	119	290	215
	9-30-92	772	72	628	121	292	217
	10-31-92	797	78	641	127	293	218
	12-31-92	853	78	715	138	301	221
	3-31-93	911	80	750	139	313	230

[a]More than 500 employees.
Source: Ministry of Ownership Transformation.

During this period the number of SOEs commercialized for capital sale rose by fewer than one hundred, though the majority of enterprises thus transformed were large enterprises. Again, the qualitative sample findings of Dabrowski et al. (1993) are instructive. During this period management and labor became disenchanted with commercialization as it became apparent that tax breaks and wage increases were not to be expected and that the Ministry of Ownership Transformation could not be counted on to pursue buyers actively. Further, it became just as apparent that privatization via liquidation offered a better opportunity because it formalized informal property rights and gave workers a larger and more active interest in the newly privatized firm than did the other privatization options (Szumanski, 1993). And it did so within a bargaining structure that was often local in character and, thus, more transparent to those with the greatest stakes.

The weakest point of the privatization program continued to be the problem of large industrial SOEs. The problem of collective action on this level was daunting and was a factor occluding possibilities for large privatization via Article 37 liquidation; it is difficult to organize several thousand workers in one enterprise to pursue an employee buyout – free riders usually exist in large groups producing communal goods. Collective action, organizing a group toward obtaining a common interest, is easier at the level of small and medium-sized firms, because exclusive benefits are more likely to result: It is easier for the individual to estimate the chances of the industries' survival and the benefits that she would reap, and it is easier for the group to accrue the capital and solidarity necessary to take over the enterprise. Organizing workers to take over the gargantuan steel mills, shipyards, and coal mines is more difficult as the prospects of recompense are smaller and less clear.

No less daunting than the collective action problem is the amount of capital represented by these SOEs. Their purchase requires a commitment of sizeable proportions for any investor. With respect to the ability of workers to give the down payment necessary for leasing, an interviewee succinctly put it "Huge properties, small salaries."

The Mass Privatization Program (Powszechny Program Prywatyzacja) was drafted during this period under Bielecki, and it represented a potential step forward toward resolution of the problem of the largest SOEs. This program aimed to disperse shares in a group of approximately four hundred SOEs to all citizens (with a larger percentage reserved for employees) to get around the problem of lack of capital and at the same time to give workers and others in society interests in rapidly concluding a politically painful portion of the economic transition. Selection and commercialization of enterprises for participation in this program gradually got under way.[10] It is significant, however, that little progress was made in getting this program through parliament at a time when the heavy sectors for which it was intended exhibited poor performance.

During the Olszewski government the fragmentation in the parliament hampered any efforts to pursue a clear economic program. Although in this period there was often much emphasis on financial reform, little progress was made in the building of the institutions needed in this crucial area. Privatization similarly languished. The government fell with a vote of no confidence by the parliament in the late spring of 1992.

Throughout this period, however, the enabling bargain between international institutions and the Polish government was sustained. Negotiations were often difficult; the Polish government's room for maneuver in the realm of macroeconomic indicators and pay raises to public employees was severely restricted by IMF conditionality. Yet the parties at this table always seemed to manage to come to agreement.

---

[10]These commercializations are *not* included in Table 8.2.

3.3 *The Suchocka government*

After a failed attempt by Waldemar Pawlak to form a government, the government of Hanna Suchocka was approved by the Sejm on July 11, 1992. Under the Suchocka government, the bargaining structures resulting from the institutions set forth in the privatization program became clearer. The parliament was still fragmented, and there were legislative delays, yet programs began to go forward. In particular, despite many setbacks, the mass privatization finally came close to becoming a reality, as the revised legislation creating the National Investment Funds was belatedly approved following an initial defeat in parliament, and a date was set for its implementation. Suchocka also managed to begin to forge a framework within which government, employers, organizations, and management could increase cooperation in the privatization of SOEs.

At the outset, the Suchocka government was faced with a strikewave. Particularly serious were the strikes in the Miedz Copperworks and the FSM auto plant. The strikes were over wage demands, and, like many other such actions in the large industries, they addressed the government as owner. The strike wave made further apparent the necessity of negotiating with labor over the future of the largest SOEs and the workers employed by them. It also underscored the vulnerability of a government playing the dual role of state and employer. The response of the relatively new Suchocka government was to refuse labor demands, but to set in motion, on July 21, wide-ranging discussions with Solidarity over the creation of a "social pact." The participants in the discussions were broadened to include a wider range of unions and representatives of producer/employer groups, particularly the Confederation of Polish Employers (the Konfederacja Pracodawcow Polskich, KPP), and the National Chambers of Commerce (Krajowa Izba Gospodarcza, KIG) though the latter would cede their seat to the KPP as the discussions progressed. It became an effort to create a viable peak agreement to rationalize national-level bargaining and to reduce labor unrest.

The negotiations for the State Enterprise Pact were concluded on February 22, 1993. Essentially, the agreement represented an attempt to restructure the national-level game toward a situation in which the dominant strategy in bargains over privatization and restructuring at the enterprise level would also be cooperation (corporatism, if you will) regardless of the size of the SOE involved. Indeed, during the Suchocka government the growth in the number of commercialized enterprises was very slight, while the number of liquidations, particularly for small and medium SOEs, continued to grow. (See Table 8.2.) The Enterprise Pact would create a structure for privatization of the larger SOEs, a structure that was designed to produce incentives for labor to surmount the collective action

222

obstacles in these larger state-owned enterprises as well. The pact did not represent an optimal outcome for any of the competing interests in the negotiation, but rather was a compromise in which all who came to the table brought something away.

In beginning the negotiations on the State Enterprise Pact, Suchocka, or at least her negotiators, seemed to understand that dissatisfaction among workers did not stem from opposition to privatization itself. Rather, most workers seem to understand that enterprises must behave differently in a market economy and that changes would have to be made. The dissatisfaction came as much from the process of privatization itself. The lengthy process burdened by bureaucratic red tape often killed privatization initiatives before they began (Kalus, 1993). Furthermore, there was often a lack of any initiative at all from managers. Three years after the political transition in many sectors and regions there was no real sense that anyone had an economic plan.

Negotiations proceeded along three lines: privatization, enterprise finance, and labor relations. The solution for privatization was to force strategic behavior upon the workforce. Self-selection prior to the pact was an option only in the liquidation proceeding, and, for reasons mentioned, this path is difficult for large enterprises especially because of the collective action problem. Under the State Enterprise Pact, firms in a healthy financial condition would have three months to choose their own privatization path from among the options available. If they do not make a decision in this period, then they would be subject to commercialization. This was favorable both to labor in giving them strategic opportunity and for government in giving them the power to review and, if necessary, to force the rapid selection of privatization paths. Further, it demonstrated commitment to moving forward on difficult cases of privatization.

Under the pact the employees would receive 10 percent of shares in the company free of charge, and some of the enterprise profits could be used to purchase stock for employees as well. The pact would make leasing easier by allowing for payment of the minimum capital contribution in installments. It would guarantee employees one-third of the seats on the new company's board, thus compensating for loss of control rights in SOEs. Also, the wage controls (*popiwek*) would be abolished. Some of the costs of transformation would be reduced by simplifying valuation and eschewing the use of consultants for this purpose.

Debt relief was also a major part of the pact. Although the pact did not offer a debt write-off, it did set up a program through which reforming enterprises will be likely to receive special assistance in reducing their financial burdens via rescheduling, "debt for equity" swaps, and forgiveness. The internationally provided Stabilization Fund (U.S.$1 billion) that was never used would be converted to a financial reform fund along with

World Bank loans, as long as the international-level bargain continued successfully (i.e., if agreement with IMF were concluded). Thus, the international-level bargain once again proved enabling in the creation of this program.

In the matter of labor relations, the Pact on State Enterprises allowed for collective bargaining over working conditions (length of workday, for example) and layoffs. It also required employers to create a "guarantee fund" for employees that would pay workers for at least three months in the event that the enterprise enters bankruptcy (or is liquidated under Article 19).

The package of laws that make up the Pact on State Enterprises and Their Transformation was introduced into the parliament. Unfortunately, the particular interests in parliament did not allow the Suchocka government to see the pact's implementation. At the end of May, Solidarity members of parliament put forward a vote of no confidence in their own government. President Walesa exercised his constitutional option, disbanding parliament and calling elections. The summer of 1993 was a period of great uncertainty, and though work continued on drafting legislation for the pact, its test in the parliament had to await new elections.

3.4 The Pawlak government

The elections of September 1993 resulted in a majority of seats in the parliament being assigned to the United Democratic Left and the Peasant Party, both representing reform-socialist interests. Furthermore, the KLD and Conservative parties, whose proposals to alter the labor code earned them "anti-union" status, won no seats in the Sejm, while the OPZZ trade union alone seated sixty-three deputies. In his first major speech, Pawlak emphasized that the reforms would continue and that sacrifices would need to be made, though his privatization minister denied any desire to be known as the "great privatizer" in Polish history.

The pact moved slowly on the legislative agenda, perhaps because the government did not have as much incentive to increase the power of the Ministry of Ownership Transformation as the ultimate arbiter in a major push toward privatization. Given the variance in interests of a "left" government, emphasizing the socioeconomic well-being of labor, the pact as negotiated gave unwanted powers and responsibilities to government. Meanwhile, strike activity did not cease. Indeed, Pawlak was faced by strikes in the mining industry, mass marches by Solidarity, and national strikewaves in March 1994. The resolution of the dilemma of the largest state-owned enterprises came no closer to realization, although plans were being considered for liquidation and attrition in certain hard-hit sectors. Labor influence had increased after it was clearly expressed at the ballot box. In 1994 it appeared that the most likely course for privatization given the then current institutional structures was inertia.

4.0 LABOR STRENGTH AND CONFIDENCE IN PRIVATIZATION

Throughout these successive post-1989 governments, the strength of labor has had to be confronted by policy makers who desire to move the largest SOEs toward private ownership. The period during which the government had the most power to shape the bargaining structures seems to have been under Mazowiecki and Bielecki with the design of privatization and stabilization policy. With the Act on the Privatization of State-Owned Enterprises, certain institutional paths were delineated, and the course of the development of bargaining structures was broadly structured. The act provided for the various methods of privatization including capital-based privatization, mass privatization, and liquidation.

The overall design of the Privatization Act emphasizing capital privatization demonstrated more concern for neoclassical economic theory and its emphasis on individual ownership than for the reality of institutional structures and the power they conferred on labor. The preference for capital privatization ignored the property rights and interests of labor and management that they would certainly desire to formalize in the new system, and it glossed over the degree to which any new owner's property rights would be attenuated by a labor code highly favorable to the interests of workers.

The most common form of privatization, liquidation via Article 37 or leasing, allows for strategic behavior at the level of the firm. This, more than anything, has allowed it to emerge as the leading mode of privatization.[11] Leasing tends to be a strategic option because it is often initiated at the firm level and payoffs are such that the firm usually ends up being owned in whole or in majority part by management or labor. It is a means of converting the de facto property rights accorded workers under the post-1989 system into de jure private property rights. It is also strategic because often the initiative to undertake a liquidation for the purpose of

---

[11]To begin Article 37 liquidation enterprise councils may initiate negotiations or must approve initiation of proceedings. When negotiations with the founding body are concluded, the Ministry of Ownership Transformation is then brought in to see if valuation is acceptable. In Article 37, on modes other than leasing, outside buyers may be recruited. In these cases – depending on valuation, of course – the enterprise can be purchased, transferred as a contribution to a new corporation usually with a domestic or foreign investor as a partner. However, by far the most frequent liquidation consists of a lease of ten years after which there may or may not be a transfer of property rights to the lessee.

225

privatization comes from within the firm. Management and labor in effect are establishing the bargaining agenda.

The success of privatization by liquidation can only be examined in relation to the problems involved with the other two methods: The lack of individual investors, the uncertainty lent to private investment by labor's power, the high transaction costs involved in preparing capital privatization, the lack of transparency due to underspecified Ministry of Ownership Transformation policy, and the parliamentary slowdown of the Mass Privatization Program's progress are a few of privatization's pains. However, the positive aspects of liquidation via Article 37 are also crucial to understanding the success of this method, not least among them the obvious advantages it provides for both bargaining parties.

The success of the liquidation track is aided by the fact that it is also a more decentralized structure. Because it requires participation of the founding body, many of these negotiations involve a local entity (usually the Voivod). (See Table 8.3.) The participants in a decentralized bargain often know one another and have a direct interest in, and knowledge of, the enterprise. In these negotiations the role of the Ministry of Ownership Transformation is to approve the deal after it has been crafted. It is thus a more decentralized method of privatization and one in which personal relationships can be used to advantage.

In the larger SOEs, the enterprise-level bargain is structured differently; privatization via employee/management buyout is not a viable policy option despite the fact that the strength of labor at this level is even greater than at the level of small and medium-sized businesses. For large industries, there is little decentralization and few strategic opportunities at the firm level in matters of privatization. The institutional structures for privatization of large firms – indeed, the futures of these firms – are murky, given this discrepancy, and I hypothesize that there is a lack of confidence in government commitment to privatization at this level. Further, I posit that data from interenterprise debt markets reflect the waning confidence of the market in the face of labor strength and government indecisiveness on privatization policy.

Interenterprise debt (IED) trading is a relatively recent phenomenon in Poland. The lack of credit evaluations and capital markets to provide information on firms and the lack of rapid legal means of collection enforcement has led to a situation in which many large firms are financing their continued existence with the money of other firms. A common means of avoiding bankruptcy is nonpayment of debts to other firms.

In Poland as a whole there is not a great problem with interenterprise debt according to Rostowski (1993). Although the amount of IED may be comparable to that in other European countries as he claims, the evidence suggests that this debt is concentrated in particular large industries,

Table 8.3. *Liquidation via Article 37: Local versus state as founding body (for SOEs in good condition), 1990 to 1993*

Year	Month	Number of SOEs privatized	State ministry as founder	Local government as founder
1990	Dec.	35	12	23
1991	Jan.	39	6	33
	Feb.	23	4	19
	Mar.	16	3	13
	Apr.	27	6	21
	May	22	11	11
	June	20	9	11
	July	54	20	34
	Aug.	31	13	18
	Sep.	34	9	25
	Oct.	34	13	21
	Nov.	28	14	14
	Dec.	56	24	32
1992	Jan.	28	10	18
	Feb.	25	12	13
	Mar.	28	12	16
	Apr.	25	8	17
	May	20	7	13
	June	17	7	10
	July	30	18	12
	Aug.	15	5	10
	Sep.	13	5	8
	Oct.	11	7	4
	Nov.	15	13	2
	Dec.	52	26	33
1993	Jan.	10	6	4
	Feb.	7	0	7
	Mar.	16	6	10
	Apr.	15	8	7
	May	12	6	6
	June	17	6	11
	July	13	4	9
	Aug.	4	1	3

Source: Ministry of Ownership Transformation.

which further endangers their very existence. An example is the situation in which many power companies find themselves. The predicament of nonpayment by some of the largest industrial power users has been mentioned elsewhere (Slay, 1992). In the fall of 1993, many power companies in Warsaw claimed that it might be necessary to halt the provision of heat and power due to the nonpayment of arrears.

In Poland the trading of IED on secondary markets began in 1991. The slow pace at which such claims could be enforced through the court system was probably an encouraging factor in the development of these markets. The prices of secondary debt give an indication of confidence in the government's ever successfully shifting the ownership of these SOEs, imposing hard budget constraints, and giving potential viability to enterprises that are not competitive in their present institutional situation. After all, the purchase of debt and the price paid for that debt represent a degree of confidence of recovering from the debtor firm which is related to an enterprise's future in navigating a market system. The data from secondary debt markets, therefore, reflect the level of confidence in the privatization and reform of the heaviest industry.

Interestingly enough, there are several points at which the price for secondary debt dropped to below 50 percent. These points coincide with the mining strikes in July 1992 and the strike waves after Suchocka's election, the general strike of December 1992 that paralyzed the Silesian mines, an initial defeat of the Law on National Investment Funds (the Mass Privatization Program) and the following low-confidence period, and the no-confidence vote on Suchocka, the subsequent election campaign, and the victory of a government of the Left. Indeed, if debt prices are regressed on a variable indicating the exercise of labor power and extreme legislative uncertainties, a statistically significant negative relationship is found. (See the appendix to this chapter.) The results suggest that the market perceived government's commitment to the privatization of large SOEs as weak in the face of labor flexing its muscle.

5.0 CONCLUSION

A discussion of bargaining over privatization cannot hope to be comprehensive in detail. The micro-bargains are extremely numerous, and meta-bargains are obscure. (The number of actual privatizations concluded has exceeded two thousand as of this writing, and negotiations with international financial institutions are confidential.) The preceding discussion is meant to show how institutional structures have been affected at each period and over time moved to reflect labor power in the largest SOEs.

228

These structures, designed to move Poland toward a system of private property rights, have been more successful when they are consistent with existing property rights interests. The reality in Poland is that labor holds a significant degree of institutional and political power. Yet, in precisely the areas of the economy in which they hold the most power, in the large enterprises, there is little opportunity for strategic labor activity in the realm of privatization. Consequently, large enterprise privatization in Poland falls short of full credibility. It is probable that little progress will be made in changing the ownership of the largest SOEs until a more constructive institutional framework for accommodating Labor's interests is developed.

APPENDIX: POLITICAL EVENTS AND THE PRICE OF INTERENTERPRISE DEBT

The dependent variable, debt price (%PRICE), is the average of weekly prices paid for heavy industry debt expressed as a percentage of face value of the debt. The data cover the period from June 2, 1992, to March 30, 1994, and come from transactions completed by Poland's four major interenterprise debt auction firms. The independent variable of interest is EVENTS, a five-point scale of political and economic events relevant to privatiziation. High values of EVENTS were assigned to the occurrence of stikewaves, changes in government, and specific events contributing to uncertainty about the privatization program, such as the announced delay of the Mass Privatization Program and the State Enterprise Pack. Although EVENTS is quite crude, especially as it is not a true ordinal scale, and therefore likely to involve measurement error, it should provide a conservative test of the null hypotheses of no relationship between interenterprise debt prices and labor and political events relevant to the credibility of privatization.

%PRICE was regressed on the constructed scale of labor and political events, EVENTS, and a time trend variable (TIME). The results obtained are shown in the accompanying table.

The results shown in the table suggest that the null hypothesis of no relationship between average sale price and political events should be rejected at the 5 percent level of significance. Substantively, the estimated coefficients indicate that, after taking account of the gradual decline over the period (approximately three percentage points every ten weeks), each point of political activity reduced the average sale price by about two percentage points. Thus, in any given week, political activity could swing the price by about eight percentage points. Similar findings resulted from estimating the model with weighted regression based on trading volumes.

229

	Dependent variable: % Price
Event	
Coefficient	−0.024
(Standard error)	(0.0098)
[One-tailed significance]	[0.009]
Time	
Coefficient	−0.003
(Standard error)	(0.00048)
[One-tailed significance]	[0.000]
Constant	
Coefficient	0.86
(Standard error)	(0.039)
[One-tailed significance]	[0.000]
R^2	0.34
Number of observations	93
Durbin-Watson Statistic	2.15

REFERENCES

Biersteker, Thomas J., "International Financial Negotiations and Adjustment Bargaining," in Thomas J. Biersteker, editor, *Dealing with Debt: International Financial Negotiations and Adjustment Bargaining* (Boulder, CO: Westview Press, 1993), 1–15.

Campbell, Robert W., *The Socialist Economies in Transition: A Primer on Semireformed Systems* (Bloomington, IN: Indiana University Press, 1991).

Dabrowski, Janusz, Michal Federowicz, Tytus Kaminski, and Jan Szomburg, "Privatization of Polish State-Owned Enterprises: Progress, Barriers, Initial Effects," in Janusz Lewandowski and Jan Szomburg, editors, *Series on Economic Transformation*, Working Paper No. 33 (Warsaw-Gdansk: Gdansk Institute for Market Economics, 1993).

Dabrowski, Janusz, Michal Federowicz, and Anthony Levitas, "State-Owned Enterprises in Their Second Year of Economic Transformation: Research Findings," in Janusz Lewandowski and Jan Szomburg, editors, *Series on Economic Transformation*, Working Paper No. 27 (Warsaw-Gdansk: Gdansk Institute for Market Economics, 1992).

Dell, Sidney, "Stabilization: The Political Economy of Overkill," in John Williamson, editor, *IMF Conditionality* (Cambridge, MA: MIT Press, 1983), 17–45.

Eggertsson, Thrainn, *Economic Behavior and Institutions* (Cambridge: Cambridge University Press, 1990).

Kalus, Adam, "Bariery Prywatyzacji," *Rzeczpospolita* 157 (3501), July 8 (1993).

Kaminski, Bartlomiej, *The Collapse of State Socialism: The Case of Poland* (Princeton, NJ: Princeton University Press, 1991).

Levitas, Anthony, "The Trials and Tribulations of Property Reform in Poland: From State-Led to Firm-Led Privatization, 1989–1991," paper presented at

Conference on Political Economy of Privatization and Public Enterprise in Eastern Europe, Asia and Latin America, Brown University, April 24–5 (1992).

Mroz, Bogdan, "Poland's Economy in Transition to Private Ownership," *Soviet Studies* 43: 4 (1991), 677–88.

North, Douglass, "Institutions," *Journal of Economic Perspectives* 5: 1 (1991), 97–112.

Ost, David. "Labor and Social Transition," *Problems of Communism* 41: May–June (1992), 48–51.

Poznanski, Kazimierz, "Restructuring of Property Rights in Poland: A Study in Evolutionary Economics," *East European Politics and Societies* 7: 3 (1993), 395–421.

Putnam, Robert D., "Diplomacy and Domestic Politics: The Logic of Two-Level Games," *International Organization* 42: 3 (1988), 427–60.

Rostowski, Jacek, "The Inter-enterprise Debt Explosion in the Former Soviet Union: Causes, Consequences, Cures," *Communist Economics and Economic Transformation* 5: 2 (1993), 131–60.

Slay, Ben, "The Banking Crisis and Economic Reform in Poland," *RFE/RL Research Report* 1: 23, June 5 (1992), 33–40.

Stark, David, "Path Dependence and Privatization Strategies in East Central Europe," *East European Politics and Societies* 6: 1 (Winter 1992), 17–54.

Stiglitz, Joseph, "The Design of Financial Systems for the Newly Emerging Democracies of Eastern Europe," Institute for Policy Reform, Working Paper Series, September (1991).

Szumanski, Andrzej, "Companies with Employee Participation as a Form of Privatization of State Enterprises in Poland," paper presented at the Conference on Privatization and Socioeconomic Policy in Central and Eastern Europe, Krakow, Poland, October 18–21 (1993).

Comment on "Institutional Structures, Labor Interests, and Evolving Privatization Bargains in Poland"

BARTLOMIEJ KAMINSKI

Lorene Allio provides a thorough and detailed analysis of Polish privatization after the emergence of the Solidarity-led government. Few would quarrel with her main message that little progress has been achieved so far in privatizing giant state-owned enterprises (SOEs). Instead of pointing out areas of broad agreement, I explore some issues that are either not covered by Allio or have been given too little emphasis. More specifically, I argue that (1) there was nothing unique about privatization in Poland, (2) the legacy of the Solidarity trade union had limited impact on the privatization process (much more important was the legacy of the last communist government-led privatization effort), (3) there were three rather than four phases in the privatization process after the collapse of communism, and (4) frustrating as a slow privatization of large SOEs may be, it has limited relevance for the transition to a market-based democracy.

1.0 IS ANYTHING UNIQUE ABOUT PRIVATIZATION IN POLAND?

In contrast to dominant commentators who either excessively focus on techniques of privatization or pay too much attention to public attitudes toward privatization, Allio seeks to link developments in privatization with broadly defined domestic and international circumstances. The latter comprises interaction between government and multilateral financial institutions. Domestic circumstances include institutional structures inherited from the political evolution in the 1980s, shaped by the struggle between the authorities and a parallel society organized around Solidarity. Within this group, the author introduces an analytically useful distinction between national and enterprise levels, each characterized by its unique bargaining structure over property rights. The privatization is conceptualized as outcomes of bargaining occurring within and between

232

these levels. Allio attributes the little progress achieved in privatizing giant SOEs to labor's holding significant institutional and political power.

Had Poland been a laggard among economies in transition from central planning, one could have looked at initial conditions, that is, those prevailing on the eve of the collapse of communism, for explanations of a different privatization path. Yet, a cursory examination of privatization in other post-communist countries would also show a relatively rapid transfer of property rights over small medium-sized SOEs to the private sector, and enormous difficulties encountered in privatizing large SOEs, the jewels in central planners' crowns. The only country that scores higher than Poland is probably the Czech Republic, although it is doubtful as their large SOEs still await substantial restructuring. One has yet to see whether investment funds will fulfill expectations and improve corporate governance (Shafik, 1994). All other countries would be ranked either at the same level or below that in Poland (for a ranking by the European Bank for Reconstruction and Development, see *The Economist,* December 3, 1994: 27). Thus, factors other than a unique set of initial conditions seem to offer explanation.

Yet this conclusion does not necessarily hold when other considerations are brought to the fore. Consider, for instance, the following question: Why is Poland not at the forefront of the privatization of large SOEs? After all, Poland was the first to launch a stabilization-cum-transformation program that effectively terminated central planning based on the economy of shortages. Notwithstanding differences in various details and implementation strategies, all other programs successfully implemented in post-communist countries have drawn heavily on the Polish program. The 1991 Czechoslovak program was similar, but its institutional component was different in putting a heavy emphasis on mass privatization. In this context, one may argue that differences in the initial conditions between Czechoslovakia and Poland, with the former having had no legacy of strong independent trade unions, enabled the Czechoslovak authorities to implement their bold mass privatization program. They did not face a credible political opposition at the enterprise level, nor were they bound by earlier legislation granting significant formal powers to workers' councils. I argue later that the difference in terms of firms' behavior, which is the most important criterion, is supposition.

2.0 THE LEGACY OF SOLIDARITY

The chapter begins with the comment that the irony of the Solidarity government's radical transformation program was that the reform "road was set to run directly through labor's garden." The implication is that Solidarity was a trade union and that dismantling of whatever was left in

Poland from central planning was against the interests of labor. Allio partly destroys the case for her thesis, however, by arguing that privatization in small and medium-sized enterprises has "progressed at an impressively rapid rate."

In hindsight, communist officials who argued during the 1980–1 upheaval that Solidarity was a political movement were right. The Solidarity program called for the implementation of industrial democracy based on worker participation and territorial self-government. This was clearly a direct challenge to the major institutional pillar of communism, one-party rule, although Solidarity activists rejected this claim at the time out of fear of Moscow's intervention.

Solidarity in the late 1980s, however, was different from that in the 1980–1 period; the ideas of workers' democracy were long gone and forgotten. Around 1986, after a full political amnesty, it had lost much of its support. Although the strikes in 1988, which had led to the roundtable negotiations, prompted many to announce a grand comeback of Solidarity, these were not strike leaders who negotiated a democratic pact with the communist authorities. The rhetoric of roundtable agreements was admittedly reminiscent of earlier Solidarity demands, but then nobody anticipated that a couple of months later Poland would have a democratically elected non-communist government. In terms of reform measures needed to revive the economy, the dividing line did not cut across the roundtable: there was a consensus that nothing short of overhauling the administrative economic system would work.

It was not a labor union that "redirected the road of Polish politics," as Allio puts it. The limited free national elections of 1989 and later free elections to local governments in early 1990 were the last two events that had witnessed political mobilization around Solidarity banners. These were not trade union issues that topped the political agenda; their common denominator was the rejection of Soviet-style socialism. And among those appointed to the Mazowiecki cabinet there were no trade union activists per se.

The above comments apply mainly to Allio's national-level bargaining. What about enterprise-level bargaining? She refers to several studies arguing that with the collapse of party rule the 1980s workers' council reforms had become meaningful at last. Indeed, the first year of the stabilization-cum-transformation program witnessed the emergence of a tripolar power structure in SOEs including workers' councils, enterprise managers, and the government entity (the so-called founding organ).

The power of workers' councils in the new post-collapse political economy has quickly evaporated, however. It has not come painlessly, as large numbers of strikes, evidenced in the chapter, clearly demonstrate. The stabilization-cum-transformation program has completely redefined the rules of the game by liberalizing prices and the foreign trade regime, and by introducing a de facto current account convertibility of the Polish currency. Contrary to earlier expectations, many SOEs have quickly adapted to new circumstances. For instance, a spectacular export expansion to OECD markets in 1990–1 was driven by the state sector. In these successful enterprises neither managers nor workers' councils were against privatization. Not surprisingly, the problem was with those firms that experienced problems in readjustment. But this is not unique to Poland – with or without the legacy of Solidarity, privatization of existing assets would obviously remain a contentious and politically difficult issue.

3.0 VICISSITUDES OF THE PRIVATIZATION PROCESS

Allio provides a very extensive discussion of legal details of the privatization process as well as its political ramifications under successive post-communist governments. Although I agree with the general thrust of her analysis, I would like to explore at some length two issues: (1) the phases of the privatization process, and (2) factors accountable for downplaying the issue of "large" privatization during the first stages of the transition in the 1990–1 period.

Instead of proposing a four-phase periodization as developed by Allio, I would break down the 1989–95 period into three phases including the Mazowiecki government period (1989–90), the post-Solidarity governments period (1991–3), and the leftist coalition government (1993–5). There are clear-cut differences between privatization policies pursued in these periods. In 1989–90 the privatization was overshadowed by other more pressing economic challenges, although the groundwork for the process was set up. The 1990–3 period witnessed a very rapid privatization of small and medium-sized SOEs, as well as significant strides in privatization of larger SOEs, whereas during the last phase the process was stalled.

The program implemented by the Mazowiecki government was criticized for paying too little attention to institutional issues including privatization. There were some valid reasons for downplaying privatization. First, privatization became a politically explosive issue because of the so-called nomenklatura appropriation of existing assets made possible by a legal framework introduced by the last communist government. Although this privatization effort was initially applauded by dissident intellectuals as the preferred solution over a self-managed system, it was widely condemned for allowing the former nomenklatura to plunder state-owned assets. Second, because of hyperinflation in the second half of 1989, macroeconomic stabilization and opening the economy to competition crowded out all other issues. As the economic system was significantly decentralized as a result of reform measures implemented in the 1980s, the Polish reformers could count on the ability of SOEs to adapt to a new domestic environment. In hindsight, they were right as many SOEs successfully reoriented and expanded their sales to the West.

As for privatization, the initial inclination of the government was to go along the path of capital privatization fashioned after the British model. Given the absence of capital markets, this did not promise to be a fast track for transferring property rights over existing assets. However, there were two major events (which can be only indirectly attributed to the Mazowiecki cabinet) with implications for the privatization process. The first was a decision to transfer ownership over small firms and other assets to local governments, which have played a major role in their privatization. The second was the law on privatization, which essentially shelved any notion of mass privatization.

The next period covers the three successive cabinets of Bielecki, Olszewski, and Suchocka. Overall, it was characterized by a consistent, pragmatic policy of privatization with a well-defined goal to enhance competition and microeconomic efficiency. Simultaneously, the focus was on hammering out the details of a large enterprise privatization scheme originally developed by Janusz Lewandowski, who was appointed Minister of Privatization. The program was finally cleared in the last days of the Suchocka cabinet.

Privatization came to a screeching halt under the Pawlak government. Although government officials argued that the actual value of assets sold to the private sector was larger than ever before, the number of enterprises privatized dramatically declined. The government seemed to have ignored an important lesson from the experience with privatization in other countries that enhancing efficiency rather than maximizing short-term government revenues should be the primary consideration (Kikeri, Nellis, and Shirley, 1992: 44). Bowing to the pressures of his anti-market political constituency, Prime Minister Pawlak shelved the privatization program for more than a year.

Thus, with the notable exception of the latest Left-coalition government, the privatization policy was consistently implemented despite well-known problems succinctly captured in a popular Polish definition of privatization: "the sale of state enterprises that no one owns, with no known value, to people with no money." On the other hand, considering that Poland is a medium-income country, with limited foreign investor interest, weak capital markets, and low regulatory capacity, it is surprising, however, that so little effort was put to other methods of privatizing management.

4.0 DOES IT REALLY MATTER WHETHER LARGE SOEs ARE PRIVATIZED?

The question addressed in this concluding section of my comment goes beyond issues raised in Allio's chapter. The fear of restoration of communism has fueled many arguments in favor of privatization. Allio quotes Jeffrey Sachs, but this view was also shared by many observers in Poland and other post-communist countries. For instance, it is argued that the transition in Russia is irreversible thanks to the success of the privatization program there. In hindsight, as far as Poland is concerned, these views seem ill-founded. The victory of parties with roots in communist Poland in the last election did not result in the reversal of economic reforms. It is only a matter of sheer speculation that they would not have won had large SOEs been privatized. Thus, the privatization for the sake of cementing the foundations of a new capitalist order does not make sense.

The striking similarities in privatization outcomes throughout most reforming post-communist countries suggest that too great a rush to include in the privatization package large, probably inherently inefficient, SOEs could destabilize the transition. Consider that the major reason that they still await privatization is that turning them into profitable companies remains a highly uncertain prospect. The alternative would be bankruptcies with massive unemployment and potential for political instabilities. Paradoxically, massive privatization in former Czechoslovakia proves the case. Despite significant strides in transferring property rights over state assets to the public, there were no significant increases in unemployment or in competition faced by SOEs, because significant restructuring of these SOEs is yet to take place.

The experience of Poland (and of many other post-communist countries) with privatization seems to suggest the limited progress in privatizing socialist giants has not affected the pace of transition to a market economy in any meaningful way. As highly respected Stanford development economist Anne O. Krueger reminds us, the growth in economies undergoing adjustment "has taken place primarily through the emergence of new activities, not through the adaptation of older ones" (Krueger, 1992: 221). She also warns that excessive preoccupation with privatization diverts capital and policy attention "from the more important problem of creating new earnings streams" (222). All in all, creating a competition-enabling environment with free entry to private operators strikes me as a much more important task than privatizing large SOEs – the challenge may be to close them rather than to privatize them.

REFERENCES

Kikeri, Sunita, John R. Nellis, and Mary M. Shirley, *Privatization: The Lessons of Experience* (Washington, DC: World Bank, 1992).

Krueger, Anne O., "Institutions for the New Private Sector," in Christopher Clague and Gordon C. Rausser, editors, *The Emergence of Market Economies in Eastern Europe* (Cambridge, MA: Basil Blackwell, 1992), 219–26.

Shafik, Nemat, "Mass Privatization in the Czech and Slovak Republics," *Finance and Development,* 31: 4 (1994), 22–4.

9

Privatization as institutional change in Hungary

LÁSZLÓ URBÁN

1.0 INTRODUCTION

Institutional change involves the replacement of one set of rules, expectations, and behaviors with another. The study of institutional change obviously requires the specification of a starting point as well as an end point. The starting point also plays an important role in theories of institutional change. In economic theory, in which change is driven by the realization of opportunities for Pareto improvements, the initial institutional arrangements determine the possible Pareto improvements. In public choice theory, in which change is driven by the interests of those in political control of the state, the existing collective choice institutions help determine which changes are favorable to officeholders. In distributional theory, in which change is driven by bargaining among various interests, the existing institutional arrangements affect the relative bargaining strengths of the interests. The privatization experience of the post-communist countries of Eastern Europe, with their differing institutional arrangements surrounding state-owned enterprises (SOEs), offers an excellent opportunity for studying the importance of the initial conditions and "path dependence." In this chapter I contribute to this effort by investigating Hungarian privatization as institutional change.

In contrast to Czechoslovakia and East Germany, Hungary and Poland began restructuring SOEs before their communist parties relinquished their political monopolies. As Lorene Allio discusses in Chapter 8, these changes gave employees an important role in post-communist privatization. In Hungary the restructuring gave a central role to managers. The process of change from 1988 to mid-1994 can best be understood in terms of the efforts of the government to accommodate managers while it pursues electoral advantage.[1] The strategic interaction between political

[1] The first free elections after the collapse of the communist system in Hungary were held in April 1990. A conservative coalition government was in office during the

László Urbán

and economic actors, and the credibility of the formal rules that result, as
developed in Chapter 2, provides the framework for analyzing the role of
politics in shaping the development of economic institutions in Hungary.

In section 2 I discuss the initial definition of property rights to Hungarian SOEs. Inclusive in this discussion is the process of "spontaneous
privatization." In section 3 I discuss the Hungarian government's privatization strategies, especially the change from reliance on direct sales to a
mixed strategy including free transfer of assets. I conclude section 4 with
obsevations on Hungarian privatization as institutional change.

2.0 INITIAL PROPERTY RIGHTS AND
SPONTANEOUS PRIVATIZATION

One might think that state ownership of assets, the starting point of
privatization, provides an adequate definition of property rights. Even
this seemingly clear definition, however, requires further qualification if it
is to be meaningfully applied to countries like Hungary or Poland. In
these countries, as a result of the reforms introduced in the 1980s, direct
central governance of SOEs had been replaced by forms of *self-
governance*. Many de facto ownership rights were delegated to "enterprise councils" in Hungary and "workers' councils" in Poland. In Hungary by 1985, two-thirds of the state enterprises were given self-governance
through enterprise councils, and only the remaining one-third continued
operation under direct state supervision. In contrast to Poland where the
internal governance structures were dominated by workers, the Hungarian self-governance was dominated by managers.[2]

From this initial situation, two very different approaches to the privatization of the assets of these enterprises were possible. One was government respect for the de facto ownership rights of these bodies and a
spontaneous process of privatization taking place as a result of managerial initiatives. The other approach was for the government to repudiate the
de facto ownership rights and *recentralize*, or at least redefine, them
under the authority of a governmental institution that would then transfer them to other economic actors. The first approach was followed during the political transformation that took place in Hungary in 1988–9.
After the free elections held in May 1990, the new government gradually
shifted to the second approach without fully abandoning the first.

following four years. The second free elections were held in May 1994, when this
coalition was defeated by the socialists. The new government promised to change the
strategy of privatization, but it had not yet done so as of October 1994.
[2]See Mizsei (1992) for a comparison of privatization in Poland and Hungary.

Privatization as institutional change in Hungary

2.1 Spontaneous privatization

In an analysis of Soviet-style economies from a property rights perspective, Jan Winiecki (1990) stresses rent maximization by economic and political actors as critical for understanding the failure of economic reforms. The apparatchiks and bureaucrats of the communist regimes are the ones who preserve rents most from maintaining the institutional status quo, and they are the groups that resist change most strongly. "Given the key positions of these groups in the STE (Soviet-type economic) system, we may predict a very high probability of failure of decentralizing, market-oriented, efficiency-increasing reforms" (Winiecki, 1990: 204). Winiecki's argument raises the following question for the Hungarian case: Why did the apparatchiks and the bureaucrats, as major beneficiaries of rent-seeking activities within the framework of the old regime, allow the reformers to gain control of the Communist Party, which finally resulted in the systemic transformation? My answer is that the most important of these actors expected the rents they could acquire within the framework of the new regime (i.e., the new structure of property rights) to be larger than the rents they could acquire within the existing property rights structure. This was possible in Hungary through the process of spontaneous privatization, which was facilitated by an institutional change initiated in the mid-1980s to undercut the position of the bureaucrats.

In 1985 the majority of SOEs were decentralized and their governance largely delegated to the so-called enterprise councils. One-half of the members of an enterprise council were representatives elected by the employees of the SOE; the other half were delegated managers. In practice, however, the top managers almost always controlled this body. The original intention of those who supported this reform was to take away the property rights from the hands of the bureaucracy, which always sabotaged and distorted market-oriented reforms as explained by Winiecki.

As a result of futher decentralization by the government in 1987, SOEs gained the right to establish corporations in conjunction with outside investors. The typical incorporation involved the SOE providing a portion of its assets as an in-kind contribution to the new corporation with another SOE or state bank as the outside investor. This kind of reorganization speeded up in 1988, when the Hungarian parliament passed a law on new forms of business associations,[3] and the government created a rather favorable environment for foreign direct investments. The "combination of decentralized decision-making rights with opening the door to

[3]Law No. 6 on Economic Associations (1988).

modern company structures other than state enterprise gave a strong impetus to self-privatisation efforts by enterprise managers" (Mizsei, 1992: 288).

In parallel with the political transformation then under way, there was thus a transformation of SOEs through corporatization and commercialization to new organizational forms. In the typical case, a large SOE transformed itself into the center of a number of smaller joint-stock companies or limited liability companies, or formed joint ventures with a foreign or domestic outside investor. Top managers of the former SOEs became top managers of the new companies as well. These companies were partly owned by different institutional investors or foreign private owners, so that the state began to give up ownership de jure as well as de facto. The state's share of legal ownership was exercised by the managers of the SOE who established the company, generally giving them managerial control.

These transformations usually did not involve domestic private ownership. The objective was to reorganize assets in a new company that did not have debt obligation, so it could get new bank loans needed for continued operations. The transformations would thus ensure that at least part of the SOE could survive commercialization and prepare the company for further ownership changes. Obviously, it was not a substitute for privatization, but it provided opportunities for enterprise restructuring before privatization and made it easier to separate viable operations from the nonviable ones.

These transformations were central to the spontaneous privatization process that gave many SOE managers, apparatchiks, and bureaucrats of the old regime legal opportunities to establish a solid economic basis for themselves within the framework of the new regime. They were able to exploit these opportunities through their control over state property and access to information. Instead of using their influence to slow down the transformation, the most competent, well-positioned, and clever individuals, who would have been the natural organizers of resistance to the new regime, found ways to establish themselves individually within the new framework. Thus the process of spontaneous privatization proved to be very beneficial politically during 1988–9, because the prospect of personal gain changed the attitudes of influential segments of the beneficiaries of the old regime toward the whole transition, so that in Hungary the transition was exceptionally peaceful.

In Hungary the spontaneous privatization refers to these early reorganizations and partial commercialization transactions. In Poland, the term "nomenklatura privatization" was used in a wider sense, referring to a variety of more or less inventive ways of asset-stripping. In Hungary sometimes the term "informal privatization" is used in this broader sense.

Informal privatization ranges on a scale from outright theft of potentially useful physical assets of an SOE during its liquidation through different forms of simple corruption to more sophisticated appropriation of assets through the creation of new corporations. The common root of all these phenomena is the well-known agency problem (Fama, 1980; Jensen and Meckling, 1976), which exists even in privately owned corporations but is more severe in SOEs. Managers tend to act not in accordance with the long-term interest of the owner because of the ineffective incentive and monitoring structures in place. Monitoring is even less effective during a fundamental economic transformation, when the old "coordination mechanisms" disintegrate, but have not yet been replaced by new ones.[4] From an economic efficiency perspective there is no problem with these transactions, because the private owners supposedly will use the assets more efficiently than the SOE did previously. Of course, inefficiency will arise to the extent that the rights to the assets lack credibility. Importantly, the distributive consequences of these transactions benefited a few insiders so excessively that it became a highly publicized and politicized issue. The new government responded by delegating more and more rights in controlling these transactions to a supervisory agency, the State Property Agency (SPA), which was established in March 1990.

Managers who implemented the early spontaneous privatization transactions were primarily interested in creating a safe and well-paid position for themselves in the newly emerging corporate sector. Nonetheless, if these spontaneous transformations had not been put under government control after a little more than a year, then they might have become a distinct privatization strategy in Eastern Europe, one whose relative efficiency it would by now be possible to assess.

As the process would have been directed by the top managers of SOEs who had strong incentives to privatize as fast as possible and in ways that helped their enterprises to survive, it is not clear whether spontaneous privatization, as distinct from informal privatization, would have been inferior to other privatization strategies on long-term efficiency grounds.

2.2 Commercialization as redefinition of property rights

Commercialization refers to the change of the legal form of a complete SOE into a corporation. The spontaneous privatization process discussed resulted in commercialization of part of the assets of a limited number of SOEs. After the free elections, the new government made the SPA the representative of the state as owner during privatization. The SPA was in charge of controlling privatization transactions, but it was not the owner

[4]On the problem of the disintegration of the old coordination mechanisms, see Kornai (1993).

243

of the state enterprises.[5] The government could have decided to change the legal form of all state enterprises into corporations by law or decree at once. Instead, a gradual approach was followed. Commercialization of the enterprises had to be initiated by the enterprise council and approved by the SPA.[6] Sometimes commercialization was closely linked to the sale of a significant stake in the company to an outside owner.

Commercialization of SOEs, with the exception of a few dozen enterprises, continued to be initiated by their managers, even after the establishment of the SPA. The managers wanted to influence the anticipated privatizations of their enterprises by participating in the process of setting the conditions of the tender to potential investors and in evaluating the tendered offers. The SPA found it expedient to rely on these initiatives. This was the so-called controlled spontaneous privatization phase in Hungary.

During this period the SPA gradually regained control over the SOEs as they were transformed into corporations. As an SOE was completely commercialized, the SPA became its major shareholder. These transformations had to be implemented according to the Law on Transformation, which involved not only a redefinition of property rights, whereby de facto ownership rights were taken away from the enterprise councils and given to stockholders, but also an initial redistribution of property rights as well. In addition to the SPA, local governments and employees of the enterprise were also entitled to shares of its stock. This distribution was prior to the actual privatization through sale or transfer of SPA-owned stocks.

Local governments in whose jurisdictions SOE sites are located are entitled to a certain ownership share in the commercialized enterprise.[7] The value of the ownership is to be determined by the value of the property (land) of the site, though the law did not specify how the value is to be calculated. The implementation was left to the SPA, which has tried to minimize to the extent possible local government's ownership share. However, local governments were allocated an average of 5 percent of the stock in each former SOE.

There are two ways in which employees (including managers) of a commercialized state enterprise are entitled to acquire its stocks under preferential conditions. The first is through "employee shares," the second is by purchasing common stocks at a discount. An employee share is a special kind of ownership instrument, which may be preferred stock,

---

[5]Law No. 7 on the State Property Agency and on handling and utilizing property belonging to it (1990).
[6]Law No. 13 on the transformation of economic organizations and economic associations (1989).
[7]Law No. 13.

but with restrictions on transferability that limit its trading to within the corporation. If the corporation is operating profitably, then the employee shareholders receive dividends. However, it is very difficult to cash in these stocks, because only other employees or the corporation itself can buy them, which they will be unlikely to do if the company is not doing well. Thus, despite the fact that employee shares can be purchased at as low a price as 10 percent of the price of the common stocks of the same corporation, they are worth buying only in the case of the best companies.

The workers and managers of the company can also buy normal shares preferentially. Preferences are not specified by law. The practice of the SPA had been that employees could buy employee shares at 90 percent discount and normal shares for 50 percent of the price. The sum of the discount on both sales cannot exceed either 10 percent (in exceptional cases 15 percent) of the equity of the given company or the wage level in the previous year of the particular employee.

Usually, the corporations provide favorable financing conditions for these purchases, so in the typical case employees (including managers) are buying altogether about 10 percent of the stock of their enterprise with very little down payment. This 10 percent average is a good indicator of the relative political power of the employees in Hungary. They are politically much weaker than in Russia or Poland, but still politically stronger than workers in the Czech Republic.

These almost automatic transfers of stocks have certainly increased the credibility of the government's intention to go ahead with privatization, allaying fears that commercialization is only a means by which the government can regain full control over the former SOEs. Yet even if the average 15 percent stake is reallocated to other owners (local governments and workers), the remaining 85 percent is still a strong temptation to use the controlling influence to intervene in the internal operations of the enterprises instead of selling them as quickly as possible.

2.3 Path dependency

In his analysis of the developing property structures in Eastern Europe, and especially in Hungary, David Stark (1993) notes the dominance of "recombinant" property. He argues that these are mixed economies not only because there are both SOEs and privately owned firms, but also because the typical firm is itself a combination of public and private property relations. He refers to the offspring of the management-initiated commercialization and privatization transactions discussed above. "Managers at the enterprise level are fragmenting property into numerous limited liability companies in orbit around corporate headquarters.

Nominally independent, majority shares of the new units are typically held by the parent enterprise in partnership with private individuals and dense institutional cross-ownership" (Stark, 1993: 1).

In explaining the development of these structures, Stark uses the perspective of evolutionary economics. Transforming property rights is about renegotiating relations among a wide set of actors to resolve their claims over different kinds of property rights. Grand schemes of privatization mistake the assignment of specific rights over property as the institutionalization of property rights. Instead, actual property relations are shaped by the interactions of new rules and past practices. This approach emphasizes the importance of path dependency in institutional development. Privatization in Eastern Europe is not taking place in a vacuum, where new organizational forms are introduced from the outside. Old institutions are collapsing and new ones are emerging, but there is a strong element of continuity in each country of Eastern Europe, he argues. In the Hungarian context, strong managerial influence on the privatization process is the major manifestation of this continuity.

3.0 AN OVERVIEW OF THE PRIVATIZATION STRATEGY

Hungarian privatization has relied primarily on direct sales rather than on free distribution to transfer nearly one-half of its state-owned assets to the private sector since 1989.[8] It is better understood as the result of the interaction of self-interested political and economic actors than as the implementation of a clearly defined grand strategy.

The economic actors include managers of SOEs and potential (mainly foreign) investors. As discussed above, the managers gained substantial influence during the early period of spontaneous privatization. Potential investors enjoyed influence because they controlled the capital needed to modernize and restructure Hungarian industry. The history of Hungarian economic development since the 1960s suggests that lasting economic reforms require the cooperation of these economic actors.

The political actors include the politicians of the government coalition and technocrats. The members of the government coalition, though inexperienced in electoral politics, eventually came to behave as if they were

---

[8]In 1989 the estimated value of state-owned productive assets in Hungary was about Ft 2 trillion (U.S.$24 billion at the time). Measured by World Bank–approved methods, 47 percent of these assets have been privatized by July 1994. Adding up revenue collected by the privatization agencies from sales transactions each year until the first half of 1994 yields a nominal sum of Ft 160 billion (*Privatizációs monitor*, August 1994), which is about Ft 250 billion (U.S.$2.5 billion) in current dollars. The discrepancy between fraction sold and revenue realized is due to the sharp decline in the value of assets since 1989 resulting from an extremely deep recession (23 percent decline in GDP between 1989 and 1993).

motivated by the self-interested desire to remain in office by gaining re-election. The technocrats include high-level bureaucrats, academics, and other professionals who had developed fairly clear views on appropriate privatization strategies through their experience with previous attempts at, and debates over, economic reform.

3.1 Initial strategy

Until early 1992, Hungarian privatization consisted almost exclusively of the sale of assets, the prefered strategy of most technocrats. Subsequently, there were more and more distributive elements included in the strategy, although these were only additions to, rather than replacements of, the reliance on sales. These new elements reflected the preference of politicians.

Consider first the views of the technocrats. Academics in Hungary were very skeptical of "mass" privatization and other forms of free distribution advocated by many observers of the East European transition.[9] Reform economists in Hungary had raised the idea of distributing ownership shares in SOEs to pension funds, holding companies, or individual citizens as early as the 1960s (Liska, 1965; Kopátsy, 1969; Tardos, 1972). These distributions were raised as "ownership reform" substitutions for privatization, which was a political taboo. During the long years of discussion, however, many theoretical and technical arguments were raised against these distributive methods so that they came to be regarded as poor substitutes for the real thing. The situation was completely different in Czechoslovakia, for instance, where discussion of these ideas, even among technocrats, was not permitted until the collapse of the communist system. By that time the conventional wisdom among Hungarian economists was that real privatization has to address not only the problem of transferring ownership rights to private actors, but also has to address corporate governance problems (although they did not use this terminology).[10] There was also a distrust of any government's ability to design effective distributive systems. Effective reorganization would be

[9]Mass privatization has been advanced by many observers as best fitting the Eastern Europen context (Borensztein and Kumar, 1991). Four arguments are offered in support of this position. First, mass privatization rapidly creates a constitutency that makes the economic transformation irreversible (Blanchard et al., 1990; Lipton and Sachs, 1990). Second, a free and equal initial distribution of stocks to former SOEs is politically desirable because it is seen to be just and fair (Fischer, 1992; Winiecki, 1992). Third, because mass privatization does not require large amounts of capital, it can go forward without substantial domestic or foreign investment. Fourth, mass privatization is pragmatic, because many of the SOEs are in such bad shape that they could not be sold for a positive price.

[10]For a discussion of corporate governance aspects of privatization in Eastern Europe, see Frydman and Rapaczynski (1991, 1994).

most likely to result from the self-interested actions of businessmen and investors who are willing to pay for the assets. The effective evaluation of assets and restructuring of companies requires real capital to be invested.

This became the dominant Hungarian technocratic view of how to achieve an effective market economy. Constructivist schemes without real commitments of money by individuals, designed by academics, and implemented by government agencies were regarded as new versions of central planning.[11] Even some key economic ministers in the new government, such as Finance Minister Mihaly Kupa and Minister for Foreign Economic Relations Bela Kadar, seemed to hold this perspective.

The dominant technocratic view in favor of sales transactions was consistent with the results of spontanteous privatization. Many SOE managers had already started to negotiate with potential investors about partial privatization of their enterprises, so they resisted a completely different approach. In addition, there was already an infant domestic consulting industry benefiting from spontaneous privatization transactions that had a stake in the continuation of the sales process.

The privatization strategy of the new government was prepared by July 1990. It stated that the predominant method of the Hungarian privatization is *sale of stocks through competitive tenders.* In response to public protest against uncontrolled spontaneous privatization, they adopted a compromise: Management-initiated privatization would continue, but under the control of the SPA. In addition to management-initiated transactions, the strategy also listed other privatization methods, like SPA-initiated and investor-initiated transactions, but all within the framework of sales through competitive mechanisms.

Why did politicians adopt the technocratic strategy in 1990? After all, politicians often make decisions against the advice of bureaucrats and academics. An additional factor is obviously a desire to gain revenue from sales for the central budget. Sales offer extra revenue without the need to increase taxes at a time of fiscal pressure. Yet, one has to keep in mind that it was not the huge budget deficit that forced them to adopt the sale strategy. In fact, the budget deficit was only Ft 16.7 billion in 1990 and 74.1 billion in 1991. It was in the years in which the budget deficit grew large (Ft 190 billion in 1992 and Ft 220 billion in 1993) that the dominant sale strategy was modified. Thus, the pressure of a budget deficit does not exlain the shift and hence does not provide a good explanation for the initial choice of strategy.

A more important factor was the government's need to service its huge foreign debt. Generating foreign exchange through the sale strategy seemed feasible in view of the apparent interest of foreign investors in

[11]An excellent example of this criticism of constructivist views is Kornai (1990).

purchasing shares in the companies offered for privatization. As in the other post-communist countries, domestic private investors did not have large amounts of capital. But Hungary was in an exceptionally favorable position compared to the other countries in terms of access to foreign direct investment because of the economic reforms it implemented during the previous two decades, which made it much easier for foreign investors to do business in Hungary. Indeed, the spontaneous privatization already made it possible for foreign investors to participate in privatization. To deny them further opportunities would have had a negative impact on Hungary's image in the West. It enabled Hungary to maintain its ability to raise new foreign funds in order to service its legacy of huge foreign debt, amounting to roughly 10 percent of the gross domestic product. In fact, the service of the foreign debt was possible in the 1990s only with the help of direct foreign investment. In return, servicing of the debt made possible the continuous inflow of direct foreign investment, the cash component of which amounted to a total of U.S.$5.8 billion by March 1994.[12]

Together, these factors may appear to provide a satisfactory explanation for why the Hungarian government accepted sales as the dominant privatization strategy. But, as all these factors were present throughout the period, they do not explain the shift in the strategy that took place in 1992. They do explain, though, why nonsale transactions only supplemented, rather than replaced, sales transactions.

The missing factor, which can help to explain the shift, is the inexperience of the new politicians who seemed to adopt more self-interested behavior after the first year or two in office. Initially, the new political elite had to discover how to behave in the new electoral situation. The new political elite, which won the first free elections after the collapse of the communist system, had little previous political experience. It took them some time to learn how to use their resources effectively to gain support for their reelection.

3.2 Political modifications

As previously discussed, the initial distribution of shares to commercialized enterprises included small allocations to local governments and employees. The subsequent addition of other distributional provisions to the privatization program shows the growing sensitivity of the members of the government coalition to their electoral prospects.

3.2.1 Compensation notes: Hungarian vouchers. The first signs of a more politically responsive approach to privatization appeared in connec-

[12]*National Bank of Hungary Monthly Report*, No. 6, 1994, p. 93.

tion with the issue of "compensation" brought to the parliament in early 1991. The whole issue of compensation to people whose property had been unjustly confiscated by the communist regime was a completely new issue when the government proposed the first law on compensation. It was raised because one of the coalition partners, the Smallholder Party, in their election campaign had promised reprivatization of the land forcefully collectivized by the communists. As they were practically a single-issue agrarian party, it was very important for them to show some progress on reprivatization.

In response to this demand by a coalition partner, the government invented the concept of "compensation notes" as a least disruptive form of reprivatization. The government did not want to risk endless legal disputes resulting from claims for the original properties by previous owners. Instead, compensation notes entitle the holder to "buy" stocks worth their face value from the SPA. The face values are set at levels that provide less than full compensation, however. After the issue was raised with respect to land, it was quickly extended to other forms of property, and after that to other kinds of grievances people held against the communist regime.

The compensation notes are freely transferable, salable, and even listed on the stock exchange. The SPA has to accept them from anybody at face value plus an interest payment to the date of redemption. The original recipients of the notes thus can use them in a variety of ways. For example, they can use the notes to buy agricultural land at special auctions, or they can use them to buy annuities from the Social Security Fund. However, in these cases the notes will ultimately be used by the holders (agricultural cooperatives or the Social Security Fund) to purchase stocks from the SPA. Altogether about Ft 200 billion (U.S.$2 billion) in notes have been issued, but only about Ft 30 billion have been redeemed by the SPA. The SPA must provide a supply of stocks matching the total value of compensation notes issued plus the interest they have earned. In light of the decreasing value of its portfolio due to the extended economic recession, providing the stocks to back up the compensation notes has posed a serious challenge for the SPA.

This difficulty is clearly shown by the secondary market value of the compensation notes. In December 1992 the notes started to be listed and traded on the Budapest Stock Exchange so that their market value became transparent to everyone. Initially, the notes traded at about 80 percent of their face value. In the first half of 1993, however, their price started gradually to decline. By the end of June 1993, the price had fallen to close to 50 percent of face value. The decline in price was a warning signal for the government, which regarded the beneficiaries of compensation as their potential supporters. They ordered the SPA to come up with more attractive stocks to be sold in exchange for compensation notes, which resulted in an upward movement of the price. During the last months of 1993, the price of the compensation notes on the Stock Exchange had been between 70 and 75 percent of face value. In 1994, especially after the election, the market price fell again to around 50 percent in June and close to 40 percent in August, where it remained throughout September and October 1994.[13] These prices reflect the suspicion that the new government will not regard the supplying of valuable stocks to back up compensation notes to be a high priority.

3.2.2 The Social Security Fund. In February 1992 the parliament decided to transfer about 300 billion Ft's (U.S.$3 billion) worth of stocks to the Social Security Fund (SSF); the transfer was to be completed by the end of 1994. The decision specified neither the composition (stocks, bonds, or physical assets and, if stocks, whether minority or majority positions, etc.) nor the management of this huge portfolio (directed by the SSF or via financial intermediaries of some sort). Politicians wanted to show that they were responsive to the financial problems of the SSF, and the pool of the privatizable state-owned assets seemed to be a natural resource for doing so. Later, when ex-communist union leaders were elected as leaders of the supervisory bodies of the SSF, the government decided to sabotage the transfer. As of this writing, practically nothing has yet been transferred to these funds.

3.2.3 Politicization of the SPA. In February 1992 the government nominated a new minister without portfolio (Tamas Szabo) to be in charge of privatization. He became the real head of the SPA, directly intervening in many of the individual transactions handled by the agency. This represented an attempt to change the direction of the internal operations of the agency from a technocratic orientation to a political one.

Nevertheless, the SPA continued to be dominated by professional technocrats in its internal operations and was headed by a board of directors, which the minister found hard to ignore. In order to guarantee complete control over the assets of the most valuable companies, the government established a fully state-owned holding company, the State Asset Management Company (SAMC),[14] which was more directly subordinated to Minister Szabo. In the fall of 1992, 160 of the most valuable companies were transferred from the SPA to SAMC.

After early 1992, the minister required that government agencies select at least half of the members of the boards of commercialized SOEs on the

---

[13]*Heti Vilaggazdasag* (Hungarian Economic Weekly) issues in 1993–4.
[14]Law No. 53 on the utilization and handling of permanently state-owned entrepreneurial assets (1992).

basis of their political loyalty and affiliation. The result was the nomination of members of the Democratic Forum parliamentary fraction to the boards of large SPA-owned corporations. This turned out to be a major vehicle for the government to preserve the loyalty of many representatives of the Democratic Forum in parliament. It may be surprising, but the government badly needed this "carrot." As the popularity of the government already began declining in late 1990, the coalition MPs were in a very difficult situation in defending the decisions of their government in front of their own constituencies. Putting them on corporate boards helped to keep their public support for the government.

3.2.4 Employee (management) buyouts. The opportunities provided for the employees of each SOE to buy minority shares under preferential conditions was already discussed above. In July 1992 the parliament enacted a new scheme in order to facilitate majority employee ownership as a new form of privatization.[15] It enables employees to buy the majority of the stocks of their corporation with the help of a special loan. The conditions of the loan are very favorable (less than a third of the market interest rate, a grace period for repayment of three years, a ten- to fifteen-year repayment period), but the banks require high collateral for financing, so the program is effectively limited to corporations with valuable assets and good prospects. Through October 1993, sixty-five companies worth about Ft 14 billion were privatized through employee buyouts (*Figyelo,* June 9, 1994). As the total stock value of these firms was about Ft 20 billion, workers took on average a 70 percent stake. The rest of the shares are held mostly by the SPA, which intends either to offer them in exchange for compensation bonds or to put them into the portfolio to be given to the social security fund.

It is worth emphasizing that the oversight by banks limits the Hungarian employee buyouts, unlike those usually occurring in the United States, to relatively strong companies rather than ones on the verge of bankruptcy. (More than half of the sixty-five companies realized a profit in 1992, which was a higher percentage than for Hungarian companies overall in that year.) It would thus appear that this program offers a real benefit to workers. In fact, however, most of the transactions are actually more accurately described as management buyouts, because within the employee organizations that formally purchase the stocks, there is almost always a managerial group in control.

Why did the government adopt employee buyouts? There is no indication that there was political pressure exerted by managers, the group most likely to gain from the program. Instead, the program appears to be

---

[15]Law No. 44. on the employee co-ownership program (1992).

the result of successful lobbying by some academics and professionals, together with the leaders of a small trade union, who were allies of the Hungarian Democratic Forum. They persuaded policy makers that the program would gain widespread support for them among skilled workers. Thus, the program appears to be part of an effort by the government to broaden its electoral support. An indication of this is the fact that the program was speeded up during the last six months before the elections in May 1994. Whereas by the end of October 1993 there were sixty-five companies privatized in the program, as was mentioned, by the end of May 1994 the number of companies involved had increased to 169 (*Privatization Monitor,* June 1994).

3.2.5 The small investor program. A final electorally motivated alteration of the basic privatization strategy by the conservative government was the so-called Small Investor Stock Purchasing Program. The idea was to offer stocks of good companies for purchase at preferential prices to small investors over a five- to ten-year period. The objective was to target social groups who had been left out of privatization to gain their electoral support with an offer of relatively good stocks at below market prices. As originally conceived, it would have been a large-scale program, almost comparable in scale to the Czech voucher program. After closer examination, however, it became clear that it was difficult to find profitable SOEs that could be offered through the program. Finally, a minority of shares in five companies were offered a month before the second parliamentary elections in spring 1994.

This program and the others described above show the attempts made by the government between 1992 and the election in 1994 to gain political support by modifying the basic privatization strategy of market sales. Even these politically motivated programs, however, could not overcome the widespread disappointment with the performance of the conservative coalition among the electorate. Moreover, there developed among the general public a perception that privatization is surrounded by corruption. This perception contributed to the resounding defeat of the conservative governmental coalition in the 1994 elections.

4.0 CONCLUSION

What does the Hungarian privatization experience suggest about institutional change? Three points stand out.

First, the post-communist privatization in Hungary reflected the years of reform efforts that had gone before it. This "path dependence" is apparent in the managerial and technocratic influence over the choice of a general privatization strategy and in the resulting combinations of public and private property relations. Managers, who had gained considerable autonomy during the pre-communist reforms, continued to play an important role in the implementation of the privatization strategy.

Second, as politicians gained experience, they came to recognize opportunities for modifying the privatization strategy for electoral advantage. The result was the addition of many distributive elements to the initial program of competitive sales. Thus, the privatization evolved according to political considerations from the initial starting conditions achieved under spontaneous privatization.

Third, the need to attract foreign direct investment to help service Hungary's huge inherited external debt and the availability of large amounts of direct foreign investment over the last four years were strong enough factors to maintain the dominance of privatization through competitive sale, even during the period of the introduction of complementary distributive mechanisms.

REFERENCES

Blanchard, Olivier, Rudiger Dornbusch, Paul Krugman, Richard Layard, and Lawrence Summers, *Reform in Eastern Europe* (Cambridge, MA: MIT Press, 1990).

Borensztein, Eduardo, and Manmohan Kumar, "Proposals for Privatization in Eastern Europe," *IMF Staff Papers* 38: 2 (1991), 300–26.

Fama, Eugene, "Agency Problems and the Theory of the Firm," *Journal of Political Economy* 88: 2 (1980), 288–307.

Fischer, Stanley, "Privatization in East European Transformation," in Christopher Clague and Gordon C. Rausser, editors, *The Emergence of Market Economies in Eastern Europe* (Cambridge, MA: Basil Blackwell, 1992), 227–43.

Frydman, Roman, and Andrzez Rapaczynski, "Markets and Institutions in Large-Scale Privatization: An Approach to Economic and Social Transformation in Eastern Europe," in Vittorio Corbo, Fabrizio Coricelli, and Jan Bossak, editors, *Reforming Central and Eastern European Economies: Initial Results and Challenges* (Washington, DC: World Bank, 1991), 253–74.

Privatization in Eastern Europe: Is the State Withering Away? (New York: Central European Press, 1994).

Jensen, Michael C., and William H. Meckling, "Theory of the Firm: Managerial Behavior, Agency Costs and Ownership Structure," *Journal of Financial Economics* 3: 4 (1976), 305–60.

Kopátsy, Sádor, "Önálló tulajdonosi szervezetekrö" (On Independent Ownership Organizations), *Pénzügyi Szemle* 16: 3 (1969), 221–39.

Kornai, János, *The Road to a Free Economy* (New York: W. W. Norton, 1990). "Transformational Recession," Institute for Advanced Study, Collegium Budapest, Discussion Paper No. 1, June (1993).

Lipton, David, and Jeffrey Sachs, "Creating a Market Economy in Eastern Europe: The Case of Poland," *Brookings Papers on Economic Activity* 1 (1990), 1–30.

Liska, Tibor, "Okonosztát," unpublished manuscript, 1965.

Mizsei, Kálmán, "Privatization in Eastern Europe: A Comparative Study of Poland and Hungary," *Soviet Studies* 44: 2 (1992), 283–96.

Stark, David, "Recombinant Property in East European Capitalism," discussion paper, Collegium Budapest, December (1993).

Tardos, Márton, "A gazdasági verseny problémái hazánkban" (Problems of Economic Competition in Hungary), *Közgazdasági Szemle* 19: 7–8 (1972), 911–27.

Winiecki, Jan, "Why Economic Reforms Fail in the Soviet System: A Property Rights–Based Approach," *Economic Inquiry* 28: 2 (1990), 195–221.

"Privatization in East-Central Europe: Avoiding Major Mistakes," in Christopher Clague and Gordon C. Rausser, editors, *The Emergence of Market Economies in Eastern Europe* (Cambridge, MA: Basil Blackwell, 1992), 271–7.

Comment on "Privatization as Institutional Change in Hungary"

KÁLMÁN MIZSEI

László Urbán's chapter is an excellent contribution to our understanding of the political economy of privatization in Hungary. It is the best and most intelligent description of the concept of Hungarian privatization and of its underlying political determinants that I have read. As a logical consequence of the exposition, the author formulates three very important (and elegantly brief) conclusions with which I tend to agree. I did not find anything amiss in his description of the privatization process in Hungary – one could find hardly anyone more competent than the author to offer this kind of assessment. I am sure that his chapter will be an important part of the reference literature on Hungarian privatization.

As the international literature on privatization is dominated by analysis heavily biased toward voucher-type privatization schemes, particularly those in Russia and the Czech Republic, Urbán's contribution is especially welcome. The fact of the matter is, however, that the jury is still out with respect to the success of the various privatization paths. Their ultimate test will be their ability to contribute to *radically changing the corporate culture* in these countries, which was badly damaged under the decades of socialism. That is, their ability to contribute to *efficient corporate governance in the large corporate sector* will be the last word about their ultimate success or failure. In the meantime, however, I am concerned about the author's quantitative assessment of the extent of privatization in Hungary so far, as there is a large discrepancy between the fraction of state assets sold and the revenue realized from sales – the numbers do not seem to add up. The author's explanation of the discrepancy (note 8) is the rapid decline of asset value in Hungary. However, the difference seems to be much too large to be explained by asset decline alone. It may well be that by taking into account the unrecorded asset stripping, we would finally end up with the total fraction sold. But the "legal" privatization certainly indicates poor performance.

Further, I am limiting my comments to some additional "historical"

256

points that have relevance to property rights in Hungary now and in the near future. Urbán raises an excellent historical question: Why did the party bureaucrats let the reformers gain as much control of the party as they did in the late 1980s? This question is especially interesting as the reform process resulted in the disintegration of the one-party power structure. His answer is also intriguing and unorthodox; however, I think an additional consideration should be kept in mind. Through the whole Kadar era, the political dynamics were greatly influenced by fear among the Hungarian Socialist Workers' Party's elite of a repetition of 1956. That, I believe, made it uniquely different from other ruling communist parties of the Soviet empire, and it certainly contributed to the willingness of the Kadar government to undertake reforms in 1968. From then on a very clear cyclical pattern developed in Hungarian politics: In periods of economic decline and crisis the party elite became relatively more receptive to ideas for reform. In those times (as in 1979) they pulled forgotten ideas out of the drawer and initiated semipublic discussions about the furthering of economic reforms. This aspect of crisis, the fear as well as the opportunity, is missing from Urbán's explanation of the historical puzzle of "Why did they give it up?" If the ruling elite knew ex ante what was to come, they would have acted differently. But they went into the game step by step, to an extent blindly, up to the point at which they had to realize that they were no longer in control. However, it is undoubtedly an important element of explanation that Urbán emphasizes: A significant part of the elite actually believed, and rightly so, that they would gain from the opening.

My final comment on this point is that one would also want to differentiate between "SOE managers" and "bureaucrats." Although the borderline between the two is often not clear in socialism, and there was a great deal of movement back and forth in the short period of the rapid changes, it was better to be an enterprise manager than to be a bureaucrat, especially if one were not young. Some bureaucrats actually lost badly in the reforms, and we cannot assume that they did not expect to lose. But Pandora's box was open, and there was not enough force to close it again.

Actually, by starting his account in the late 1980s, Urbán keeps unstated an important story from the perspective of property rights development in Hungary. Privatization, in the broader perspective, did not start at the end, but rather at the beginning, of the 1980s. At that time, by allowing only informal forms of private property to emerge, the political elite had a double impact on the property rights of the 1990s. First, it allowed entrepreneurial spirit to flourish earlier than in most of the other Eastern European countries. Therefore, by the time "real" capitalism was made possible, a quite sizeable part of the Hungarian population experienced part-time or full-time private entrepreneurship, already had a stake in law-and-order and in capitalism itself, and viewed the market economy as something natural and good. On the other hand, the bad news from this shy, private entrepreneurship was that a large part of this middle class learned to live on the edge of legality, as the legal status of these early private units was awkward; tax and other regulations also forced them to be "entrepreneurial" in terms of arranging permissions and in avoiding state rules and taxes. A new entrepreneurial culture was thus socialized in such a way so as almost naturally to absorb the illegalities of the managerial privatization beginning in 1988. Again, the rules and entrepreneurial morality were not clearly defined; the attitude of the "fox" toward state rules emerged. In view of the circumstances, these attitudes and behaviors are understandable. Yet they pose a very important question: How will law and order, and thus property rights, be strengthened in a society that has learned in three consecutive waves of private business creation that one has to cheat the state to succeed, and that this cheating is, after all, not a very immoral thing?

I agree with Urbán's characterization of the Hungarian privatization flow: It was initially a strongly managerial one, and then, after the 1990 elections, it became gradually more centralized. This flow suggests that political competition may not be conducive to managerial privatization, as it appears defenseless to attacks from politicians. Indeed, it raises the question of whether decentralized, manager-led privatization had even the slimmest chance to survive as the main privatization process in Hungary or elsewhere. If the answer is a clear no, it means that all of us who tried to protect managerial privatization did it wrong politically and perhaps would have been better advised to design something politically more feasible after all. At the least, the advocates of managerial privatization could have done a better job in codifying more precisely the rights of the managers in the process. Such formalization would have at least made political attacks more difficult, though one may doubt that even then the design could have survived democratic politics.

Urbán points to path dependency as part of his explanation. Stark's perspective is especially applicable when looking at Hungary. Moreover, the institutional heritage of any given country almost certainly has an impact on the way its new institutions are shaped. We should remember, however, that policy design may also have a major impact over the shaping of new institutions. As much as Hungary serves up plenty of examples for advocates of path dependency, the last five years in Russia, Poland, and the Czech Republic provide ample support for those who believe in the strength of human action. The design of the Polish stabilization program and of the Czech and Russian privatization schemes illustrates that in extraordinary times the elites have an extraordinary opportunity to shape and reshape institutions to an extent that may sometimes make sociologists feel very uneasy.

10

Marketization and government credibility in Shanghai: Federalist and local corporatist explanations

STEVEN LEWIS[1]

1.0 INTRODUCTION

Why do people risk investing in the People's Republic of China? China's cities and countryside have soaked up a tidal wave of new factories, stores, and offices since reforms began in 1978. The high levels of economic growth during this period – an annual average increase in gross domestic product of 8.8 percent from 1978 to 1992 (Perkins, 1994: 24) – correspond to these phenomenal levels of foreign and domestic investment. But with one-party communist rule and no independent professional judiciary to define and enforce their property rights, these investors may appear to be taking a big gamble. Are they simply intoxicated with the desire to ride that wave of high economic growth?

Or perhaps investors are sober after all, and perhaps property rights in China are more credible than they may at first appear. Recent works by political economists and China studies specialists suggest some intriguing institutional explanations for the source of credible property rights. These explanations differ from previous theories in that their authors see the apparent stability of China's marketization reforms as relying on both formal institutions (e.g., of laws and regulations) and informal institutions (e.g., of norms and conventions).[2] The incorporation of social

---

[1]The author wishes to thank the following scholars for their useful comments at various stages in the writing of this chapter: Lorene Allio, Harry Broadman, Daniel Diermeier, Mariusz Dobek, Joel Ericson, Timothy Frye, George Horwich, Xiaobo Hu, Brendan Kiernan, William Kirby, Jack Knight, Y. Y. Kueh, Melanie Manion, Victor Nee, William Riker, Andrew Sobel, and Richard Suttmeier.

[2]Note, however, that such theories of the institutional sources of stability, including the two types of explanation discussed here, often do not explain the mechanism by which these institutions change. I discuss this problem and propose a test of the usefulness of general theories of change in property rights elsewhere (Lewis, 1996). For a discussion of the merits of various types of explanations for institutional change see Knight (1992) and Chapter 12 in this volume.

norms and conventions into the study of marketization makes these theories unique. The consideration of such informal institutions may help explain the high levels of investment in an environment without a formal, legal basis for secure property rights. And yet, oddly enough, the names of these two types of explanation refer to the property institutions of the very formal and very legalistic Western advanced industrial economies: "market-preserving federalism" and "local corporatism."

In this chapter I examine the usefulness of the market-preserving federalism and local corporatism theories in finding the elusive source of credibility behind investment in a marketizing China. The study of investor rights in China is important for the study of property rights in general. China is a neglected case in the study of marketization in the former centralist planned economies (CPEs). As such it may be useful in evaluating the validity of those studies of marketization in the CPEs that focus on the formal, legal sources of credible property rights (e.g., constitutional revisions, formal privatization auctions, and voucher plans). If China's property rights are credible and dependent on such informal institutions as norms and conventions, then theories of stable marketization in the former CPEs that focus solely on formal institutions may lack validity, or at least generality.

I test the usefulness of the market-preserving federalism and the local corporatism theories. Market-preserving federalism argues that competition among autonomous, local governments provides the security and stability required for investment. Informal relationships between levels of government are essential here in that they provide the credible guarantee that higher-level governments will not intervene in this competition. Local corporatism argues that the competition created by the decentralized fiscal structure of government and the presence of personal ties between local government leaders and investors provides credibility.

By looking at the case of local economic development zones and foreign investment in Shanghai, I overcome problems in the generality of these two explanations. Inexplicably, previous market-preserving federalism explanations have relied on macro-level data. But, as the key actors in federalist explanations are local governments, the interaction of these units of analysis must be studied. Local corporatist explanations have relied on studies of towns and local enterprises in China's countryside. And although the Township and Village Enterprises (TVEs) are the most dynamic actors in China's export economy, the urban coastal areas, and their suburbs, are the location of most investments and much economic growth.

Why Shanghai? Although it has lost much of the international prominence it enjoyed as the industrial and financial capital of Asia under the colonialist Western powers and Japan, Shanghai still commands attention as China's most populous and wealthiest city, and its largest industrial and financial center. Only 1 percent of China's population live in Shanghai, yet Shanghailanders produce 7 percent of China's industrial products, buy and sell 12 percent of goods, ship 22 percent of all products, and raise 12 percent of China's fiscal revenue (STJ, 1995: 15). The case of Shanghai's investment institutions, therefore, is an important one for theories of property rights to be able to explain, and the variety of administrative institutions controlling investment among Shanghai's political subunits provide an excellent set of cases for testing the various theories.

Why foreign investment? First, foreign-invested enterprises and foreign-funded projects have become influential in China's economy, particularly in coastal areas. They not only account for a large part of industrial production, land development, and housing construction, but they are also important sources of tax revenues. Second, because the majority of foreign-invested enterprises are equity joint ventures with domestic companies, and because there are considerable fiscal and financial incentives for Chinese enterprises to form such mergers, the division between the domestic economy and the international economy has become difficult to distinguish. Investors are able to exploit ambiguities in formal laws and such informal institutions as personal connection networks (*guanxi*) to set up enterprises of "hybrid" property forms. The exact nature of ownership of these is often unclear to investors, officials, and researchers alike (Gold, 1989; Nee, 1992; Su, 1992). In sum, foreign investment property forms have become an essential and influential portion of China's economy and therefore deserve systematic study.

Section 2 describes a test of the market-preserving federalist explanation for the source of credible property rights in a marketizing China. The evidence clearly shows that the growth of local economic development zones and foreign investment comes from local government actions to decentralize investment authority. Foreign investment flows to those localities that are both economically more competitive and more decentralized. The evidence also suggests a source of the credible guarantee of nonintervention by higher-level governments: informal norms of local independence and conventions of authority between individual leaders at different levels. Section 3 describes a partial test of the "local corporatist" explanation. The results show that investments are not likely to be dependent on fiscal relations between governments, but that they are clearly influenced by informal networks of relations between local government leaders and investors.

2.0 MARKET-PRESERVING FEDERALISM

Federalism is often referred to in terms of the political stability imparted by its formal institutional components: constitutions, laws, and regulations. But political economists have recently begun to focus on the effects that such stability gives to markets and economic development. Attempts to explain the political sources of economic growth made by China scholars often implicitly make similar arguments.

The keys to credible property rights within a federalist system are the autonomy of local authorities to regulate markets and the free mobility of capital, services, and goods among competing local political units. "Federalism" here is defined as having three general characteristics (Riker, 1964; Weingast, 1995); the definition of "market-preserving federalism" includes these three as well as two additional characteristics.

First, there must be multiple layers of government ruling the same land and the same people. Second, each level of government must maintain a well-defined scope of authority such that it is autonomous within its area of authority. Third, there must be a "guarantee of autonomy" for each level of government that credibly prevents the intervention of other levels of government. "Market-preserving federalism," however, demands a fourth characteristic, a "locus of economic regulatory authority" with two requirements: "first, that the authority to regulate markets is not vested with the highest political government in the hierarchy; and second, that the lower governments are prevented from using their regulatory authority to erect trade barriers against the goods and services from other political units" (Weingast, 1995: 4). This fourth characteristic guarantees that the political decentralization of federalism extends to economic affairs as well. It prevents the establishment of politically created monopolies that stifle competition across political units. The fifth characteristic is that the local governments must face a hard budget constraint such that they are not bailed out of fiscal problems by the central government, or through their own printing of currency (Weingast, 1995).

According to the "federalist" explanation, the new property rights institutions in a marketizing CPE are more credible if the primary regulating authority governing their definition and enforcement is local government authority, and if these local authorities are prevented from erecting barriers to the free flow of goods, services, and capital among their jurisdictions. Such federalism would be "market-preserving" if localities that arbitrarily or inconsistently defined and enforced property rights forms would, over time, lose trade and investment to localities that more credibly defined and enforced them. In such a system, local governments have a strong incentive to support changes toward more marketized forms of property in order to maintain their revenues. The keys to a federalist explanation of the credibility of property rights institutions in marketizing CPEs, however, are competition among local governments and the *credible guarantee* of both the autonomy of local authority to regulate markets – a barrier to future intervention by central governments – and the free mobility of capital and goods among local political units.

Is a change toward a more federalist system the source of credibility underlying China's rapid economic growth? In the next section I test this by looking for the presence of the key elements of "market-preserving federalism" in Shanghai's foreign investment environment. First, are local-level governments relatively autonomous in terms of foreign investment regulation authority, and do they compete with one another? Second, is commerce among local jurisdictions unrestricted by trade barriers? Third, are there hard budget constraints imposed on local governments? Finally, is there a plausible institution that guarantees the autonomy of local foreign investment authority? If these federalist institutions do exist, they may be the source of the apparent credibility of property rights in China. In the following section I test the federalist argument more explicitly by comparing the variation in foreign investment with the variation in decentralization and economic competitiveness across the counties and districts of Shanghai.

I conclude that a system very much like market-preserving federalism is emerging in China. First, the presence of a large number of local-level economic development zones indicates that there is indeed competition among local governments. Second, the central government's lack of control over the development zone creation process provides clear evidence of a high degree of local government autonomy. There is also some evidence that informal institutions of cooperation among local leaders, and between local leaders and central leaders, provide a credible guarantee against central intervention in the local investment environment. Third, there do not seem to be barriers to trade among localities, and local governments are faced with hard budget constraints imposed by higher authorities. And, as predicted by the theory, foreign investment data show that foreign investors have been attracted to those counties and districts that have both economically viable projects and more decentralized authority in terms of investment regulation.

In sum, my analysis, the first using such micro-level data from Shanghai, shows that the essential features of a "federalist" system of property rights were in place in Shanghai's subjurisdictions by 1992. Overall, the decentralization of investment regulation in China has produced competition between local governments to attract foreign investment projects, and this competition is also largely unconstrained by central authority. The fact that foreign investors have clearly responded to the relative protection afforded by such competition reflects the credibility of property forms in this emerging "federalist" system.

2.1 Federalism and local investment autonomy in China

The theory of "market-preserving federalism" predicts that foreign investment will flow mainly to areas that are economically more competitive and more decentralized in terms of investment regulation. If foreign investment and local development zones are mainly found in the less competitive, more centralized areas of Shanghai, then this explanation can be refuted. In addition, if there are no signs that local governments operate under hard budget constraints and that they erect barriers to the free flow of goods, labor, and capital, then these explanations are refuted. Finally, there must be the presence of some sort of institution that "guarantees" the autonomy of local governments from the intervention of higher-level governments. As China's constitution affords no such guarantee, the institutional "guarantee" must be an informal one.

Consider the proliferation of local economic development zones as a measure of the decentralization of investment authority in China. Even if only the economic development zones that are officially sanctioned by the central government are examined, China's decentralization of tax and investment authority to such zones has been wide in scope and large in influence. Because they have only been partially dealt with elsewhere (Crane, 1990; Reardon, 1991; Kueh, 1992; Sang, 1993), it is worthwhile noting the diversity of their powers here (see Appendix), using more recent information supplied by the highest central government authority, the State Council (GBM, 1992).

China's "open cities" number 339, have a population of 320 million (about a quarter of the Chinese population), and cover some 500,000 square kilometers. They produce about 60 percent of China's gross domestic product. Foreign-invested enterprises actually in operation in these areas numbered some 39,000 by the end of 1992, with another 110,000 contracted to open. Exports from these enterprises totaled U.S.$8.5 billion for the first half of 1993, about 25 percent of China's total exports (CD, 1993a). Shanghai's three Economic and Technological Development Zones (ETDZs) and the Pudong New Area are the source of most of Shanghai's exports.

The diversity of the benefits that each type of zone is allowed to offer foreign and domestic investors suggests that such decentralization is not proceeding according to central plan. Altogether, there are eleven different types of "special economic zones" recognized by State Council directives since 1978, including zones for the export of high-technology and agricultural products and for the exchange of goods in areas bordering the Siberian frontier (GBM, 1992). Many overlap in jurisdiction and duplicate their respective regulatory authority over investment. Some have clear temporal constraints, whereas others have none. All are ambiguously defined. Overall, it is hard to imagine how such contradictions could be the product of a plan by central leaders and bureaucrats to decentralize regulatory authority over foreign investment. The timing of their creation, moving from the first SEZ in the border area near Hong Kong to the coastal areas of Fujian and Shanghai and finally to the border trading posts of the Siberian frontier, seems to parallel the restoration of political and economic ties with British Hong Kong, Western countries, Japan, Taiwan, and, most recently, Russia.

But in order to test this "federalist" explanation, consider the growth of the many local-level "development zones" and their own diversity and complexity. Indeed, if such a system is emerging in China today then its effects must be evident at the lowest levels of government. There is strong evidence that the central government, and even provincial and municipal governments, no longer control the "development zone" creation process. The credibility of the foreign enterprise property rights within their jurisdictions are thus defined and enforced by county-, district-, and even township-level authorities. The State Council Office of Special Economic Zones has put the total number of legal and illegal zones at twelve hundred (CD, 1993b), the State Land Administration at around two thousand (CD, 1992), and the State Planning Commission at around three thousand (XW, 1993). One influential economist who is knowledgeable on the issue estimates that there are around eight thousand "development zones."[3]

In an effort to return the flow of surplus capital toward its own development projects, the State Council has tried to close down these zones. But there is not even consensus at the central government level on which zones are "legal" and which are "illegal." The State Council's Special Economic Zones Office has stated that it hopes to preserve some 130 centrally approved development zones, and some 470 provincial- and municipal-level approved zones (CD, 1993a). The State Planning Commission, however, estimates that there are only about one hundred centrally approved zones, and some three hundred to four hundred provincially and municipally approved zones worth keeping (XW, 1993).

The deterioration of central regulatory authority over the provinces, the autonomous regions, and the three municipalities has been followed by an erosion of the authority of even those levels of government. Subordinate county- and district-level governments have assumed regulatory authority over foreign investment. Except for the three economic and technological development zones (ETDZs) and the special bonded trade and export-processing zones within the Pudong New Area – all approved by the State Council (see the appendix to this chapter) – evidence sug-

[3]Interview, November 1993.

gests that Shanghai's municipal government has itself lost control over many foreign investment projects to its counties, districts, and townships. In terms of center-granted special economic authority, Shanghai Municipality, a Coastal Open City and Coastal Economic Open Area, comprises one special economic area, the Pudong New Area, three ETDZs (Hongqiao, Minhang, and Caohejing), one New High Technology Products Open Area, One Export Processing Zone, and one Bonded Trade Zone. Aside from these there are thirteen urban districts and six suburban counties in which there are sixteen county-level industrial zones (*gongye xiaoqu*) and 196 township-level industrial zones recognized by the municipal government (*WHB*, 1993). These industrial zones, however, have not been authorized to offer special tax incentives for foreign investors. There do not seem to be accurate official records of the number of municipal-government–sanctioned or self-created "development zones" offering special tax breaks to foreign investors. City officials and scholars who study Shanghai's industrial economy do not know the total extent of "development zone" decentralization even within the municipality.[4]

From an original data set derived from foreign enterprise registration forms, it can be seen that between 1988 and 1993 foreign enterprises have invested in at least ninety-nine "special economic zones" that have not been officially approved by the central or Shanghai municipal governments.[5] The simple fact that these zones go by twenty-eight published types of titles suggests that the decentralization of investment regulation authority has not been a uniform, planned process. Simple descriptors have given way to all-encompassing ones: "Industrial Development Zones" and "Economic Open Development Zones" gave way to "Com-

[4]Based on interviews with Chinese scholars who study the management of local and foreign-invested industry and with officials from municipal- and county-level foreign trade and investment commissions, conducted November 1993 and March through June 1994.

[5]These data were collected and compiled using the foreign-invested enterprise start-of-operations (*kaiye*) announcements, published by the Shanghai Administration of Industry and Commerce (SAIC) in *Jiefang Ribao* (Liberation Daily), Shanghai's official newspaper. (Shanghai's SAIC appears to be the only agency that publishes such announcements.) The announcements contain much useful registration data on enterprises that have already begun operation: name of the enterprise, address, property form (joint-equity venture, cooperative, wholly foreign-invested, foreign-share–issuing public stock company, and public-stock-company–created enterprise), scope of economic activity (specific industry, trade, etc.), registered capital in the currency in which it was deposited in the People's Bank of China, corporate board members and officers, original date of operation and set time limit for dissolution, and SAIC registration number. These announcements also contain notices filed when enterprises "modify" (*biangeng*) their registration data. For this study I was able to codify start-of-operation announcements from 1988 through February 1994, creating the first data set of its kind for the study of foreign investment and "economic development zones" in China.

prehensive Industrial Open Development Zones" and "Private Economy Investment Open Development Zones." Others beckon to select groups of investors: "Taiwan Investment Industrial Zones," "Foreign Investment Industrial Courts," and "Scientific and Technological Court Zones." The diversity of names and benefits offered in these "zones" suggests a drive by local governments to distinguish themselves from other, competing localities.

Some of these zones openly advertise their investment benefits in Shanghai's official newspapers, including such benefits as the reduced 15 percent enterprise income tax rate, and others that clearly go against central government and municipal government mandates (*JR*, 1992). In addition, during the last few years at least eight private economy development zones have sprung up in Shanghai's counties at the initiative of village- and county-level leaders (Cheng, 1993). Interviews with local officials and private economy zone land development company managers – often the same individuals – indicate that such zones have successfully offered foreign investors the same special benefits that they offer domestic private investors.[6] In addition to the tax benefits and low land prices, they may also offer incorporation rights to investors who do not manufacture or even locate a headquarters within their jurisdiction. As with other federal systems, it is possible to locate a corporation's headquarters in the jurisdiction with the lowest corporate income tax rate and conduct business and operations within other localities.[7]

There is some evidence to suggest that Shanghai's municipal-level officials are aware of the apparent illegal benefits offered by the suburban "development zones" and that they are trying to give them legitimacy through mergers with "official" special economic jurisdictions that are recognized by the central and municipal governments. The "Xinghuo Industrial Zone," which has been referred to as the "Xinghuo Technical Development Zone" and the "Xinghuo Development Zone" in foreign enterprise investment registration materials and in official maps (PXG, 1993), has been annexed by the Pudong New Area, although some thirty kilometers and one county separate the two (*JR*, November 1993b).

Through increased inspections and regulation, the Shanghai municipal

---

[6]Based on interviews with township-level officials and "private economy zone" and land development company leaders in two of Shanghai's counties, April and May 1994.

[7]An interview with a township-level official who oversees a private economy development zone indicates that such authority can extend across provincial and municipal boundaries, albeit with more difficulty, than across district and county boundaries within Shanghai municipality. In this case, the zone collects flat "registration" fees and "administration" fees, as a percent of taxable profits, from hundreds of domestic investors and a few foreign investors.

government has been successful in eliminating the "development zones" created in urban areas. Whereas most of the thirteen urban districts were advertising district-created "development zones" and "technology development zones" in 1992 and 1993, by 1994 urban districts were no longer able to offer, or at least to advertise, such benefits to foreign investors.[8] As interviews with county- and township-level foreign investment administration officials in four of Shanghai's six counties reveal, some of the rural counties of Shanghai, however, began advertising the creation of special "zones" in 1991. By 1993 virtually every township had joined in the process.[9] Most counties and townships simply converted their old "industrial" zones into "development zones" and began competing with each other to offer lower land prices and tax benefits. It appears that any government authority that controls land use rights can set up a "land development company" and an "economic development zone." In some localities, county-level government agencies even compete with each other to set up unofficial "zones" on land they control.

The second and third elements of the "federalist" explanation are easily supported by the evidence. As others have noted, hard budget constraints on local government authorities exist throughout China (Oi, 1992; Wong, 1991, 1992), and their presence can be most clearly seen in the existence of fiscal contracts between lower and higher levels of government (Qian and Weingast, 1995). Interviews with government officials in the suburban districts and counties of Shanghai clearly reveal that there are indeed hard budget constraints (and fiscal contracts) as well as a lack of trade barriers between the localities. Although the maintenance of the "household residency permit" system means that the mobility of labor is somewhat constrained, in general there are few barriers to the movement of capital or goods.

Finally, market-preserving federalism demands a fourth element: an institutional mechanism that "guarantees" the nonintervention of higher levels of government. Federalist theories rely on the existence of such informal institutions as party coalition arrangements or on popular attitudes toward intra-government relations to explain the "guarantee" that keeps central or higher-level authorities from overwhelming lower-level authorities (Weingast, 1995).

In China's case, the answer may lie in the weakness of the formal and informal institutions supporting centralism. Formal central authority rests on the ambiguous powers given to the central government in China's constitution, and any informal institutions supporting centralism are colored by such disastrous central authority campaigns as the Great Leap

[8]Interview with foreign investment consultation company manager, June 1994.
[9]Interviews conducted March through June 1994.

Forward in the late 1950s and the Cultural Revolution of 1966 to 1976. As historians point out, central authority over economic activity was virtually nonexistent during the imperial periods, and ineffective during the Republican period of 1911 to 1949 (Kuhn, 1986; Kirby, 1984). Central fiscal control over provinces, municipalities, and autonomous regions was only strong during the two decades between 1957 and 1978 (Oi, 1992; Wong, 1991, 1992). Viewed historically, strong local government is the norm and centralism the aberration in China.

Shanghai has a history of clear independence from central authority as a colony for nearly a hundred years. Many of the senior local government leaders and officials who oversaw decentralization efforts in the early and mid-1980s were trained as cadres in the 1940s and early 1950s, when Shanghai's authorities had more regulatory control over its economy than in later decades. Shanghai's county- and township-level officials are naturally even more inclined to think and act independently of municipal authorities because many of Shanghai's rural counties were only annexed by the municipal government in the 1950s and 1960s. Shanghai's county seats often have recorded histories as trading and cultural centers of as long as a thousand years. This is in contrast to the city of Shanghai, which only became a large commercial center during the 1890s, and a financial and cultural center in the 1920s and 1930s. Interviews with county officials reveal that Shanghai's county governments often competitively construct their economic policies with an eye on developments in the neighboring counties of Zhejiang and Jiangsu provinces.[10]

Certainly individuals and local governments in Shanghai have long favored a return to the decentralized authority that their predecessors enjoyed, but how did they know that central authorities were not going to recentralize regulatory authority in the future? Evidence suggests that changes in two sets of informal institutions caused local authorities to act as if they believed central authorities would not try to recentralize their authority.

The first is the set of informal institutions that induce cooperation between Shanghai's municipal authorities and central government leaders. After the reorganization of central government and Communist Party ranks subsequent to June 4, 1989, Shanghai's mayors and party secretaries rose to lead the central authority. The current president and party general secretary, Jiang Zemin, was the former party secretary of Shanghai in the 1980s, and the vice premier responsible for government economic policies, Zhu Rongji, was the former party secretary and mayor of Shanghai. The secretive nature of central government and Communist Party politics prevents a clear understanding of the influence of any

---

[10]Interviews with officials in four Shanghai counties, March through June 1994.

"Shanghai faction" in central ranks. It can reasonably be assumed, however, that central leaders have a more realistic understanding of Shanghai's reform needs, and those of coastal areas in general, than did previous central leaders. It can also be assumed that Shanghai's current leaders enjoy avenues of communication previously denied their predecessors in the 1980s. The possibilities for cooperation are thus made more numerous, and from this the growth of informal institutions governing relations between Shanghai and central authority could develop.

Paramount leader Deng Xiaoping's visit to Shanghai and the Southern Coast areas in January and February 1992 provided an opportunity for both central and municipal authorities to signal their commitment to the increase in investment and the changes in property rights institutions begun in 1990 and 1991. County- and district-level leaders must have been even more encouraged by the reaction of municipal authorities to Deng's visit. These governments were encouraged by the strategic way in which the city government published – against central government and party orders[11] – the intraparty speech made by China's senior informal leader Deng Xiaoping on an inspection tour of Shanghai in January 1992, in which he simply said, "Shanghai should open up more" (Deng, 1993). Central leaders who owed their ascension to Deng's approval could hardly impose restrictions after his speech had been published by city leaders, and county- and district-level leaders must have been impressed by the strategic use of Deng's statement made by their superiors. Informal ties between former Shanghai officials who had become senior central-government leaders and current Shanghai officials and the strategic steps taken by city officials to commit themselves to the decentralization of regulatory authority must surely have contributed to expectations that local authority would not be recentralized.

The second set of informal institutions that may have contributed to the "guarantee" of the autonomy for local regulatory authority are those institutions facilitating coordinated action among local authorities at the county and district level. County-level leaders have an informal organization that operates at the central government level, an annual conference, and Shanghai's municipal leaders formally meet several times each year with county- and district-level party and government officials. China's counties and districts have even established official "sister" relationships with each other. Baoshan District, for example, has established educational and informational exchange agreements with thirty other local governments since 1984 (BDZ, 1993). From these meetings it can be reasonably assumed that local leaders have at least developed lines of communication with each other such that the possibility of coordinated,

---

[11]Interviews with city economic management authority officials, June 1993.

collective action might exist. Shanghai's six county-level party secretaries, for example, might thus find it relatively easy to coordinate strategic actions to force municipal leaders to decentralize regulatory authority.

Although there is no evidence that such coordination occurred or that such informal institutions exist, the internal monitoring costs of collective action among a mere six actors must be low. In sum, the existence of a strong history of local autonomy and of the strategic action of municipal leaders in their dealings with central leaders suggests that an informal guarantee of autonomy does exist. The opportunity (albeit not the evidence thereof) of effective, concerted strategic action by subordinate officials suggests the presence of an additional informal "guarantee" of local autonomy. The results of this local-level study thus complement research done using macro-level data (Qian and Weingast, 1995).

2.2 Testing the federalist explanation: Decentralization or simply economic advantage?

Clearly many factors enter into an investor's determination of the best location for investment. To test the strength of the federalist explanation, I look at how that explanation compares with an intuitive and persuasive alternative explanation: Foreign investors simply look for areas where potential Chinese business partners provide more lucrative opportunities. The quality of the available set of business partners is important because most foreign investors set up joint-equity ventures. To test the validity of each theory, I consider measures of foreign investment, industrialization, and enterprise competitiveness across the suburban counties and districts of Shanghai in 1992.

Why 1992? In this year foreign investment first began to flow to China in substantial amounts, and in this year local governments first began to set up their own, local "development zones" to entice foreign investors. But not all localities decentralized equally. Through interviews with foreign investment officials in four of Shanghai's six counties and districts, and through an examination of the existence of such local development zones in these counties and the urban districts, I can construct a rough ranking of the decentralization of investment authority within each county or district.

Chuansha/Pudong, Jiading, and Shanghai/Minhang counties, along with the three small ETDZs (see Figure 10.1), decentralized investment authority to subordinate towns and townships in 1991 and 1992.[12] Songjiang and Qingpu counties began decentralization in 1992. The urban districts, Baoshan District, and Nanhui, Jinshan, and Chongming coun-

[12]In 1992 most of Chuansha County became the Pudong New Area (with the remainder following in increments) and Shanghai County became Minhang District.

271

Figure 10.1

ties did not begin decentralization until 1993. To test the federalist explanation, compare the varying success of these three levels of local jurisdictions in attacting foreign investment during this crucial year of investment growth.

First, compare the number of new, operating foreign enterprises with the number of existing industrial enterprises, and the expression of this as a percentage in the third column. Clearly the pure size of the industrial economy (most foreign investment is in manufacturing) is not so important to foreign investment. In Chuansha County the number of new foreign-invested enterprises in 1992 nearly equaled half the number of

272

existing industrial enterprises, whereas in Chongming County they numbered only about 3 percent of the latter.

Second, consider the alternative explanation, that foreign investors seek the areas with the most lucrative types of partners. I argue that the average industrial exports, in RMB millions, and the average industrial production value, in RMB millions, of industrial enterprises is an accurate measure of the potential viability of joint ventures. Informal interviews with both foreign investors and Chinese industrial enterprise leaders support this assertion. Foreign investors often ask potential business partners about their productivity and export potential (especially as manufacturing exports are the best way for foreign investors to receive returns in hard currencies). And the data in Table 10.1 show a rough correlation between foreign investment and enterprise competitiveness. Counties with enterprises that perform comparatively poorly do not seem to attract much foreign investment. Investors do seem to be very interested in areas with more potential for lucrative partners.

Yet, if we consider these measures of competitiveness and the rough ranking of decentralization of the various counties and districts something different seems to be occurring. First, the cases where jurisdictions are both very decentralized and where the enterprises are very competitive can be set aside: Chuansha, Jiading, Shanghai, and Songjiang counties and the ETDZs. Their comparatively high levels of foreign investment are likely to be overdetermined. Cases of late decentralization and poor performance are also not very instructive: Fengxian and Chongming counties.

Now consider the interesting cases where areas are both administratively centralized and yet economically competitive, or where they are decentralized and yet not economically competitive. Baoshan District, Jinshan County and the original urban districts are examples of the first case. All of these areas are economic overachievers in the Shanghai area, largely due to the presence of very large central- and municipal-government industrial factories (steel mills in Baoshan, petrochemical factories in Jinshan, a range of such in the urban districts). In fact, outside of the three small ETDZs, Baoshan is one of the most advanced localities in all of China. And yet foreign investment did not flow there in 1992. The same is true of Jinshan County and the urban districts.

The key here is that in these three areas county-level leaders were successful in forcing foreign investors to come to bargain at their own tables. Foreign investors were not allowed to negotiate among subordinate town and township leaders. As interviews reveal, the government of Baoshan has also been particularly effective in forcing domestic individual investors to go to a monopolistic "private economy zone." The result, as with foreign investment, is a proportionately small share of the invest-

Table 10.1. *Investment, industrialization, decentralization, and enterprise competitiveness across suburban counties and districts of Shanghai Municipality, 1992*

Jurisdiction	(A): Number of new, operating foreign-invested (F.I.) enterprises, 1992[a]	(B): Number of industrial enterprises[b]	A/B (%)	Average industrial exports in RMB millions[c]	Average industrial production in RMB millions[d]	1992 decentralized F.I. authority?
Main urban districts	614	5,771	10.6	2.37	20.82	No
Chuansha County/Pudong[e]	356	827	43.0	3.04	14.59	Yes
Jiading County	168	864	19.4	1.99	18.07	Yes
Shanghai County/Minhang[f]	114	698	16.3	1.81	9.35	Yes
Baoshan District[g]	72	727	9.0	2.47	35.02	No
Fengxian County	72	812	8.8	1.05	5.80	No
Songjiang County	67	591	11.3	2.00	9.28	Yes
Nanhui County	66	1,031	6.4	1.07	5.56	No
Qingpu County	63	665	9.4	0.92	5.55	Yes
Jinshan County	62	556	11.5	1.63	17.01	No
ETDZs[b]	56	120	46.6	9.30	69.54	Yes
Chongming County	31	845	3.6	1.00	5.83	No

[a]Derived from Shanghai SAIC foreign-invested enterprise registration data.

[b]Number of industrial enterprises run by county, district, neighborhood, town, and township governments (excluding only enterprises run by the municipal level of government and by village-level governments) (STJ, 1993b: 55–71).

[c]Derived by dividing the total value of industrial exports, in 1990 prices, by the number of industrial enterprises as in note b (STJ, 1993b: 55–71).

[d]Derived by dividing the total value of industrial production, in 1990 prices, by number of industrial enterprises as in note b (STJ, 1993b: 55–71).

[e]Chuansha County became most of the Pudong New Area in 1992.

[f]Shanghai County became Minhang District in 1992.

[g]Baoshan County became an urban district in 1989, but it still continues to publish its economic data as a unit separate from other urban districts.

[h]Includes the Economic and Technological Development Zones of Caohejing, Minhang, and Hongqiao.

ment pie. The comparison of Jiading County and Baoshan District in 1992 is particularly instructive. The two were similar in terms of the size and performance of industry, and yet Jiading (an area even more remote from the urban center) attracted much more foreign investment than did Baoshan. The key here is that Jiading was already quite decentralized in terms of investment authority by 1992. Now consider the case of Qingpu County, an area relatively decentralized and yet not economically competitive. It managed to attract the same proportion of foreign investment as Baoshan did, but foreign investors here signed on with enterprises that were clearly inferior performers to those of Baoshan. The key factor, again, is decentralization.

2.3 The possibility of a federalist system in China

The analysis of foreign investment presented in this section supports the federalist explanation for the rise in the credibility of new property forms in China since reforms began in 1978. The results of this local-level study thus complement research done using macro-level data (Qian and Weingast, 1995; Montinola, Qian, and Weingast, 1995). Shanghai's municipal-, county-, district-, and township-level authorities acted to decentralize the regulation of foreign investment in the late 1980s and early 1990s. In doing so they established a system in which the competition between localities helps give credibility to investor property rights.

3.0 TESTING THE LOCAL CORPORATIST MODEL OF CREDIBLE PROPERTY RIGHTS

The keys to "local corporatist" theories that explain the growth of credible property rights institutions in marketizing CPEs are local government dependence on revenues from new forms of property rights or the strength of informal ties between investors, local government officials, and financial organizations. Unlike traditional theories of "corporatism" that seek to explain the high economic growth in advanced industrial democracies as the product of informal coalitions among government agencies, labor groups, and corporate managers, the "local corporatism" variant proposed by China scholars sees high economic growth as coming from the "fiscal dependence" of governments on "profit-sharing" fiscal institutions and the informal, cooperative ties among local governments, enterprise managers, and financial organizations (Nee, 1992; Nee and Su, 1994; Oi, 1992; Walder, 1992).

Although these explanations have not been formalized, a game-theoretic model such as that presented in Chapter 2 on commitment and the credibility of property rights might support such an effort. As that

275

model demonstrates, the credibility of new property forms rests on a counterintuitive notion: Governments can actually increase the credibility of property forms in the eyes of investors by raising the rates of taxation on them so that the government is more dependent on the revenue they provide. Investors may believe that governments will protect their property rights because they do not wish to harm an important source of revenue. One source of credibility in the theories of local corporatism proposed by China scholars comes from such fiscal dependence. These theories attempt to do more than merely explain the credibility of new property forms as the result of changes in fiscal institutions. They also try to explain the relatively high economic performance of township-level enterprises as the result of such informal institutions as social network norms (*guanxi*) and personal relationships.

As with the testing of the federalist theory in section 2, I test the "local corporatism" theory by examining the changes in formal institutions of fiscal relations between the various levels of government in Shanghai. I also look at changes in the informal institutions of "corporatist" cooperation between foreign investors, local government officials, and local bank and credit cooperative managers. Does increased dependence on such marketized forms of property as foreign ventures, ceteris paribus, lead to increased credibility and further investment? Following this logic, jurisdictions with high levels of fiscal dependence on marketized property forms are expected to attract more foreign investors; those that are more dependent on traditional state-owned property forms should be less successful in attracting foreign investment. I do not propose to test the variation of the "local corporatist" model that hypothesizes that the credibility of property rights rests solely on personal ties and network norms. Such a test could only come from surveys or systematic case studies of relationships between individuals in local enterprises, governments, and financial organizations (Nee and Su, 1994).[13] To test the theory that the credibility of foreign investment institutions rests on both fiscal dependence and informal and personal ties, I look for signs of both fiscal dependence and evidence that the registration and operation of foreign ventures rests on informal institutions.

---

[13]For an exploratory attempt at determining the strength of informal ties between foreign investors and local government officials, see Lewis (1996). In this work the lists of the members of the board and the executive officers of foreign enterprises are compared with lists of party cadres and government leaders at the county, town, and township levels in the suburban counties of Shanghai, and with the lists of the other foreign-invested enterprises in that locality. A survey of 222 such enterprises in Baoshan District suggests that such formal ties between enterprises and investors are rare (less than 10 percent of the cases), but that ties among foreign investors are fairly extensive (more than 20 percent of the cases).

3.1 Fiscal dependence and local government

Are Shanghai's levels of government fiscally dependent on marketized forms of property? Since 1980 there has been a dramatic change in the proportion of city revenue coming from state enterprises and taxes. In 1980, revenues from taxes were 5.8 billion RMB, and those from state enterprises were 11.4 billion RMB. By 1987, the figures were more than reversed: tax revenue had increased to 11.4 billion RMB, whereas state enterprise revenues fell to 4.8 billion RMB. By 1992, tax revenues had swollen to 18.3 billion RMB, whereas revenues from state enterprises had fallen to a mere 650 million RMB. In recent years, the distribution of enterprise profits in Shanghai has shifted toward marketized forms. In 1987 state enterprises reported profits of 1,067 million RMB, collectives reported profits of 173 million RMB, and foreign/private firms reported profits of 81 million. By 1992, state enterprise profits had fallen substantially to 622 million RMB, collective profits fell somewhat to 137 million RMB, and profits of foreign/private firms rose to 546 million RMB. Thus, overall, Shanghai has become more dependent on taxes as a revenue source, and foreign/private firms have become a relatively more important potential tax base.

Changes in formal fiscal institutions suggest that those jurisdictions that are more dependent on new forms of property should be more likely to attract foreign investment. Shanghai's fiscal institutions saw a major change in 1988 when the municipal government signed a five-year "fiscal contract" (*caizheng baogan*) with the central government in 1988 (*SJN*, 1989). Under the arrangement, for the first three years the city was obligated to pay its budget expenses as well as a set amount of funds to the central government, with the remainder retained by municipal authorities. For the last two years, the amount committed to the central government was increased 65 percent, and the remaining funds split between central authorities and municipal authorities. When the first "fiscal contract" expired in 1992, central and municipal authorities began new negotiations, with no new five-year contract emerging. Shanghai did, however, obtain the same terms that it had in 1992 for 1993.

In turn, municipal authorities established a five-year fiscal contract system with subordinate counties and districts, setting up two different systems of fiscal responsibility.[14] The first type of system saw some of the counties and districts paying local budget expenses and a base amount to city authorities equal to what they had handed over in 1987. Remaining funds were split according to percentages established for each individual county and district. For the first three years of this system Jinshan and

[14]As with the central-municipal contract for 1993, those between the municipal-level and subordinate jurisdictions were the same in 1993 as in 1992.

277

Steven Lewis

Table 10.2. *Foreign investment in Shanghai: Percent of total new operating enterprises by type of fiscal jurisdiction, 1988–93*

Jurisdiction	1988 (%)	1989 (%)	1990 (%)	1991 (%)	1992 (%)	1993 (%)
Original urban districts	48	56	51	41	35	35
Special economic areas[a]	14	12	10	20	24	27
Other counties/districts	31	28	33	36	36	32
Jinshan and Chongming counties	7	4	3	3	5	6

[a]Includes the Pudong New Area and the Economic and Technological Development Zones at Minhang, Caohejing, and Hongqiao.
Source: Data derived from Shanghai SAIC foreign-invested enterprise registration forms.

Chongming counties, and two urban districts, could retain all remaining funds. Other city districts, mainly the comparatively wealthy, heavily commercial and industrial urban districts, could retain between 75 and 85 percent of remaining funds. During the remaining two years, all of the counties and districts in the first system could retain only one-half of remaining revenues, with the base amount increased to the amount that unit had paid in 1990. The second system, which was used for all of the other urban districts and most of the counties, was the same except that the base amount increased by 1 percent each year during the first three years. Clearly, Jinshan and Chongming counties, Shanghai's most remote and agricultural counties, were the most favored counties under the new fiscal system, with the other counties also receiving more benefits than the more wealthy urban districts. The Pudong New Area, established in 1990, and the ETDZs were allowed to retain all funds remaining after their contracts were filled and thus enjoyed the greatest benefits among all jurisdictions. Finally, each county and district established similar fiscal contracts with subordinate township and neighborhood governments.

The evidence presented in Table 10.2 does not seem to support the fiscal dependence hypothesis: Those jurisdictions most dependent on tax revenues did not receive most of the foreign investment ventures.

Much of the foreign investment has gone to the special economic jurisdictions, such as the Pudong New Area, the EDTZs and the Bonded Trade Zone, and the rural counties that had fairly favorable fiscal terms. Urban districts, which generally had unfavorable fiscal terms in their fiscal contract, attracted a decreasing percentage of foreign investment, and Jinshan and Chongming counties, which had very favorable fiscal terms, have seen smaller shares of new foreign investment. Clearly, foreign investors have not been more attracted to jurisdictions that are more dependent on their investments as potential sources of revenue.

This may be so for several reasons. First, most investors probably do not consider the strategic value of taxes on their investments. Because many jurisdictions offer three- to five-year income tax holidays, and because many investors only intend to engage in short-term manufacturing, the connection between taxes and government behavior may not seem clear to investors. In fact, foreign ventures do end up contributing large amounts to local government coffers, through various kinds of taxes, but it is easy to see why individual investors would not initially see this connection because of the tax holiday benefits. Second, foreign investors may simply have no way of knowing in which jurisdictions their tax payments would have the most influence. The clearest measure of fiscal dependence would be to examine the actual amount of funds paid to higher levels of government as a percentage of total revenues collected, but because the officials of many jurisdictions consider such information to be an "economic secret," systematic analysis is not possible.[15] But, to the extent that the formal institutions controlling the amount that each jurisdiction has to pass on to higher authorities reflect the actual amounts paid, which is very likely if higher authorities possess only approximate information on the levels of economic activity going on at lower levels, the evidence suggests that fiscal dependence is probably not the source of credibility of any "local corporatism" in Shanghai.

3.2 Local government, investors, and informal institutions

Do informal institutions and personal relationships influence foreign investment in Shanghai? Evidence indicates that informal institutions and personal arrangements of several forms play a significant factor in the foreign investment registration and regulation enforcement processes. First, investors who are nominally foreign actually may be domestic investors bringing capital back home in a way that maximizes the benefits that such capital can attract. Domestic enterprises have several indirect ways that they can become foreign-invested (*sanzi*) enterprises. Bribes are an informal, though nonsystematic, means of obtaining foreign investment benefits, but larger, export-oriented enterprises have found a formal, legal means to do so: invest in Hong Kong or abroad, and then reinvest in Shanghai as a foreign investor. Research shows that by 1994 nearly one thousand Shanghai enterprises had invested abroad and are

[15] Although Shanghai's suburban counties publish such statistics in statistical indexes, none of the original urban districts do so. The Pudong New Area and the ETDZs also publish indexes, but these do not include fiscal data. Interviews conducted with urban district officials reveal that they are extremely reluctant to discuss their fiscal obligations to municipal authorities.

capable of using this technique (Ou and Jin, 1992). This path has been made easier by central government plans to increase mainland investment in Hong Kong before 1997 in order to facilitate the territory's incorporation within the mainland political and economic system. Unfortunately, only anecdotal evidence exists to show that this type of "returned-investment" behavior occurs (TEIU, 1993).

Second, there are many indications that the foreign enterprise registration process is open to strategic behavior designed to circumvent regulatory restrictions on the size and scope of foreign ventures. The fact that the annual percentage of contracted capital for foreign enterprise ventures that actually comes from abroad varies so widely suggests that enforcement of this regulation is inconsistent: 1989 (117 percent), 1990 (47 percent), 1991 (40 percent), and 1992 (23.5 percent) (*STJ*, 1990: 310, 1991: 334, 1993a: 57–60). Although foreign partners in joint equity and cooperative ventures are supposed to provide at least 25 percent of the total investment, they seem rarely to do so. One urban district reported U.S.$100 million in contracted ventures in the first three quarters of 1993, but announced that these ventures were only backed up by U.S.$500,000 from overseas (*SS*, 1993).

Third, undercapitalization by ethnic Chinese investors from Hong Kong, Macau, Taiwan, and Singapore provides the most solid evidence that personal relations and such informal institutions as the cultural norms of negotiation and conflict resolution influence the definition and enforcement of property rights in Shanghai. Because these Chinese are not only warmly received as foreign investors as a consequence of the Communist Party policy designed to gather allies in its conflict with Nationalist authorities on Taiwan, but also because many of them share a common language, they are more capable than other foreign investors of behaving strategically and exploiting the weaknesses of the foreign investment system. By the end of 1992, these non-mainland Chinese had contracted 67 percent of the direct investment projects in Shanghai, representing 62 percent of total foreign direct investment. Although they contributed 45 percent of the actual investment in foreign enterprises, on average they contributed only 17 percent of their contracted amount of capitalization, much lower than amounts for investors from other countries and regions (*STJ*, 1993: 57–61). Also, among foreign industrial enterprises in 1992, some 38 percent were joint ventures between mainland and overseas Chinese, and yet these enterprises produced only 18 percent of the industrial output and 11 percent of the total amount of tax and profits of industrial foreign enterprises. Contributing to monitoring problems is the fact that 65 percent of these industrial joint ventures are between overseas Chinese and collective enterprises, which operate outside of state production plans and are therefore relatively loosely controlled by city and local governments (*STJ*, 1993: 40). Furthermore, even greater disparities between real and actual investment exist in the more independent areas of Shanghai. The Pudong New Area's foreign enterprises on average only saw 6 percent of their contracted investment coming in from abroad in 1992, although Shanghai has a rate of 23 percent overall (*STJ*, 1993: 110–14).

Although the case of Shanghai presents local-level evidence that nullifies the hypothesis that the credibility of new property forms in marketizing economies comes from fiscal dependence, on which some theories of "local corporatism" seem to stand, there is strong evidence showing that the foreign investment process is subject to such informal institutions as cultural norms of communication and to the influence of personal relationships, as many "local corporatism" theorists contend.

4.0 CONCLUSION

This study of Shanghai's reforms demonstrates that formal institutional changes to decentralize regulatory authority over economic activity clearly influence the credibility of new property forms. Such changes, however, are at least facilitated by, and perhaps dependent on, changes in informal institutions, as this study's testing of the "local corporatism" theories demonstrate. A federalist theory for why China has succeeded in its marketization efforts must offer a plausible explanation for the nonintervention of central authorities to recentralize the reform process, and this explanation must rely on changes in informal institutions to provide that "guarantee" of nonintervention. In this chapter I offered several such plausible explanations. Furthermore, this study shows that "local corporatist" theories for China's success cannot rely on the "fiscal dependence" created by "profit-sharing" changes in formal taxation institutions as the hypothesized "guarantee" of cooperation among government, corporate, and financial actors. Evidence presented here indicates that such "dependence" does not exist, and therefore such theories must rely on other types of behavior to explain cooperative action. As informal institutions certainly played a significant role in changes in foreign investment institutions in Shanghai, the "local corporatism" hypothesis relying on informal institutions and personal relations to give credibility to property forms has some support.

Steven Lewis

APPENDIX: TYPES OF SPECIAL ECONOMIC
JURISDICTIONS IN SHANGHAI MUNICIPALITY
RECOGNIZED BY CENTRAL GOVERNMENT
IN MID-1990s

1. Shanghai as a "Coastal Open City" (yanhai kaifang chengshi)

Set up by State Council directive in 1984, "Coastal Open Cities" comprise fourteen coastal ports (95 percent of China's port capacity), stretching from Guangzhou in the far south to Shanghai in the east and Dalian in the Northeast. Their powers are mainly limited to offering more attractive conditions for certain types of industry that invest in their original urban districts (lao shi qu): limited land-use transfer authority; the right to waive local income tax and local government fees; no import tariffs on equipment to be used in joint-venture enterprises; the 15 percent tax rate for large-scale (U.S.$30 million and above) and long-term foreign ventures investing in energy, transportation, and port and urban construction projects; and a reduced income tax rate (80 percent of the basic rate, which is determined by the central government) for enterprises investing in production-oriented ventures.

2. Shanghai's Economic and Technological Development Zones (ETDZs) of Coastal Open Cities (yanhai kaifang chengshi de jingji jishu kaifa qu)

ETDZs were set up by State Council directive in eleven Coastal Open Cities in 1984 and 1985, with three zones from Shanghai (Minhang, Hongqiao, and Caohejing ETDZs) added in 1986 and 1988 and ETDZ powers given to Shanghai's Pudong New Area upon its creation in 1990. Two more ETDZs were added in 1992 and seven more in 1993, for a total of twenty-seven total development zones across China (JR, 1993a). Formally, their laws of incorporation were designed to attract foreign investors from the science and technology industries. The ETDZs have much the same authority as the Coastal Open Cities, except that they are administratively subordinate to their host Coastal Open Cities. Their special industry investors can get the lowest income tax rate (15 percent) but cannot import production or office equipment without paying tariffs.

The influence of the ETDZs on the decentralization of tax and investment authority has been large, however, because of the means by which the Coastal Open Cities were able to deal with the sale of their land-use rights. In imitation of high-tech industrial parks such as those found in America and Europe, the EDTZs were designed to gather together foreign investors into small production-oriented zones. As this required that

282

they be built outside of the cities, and thus outside of the land used by urban industrial work units, Coastal Open Cities were thus allowed to devise a new property form: the state-owned land development corporation. The registration of these companies, and the regulation of their land use, are supposed to be handled by central authority, the Land Administration Bureau. By the early 1990s, when surplus domestic capital could be moved between localities and banks more freely, and as central and local authorities began to decrease their monitoring of rural localities, thousands of nonsanctioned land development companies and "development zones" had sprouted up around China, including in Shanghai's urban districts and rural counties. With the removal of restrictions on foreign investor participation in the land development business in 1992, hundreds of joint-venture and wholly foreign-owned development companies have been formed in the Shanghai area.

3. Shanghai's Coastal Economic Open Areas
(yanhai jingji kaifang qu)

These areas were first recognized for the Yangtze River area in 1985 – including the rural counties of Shanghai – the Liaodong Peninsula in the Northeast in 1988, the Jinan area of East China's Shandong Province in 1990, and much of Guangdong Province in 1992. The powers given to these areas were the first attempts to increase the benefits offered to domestic investors, mainly to encourage export processing. Export processing enterprises could obtain more export rights and reduced tariffs, as well as no tariffs on the import of equipment for production. Scientific- and technology-oriented investments received the 24 percent income tax rate. Also, as with the above forms, large-scale foreign investments in infrastructure could get the 15 percent income tax rate. Using their new authority as Coastal Economic Open Areas, or as Coastal Open Cities – as many such cities are both – they have set up industrial districts (*gongye qu*) in farming areas in the outlying districts and counties of Shanghai and other areas of China. Some of these districts became unofficial "development zones" in the 1990s.

4. Shanghai's Pudong New Area (Shanghai pudong xinqu)

In terms of the benefits it is allowed to offer to investors, especially the 15 percent tax rate for "export-oriented" enterprises, Pudong is the same as the Special Economic Zones of Shenzhen, Zhuhai, Shantou, and Xiamen. Yet, administratively it is still subordinate to the Shanghai city government (Sang, 1993). In terms of revenue collection, however, Pudong is different from other city districts in Shanghai in that it was allowed to retain all of the funds collected beyond its annual contract with the city government, but only during the eighth Five-Year Plan (1991–5). It is also allowed to control for its own development the foreign currency earned by its export-oriented enterprises, which has led to the development of a new state-owned development bank. In July 1995 the State Council publicly approved the extension of special tax breaks for Pudong's businesses for the next five-year period (Faison, 1995).

5. Shanghai's New High-Technology Products Open Area
(gaoxin jishu chanye kaifa qu)

In 1988 the State Council recognized Beijing's "Experimental District for the Open Development of New Technology Products" (*xin jishu chanye kaifa shiyan qu*), and in 1993 it approved twenty-six more: twenty-one in large cities and Open Cities, two in Economic and Technology Development Zones (including Shanghai's Caohejing), and three in Special Economic Zones. These areas extended the benefits available to foreign and Chinese investors in SEZs and ETDZs to all investors doing research and production related to a few high-technology fields. These areas are also different in that their authority is directly subordinate to the central government. They are subject to many detailed conditions relating to such factors as the ratio of researchers per other staff and workers, and the amount of research funding as a percent of total enterprise income.

6. Shanghai's Bonded Trade Zone (baoshui qu)

The first Bonded Trade Zone was approved for Shanghai's Pudong New Area in 1990, followed by zones in Tianjin, a Coastal Open City, the Shenzhen, and Shantou SEZs in 1991, and by zones in Guangzhou and Dalian, Coastal Open Cities, in 1992. The main benefit that they can offer foreign investors is a low enterprise income tax rate for entrepot trade, and the lowest tax rate (15 percent) for export processing enterprises. Foreign investors engaging in entrepot trade in the Bonded Trade Zone of Shanghai and the Shenzhen and Shantou SEZ zones also benefit from the 15 percent income tax rate because the Bonded Trade Zones are located within SEZs or SEZ-like areas that are able to offer such lower rates. The level of autonomy of these zones is unclear: Although they can only be established by State Council approval, their administration, and thus investment authority, is under local government control. The Waigaoqiao Bonded Trade Zone in Shanghai's Pudong New Area has seen the registration and opening of hundreds of wholly foreign-owned enterprises since it was established.

REFERENCES

BDZ (*baoshan difang zhi*/Baoshan Local Gazette). *Baoshan nianjian 1993* (Yearbook of Baoshan, 1993). (Shanghai: Shanghai kexue zaji chubanshe).

CD (*China Daily*), "Authorized Use of Land Required to Curb Abuse," December 10 (1992), 1.

"Praise for China's Decade of Progress," November 23 (1993a), 4.

"State Closes 1,000 EDZs to Better Efficiency," August 13 (1993b), 1.

Cheng Baorong, "Shanghai geti siying jingji fazhan xianzhuang, wenti jiqi duice" (Shanghai's Individual and Private Economy's Development Situation: Problems and Counter-Measures), unpublished manuscript, Shanghai Academy of Social Sciences, Economic Research Institute (1993).

Crane, George, *The Political Economy of China's Special Economic Zones* (New York: M. E. Sharpe, 1990).

Deng Xiaoping, *Deng Xiaoping wenxuan* (Selected Works of Deng Xiaoping) (Beijing: Renmin chubanshe, 1993).

Faison, Seth, "China to Keep Coast Areas' Special Status: East Shanghai Zone Is Haven from Taxes," *New York Times*, July 7 (1995), C2.

GBM (Guowuyuan bangongting mishuju/Secretariat Department, State Council Office), *Zhongguo jingji gaige kaifang shiyan qu* (China's Economic Reform Open Experimental Areas) (Beijing: Zhongguo qingnian chubanshe, 1992).

Gold, Thomas B., "Urban Private Business in China," *Studies in Comparative Communism* 22: 2–3 (1989), 187–201.

JR (*Jiefang ribao*/Liberation Daily), "Gudong siying qiye jin kaifa xiaoqu" (Stimulate the Entrance of Private Enterprises into Development Mini-Zones), March 22 (1992).

"Guowuyuan xin pi qige kaifaqu" (State Council Approves Seven New Development Areas), May 5 (1993a).

"Xinghuo gongye qu naru Pudong xinqu" (Xinghuo Industrial District Incorporated by Pudong New Area), November 26 (1993b).

Kirby, William C., *Germany and Republican China* (Stanford, CA: Stanford University Press, 1984).

Knight, Jack, *Institutions and Social Conflict* (Cambridge: Cambridge University Press, 1992).

Kueh, Y. Y., "Foreign Investment and Economic Change in China," *China Quarterly* 131 (1992), 637–90.

Kuhn, Philip A., "The Development of Local Government," in John K. Fairbank and Albert Feuerwerker, editors, *The Cambridge History of China*, Vol. 13: *Republican China, 1912–1949, Part 2* (Cambridge: Cambridge University Press, 1986), pp. 329–60.

Lewis, Steven, "Testing General Theories of Change in Property Rights: Privatization Experiments and Economic Development Zones in China," Ph.D. dissertation, Washington University, St. Louis (1996).

Montinola, Gabriella, Yingyi Qian, and Barry Weingast, "Federalism, Chinese Style: The Political Basis for Economic Success in China," *World Politics* 48: 1 (1995): 50–81.

Nee, Victor, "Organizational Dynamics of Market Transition: Hybrid Forms, Property Rights and Mixed Economy in China," *Administrative Science Quarterly* 37: 1 (1992), 1–27.

Nee, Victor, and Sijin Su, "Local Corporatism and Informal Privatization in China's Market Transition," in Victor Nee and Thomas Lyons, editors, *The*

Economic Transformation of South China: Reform and Development in the Post-Mao Era (Ithaca, NY: Cornell University East Asia Series 70, 1994).

Oi, Jean C., "Fiscal Reform and the Economic Foundations of Local State Corporatism in China," *World Politics* 45: 1 (1992), 99–126.

Ou, Zhiwei, and Fang Jin, *Kuaguo jingying zhi lu* (The Road to Multi-national Management) (Shanghai: Shanghai shehui kexueyuan chubanshe, 1992).

Perkins, Dwight, "Completing China's Move to the Market," *Journal of Economic Perspectives* 8: 2 (1994), 23–46.

PXG (Pudong xinqu guanwei bangongshi xuanchuan chu/Propaganda Section, Pudong New Area Management Committee Office), *Shanghai Pudong xinqu* (Shanghai Pudong New Area Map) (Shanghai: Zhonghua ditu xueshe, 1993).

Qian, Yingyi, and Barry Weingast, "China's Transition to Markets: Market-Preserving Federalism, Chinese Style," Essays in Public Policy 55, Hoover Institution on War, Revolution and Peace, Stanford University (1995).

Reardon, Lawrence C., "The SEZs Come of Age," *China Business Review* November–December (1991), 14–20.

Riker, William H., *Federalism: Origin, Operation, and Significance* (Boston: Little, Brown, 1964).

Sang, Bin Xue, "Pudong: Another Special Economic Zone in China? – An Analysis of the Special Regulations and Policy for Shanghai's Pudong New Area," *Northwestern Journal of International Law & Business* 14: 1 (1993), 130–60.

SJN (*Shanghai jingji nianjian 1989*/Shanghai Economic Yearbook 1989) (Shanghai: Shanghai shehui kexueyuan chubanshe, 1989).

SS (Shanghai Star), "District Absorbs Overseas Investments," November 26 (1993).

STJ (Shanghai tongji ju/Shanghai Bureau of Statistics), *Shanghai gongye nianjian* (Shanghai Industry Yearbook) (Shanghai: Shanghai tongji ju, 1993b, 1992b, 1989, 1988).

Shanghai Pudong xinqu tongji nianjian (Statistical Yearbook of Shanghai's Pudong New Area) (Beijing: Zhongguo tongji chubanshe, 1993c).

Shanghai shi duiwai jingji tongji nianjian (Foreign Economic Statistical Yearbook of Shanghai) (Shanghai: Shanghai tongji ju, 1993a).

Shanghai tongji nianjian (Shanghai Statistical Yearbook) (Beijing: Zhongguo tongji chubanshe, 1990, 1991, 1992a, 1995).

Su, Sijin, "Hybrid Organizational Forms in the Mixed Economy in South China: 'One Firm, Two Systems,' and Their Dynamic Process," paper presented at the Cornell University Symposium on "The Great Transformation in South China and Taiwan: Markets, Entrepreneurship, and Social Structure," October 16–18 (1992).

TEIU, "Country Report: China and Mongolia, Third Quarter 1993." (London: The Economist Intelligence Unit, 1993).

Walder, Andrew, "Property Rights and Stratification in Socialist Redistributive Economies," *American Sociological Review* 57: 4 (1992), 524–39.

Weingast, Barry, "The Economic Role of Political Institutions: Market-Preserving Federalism and Economic Growth," *Journal of Law, Economics and Organization* 11: 1 (1995), 1–31.

WHB (Wenhui Bao), "Hujiao gongye xiaoqu chengpi jueqi" (Shanghai's Suburban Industrial Small Zones Rise Up One after Another), October 5 (1993).

Wong, Christine, "Central-Local Relations in an Era of Fiscal Decline: The Paradox of Fiscal Decentralization in Post-Mao China," *China Quarterly* 128 (1991), 691–715.

"Fiscal Reform and Local Industrialization: The Problematic Sequencing of Reform in Post-Mao China," *Modern China* 18: 2 (1992), 197–227.

XW (Xinmin Wanbao/Xinmin Evening News), "Guojia ji kaifaqu jianshe chengxiao zhuozhu" (Achievements in the Construction of State-Level Development Areas Are Outstanding), November 9 (1993).

Federalist and local corporatist theories: A comment on an empirical test

VICTOR NEE

Why has the Chinese economy maintained such a spectacular rate of economic growth? This is the question that motivates Steven Lewis's case study of Shanghai's move to reclaim its former status as the financial center of continental East Asia. His account describes the institutional changes that have paved the way for Shanghai's transition to a market economy. The description in turn provides evidence to test theories of sustainable growth. It is the first empirical test of new institutionalist explanations of sustainable economic growth in China. This comment first discusses the theories he tests and then focuses on the implications of his results.

Federalist theory, extending new institutional economics, emphasizes the economic role of political institutions, but focuses analytic attention on the emergence of a market-preserving federalism in which local governments act as a counterbalance to the central state, limiting the state's ability to expropriate economic surplus (Weingast, 1993). The main argument of federalist theory posits that a political order in which multiple levels of government coexist within a framework ensuring autonomy for lower levels of government fosters competition between local governments for capital and labor. In the competition to attract and retain capital, political actors have an incentive to demonstrate credible commitment to maintaining an institutional environment favorable to economic growth. Federalist theory assumes a market economy in which capital and labor are free to move to the most advantageous sites (Riker, 1964). It has difficulty, therefore, in explaining why local political actors constrain rent-seeking activities to invest in market-oriented growth in the nonmarket setting of China during the early stages of reform. Lewis's decision to focus his case study on the role of foreign investment was the appropriate research design to test federalist theory. Once a market economy is more or less in place, however, competition among lower governmental units imposes constraints on their predatory behavior through the exit power of capital and labor.

Federalist and local corporatist theories

Another limitation of federalist theory it that it assumes a legal-rational institutional framework in which laws regulating property rights apply to both economic and political actors. Such is not the case in China, where traditionally political authority defines itself above the rule of law. Lack of a tradition of legal-rational authority and institutionalized procedures for litigation and enforcement of contracts results in widespread uncertainty over rights to economic surplus specified by contractual agreement with government, whether central or local. Competitive pressure among local governments for investment and market share may limit predatory behavior by government, yet this in itself does not give rise to secure rights over property and credible commitment to contracts. In a system of *kadijustice,* economic actors seek to cement formal agreements and contracts in a framework of informal understanding and trust secured by ongoing personal connections. The limitation of federalist theory applied to the post-communist context – the assumption of an existing market economy and established legal-rational institutional framework – is what gives rise to interest in local corporatist theory.

In corporatist models, local government provides essential backing for firms operating in an institutional environment of partial reform. For many local firms (especially township firms) at the bottom of the hierarchy of industry, local government's backing is crucial because it provides firms with valuable network ties needed to secure factor resources and stronger negotiating positions with respect to larger state-owned and foreign firms. Such services provided by local government should be distinguished from redistribution, in which resources are appropriated by administrative fiat from the periphery to the center and distributed back to the periphery. In the corporatist role, local government seeks to promote economic development, and if this requires limitations on redistribution, it willingly does so lest it loses out in the competition for investment capital and market share.

Although corporatist accounts share the same emphasis on the role of local government, they nonetheless differ in their specification of the causal mechanisms that explain sustainable growth. Broadly speaking, one variant of the corporatist model employs state-centered analysis while the other conceives of local corporatism as a social institution. As Lewis points out, the state-centered approach stresses the importance of fiscal decentralization in providing incentives for political actors to pursue local strategies favorable to economic growth. The "local state corporatist" model claims that sustained economic growth can obtain as long as there are secure property rights for some government unit and sufficient incentives for that unit to pursue growth. According to this view, individual agents need not have rights over the firm's profits for economic growth to occur, because there is no inherent reason why secure property rights will

289

be an incentive only if they are assigned to private interests (Oi, 1992). China's fiscal reform provides local governments rights over income generated by nonstate firms, creating strong incentives for local officials to foster economic development. Local governments have taken on characteristics of a multidivisional firm, with state officials acting as the equivalent of a board of directors. They plan and coordinate economic activities in their territorial jurisdiction, making all investment decisions, taking risks, and finding ways to bail out firms in financial trouble. Political actors are the real entrepreneurs in state-centered analysis, as it is the local government that is responsible for shaping the outcome of reform.

The state-centered approach treats markets as a background factor, rather than as an explanatory variable. The success and survival of firms is still determined by the socialist state, albeit its local agents. Firms readily conform to a script written for them by local state officials, playing no autonomous role. Rather than seeing the shift to markets as the source of improved economic performance, it attributes the success of Chinese reforms to more effective monitoring and enforcement by local government of industrial property it owns compared to that of the central state. This is why state-centered analysis emphasizes the reassignment of property rights within the state hierarchy to explain sustainable growth (Walder, 1992). It assumes that the cost of information to political actors is sufficiently cheap at the local level to enable government to act as the board of directors of a multidivisional firm. Yet, even at the level of local communities and municipalities, the cost of information for political actors increases exponentially as the division of labor becomes more complex and the number of firms grow in the wake of rapid industrialization.

Missing from the state-centered approach to explaining sustainable growth in the industrial economy of China are the economic actors and key features of institutional change that distinguish the decentralization process in the post-Mao China from that of the Maoist era. These include economic institutions like profit sharing, the implementation of open-door policies leading to integration with the world market economy, the presence of foreign investors as economic actors, the birth and growth of private and semiprivate business that compete with publicly owned firms, and the evolution of informal rights to property leading to the ascendancy of the profit motive in an emergent mixed economy (Lyons and Nee, 1994).

By contrast to the state-centered model, local corporatist accounts argue that economic actors and firms embedded in local communities, backed by corporatist governments, fueled the economic growth in China. By local corporatism, I refer to the matrix of social institutions giving rise to a "loosely coupled" coalition between local government, financial institutions, firms, and employees aimed at promoting market-oriented growth. In local corporatist arrangements there is a gap between the formal rules of the game and what political and economic actors actually agree to do in informal settings. This separation between formal and informal institutions provides corporatist arrangements with the flexibility to adapt quickly to unexpected changes in the institutional environment without first obtaining approval from superordinate state agencies. The speed of response to changing circumstances enables economic and political actors to adjust to new opportunities in a market environment defined by uncertainty about the fundamental rules of the game and inconsistent monitoring and enforcement of formal rules by the central state.

Bounded rationality and opportunism are commonplace even in small communities (Popkin, 1979). For this reason, the local corporatist model emphasizes the importance of repeated exchange, social norms, and networks of personal ties that link political and economic actors in communities and municipalities. Trust needed for maintaining credible commitment is fostered by a thick web of personal ties. In settings in which information is shared by actors, not only are metering costs lower, but trust is more readily enforced by credible sanctions. Malfeasance and opportunism are punished by sanctions leading to exclusion from the core group of political and economic actors in local corporatist orders. In other words, reputation matters when a web of personal connections provide the critical social capital needed to be a participant in economic transactions.

Local corporatist theory readily combines with federalist theory. It assumes ongoing parameter shifts in the institutional environment resulting in change in the comparative costs of governance (Nee, 1992). The expansion and thickening of market institutions drives the shifts in parameters altering the comparative advantage of alternative governance structures in the Chinese industrial economy. Competition for investment and trade between corporatist governments results in the evolution of local institutions, formal and informal, more apt to attract investment capital and promote economic growth. As the mix of property rights shifts toward a greater representation of private and semiprivate property forms, the role of local government incrementally changes from socialist redistribution to that of third-party enforcer of contracts. Local corporatist arrangements have a comparative advantage under conditions of partial reform when the existing institutional framework has yet to be supplanted by an institutional framework consistent with the needs of a modern market economy. Under such circumstances, informal arrangements worked out by political and economic actors, backed by enforceable trust, are crucial because they maintain a framework conductive to credible commitment between political and economic actors.

Lewis's chapter provides an illuminating and persuasive analysis of the importance of competition for foreign investment in the dynamics of institutional change at the local level. He describes the evolution of an institutional framework favorable to foreign investment in Shanghai to test theories of sustainable growth in China. Lewis provides persuasive evidence showing how regulatory power over foreign investment devolved to lower levels of government. In order to attract foreign investment, government units in the Shanghai area vie with one another to offer favorable terms.

Lewis's study tests the state-centered corporatist hypothesis by asking whether fiscal dependence on tax revenues from marketized firms correspond to government providing a more favorable institutional environment for foreign investors. The distinctive feature of state-centered analysis is its sole emphasis on political actors and institutions in explaining sustainable growth. It claims that the fiscal dependence on tax revenue from marketized firms explains the needed change in incentives to sustain economic growth. Lewis's research design is both simple and ingenious. He reasons that if the fiscal dependence hypothesis holds, then he should find the highest concentration of foreign investment in districts most dependent on marketized firms for tax revenue. His data show instead that foreign investment is most concentrated in districts that provide more favorable terms to foreign investors, but these are not the same districts that are most dependent on tax revenues from marketized firms. Consequently, he rejects the fiscal dependence hypothesis of state-centered analysis.

In conclusion, rather than focusing only on changes in incentives for political actors, the new institutionalist corporatist approach maintains that economic actors and firms embedded in local communities and municipalities, backed by corporatist governments, fueled the economic growth in the coastal provinces of China. Local corporatist theory highlights the economic role of social institutions, in combination with political institutions, in explaining sustainable growth in the Chinese industrial economy. Federalist and local corporatist theories differ from state-centered explanations in that they account for improvements in incentives for both political and economic actors; hence they explain why corporatist arrangements are self-enforcing and result in flexible cooperation between government and firm in a manner that can sustain economic growth in an otherwise uncertain institutional environment.

REFERENCES

Lyons, Thomas P., and Victor Nee, *The Economic Transformation of South China: Reform and Development in the Post-Mao Era* (Ithaca, NY: Cornell East Asia Series, Cornell University, 1994).

Nee, Victor, "Organizational Dynamics of Market Transition: Hybrid Forms, Property Rights, and Mixed Economy in China," *Administrative Science Quarterly* 37: 1 (1992):1–27.

Oi, Jean C., "Fiscal Reform and the Economic Foundations of Local State Corporatism in China," *World Politics* 45: 1 (1992), 99–126.

Popkin, Samuel, *The Rational Peasant* (Berkeley, CA: University of California Press, 1979).

Riker, William H., *Federalism* (Boston: Little, Brown, 1964).

Walder, Andrew G., "Corporate Organization and Local Government Property Rights in China," in V. Milor, editor, *Changing Political Economies: Privatization in Post-Communist and Reforming Communist States* (London: Lynne Rienner, 1992), 53–67.

Weingast, Barry, "Constitutions as Governance Structures: The Political Foundations of Secure Markets," *Journal of Institutional and Theoretical Economics* 149: 1 (1993), 286–311.

11

Learning about the economy: Property rights and the collapse of the East German industrial economy

HANNES WITTIG[1]

1.0 INTRODUCTION

When the wall that had divided the two German states came down, the world expected the formerly communist East Germany to make rapid economic progress. The German Democratic Republic (GDR) would fare much better when exposed to capitalism, it was presumed, than her former communist allies and trading partners. Not only had the GDR apparently enjoyed economic leadership within Comecon, the communist trading bloc, it was also endowed with a powerful sister state that would help it over initial economic difficulties and soften the political and social difficulties associated with a radical transformation process.

These expectations were brutally disappointed. The GDR experienced a more dramatic economic decline than has ever been experienced by any other industrial nation in history (Sinn and Sinn, 1992). Within months, the number of industrial employees fell from around 3.2 million to around 800,000 (Statistisches Bundesamt, June 1992). Between the first half of 1990 and the third quarter of 1991, industrial production in the GDR declined by approximately 70 percent (Monatsbericht der Deutschen Bundesbank, November 1991). Moreover, even a few years after the collapse, recovery was still very slow. Instead of contributing U.S.$400 billion to the public purse, as experts had predicted, actual revenues from the privatization of East German firms were negative (Sinn and Sinn, 1992). In the spring of 1994 the debt of the national privatization agency, the Treuhandanstalt, was around U.S.$150 billion. Without

[1] This chapter was presented as a paper at the Annual Research Conference of the Association of Public Policy Analysis and Management held October 28–30, 1993, in Washington, DC. The author wishes to thank Edward Bird, Hans-Werner Sinn, and Susanne Lohmann for comments. The chapter benefited substantially from extensive discussions and joint work with Daniel Diermeier. The usual disclaimer applies.

much exaggeration one might say that one of the largest industrial sites of the world had vanished.

A variety of explanations have been offered for the puzzling discrepancy between promising starting conditions and disastrous outcomes. Some of these explanations are normative in the sense that they identify the short-comings of the economic policies chosen by the West German government and suggest better solutions (Akerlof et al., 1991; Sinn and Sinn, 1992). Most of these explanations emphasize in particular the dramatic rise of the real wage caused initially by the currency union itself and subse-quently by a lack of discipline on the part of trade unions in the year following reunification when collective bargains aimed at a rapid equaliz-ation of East and West German wage levels were made.[2] The explosion of the real wage, it is argued, was decisive in the destruction of East German industrial competitiveness.

Although it is undoubtedly true that high real wages contributed to the economic collapse, this approach does not address the question of why no precautionary policies were adopted by the West German government. As is evident from the literature on labor economics, trade union behavior is quite well understood. Unions can be reasonably modeled as wage-generating mechanisms where output depends on a certain number of input factors, most importantly on the wage elasticity of the labor de-mand curve (which in turn depends on labor productivity) and on the reservation utility for laid-off workers (which in turn is typically depen-dent on government policies such as the level and duration of unemploy-ment benefits and the extent of government-provided employment oppor-tunities).[3] By an appropriate choice of policies, government can influence, if not predetermine, the outcome of wage bargaining even within an institutional framework of autonomous collective bargaining (*Tari-fautonomie*) such as has been a cornerstone of the West German social market economy (*Soziale Marktwirtschaft*).[4]

Why then did West German government leaders forgo their chance to choose policies so as to avoid the disastrous outcomes of free union bargaining in East Germany?[5] Here a version of the theory of politically

[2] In the absence of capitalist private property Eastern employers' associations offered only weak resistance.

[3] For these results see, for instance, McDonald and Solow (1981), Oswald (1985), and more recently Calmfors (1992) or Layard, Nickell, and Jackman (1991).

[4] The interaction between government and collective bargaining has been explicitly modeled as a macroeconomic game by authors such as Calmfors and Horn (1985), Gylfason and Lindbeck (1986), and Holmlund and Lundborg (1988).

[5] Indeed, the West German government had even more than its usual set of choice variables at its disposal: The State Treaty in which the basic institutional arrangements were made passed the German Bundestag with a majority that would have well al-lowed for (temporary) constitutional amendments.

induced business cycles as pioneered by Nordhaus (1975) may be of help.[6] Chancellor Helmut Kohl, being in a highly precarious political situation, it is argued, consciously committed this omission – discounting future election results – in order to win the first free elections in the GDR in March 1990 as well as the first all-German general elections in the fall of 1990. Being under threat from within his own party, and facing a social democratic opposition candidate who was clearly leading the polls at the time, Kohl deliberately refrained from choosing policies that would impose tangible short-term burdens on East German voters but that might have been more beneficial in the long run.[7] In this light, one would have to discount Kohl's infamous television promise of "flourishing landscapes" (*blühende Landschaften*) in East Germany on the evening before the State Treaty was enacted. Also, the short-term perspective would serve to explain his consistent refusal to admit that he was going to raise taxes for the financing of reunification, which he obviously did shortly after his glorious victory in the fall elections of 1990.

This story relies on the implicit assumption that Kohl did in fact know about the dismal state of East German industry at the time when crucial decisions were taken.[8] Yet, it is not at all obvious that the West German government could have known the *extent* of the productivity gap. How could they have found out other than by gathering expert opinion from macroeconomic research institutes or by hearing the voices of interest groups? How could they have updated their unduly optimistic prior beliefs about East German productivity?

The analysis presented here suggests that the peculiar circumstances of German unification, especially the complicated political and legal problems regarding the role of the former allied powers, the limited influence of the West German government on privatization in East Germany, and the perception of time pressure by the West German government, led to a decision sequence in which the usual political and economic institutions that have helped to sustain the economic success of the old West Germany could not function properly. In particular, those channels by which infor-

---

[6] The first stream of work on political business cycles assumed myopia on the part of either voters (Nordhaus, 1975) or parties (Hibbs, 1977). The second stream, beginning with Hamada (1976), Kydland and Prescott (1977), and Barro and Gordon (1983), has been explicitly game theoretic, incorporating rational expectations so that neither economic and political actors nor voters are systematically fooled in equilibrium. For an overview, see Alesina (1995).

[7] The political scenery in the crucial months is well described in Herles (1990).

[8] It also shares the notorious weakness of theories of politically induced business cycles, their dependence on the assumption of a myopic electorate. In contrast, the explanation developed in this chapter will be compatible with rational behavior on the part of all participants.

mation about the state of the private economy is transmitted from economic to political decision makers either were not available or did not function properly in the case of the East German economy. Government acted on an initial misperception, I argue, and there was no feasible mechanism through which this misperception could be corrected before important economic policy decisions were made.

That does not mean, however, that the dismal state of the GDR economy was completely unknown in West Germany. On the contrary, it had soon become apparent to that very group of economic actors who were expected to be the engines of East German growth and who had, in search of opportunities for profitable acquisitions and investment, flooded East Germany in the immediate wake of the fall of the wall: West German entrepreneurs. How then, if knowledge about the true productivity of East German industrial facilities was available before government decisions were taken, did the misperception guide policy? Why did the government not gather this information from entrepreneurs? Why did it base its decisions on a faulty perception of East German industrial productivity?

My answers to these questions derive from an argument about the credibility of the private information offered by entrepreneurs. The government realized that entrepreneurs had an economic incentive to claim low productivity for East German industry so as to obtain favorable economic policy. If property rights in East Germany had been sufficiently clear to permit the alienation of industrial assets, then the absence of investments by entrepreneurs would have made their claim more credible: Not investing when productivity is high involves an opportunity cost to entrepreneurs in terms of forgone profits. Property rights were not sufficiently clear to allow alienation, however. Consequently, claiming low productivity was costless to entrepreneurs and therefore was "cheap talk" that lacked credibility with the government.

The analysis of this "pathological case" helps throw light on the role of effective property rights in the more normal workings of political-economic institutions. Entrepreneurs have a strong incentive to search for profitable investments. Their efforts produce vast amounts of decentralized information about the specifics of "time and place" that would be extremely costly and time-consuming for government to discover through either its own agents or independent auditors (Hayek, 1945). Effective property rights give the entrepreneurs the opportunity not to invest, which enables them more credibly to convey their information to policy makers. Although more credible information does not guarantee that disastrous economic policies will be avoided by self-interested policy makers, it enables them to make more informed choices.

2.0 POSITIVE POLITICAL THEORIES
OF PROPERTY RIGHTS

The positive political theory of property rights has a short history. Whereas the importance of property rights has been long recognized in economics (Alchian and Demsetz, 1973; Demsetz, 1964, 1967; Eggertson, 1990), economic theories of the origin and stability of property are of only limited use in a political-economic analysis, because they typically do not recognize government officials as strategic actors (Riker and Sened, 1991).

The main challenge of a positive theory of property rights is to demonstrate how political actors, especially rulers, have an incentive to respect property rights despite their ability to violate them for immediate gain. Following such an approach, which is presented in Chapter 2, property rights are conceptualized as endogenously arising from the strategic interactions of political and economic actors.

In the following presentation, I present an interpretation of the role of property rights that is theoretically independent from the usual economic arguments and yet fits nicely within a positive theory of property rights. My main thesis is that, in an economy with an established system of property rights, a government that makes macroeconomic decisions can learn about the state of the economy from the investment decisions of entrepreneurs that in turn depend on secure property rights.

I then apply this interpretation to the case of East German unification. I argue that the usual information transmission through investment was not available in East Germany due to ill-defined property rights. The government thus had to rely on its prior information concerning the state of the East German economy, with fatal consequences for growth and employment in the unified Germany. In this sense the government neither made a "mistake" nor did it not understand the consequences of its actions. Rather it had to make a decision under extreme uncertainty. These decisions turned out to be inefficient ex post, although they were reasonable ex ante.

On the one hand, this approach permits the incorporation of the case of German unification into a broader theoretical context. On the other hand, the unusual case of German unification gives insights into the "normal" functioning of property rights from the perspective of political economy. In this sense I use a "sick" institution to understand how a "healthy" institution works.

3.0 INVESTMENT AS SIGNALING

In my analysis I use insights from the game theoretic literature dealing with interaction under incomplete information. Signaling games in particular have proved to be very useful, because they generate important insights into the strategic complexities of information transmission.[9]

3.1 Strategic signaling

In the archetypical signaling model (Spence, 1973), there is a sender and a receiver. The sender has some private information about the state of the world, also referred to as the sender's "type," that is valuable to both actors. The sender then can send a signal to the receiver after which the receiver picks an action that has consequences for both actors. Both actors are assumed to maximize expected utility. In addition, the receiver is supposed to update her prior belief about the state of the world rationally; that is, she is assumed to use Bayes' Rule taking account of the strategic incentives of the sender to send a particular message.

One of the main insights of this literature is that a sender with private information may be unable to transmit this information credibly, although both actors would be better off if they were to act in a situation in which this information were publicly available. The problem the sender faces in credibly transmitting her information stems from the fact that the receiver will take account of a sender's incentives to lie about her type. In certain circumstances, this may lead to the receiver picking an action that makes both actors worse off than under complete information.

Whether this credibility problem can be solved, or at least mitigated to some extent, depends on the particular signaling mechanism. The theoretical literature on signaling games has demonstrated that the degree to which a signal is costly is critical. If signals are costless ("cheap talk"), then the degree to which they transmit useful information depends on how far the preferences of sender and receiver are different. If they differ greatly, then no credible information can be transmitted and the receiver has to act on her prior beliefs.[10] The most relevant case for our analysis occurs when both actors incur welfare losses if both act on their priors. Thus, while it may be in the sender's interest to convince the receiver to take an action that would be beneficial for both, the informational asymmetry of the decision problem precludes an optimal outcome. The reason for this dilemma, of course, is that the receiver realizes the sender's incentives to misrepresent her private information, and the sender cannot credibly communicate that she speaks the truth.

If, however, signals are costly; that is, if the benefits associated with a

[9] There is a rich literature on signaling games both in economics and political science. For overviews on applications in political science, see Austen-Smith (1992) and Banks (1991).

[10] The seminal paper for the analysis of costless signaling is Crawford and Sobel (1982).

particular signal depend on the sender's type, then credible information can be transmitted more easily. In fact, under some conditions it is possible to have separating equilibria, in which the receiver is fully aware of the sender's information.[11] Although efficiency losses may occur even if all the information is transmitted, more informative equilibria tend to have better welfare properties.

3.2 Information transmission through investment

This general framework can now be used to shed light on the role of property rights in an economy in which a central government influences the parameters of production, for example, the price of labor directly or indirectly through the mechanism of union collective wage bargaining, and through policy decisions in such areas as social spending, unemployment benefits, taxation, and public borrowing.

Following the approach of positive political economy, I do not assume that governments are benevolent dictators interested in maximizing global efficiency. Rather, I assume that governments have interests of their own. These interests can be thought of as induced by an underlying political process in which the desire to stay in office as well as the details of the electoral system and the bargaining process over policy outcomes critically matter.

While recent political economy models have shed important insights on the interaction between economic and political actors (Baron, 1995; Banks and Weingast, 1992) that induce preferences for a government, I leave this interaction implicit in order to focus on the signaling aspect of property rights. I assume that the government's preferences can be represented by a single-peaked utility function on government revenue. This implies that the government has a preferred level of revenue that might be a consequence of a trade-off between the political benefits of government spending and the political risks of expropriating wealth from voters.[12] This assumption is also consistent with a benevolent government interested in providing a public good, but facing a trade-off with respect to deadweight losses due to taxation.[13]

---

11 The seminal work on costly signaling is Spence (1973).

12 This assumption is by no means innocuous. Standard results in the social choice literature imply that collective preferences need not satisfy even minimal rationality requirements like acyclicity or transitivity, let alone single-peakedness (for an overview, see Schofield, 1985). The assumption can more easily be defended if the relevant policy space in the case considered has a single dimension. Whether this assumption is justified is an empirical question that has to be decided on a case-by-case basis. In our application, German politics, there is ample evidence that a single Left-Right economic dimension underlies the policy space (Laver and Schofield, 1990).

13 This interpretation was suggested to me by Susanne Lohmann.

In the model I assume that local entrepreneurs have private information about the characteristics of investment objects, such as the productivity of certain assets. This information, however, is unknown to the central government, because it would be prohibitively costly for the government to obtain this information. The government has some prior belief about the productivity of the economy in the next period. These beliefs are common knowledge.

Under normal conditions firms buy through investment their production capabilities for the next period. The amount of this investment depends on the entrepreneurs' private knowledge about the future productivity of these assets and their perception of the economic framework the government will create in response to the investment. By observing the amount of investment, the government updates its beliefs about the next period's economic output and, accordingly, decides on parameter values that are relevant to future production because they affect factor prices (through unemployment benefits, rules on wage bargaining, employment subsidies, health care, or social security cost sharing arrangements) or influence expected revenues (through tax levels, price ceilings, or export restrictions). Finally, the entrepreneur chooses a level of production depending on her investment and the parameters selected by government.

In standard signaling games, a formal analysis of this interaction often gives equilibriums in which no information is revealed to the government. These equilibriums are called "pooling equilibriums," because all types pick the same action, either investment or noninvestment, depending on the costs of investment, and the government does not update its beliefs but rather acts on its priors. For some parameter configurations, however, equilibria exist in which investment decisions do convey credible information about the state of the economy. In these equilibria, so-called separating equilibria, entrepreneurs invest when productivity is sufficiently high and abstain from investment otherwise. In separating equilibria governments are fully informed about the state of the economy and pick an action so that, though entrepreneurs anticipate the consequences of their actions taking account of higher factor prices, they still have an incentive to invest in the case of high productivity.

Although all actors typically benefit from the ability to signal the value of assets through investment, there are some efficiency loses due to incomplete information even if, as in a separating equilibrium, the costly signal removes all uncertainty about the value of an asset.[14] The reason is that a single investor faces a trade-off between inducing the government to set a lower tax rate by strategic underinvestment and purchasing enough capacity in order to maximize profits in the next period. In equilibrium, individual entrepreneurs will typically underinvest.

[14] This is a typical feature of signaling models: see, for example, Banks (1991).

If there are many investors, however, then it may be the case that the marginal informational impact of a single entrepreneur's decision on the government's belief may be rather small, while the entrepreneur alone suffers the consequences from underinvestment. In this situation, it may be optimal for investors to refrain from strategic underinvestment and invest sincerely, thereby revealing information about the economy through "informational externalities" of investment. In this sense, one can conjecture that the traditional assumption that investment is non-strategic with respect to governments can be recovered as a limiting case.

The key feature of this investment model is that, because an investment decision has consequences for the level of production and thus for the next period's profits, it is formally equivalent to a costly signal in a game of asymmetric information. For the investment to have these economic consequences, however, it is critical that the investor has well-defined property rights to the investment. Otherwise, no credible information will be transmitted, and the government has to act on its prior beliefs. This is evident in the case of separating equilibria where on the equilibrium path entrepreneurs abstain from investing. Abstention can only transmit information, however, because entrepreneurs *could* have rationally invested in the case of high productivity.

This model provides a rationale for the stability of property rights: Under normal circumstances they are part of a mechanism for transferring knowledge about the productivity of assets to the government so that it is not necessary for government to own productive resources itself in order to design and implement its most desired policy. In contrast, arbitrary interference with private property introduces uncertainty about the value of particular investments and thus decreases the information content of investment decisions.[15]

There may be many reasons why investors cannot credibly transmit their information. One was already pointed out. Ceteris paribus, insecure property rights decrease the amount of credibly transmitted information. The reason is that in our context secure property rights ensure that an investor knows that he alone will suffer the consequences or enjoy the benefits of an investment decision. This feature is critical for an investment to be a costly signal. In extreme cases potential investors may not be able to invest in a particular area at all. Rather, they may only have the option to announce that they will or will not invest in future periods.

[15] I pointed out earlier that this analysis focuses on the incentives to honor property rights but does not give sufficient conditions under which those rights will be secure. In fact, in a single-shot interaction, a government may have an incentive to violate property rights *after* a firm has produced some output. But this behavior then may be anticipated by the entrepreneurs who consequently will refrain from investing so that a Pareto-inferior outcome results. The commitment problem and possible solutions to it are discussed in Chapter 2.

Such an announcement, however, is only "cheap talk" and is recognized as such, because, in the absence of signed contracts, an investor can choose actions not consistent with announcements. Hence this situation corresponds to a costless signaling game. Because by assumption entrepreneurs want to maximize profits and governments want to extract some revenue,[16] a standard result in the theory of costless signaling (Crawford and Sobel, 1982) indicates that no credible information can be transmitted in equilibrium. In this case a government can no longer rely on credible information being transmitted through investment and has to act on its priors.

4.0 GERMAN UNIFICATION: A CASE STUDY

In this section I apply the investment-as-signaling framework to the specific problems of German unification. In particular, I argue that during the unification process information about the state of East German industries, though available to entrepreneurs, could not be credibly transmitted to the (West) German government. The (West) German government had to make policy decisions influencing, among other things, next-period production in East Germany, when investment in East German industries was legally not possible or, later, was plagued by uncertain property rights.

Without the opportunity to invest, West German entrepreneurs who had already acquired detailed information about the state of the East German economy could only "warn" the government not to set unemployment benefits or the exchange rate between East and West German currency too high, for instance. These warnings, however, were only speeches, "cheap talk," and because the government, rationally, recognized that future investors had an incentive to demand lower unemployment benefits and exchange rates no matter what the true state of the economy, it discounted these warnings and acted on its priors that, unfortunately, were too optimistic concerning the economic potential in the East. Entrepreneurs could purchase production capabilities only when it was already too late, after the government had already made critical policy decisions.

In order to make this model applicable to German unification I have to establish at least three facts:

1. That the West German government misjudged the productivity of East German industries
2. That West German entrepreneurs had acquired detailed information about the state of East German industries

[16] I ignore the trivial case in which the preferences of governments and entrepreneurs completely coincide.

303

3. That this information could not be signaled through investment in existing East German industries

Note that with regard to fact (3) it is critical to establish that West German firms, or any "foreign investors," could not purchase existing East German firms. Neither green field investment nor investment in nonindustrial sectors reveal any information about the state of East German industry.

4.1 Government misjudgment

Let me begin by reviewing the misjudgments of East German economic prospects that prevailed in early 1990, the time when fundamental decisions about the socioeconomic framework for unification were made. In February 1990 the leading forecasting institutes of West Germany projected East German productivity to rise from about half to between 70 and 80 percent of West German industrial productivity within one year (IFO-Schnelldienst, July 1990: 20; DIW, July 1990).

The economic and currency union, it was expected, would act as a "productivity whip" (IFO-Schnelldienst, July 1990: 10).[17] Massive improvements were expected from better management and organization, assortment and product screening, technology transfer, and increased reliability of industrial suppliers. Similar predictions could be heard from key advisers to the German government like Hans Willgerodt (1990) or Horst Siebert (1990, 1991), chairman of the internationally renowned Kiel World Economic Institute.

The result of these expert opinions was that during the first half of 1990 politicians in Bonn believed in growth rates of around 10 percent and in a "new, if not more successful, economic miracle."[18] Government officials expected "the whole thing if properly handled" to be a giant "10-year stimulus program" (*Konjunkturprogramm*) for the two German economies (*Der Spiegel*, February 7, 1990: 29). By midyear 1990 Federal Economic Minister Haussmann was still confident and expected full employment in East Germany in the near future (*Der Spiegel*, July 27, 1990: 80). The president of the Federal Unemployment Agency (Bundesranstalt für Arbeit) expected the number of unemployed to settle at between 100,000 and 300,000 persons (*Der Spiegel*, May 19, 1990: 20).

One can only speculate why the West German government and the research institutes were so optimistic. For the application of the model this is irrelevant, as these optimistic expectations correspond to prior beliefs, and are thus exogenous to the model. Establishing, as this record

---

[17] All translations are by the author.
[18] Assertion made by Liberal Party chairman Graf Lambsdorff in a speech before the German Bundestag (Deutscher Bundestag, April 27, 1990: 16,411).

does, that the West German government did in fact overestimate the productivity of East German industries, and that this expectation was common knowledge, is all that is required for application of the model.

4.2 Private information

While political decision makers had rather optimistic beliefs about the future of the East German economy, skepticism soon prevailed among the key economic agents: West German industrialists. But why would it matter what West German industrialists believed about East German firms? For one thing, private firms are bearers of private knowledge about optimal technologies, products, and costs in a decentralized economy. Moreover, there existed rather dense economic interchange between West German firms and East German Kombinate before the fall of the Wall. Most importantly, East Germany was flooded by agents of West German firms searching for opportunities for favorable joint ventures and acquisitions. West German entrepreneurs initially shared the government's optimistic expectations and thus were willing to incur the search costs associated with acquiring detailed information about potential East German acquisitions. This mixture of curiosity and business interest, however, disappeared quickly. In newspaper interviews leading CEOs voiced their shock at what they had seen. The following statement by a representative of the West German textile industry is typical (*Wirtschaftsdienst*, June 1990: 291): "It can indeed hardly be believed that existing industrial capacities in the GDR, even if modernized and rationalized, will ever be able to sell their production." A West German consultant in May 1990 did not see a single reason why one should invest in productive sites in the East (*Der Spiegel*, May 19, 1990: 21). By the end of March the leading German news magazine, *Der Spiegel* (March 12, 1990: 140), had already summarized the mood among West German industrialists with the statement that as a productive site the GDR was "out."[19]

As is already obvious from these statements, West German industrialists voiced their concern about the future of East German industries at an early date. However, they were unable to back up their words by costly signaling. Legal restrictions on the acquisition of property rights in the East precluded any investment. Thus the firms' abstention from acquisition of East German industrial facilities, which under normal circumstances would have credibly signaled low expected productivity in the East, could quite obviously not carry any information about the actual state of the East German economy, because investment was not legally

[19] To be sure, there was extensive activity in the East by West German entrepreneurs. But these activities were almost exclusively restricted to the opening of distribution centers and the planned construction of "green field" sites (Hagedorn, 1990: 159).

and economically possible. If a firm can invest, but chooses not to, then this choice transmits information about the expected productivity of the investment. But if it is unable to invest due to legal restrictions, then refraining from investment cannot transmit any information.

It is worth pointing out that *initially* West German entrepreneurs did share the general optimism about an impending "economic miracle."[20] After all, this was the reason they were willing to incur search costs to learn about the state of East German facilities. However, although individual entrepreneurs were able to acquire information about a particular site at relatively low costs given the expected profits, a similar fact-finding mission is impossible, or at least prohibitively costly, when a government needs information about the state of a whole economy. Thus, while entrepreneurs were able to update their beliefs about East German industries quickly, this was not possible for the West German government, because the usually reliable mechanisms for information acquisition could not function properly in the political context of German unification.

4.3 Blocked transmission

The main impediment in the way of investors was the still existing East German government. International negotiations concerning German national sovereignty, the so-called 2+4 negotiations between the two Germanies and the former Allied Powers (France, Great Britain, United States, and the Soviet Union), slowed down the unification process and helped sustain a lame-duck East German government that, up to March 1990, was still controlled by former Communists and tied up in roundtable (*Runder Tisch*) discussions in which policies had to be approved of by a committee that was dominated by left-wing bourgeois opposition groups (Thaysen, 1990).

The West German government, at least according to its own perception, however, had to act fast. First, there was the issue of migration pressure since the opening of the inner German borders. In the month of January alone, fifty thousand East Germans "immigrated" to the West. Second, West German foreign policy makers perceived a "window of opportunity" for unification and were anxious to seize the opportunity given the uncertainty about Gorbachev's political future (Teltschik, 1991). The brief review of the most important dates in the process of German unification presented in Table 11.1 helps to clarify the sequence of events.

As can be seen from this table, German unification was a realistic expectation very soon after the fall of the Berlin Wall. But it took more

[20] Thus the situation was consistent with the standard modeling assumption of common prior beliefs.

Learning about the economy

Table 11.1. Chronology of German unification

Date	Event
November 19, 1989	Fall of the Berlin Wall
December 12, 1989	Prime Minister Modrow and Chancellor Kohl agree to form a "contractual community" (*Vertragsgemeinschaft*)
March 1, 1990	Establishment of the Treuhandanstalt
March 18, 1990	First free elections in the GDR lead to a clear victory for Christian Democratic parties
May 5, 1990	Start of the "2 + 4" negotiations
May 18, 1990	Ratification of the State Treaty on the establishment of a common currency, and common economic as well as social policy by the German Bundestag
June 17, 1990	Second Treuhand Law
July 1, 1990	Enactment of State Treaty, leading to a common currency
August 31, 1990	Unification Treaty ratified by the Bundestag
October 3, 1990	German unification
December 2, 1990	Bundestag election (first general elections in the unified Germany)
March 4, 1991	"2 + 4" Treaty ratified

Source: Adapted from Sinn and Sinn (1992: 15–17).

than a year until a legal framework for the unification was finally established. During this period the West German government had to make policy decisions that were expected to have consequences not only for West, but also for East, German industries. Among those decisions were the exchange rate between East and West German currencies and the related question of the debts of East German industries, the adoption of the West German social security system including the level of pension entitlement, unemployment benefits, public assistance payments, public subsidies, public borrowing rates, the immediate adoption of the West German wage bargaining system, and, finally, taxation.

It is clear that these government decisions directly or indirectly influence production parameters, especially the costs of labor and capital. Although some of the decisions, for example, those about tax and subsidy rates,[21] can be changed relatively easily, this is not the case for entitlements created through the social security system or for even more far-reaching decisions such as the adoption of the West German wage bargaining system. More-

[21] This, of course, is an overstatement for the sake of argument. Once taxes, and especially subsidies, are established, special interest groups will try to protect their prerogatives.

over, most of these decisions, especially those concerning social security, were part of the State Treaty of early summer 1990.

The West German government, however, had only limited control over the East German privatization measures before the fall of 1990. The Treuhandanstalt, the central state privatization agency, was created in March 1990 by the GDR chamber of deputies that was still controlled by the members of the German Communist Party. No elections had taken place, and the composition of the chamber still represented the old socialist system. The First Treuhand Law prescribed that the old GDR industrial complexes (so-called *Kombinate*) transform themselves into capital companies with the eventual goal of selling their shares. According to government sources, however, the true intention of the law was to prevent "foreign" takeovers, that is, purchases by West German entrepreneurs (*Der Spiegel,* July 28, 1990: 69). Treuhand posts were held by former communist state officials until August when the leadership was nearly completely changed. By midyear 1990 only a quarter of the Kombinate had been transformed into capital companies (*Der Spiegel,* July 28, 1990: 69). No privatization occurred before the end of June when the Second Treuhand Law, now under a freely elected government, explicitly entrusted the Treuhand with the privatization of East German industries.[22] By this time, however, the State Treaty was already in effect and solidified in a common economic and social system.

It might be argued that, although investment was legally impossible before the fall of 1990, German entrepreneurs, especially those with good government connections, could have engaged in informal agreements with either the East or the West German government promising to invest in East German industries. The actual refusal to engage in such potential agreements then would be functionally equivalent to abstention from investment in normal circumstances and thus make the entrepreneurs' dismal judgment concerning the future of East German industries credible.[23] Note that simply pointing out that such arrangements did not abound misses the point of the argument, because it would be precisely the lack of such arrangements that would serve to signal low productivity in equilibrium. Crucial to this argument, however, is the demonstration that such informal arrangements were possible.

The critical feature of investments as costly signals, however, is that they are sunk. If firms do not invest sufficiently, then they suffer opportunity costs. Intentions to invest at a future time, in contrast, can always

[22] Previous legislation concerning joint ventures of East German with foreign firms passed in March 1990 had been highly restrictive with respect to Western majority shareholdings and referred to the joint funding of new firms rather than the acquisition of existing GDR-production facilities.
[23] This possibility was brought to my attention by Edward Bird.

be reneged. In order to make them equivalent to costly signals, informal arrangements must be enforceable. In the case of investment in East Germany, enforcement relying on legal sanctions was impossible. Informal sanctions, however, typically rely on the possibility of punishing defectors by shunning them in future interactions. A potential defector then has to compare the myopic incentive to renege with the opportunity costs of lost future cooperation. Thus, informal enforcement depends on the possible gains from repeated future interaction.

The unique case of German unification, however, can hardly be subsumed under a model of repeated interaction. After all, the East German administration was clearly recognized as a lame-duck government. Further, under normal circumstances, as in a future unified Germany with a functioning legal system, there is no need for credible intentions to invest, because ordinary investment is possible. Therefore, the opportunity costs for reneging were small if not zero.[24]

Investment in the East was virtually impossible until the fall of 1990, and it remained difficult and highly uncertain even after unification thanks to the restitution clause of the Unification Treaty. This clause required the restitution of all formerly private property in East Germany to legitimate private claimants with the exception of expropriations during the Soviet occupation.[25] Although local authorities that had to decide on restitution claims had yet to be constituted, and knowledgeable personnel were scarce, nearly every potential production site in East Germany was subject to some restitution claim. Frequently, multiple restitution claims to the same property were made so that the restitution clause effectively led to a nearly complete blockade of investments and acquisitions. In March 1991, when the German cabinet decided on an acceleration amendment,[26] irreversible delay had already taken effect. Even in

---

[24] As a final possibility, governments may choose to increase opportunity costs for reneging by linking a defection with respect to investment intentions to other mutually beneficial interactions, such as subsidies and government contracts. Here the question is whether such punishments are credible, as governments may also suffer if such interactions are terminated. This may depend on a variety of economic and political factors including the possibility of switching to a different supplier and the political cloud around the firms involved. Obviously, further research is necessary to resolve this point unequivocally.

[25] The details of restitution are not the topic of this chapter. For an overview of the economic effects, see Sinn and Sinn (1992). To my knowledge there is no explicit analysis of the political reasons to choose restitution rather than a compensation solution. Such an analysis, I believe, has to take account of West German coalition politics in the face of an impending election focusing on the German Liberal Democrats (FDP), the junior member of the governing coalition, whose leader Hans-Dietrich Genscher played a critical role in the decision to adopt a restitution solution.

[26] Restitution claimants could no longer legally prevent the Treuhand from selling their alleged former property to potential investors, but were referred to later entitlement.

June 1992 only 4.4 percent of about 2.5 million restitution claims had been dealt with conclusively (*Süddeutsche Zeitung,* June 1, 1992: 5).

Note that while the restitution decision undoubtedly aggravated the problem of economic development in the East, my main argument, that it prevented the transmission of credible information by restricting investment, is independent of the details of the restitution policy. Investment was impossible during the critical time between the fall of the Wall and unification, no matter how the question of private property was solved eventually.

5.0 CONCLUSION

This application of the investment-as-signaling framework is intended to provide some new insight into the particular features of the German unification process. As such it competes with a variety of other analyses. It is not intended as the "explanation" of the economic decline in East Germany. In fact, I do not know what it means to explain a singular event such as the economic aspect of German unification. At best, my reconstruction of the events of German unification provides a case study that is consistent with theoretical expectations. Thus, I claim that we can gain insights into the normal functioning of political-economic institutions from the study of this "pathological" case.

In normal times governments use research institutes, discretionary investigations, and regulatory agencies to learn about economic activity not organized in markets. Might such mechanisms have substituted for secure property rights to permit either private investors to convey their knowledge credibly or government to correct faulty misperceptions?

I think it improbable. The overoptimistic misperception of the state of the East German economy was very deeply ingrained among politicians. It was not only shared but nourished by expert opinion from the leading macroeconomic policy research institutes. The legal framework for regulatory agencies did not exist. By way of a costly signal, business could have offered to finance auditors to verify their assessments. Even disregarding Hayekian doubts about the quality of information aggregation through auditors, however, severe obstacles would have hindered use of this approach. Independent audits would have had to be extremely extensive to convey the same amount of information that would have been transmitted by the absence of investment. An army of auditors would have been needed to provide on a timely basis close firm-level scrutiny of what was then one of the world's largest industrial economies. Further, it is unclear how agents of the West German government could have collected information in a region that was still sovereign foreign territory.

Other mechanisms remain conceivable, nevertheless. Business could have made its future actions contingent on government action. One possibility is that business could have committed to invest in response to legislation that led to low wages in the East. Another possibility is that business could have offered government some sort of bond, such as the acceptance of higher taxes, against its signals being deceptive.

Yet, substantial collective action problems among a diverse business community that itself had to update strong prior beliefs about the state of East German industry had to be overcome. Indeed, only individual firms can plausibly commit to investment.[27] It probably would have been more feasible for industrial organizations to offer a bond, but even this mechanism would have been difficult to implement in such a way that the promise of political acquiescence to higher taxes in the event of a deceptive signal would have been credible. Ironically, the same decentralization that works so well in normal times to convey information to the government about the state of the economy hinders the use of alternative mechanisms for information transmission during exceptional times.

REFERENCES

Akerlof, George A., Andrew K. Rose, Janet L. Yellen, and Helga Hessenius, "East Germany in from the Cold: The Economic Aftermath of Currency Union," *Brookings Papers on Economic Activity* 1 (1991), 1–101.
Alchian, Armen, and Harold Demsetz, "The Property Rights Paradigms," *Journal of Economic History* 33: 1 (1973), 16–27.
Alesina, Alberto, "Elections, Party Structure, and the Economy," in Jeffrey S. Banks and Eric A. Hanushek, editors, *Modern Political Economy* (Cambridge: Cambridge University Press, 1995), pp. 145–70.
Austen-Smith, David, "Strategic Models of Talk in Political Decision Making," *International Political Science Review* 13: 1 (1992), 45–8.
Banks, Jeffrey S., *Signaling Games in Political Science* (New York: Harwood Academic Publishers, 1991).
Banks, Jeffrey S., and Barry Weingast, "The Political Control of Bureaucracies under Asymmetric Information," *American Journal of Political Science* 36: 2 (1992), 509–24.
Baron, David P., "The Economics and Politics of Regulation: Perspectives, Agenda, and Approaches," in Jeffrey S. Banks and Eric A. Hanushek, editors, *Modern Political Economy* (Cambridge: Cambridge University Press, 1995), pp. 1–62.
Barro, Robert J., and David B. Gordon, "Rules, Discretion and Reputation in a Model of Monetary Policy," *Journal of Monetary Economics* 12: 1 (1983), 101–22.

[27] The collective action problem also explains why industry-level collective bargaining usually only covers wages and not some mix of wages and employment even though the latter would arguably be Pareto superior in most circumstances. Note, for example, the current German debate over "Bündnis für Arbeit," a pact between unions and businesses involving the exchange of lower wages for higher employment.

Calmfors, Lars, *Wage Formation and Macroeconomic Policy in the Nordic Countries* (Oxford: Oxford University Press, 1992).

Calmfors, Lars, and Henrik Horn, "Classical Unemployment, Accommodation Policies and the Adjustment of Real Wages," *Scandinavian Journal of Economics* 87: 2 (1985), 234–61.

Crawford, Vincent, and Joel Sobel, "Strategic Information Transmission," *Econometrica* 50: 6 (1982), 1431–51.

Demsetz, Harold, "The Exchange and Enforcement of Property Rights," *Journal of Law and Economics* 7: October (1964), 11–26.

"Toward a Theory of Property Rights," *American Economic Review* 57: 1 (1967), 347–59.

Eggertsson, Thrainn, *Economic Behavior and Institutions* (Cambridge: Cambridge University Press, 1990).

Gylfason, Thorvaldur, and Assar Lindbeck, "Endogenous Unions and Governments: A Game-Theoretic Approach," *European Economic Review* 39: 1 (1986), 5–26.

Hagedorn, Jobst R., "Viele Unternehmen wollen aktiv werden" (Many Firms Want to Engage Themselves), *Der Arbeitgeber* 42: 4 (1990), 159–60.

Hamada, Koichi, "A Strategic Analysis of Monetary Independence," *Journal of Political Economy* 84: 4, part 1 (1976), 677–700.

Hayek, F. A., "The Use of Knowledge in Society," *American Economic Review* 35: 4 (1945), 519–30.

Herles, Wolfgang, *Nationalrausch: Szenen aus dem gesamtdeutschen Machtkampf* (National Frenzy: Observations about the Struggle for Power in Reunited Germany) (Munich: Kindler, 1990).

Hibbs, Douglas, "Political Parties and Macroeconomic Policy," *American Political Science Review* 7: 4 (1977), 1467–87.

Holmlund, Bertil, and Per Lundborg, "Unemployment Insurance and Union Wage Setting," *Scandinavian Journal of Economics* 90: 2 (1988), 161–72.

Kydland, Finn E., and Edward C. Prescott, "Rules Rather than Discretion: The Inconsistency of Optimal Plans," *Journal of Political Economy* 85: 3 (1977), 473–91.

Laver, Michael, and Norman Schofield, *Multiparty Government* (Oxford: Oxford University Press, 1990).

Layard, Richard, Stephen Nickell, and Richard Jackman, *Unemployment: Macroeconomic Performance and the Labour Market* (Oxford: Oxford University Press, 1991).

McDonald, Ian M., and Robert M. Solow, "Wage Bargaining and Employment," *American Economic Review* 71: 5 (1981), 896–908.

Nordhaus, William D., "The Political Business Cycle," *Review of Economic Studies* 42: 2 (1975), 169–90.

Oswald, Andrew J., "The Economic Theory of Trade Unions: An Introductory Survey," *Scandinavian Journal of Economics* 87: 2 (1985), 160–93.

Riker, William, and Itai Sened, "A Political Theory of the Origin of Property Rights: Airport Slots," *American Journal of Political Science* 35: 4 (1991), 951–69.

Schofield, Norman, *Social Choice and Democracy* (Heidelberg: Springer, 1985).

Siebert, Horst, "The Economic Integration of Germany," Institut für Weltwirtschaft, Kiel, working paper no. 160a (1990).

"German Unification," *Economic Policy* 13: October (1991), 287–340.

Sinn, Gerlinde, and Hans-Werner Sinn, *Jumpstart: The Economic Unification of Germany* (Cambridge, MA: MIT Press, 1992).

Spence, Michael, "Job Market Signaling," *Quarterly Journal of Economics* 37: 3 (1973), 355–74.

Teltschik, Horst, *329 Tage: Innenansichten der Einigung* (The 329 Days of German Unification: View from the Inside) (Berlin: Siedler, 1991).

Thaysen, Uwe, *Der Runde Tisch, oder, Wo blieb das Volk? Der Weg der DDR in die Demokratie* (The Round Table, or, Where Were the People? The Path of the DDR to Democracy) (Opladen: Westdeutscher Verlag, 1990).

Willgerodt, Hans, et al., *Gutachten: Vorteile der wirtschaftlichen Einheit Deutschlands* (Study: Advantages of the Economic Unification of Germany) (Cologne: Volkswirtschaftliches Institut der Universität, 1990).

Government documents

Beschluss zur Gründung der Anstalt zur treuhänderischen Verwaltung des Volkseigentums vom 1.3.1990, Gesetzblatt der Deutschen Demokratischen Republik, Teil I, No. 14, 8: 3 (1990), 107.

Gesetz über die Gründung und Tätigkeit privater Unternehmen und über Unternehmensbeteiligungen vom 7.3.1990, Gesetzblatt der Deutschen Demokratischen Republik, Teil I, No. 17, 16: 3 (1990), 141–44.

Gesetz zur Privatisierung und Reorganisierung des volkseigenen Vermögens vom 17.6.1990, Gesetzblatt der Deutschen Demokratischen Republik, Teil I, No. 33, 22: 6 (1990), 300–3.

Verordnung zur Umwandlung von volkseigenen Kombinaten, Betrieben, und Einrichtungen in Kapitalgesellschaften vom 1.3.1990. Gesetzblatt der Deutschen Demokratischen Republik, Teil I, No. 14, 8: 3 (1990), 107–8.

Vertrag über die Schaffung einer Währungs-, Wirtschafts-, und Sozialunion zwischen der Bundesrepublik Deutschland und der Deutschen Demokratischen Republik vom 18.5.1990, Bundesgesetzblatt, Teil II, No. 20, 29: 6 (1990), 537–67.

Vertrag zwischen der Bundesrepublik Deutschland und der Deutschen Demokratischen Republik über die Herstellung der Einheit Deutschlands vom 31.8.1990, Bulletin der Bundesregierung, No. 104, 6: 9 (1990), 877–1120.

Misinformation, insecure property rights, and the collapse of the East German economy

SUSANNE LOHMANN

Political decision makers often face the problem of using information about the state of the economy that is not known to anyone in its totality: After all, market information typically does not exist "in concentrated or integrated form, but solely as the dispersed bits of incomplete and frequently contradictory knowledge which all the separate individuals possess" (Hayek, 1945: 519). Dispersed information can be aggregated in a number of ways. For example, prices resulting from trading in markets transmit private information held by market participants. Similarly, international capital movements or sector-specific investment patterns reveal some of the private information that shaped investors' expectations about future economic prospects.

In this volume Hannes Wittig develops a novel hypothesis: The degree to which private information pertinent to political decisions is aggregated depends on whether property rights are secure. The status of property rights thus determines whether political decisions will be made in an informed manner. Wittig identifies a hitherto unrecognized benefit of secure property rights: Whereas the literature emphasizes the importance of property rights for credible commitment and policy stability, he emphasizes their informational role.

This point is made in the context of a simple signaling model that can be conceptualized as follows. (See Table 1.) A government can choose to follow either an active or a passive policy. The optimal policy depends on economy's future prospects. If these are good, then the government desires to follow a passive policy, whereas the government would like to respond to unfavorable prospects with an active policy. Initially, the government does not know for sure the economy's prospects; its prior beliefs are that they are favorable. In the absence of further information the government would thus follow a passive policy.

Firms are privately informed about future economic prospects. Their investment decisions depend on their expectations about the profitability

314

Table 1. *No investment under insecure property rights*

Property rights	Economic prospects	Investment	Policy
Secure	Good	High	Passive
	Bad	Low	Active
Insecure	Good	Zero	Passive
	Bad		

of investment projects, and profits are expected to be high if property rights are secure and economic prospects are good, low in the case of secure property rights and bad economic prospects, and zero if property rights are insecure.

Even though the government cannot directly observe economic prospects, it can form inferences based on its observations of firms' investment behavior. Given the assumptions made so far, it immediately follows that the government follows an active policy only if property rights are secure and investment levels are low; only in this case can the government infer that economic prospects must be bad. The government follows a passive policy in all other cases – either because it infers that economic prospects are favorable (in the secure property rights case), or because the firms' investment decisions are uninformative (in the insecure property rights case). In the latter case political decision making is biased toward the passive policy, which is suboptimal if economic prospects are in fact unfavorable.

The assumption that investment levels are zero in the case of insecure property rights is not very plausible on either empirical or theoretical grounds. Arguably, the probability of expropriation is not generally equal to one. There usually exist at least some investment projects whose expected profitability is strictly positive even taking into account the risks associated with insecure property rights. For this reason, it seems reasonable to modify Wittig's model as follows (see Table 2): Suppose firms invest less if property rights are insecure than if they are secure; but in either case they invest more if economic prospects are good than if they are bad. This seemingly innocuous modification leads to a dramatic change in the conclusions. Now the firms' private information is fully aggregated under both secure and insecure property rights, and the policy bias is eliminated: The government's decision is optimal independent of the status of property rights.

It is worthwhile reflecting for a moment on the factor that drives the result of zero information aggregation in the original Wittig model. Con-

Table 2. *Some investment possible under insecure property rights*

Property rights	Economic prospects	Investment	Policy
Secure	Good	High	Passive
	Bad	Low	Active
Insecure	Good	Low	Passive
	Bad	Zero	Active

sider a simple signaling game with multiple senders and one receiver. The senders have information about the state of the world. The receiver makes a decision. The senders' and receiver's payoffs depend on the interaction between the state of the world and the decision. Thus, the senders have information pertinent to the receiver's decision, and both the senders and the receiver have a stake in allowing the senders' information to be used in the receiver's decision. In this situation, the senders may have incentives to signal their information to the receiver, and the receiver may have incentives to condition her decision on the senders' signals. It is well established that the following two features affect the degree to which the senders' information is revealed to the receiver (see Lohmann 1993 and the references therein). First, if there are multiple senders and the decision in question has the characteristics of a collective good, then the provision of costly informative signals is subject to a free rider problem. Second, senders whose interests conflict with those of the receiver may have incentives to send deceitful signals. (Of course, the receiver, being rational, sees through their manipulations.)

Wittig suggests that the above-mentioned factors prevent the "full-information policy" from being achieved in the insecure property rights case. In fact, the driving factor appears to be one identified by Hopenhayn and Lohmann (1994): "Political decisions will tend to be biased if information flows to political decision-makers are 'coarse' relative to the 'complexity' of the political environment." This insight can be expressed as follows: Private information may fail to be fully aggregated if the dimensionality of the senders' "message space" is low relative to the dimensionality of the receiver's "decision space."

According to the model presented in Table 1, the information that is to be transmitted – good/bad economic prospects – is binary in nature, as is the government's decision to follow a passive/active policy. In the case of secure property rights, the firms' message space is also binary: They can choose between high/low investment levels. As a consequence, their private information is fully aggregated. In the case of insecure property rights, firms send one message independently of their private information: zero investment. Lack of differentiated action implies zero information aggregation, and a policy bias results. In the modified model presented in Table 2, the firms' message space is binary both for secure and insecure property rights. As a result, the firms' private information is fully aggregated, and the government's policy decision is optimal.

The link between coarse information flows, complex policy decisions, and policy bias continues to hold if we modify the above model to allow for higher-dimensional message and decision spaces. Suppose that economic conditions can range from bad to good on a continuum, and let the optimal policy vary continuously with economic prospects. Consider first the situation in which the firms' message space is binary: They are restricted to choose between two levels of investment, high/low in the case of secure property rights, and low/zero in the case of insecure property rights. The government follows the policy that is optimal conditional on the firms' investment behavior. Except in knife-edge cases, government policy is not unconditionally optimal: Once again a policy bias is obtained. On the other hand, if the firms' message space is continuous in the sense that optimal investment levels vary continuously with future economic prospects, then the firms' private information is fully aggregated, and government policy is unconditionally optimal.

The discussion so far suggests that the degree to which dispersed information pertinent to political decision making is aggregated depends on the range of differentiated activities in which market participants – firms, workers, and consumers – can engage (given that their observed activities function as signals). It is intuitively plausible that market activities are more highly differentiated if property rights are secure, and more limited in scope if property rights are insecure. This proposition implies that the status of property rights has informational implications, as suggested by Wittig's informational hypothesis. A rigorous development of this argument is beyond the scope of this comment.

Moreover, implicit in Wittig's argument is the notion that there are no other political channels of information aggregation. Even if firms are "mute" in matters of investment, they surely have access to other modes of expression. For example, they can lobby the government, enhancing the credibility of their lobbying messages by exerting costly lobbying efforts. Indeed, Lohmann (1995) develops a signaling model of lobbying, showing that information can be fully aggregated even in the presence of a free rider problem and conflicts of interest. There exist numerous other political mechanisms of information aggregation (Lohmann 1993, 1994a, 1994b). Workers and consumers can transmit information through costly political action or emigration; and they can respond at relatively low cost to public opinion polls or cast protest votes (or abstain) in elections.

There exists an intriguing parallel to Wittig's informational hypothesis in the political arena. Free societies grant their citizens numerous rights, among them the rights to engage in free speech and to vote in regularly scheduled elections. Such "political property rights" ensure that information about the people's preferences is aggregated in a relatively unencumbered way (at least in comparison to unfree societies). As a result, both voters and politicians can make more informed decisions. Based on publicly revealed information, voters can dismiss unresponsive or unrepresentative politicians; and politicians can respond to voter sentiment and implement representative policies, thereby furthering their chances of re-election.

As a final point, let me raise an issue of evidence. Wittig cites statements by businesspersons that appeared at the time in publications like *Wirtschaftsdienst* and *Der Spiegel* as indicating their gloomy assessments of East German conditions, which subsequently turned out to be correct. Is there any evidence that the government did in fact treat these statements as uninformative "cheap talk," that is, as incredible because of their lack of costliness? Or is it possible that government decision makers believed these assessments but nevertheless chose policy on the basis of other considerations?

In conclusion, Wittig offers a novel and potentially powerful hypothesis about the importance of secure property rights for the informational value of the signals sent to policy makers by economic actors. As indicated in this comment, however, considerable room remains for refining and testing the hypothesis.

REFERENCES

Hayek, Friedrich A., "The Use of Knowledge in Society," *American Economic Review* 35: 4 (1945), 519–30.

Hopenhayn, Hugo, and Susanne Lohmann, "Delegation and the Regulation of Risk," mimeo, University of Rochester and UCLA, revised August (1994).

Lohmann, Susanne, "A Signaling Model of Informative and Manipulative Political Action," *American Political Science Review* 87: 2 (1993), 319–33.

"Information Aggregation Through Costly Political Action," *American Economic Review* 84: 3 (1994a), 518–30.

"The Dynamics of Informational Cascades: The Monday Demonstrations in Leipzig, East Germany, 1989–91," *World Politics* 47: 1 (1994b), 42–101.

"Information, Access and Contributions: A Signaling Model of Lobbying," *Public Choice* 85: 3–4 (1995), 267–84.

12

Post-communist privatization as a test of theories of institutional change

LORENE ALLIO, MARIUSZ MARK DOBEK,
NIKOLAI MIKHAILOV, AND DAVID L. WEIMER[1]

1.0 INTRODUCTION

Institutional change poses a challenging intellectual puzzle. If one defines an institution as a set of stable and widely shared expectations about how economic, political, and social actors will constrain their behaviors in some specified circumstances, then one must account for how new expectations come to be stable after supplanting the old ones. In the language of game theory, one faces the problem of understanding how the strategies of players move from one equilibrium to another. Particularly perplexing is how institutional change can produce expectations that new behaviors will be stable. This question is especially important with respect to property rights because the credibility that they will persist fundamentally affects such economic behaviors as investment and the preservation of assets. In this chapter we attempt to gain a better understanding of institutional change by looking at the experiences of post-communist countries in moving from state to private ownership of the means of production.

The investigation of institutional change in Eastern Europe and the former Soviet Union benefits from a fortuitous mix of common and variable factors across the countries of interest. The most significant common factor is that these countries all begin with a preponderance of state ownership and a stated intention to privatize. The important variables include differences in formal political, and informal social, institutions. Looking at the courses of change across countries offers the possibility of determining the relative merit of the major competing theories of the driving force of institutional change: *Pareto efficiency* versus *governmental self-interest* versus *distributional advantage*. It also offers an oppor-

[1]The authors wish to thank Jeffrey Banks, Randall Calvert, Timothy Frye, Jack Knight, Steven Lewis, and Andrew Rutten for helpful comments on various aspects of this chapter.

tunity for investigating the relationship between changes in informal and formal institutions.

2.0 THEORIES OF INSTITUTIONAL CHANGE

We consider three general theories of institutional change. The first, which we label the *economic* theory, posits that institutional changes occur as if they were the realization of opportunities for Pareto improvements. The second, which we label the *public choice* theory, introduces the incumbent government as a strategic actor with interests that may not be consistent with Pareto efficiency. The third, which we label the *distributional* theory, sees institutional change as the by-product of distributional conflict. In this section we briefly outline each of these theories and its implications for the efficiency of institutional change. In particular, we wish to frame hypotheses that distinguish among these theories and that we can test, to the greatest extent possible, with the privatization experiences of post-communist countries.

Institutional change involves the movement from one set of mutually shared expectations about social behavior to another. We specify hypotheses in terms of the efficiency of these moves. Several terms are relevant to our discussion: Pareto efficiency, potential Pareto efficiency, and Pareto improving.

In its neoclassical use, Pareto efficiency applies to the comparison of alternative equilibria. An equilibrium is Pareto efficient if no other equilibrium exists that would make at least one person better off without making anyone else worse off. It is based solely on people's preferences over alternative equilibria, ignoring the dynamics of movement from one equilibrium to another. An equilibrium is potentially Pareto efficient relative to the status quo equilibrium if it offers a sufficient excess of benefits over costs (net benefits) so that, with costless redistribution, it would be possible to make someone better off without anyone else being worse off. Potential Pareto efficiency is the standard criterion for ranking alternative equilibria in applied welfare economics: An equilibrium is considered efficient if it maximizes net benefits.

As we are interested in institutional change, we use dynamic Pareto efficiency to apply to preferences over *moves* from one equilibrium to another: A move, perhaps staying with the status quo, is Pareto efficient if no other move could make someone better off without making anyone else worse off. A move is Pareto improving if it actually makes at least someone better off without making anyone else worse off. An equilibrium may be inefficient in the neoclassical sense that some alternative is Pareto

Table 12.1. *Competing theories of institutional change*

Theory	Central mechanism	Refutation
Economic	Change occurs as if it is the result of mutually acceptable (Pareto-improving) contracting among relevant economic actors	Institutional change that is not Pareto improving
Public choice	Change results from actions taken by government as strategic actor interested in revenue and electoral prospects	Institutional change that neither satisfies a pressing revenue constraint nor advances the electoral prospects for the government in power
Distributional	Change results as the by-product of "bargaining" among actors with asymmetric resources seeking distributional gains	Institutional change that disadvantages the strongest organized interests

superior, whereas a movement from the status quo to the alternative is not Pareto improving because of the costs of reaching a collective decision to make the move and distribute the resulting net gains.

As these concepts depend on the institutional rules and endowments embodied in the status quo, they have both normative and positive implications.

The use of the potential Pareto efficiency standard in applied welfare economics does not necessarily correspond to the maximization of social welfare, especially if the status quo involves great disparities in wealth or opportunity. Daniel Bromley (1989) argues strongly that analysts should impose an explicit social welfare function to take account of distributional values in comparing the desirability of alternative institutions. In our analysis, although we recognize the limitation of potential Pareto efficiency as a normative standard, we nevertheless find it useful in distinguishing among the theories.

The major theories of institutional change imply what Douglass North (1990) calls "path dependence." With respect to the economic theory, for instance, the feasible set of potential Pareto-improving moves obviously depends on the status quo. More generally, the costs and benefits of possible institutional changes are measured relative to the existing formal and informal institutions. Understanding the existing institutional environment is thus essential for understanding institutional change.

We next draw on these concepts to explain the three competing theories of institutional change presented in Table 12.1: the economic, public choice, and distributional theories.

2.1 The economic theory

The economic theory of institutional change sees new institutions emerging as the result of contracting among economic actors (North and Thomas, 1973; North, 1981, 1990). In its "naive" form, the economic theory posits institutional change as resulting from the realization of opportunities for Pareto improvements in the formal and informal rules governing social interaction (Eggertsson, 1990). The opportunities arise because of changes in relative prices or the introduction of new production or monitoring technologies. For example, Harold Demsetz's (1967) theory of the evolution of property rights attributes changes in property rules to the internalization of externalities that become relevant because of changing economic conditions such as increases in the relative prices of natural resources.

The more sophisticated version of the economic theory considers transaction costs (North, 1990).[2] These are the costs associated with reaching a collective agreement to change from one institution to another. The transaction costs may trap participants in an institution that is Pareto inefficient in the neoclassical sense because the move to a superior institution is not Pareto improving. Those with stakes in particular rules bargain in an effort to obtain desirable changes and block, or seek compensation for, undesirable ones. For example, with respect to property rights, Gary Libecap (1989) argues that the likelihood of agreement on institutional changes depends on a number of factors relevant to bargaining among stakeholders: the size of the potential gains at stake, the number of interested parties, the heterogeneity of the parties with respect to information and circumstances relevant to the proposed change, the distribution of gains under the current rules, and the distribution of gains under the proposed rules.

The economic theory predicts that institutional changes will be Pareto improving. Neoclassically efficient institutional forms may not be adopted because of transaction costs, but any institutional changes that do occur will be Pareto improving. Thus, *observation of institutional changes that are not Pareto improving refutes the economic theory.* As

[2]For an overview of the nature of transaction costs in bargaining, see Heckathorn and Maser (1987).

North (1990) notes, however, people have imperfect cognition that may lead them to make mistakes in the sense of adopting institutional changes that appear Pareto improving ex ante but turn out to be Pareto inferior ex post. Therefore, in applying this test, the appropriate empirical condition is that the adopted change be recognized as inefficient ex ante.

2.2 *The public choice theory*

The state plays a passive role in the economic theory of institutional change. Several writers in the economic tradition, including North and Thomas (1973) and North (1981), developed a parallel theory in which the state has a strategic role in institutional change. Several recent studies of changes in property rights develop and apply the micro-foundations of this approach, which we label the public choice theory of institutional change (McChesney, 1990; Riker and Sened, 1991). Its key notion is that the government controlling the state selects formal rules to promote its own goals.

The goals of the government may very well include economic efficiency to facilitate economic growth. But they may also include more immediate goals, such as the generation of revenue, foreign exchange, and the maintenance of political support, that may be inconsistent with economic efficiency.[3] If the government adopts rules to promote these latter goals, then the resulting institutional change may be inefficient. Thus, there is a basis for distinguishing between the public choice and economic theories.

In order to arrive at testable implications, we must be more specific about governmental goals. We assume that, though the government in control of state institutions seeks to promote its long-term security by promoting economic growth, it pursues its short-term security by enhancing its electoral prospects, subject to fiscal constraints imposed by the need to raise revenue to finance public expenditures. Thus, *observation of institutional change that is neither electorally advantageous for the government in power, nor consistent with important fiscal constraints that it faces, refutes the public choice theory.*

A broader interpretation of the public choice theory would include gaining the support of important interest groups as instrumental to achieving other governmental goals. Unfortunately, this broader interpretation would allow the public choice theory to encompass the distributional theory, at least with respect to changes in formal rules. In order to be able to distinguish between the theories, which seem to contrast

---

[3]Even the selection of privatization strategies in the United Kingdom under the Thatcher government, which seemed committed to economic efficiency as a principle, appears to have been greatly influenced by electoral concerns (Dobek, 1993).

most in terms of the centrality of the role of government, we adopt the narrower interpretation. We thus subject the public choice theory to a somewhat stricter test than those applied to the other theories.

2.3 The distributional theory

As elaborated most fully by Jack Knight (1992), the distributional theory posits institutional change as the by-product of conflicts among interests over distributional gains. Bargaining among interested parties establishes rules that distribute distributional gains. The distributions, which reflect the bargaining power of the various parties, need not be efficient. Either changes in the distributional consequences of rules resulting from changes in relative prices or technologies or changes in the bargaining power of interests can induce institutional change.

Its advocates see the distributional theory as applying to incremental changes in both formal and informal institutions (Knight, 1992; North, 1993). Yet, in informal bargaining, unless the advantaged party has the ability to impose an outcome on the less advantaged one, we would expect the less advantaged party to do at least as well as the status quo so that outcomes would not be Pareto inefficient, though gains could be grossly asymmetrical. Informal bargaining that imposes costs on those not party to the bargain could lead to Pareto-inefficient changes. More importantly, however, it is through bargaining over the use of the coercive powers of government to change formal institutions that advantaged parties have the opportunity to gain at the expense of less advantaged parties. It is not distributionally motivated bargaining per se that leads to Pareto inefficiency, but rather the inability of all affected parties to guarantee themselves at least the status quo.

With respect to changes in formal rules, the bargaining powers of the various interests reflect their relationships to the government. Interests can provide or withhold electoral support, information, or material contributions. They may be able to make credible threats to initiate politically or economically disruptive actions that are costly to the government. The capabilities of interests for conferring benefits and threatening the imposition of costs on the government usually depend on the extent to which the interests are organized.

Organizing individuals with similar interests is typically difficult because of the collective action problem (Olson, 1965). Individuals have an incentive to "free ride" by shirking with respect to their contributions to the organization if the contributions are costly and they cannot be easily excluded from the benefits gained by the organization. Mancur Olson (1982) argues that once interests discover mechanisms to overcome the collective action problem, they tend to persist. The nature of the interests of these organizations affects the efficiency of institutional change. Their interests may be "encompassing" and consistent with economic efficiency or "special" and detrimental to it. With respect to the transition from socialism, for example, Olson (1992) argues that economic growth initially declines because of the shift from a strong socialist organization with predominantly encompassing interests (the Communist Party) to weak organizations with special interests. The reemergence of strong organizations with encompassing interests would set the stage for a resumption of growth.

With respect to privatization, we test the distributional theory by predicting that institutional changes will reflect the relative strengths and interests of organized groups within society. *Observation of institutional changes that disadvantage the strongest organized groups refutes the distributional theory.*

2.4 Distinguishing among the theories

What would be an ideal test for distinguishing among the theories? Imagine a society facing three alternative rule changes. Rule E is efficient relative to the status quo, relatively favorable to the weakest organized interests, and electorally disadvantageous for the government. Rule P is inefficient relative to the status quo, relatively favorable to the weakest organized interests, and electorally advantageous for the government. Rule D is inefficient relative to the status quo, relatively favorable to the strongest organized interests, and electorally disadvantageous for the government. Observing the choice of E, P, or D would strongly favor the economic, public choice, or distributional theories, respectively.

Unfortunately, the world rarely offers circumstances in which the available choices can be identified so clearly and so neatly distinguish among the theories. In the analysis that follows, we first attempt to reject theories according to the refutations in Table 12.1. When this does not leave a single theory, we resort to a less clear-cut weighing of evidence in support of the theories. For example, though efficient change is possible under all three theories, it is central to the economic theory. Hence, absent strong evidence of relative distributional gain for the strongest organized interests or clear electoral advantage for the government, we would interpret efficient change as tending to support the economic theory. With respect to inefficient change, we attempt to weigh the relative gains to organized interests versus the electoral advantage of the government in an effort to distinguish between the distributional theory and the public choice theory.

3.0 THREE TESTS OF THEORIES
OF INSTITUTIONAL CHANGE

Our empirical focus is on privatization in the post-communist countries.[4] In the following sections we attempt to determine the relative usefulness of the theories of institutional change for interpreting the resolution of three important privatization issues in the post-communist countries: informal privatization, majority employee ownership, and corporate control in the context of privatization strategies. Implicit in each of these issues is an argument about efficiency that helps us make use of the refutable implications of the theories.

3.1 Informal privatization

We use the term "informal privatization" to refer to the reallocation of de facto ownership and use rights to state-owned assets by the managers of state-owned enterprises (SOEs) and the bureaucrats who oversee them. We refrain from labeling this process "spontaneous privatization," its common name in the privatization literature, to avoid confusing it with the legal exercise of managerial discretion over the organizational transformation of SOEs within formal privatization programs. (See the discussion of Hungarian spontaneous privatization in Chapter 9.) Informal privatization is not just spontaneous but also de facto rather than de jure.

Informal privatization started long before other forms of ownership transformation in several Eastern European countries and the Soviet Union. It occurred on a massive scale only in those countries in which the old communist elites consciously opted for the liberalization of political and economic systems to strengthen regime legitimacy and improve the performance of faltering economies. In countries like East Germany and Czechoslovakia, where the ruling parties displayed strong adherence to rigid ideological dogmas right up until they were ousted from power, informal privatization did not take root.

As informal privatization cannot be considered a result of a coherent government policy, the public choice theory of institutional change is of less use for understanding this method of ownership transformation than are the economic or distributional theories. The role of governments in informal privatization, at least initially, was limited. The governments relaxed rigid controls over the economic activities of enterprises that existed under the system of central planning, thereby creating opportunities for informal institutional changes in property rights. But the

[4]A more precise term would be "desocialization," the relinquishing of state ownership of the means of production, rather than privatization, which in common use also includes "debureaucratization"; see Donahue (1989: 215).

process of change in property rights was driven primarily from below by SOE managers. Most often managers acted in alliance with the bureaucrats from the ministry that had established their enterprise and with at least some of the enterprise's employees.

The economic theory of institutional change predicts that the informal changes in property rights that take place during informal privatization will be driven by efficiency considerations. According to this theory, the new forms of property rights emerging from informal privatization should be more efficient than the old ones that existed under the system of central planning.

The distributional theory stresses the importance of resource asymmetries among major societal actors. It predicts that informal changes in property rights during informal privatization would be most beneficial for advantaged groups within society.

Informal privatization in countries of Eastern Europe and the Soviet Union proceeded along several routes. The methods of ownership transformation described by Jadwiga Staniszkis (1991) in her article about "political capitalism" provides a fairly complete picture of the different forms of informal privatization in Poland.

One of these forms involved the use of the equipment and other assets of SOEs by companies set up by the managers of the SOEs. In this way, the managers were able to shift certain costs of production to the parent firm, disregard regulations constraining the state enterprise, and sometimes even avoid taxation of the resulting high profits.

Another form involved the creation of managers' private companies that performed certain functions of the SOE. As the managers retained their jobs in the state firm, they were able to pressure prospective clients by linking the contracts for their private firms with access to the products of their SOEs, which often enjoyed monopoly positions in the economy.

Probably the most often encountered form of informal privatization consisted of selective leasing of parts of SOEs to private companies either partially or fully owned by the management of the parent firm. In this way, these companies gained access to the most advanced equipment and, again, could shift some of their costs to the SOE.

Finally, in those cases in which an SOE went bankrupt and the state could not find a private company willing and able to buy most of its assets, a special kind of company owned by private persons and the Treasury was created. Representatives of the Treasury provided a sort of protective umbrella for the company, making it easier to get supplies, subsidies, and tax advantages.

In Hungary, when roundtable negotiations opened the possibility of political transition, the managers of SOEs and the high-ranking bureaucrats gained a unique opportunity to appropriate state property without intervention from state actors. The government was virtually paralyzed by the agreement reached at the roundtable stating that the last communist parliament "should pass no legislation that would preempt the ability of the subsequent, newly elected Parliament to carry out its mandate" (Stark, 1990: 363).

Informal privatization was usually started by the decision of the enterprise council that consisted of representatives of the workers and managers to create a new joint-stock company, which later traded its shares for the assets of the SOE. By mid-1990, "40 percent of state enterprises in industry, trade, and construction had founded several hundred such companies with an average of ten percent of their assets" transferred to the newly established firms (Frydman, Rapaczynski, and Earle, 1993: 132).

As in Poland, in many cases, enterprise directors and members of the Hungarian Communist Party and state apparatus were able to carve out the most profitable parts of the SOE business for themselves and shift some of the operating costs to the parent enterprise.

In the former Soviet Union, informal privatization was initially channeled through the legal form of cooperatives. The emerging firms, however, bore little resemblance to real cooperatives with equal shares and control among members; rather, they were effectively equivalent to management buyouts of sections of state enterprises (Filatotchev, Buck, and Wright, 1992). Beginning in 1989, the so-called small enterprises and leased enterprises became the predominant form of informal privatization (Johnson and Kroll, 1991). With the virtual collapse of central authority in the aftermath of the coup in August 1991, managers of SOEs both in Russia and Ukraine acquired de facto independence from ministerial control and were able to use this independence to promote their personal interests.

Although the methods of informal privatization differed from each other in many respects, they shared at least two common characteristics. First, none of these ownership forms represented de jure private property. Second, the new firms almost always retained the vital link with their parent state enterprises that allowed them to gain access to cheap supplies and shift some of their costs to the state budget. As a result, the success of these new firms was determined not so much by technological innovation, high quality of products, or superior organization, but rather by their exclusive access to attractive markets, information, and supplies at below market prices made possible by the dual status of the owners. Such companies often operated in markets closed to domestic or foreign competitors, dealing primarily with the state sector and foreign trade, where they were able to exploit the monopoly positions of their founding SOEs (Staniszkis, 1991). The incomplete nature of ownership and the absence of a guarantee of its permanence explain why owners rarely invested their own money in such entities, but instead put great effort into finding ways of shifting costs to the state sector. The extensive use of cost-shifting opportunities contributed to the rapid deterioration of the financial condition of the parent SOEs and thus negatively affected the overall performance of the economy.[5]

Informal privatization, which appears economically inferior to other possible strategies of ownership transformation, is not driven by efficiency considerations. Although a complete and de jure transfer of SOEs to private ownership through informal privatization might well be potentially Pareto improving, the partial and de facto transfers that did occur were certainly not. The economic theory of institutional change is thus refuted by the empirical evidence from the process of informal privatization in post-communist countries. The distributional theory, on the other hand, is supported by the empirical evidence, as informal changes in property rights clearly benefited those actors (primarily managers of SOEs) who had significant informational and organizational advantages.

It is also useful to look at what happened with informal privatization after the communists lost power in Hungary, Poland, and the Soviet Union in light of the three theories of institutional change.

The first democratically elected governments in Poland and Hungary realized the danger that "the kind of economic system that may arise from such privatization would not only have the old oligarchy at its helm but may well have more in common with the old shortage, soft-budget constrained economy than with dynamic market economics" (Stark, 1990: 370). In addition, the governments could not ignore public reaction evoked by informal privatization that was overwhelmingly negative (Slay, 1992). It came as no surprise, therefore, that the new Polish and Hungarian governments immediately established state organizations for supervising the privatization process (State Property Agency in Hungary; Ministry of Ownership Transformation in Poland), put an end to uncontrolled transfer of state property to managers of SOEs and high-ranking Communist Party and state officials, and introduced other strategies of ownership transformation. Neither of the two governments, however, seriously tried to reverse informal privatization where it had already occurred and renationalize the former state property.

In Russia and Ukraine, it was much more difficult for the governments to reestablish control over SOE managers. The Russian government chose

---

[5]Administered prices create arbitrage opportunities for those who have access to supplies priced administratively below market levels. In 1989, all industrial prices were administered in Poland and the Soviet Union, whereas only 15 percent of all prices were administered in Hungary (Bruno, 1993: 15). It is likely, therefore, that informal privatization involved greater inefficiency in Poland and the Soviet Union than it did in Hungary.

to solve the problem by introducing a large-scale privatization program based on free distribution of ownership shares to the whole population. (See Chapter 4.) This strategy was supposed to limit drastically the amount of cost-shifting from mixed or private firms to SOEs, simply because the number of companies left in state ownership would be much smaller.

The post-communist governments in countries in which informal privatization was under way tried to put an end to this method of ownership transformation. Such efforts were most successful in Poland and Hungary, less so in Russia and Ukraine. How would the three theories of institutional change explain this radical shift in government policies?

An explanation consistent with the economic theory would have to stress the importance of imperfect information available to the government during the early stages of informal privatization. The proponents of this theory may, for instance, argue that when all the deficiencies of this method of ownership transformation were finally realized, the government put an end to informal privatization because it was inefficient. The major problem with such an explanation is that the drawbacks of informal privatizations became obvious to everyone long before the fall of the communist governments, but no actions against this form of ownership transformation were taken at that time. The economic theory of institutional change is thus not only incapable of explaining why such an inefficient method of ownership transformation occurred in Poland, Hungary, Russia, and Ukraine, but it also cannot explain why informal privatization was slowed down or completely stopped in these countries when the democratic governments came to power.

The public choice theory of institutional change is able to provide at least a partial explanation for the change in government policy. As all the governments after the fall of the communist regime have to be accountable to the electorate, public attitudes toward informal privatization could no longer be ignored as they had been under the last communist governments. Because the public strongly resented this method of ownership transformation, which benefited primarily the old communist nomenklatura, the democratic governments had a strong incentive to put an end to it. As this method of privatization was also inefficient and caused a substantial decline in government revenues from SOEs, there were no counterincentives that could have prevented the radical shift in government policy with respect to informal privatization.

An explanation consistent with the distributional theory of institutional change would also stress the importance of elections for government choice of privatization strategies. Under a democratic system of government the influence of the general public increased dramatically. Knight (1992) points out that the desire to stay in power may motivate governments to pay attention not only to the interests of those directly affected by particular institutional rules, but also to the opinions of those who are not directly affected and have no particular distributional interests in the form that the rule takes. Those not directly affected may prefer socially efficient institutions to those that give distributional advantage to the most influential actors. Thus, according to the distributional theory, if all of the electorate with the exception of those who directly benefited from informal privatization were opposed to this method of ownership transformation, then the democratic governments in post-communist countries whould have been under considerable pressure to curb unpopular and inefficient privatization policies. Unfortunately, this explanation is not inconsistent with the public choice theory.

Another explanation consistent with the distributional theory distinguishes between past and future gainers from informal privatization. Three factors suggest that the private gains from informal privatization declined over time. First, it is reasonable to assume that the most attractive opportunities for gain were pursued first, so that over time the quality of the remaining opportunities declined. Second, price liberalization reduced the advantages of informal privatization by reducing the opportunities for arbitrage between administered and market prices. Third, the informational advantages enjoyed by managers and bureaucrats declined as the old planning system faded. If potential gains did indeed decline, then much less was at stake for those who had not yet engaged in informal privatization than for those who had already done so. Further, it is likely that those who had already gained had converted their old assets of declining value (information and position) into a new asset (wealth) of continuing value in the new system. Therefore, it is consistent with the distributional theory that informal privatization was stopped rather than reversed.

The distributional theory, in contrast to the other two theories of institutional change, also allows us to make predictions as to which of the post-communist governments would be most successful in putting a quick end to informal privatization. In those countries in which the governments are relatively strong and the managers' organizations are relatively weak (Hungary and Poland), implementation of government decisions to end informal privatization would not be particularly difficult. On the other hand, in countries with relatively weak central governments and strongly organized managers (Ukraine and perhaps Russia), attempts to end informal privatization without significant side payments to enterprise insiders are unlikely to succeed.

Thus, overall, the distributional theory appears to outperform the two alternative theories in explaining the occurrence and subsequent control of informal privatization.

3.2 Majority employee ownership

Another method of privatization that may lead to inefficient outcomes is majority employee ownership. Several recent reviews summarize the findings of a large theoretical, though less developed empirical, literature on producer cooperatives (Hannsman, 1990; Nuti, 1992; Bonin, Jones, and Putterman, 1993). These reviews identify a number of sources of potential inefficiencies of firms owned and managed by workers relative to capitalist firms operating in equally competitive product markets: restrictive employment practices, reduction of output in situations of market power, less complete risk diversification, distorted responses to product and factor price changes, distorted project selection, underinvestment and undercapitalization, and high costs of internal governance.

Some of the potential deficiencies of worker-managed firms are less relevant to the post-communist setting than others. The alleged restrictive employment policies pursued by worker-owned companies is one example. The most famous model of the labor-managed firm, which was developed by Ward (1958) and refined by Vanek (1970), Meade (1972), and several others, assumes that "instead of attempting to maximize profit, the labor-managed firm operates under the principle of maximization of net income per laborer" (Vanek, 1970: 19). Income per member in worker-managed companies cannot be lower than the supply price of labor outside the enterprise (or members would leave), but it can be higher than the market wage. As a result, employment levels in producer cooperatives will always be "equal to or lower than that provided in the same conditions by a capitalist enterprise" (Nuti, 1992: 4).

This potential problem will not affect most employee-owned enterprises in Eastern Europe, Russia, or Ukraine in the near future. It may affect growing firms, but there are very few expanding employee-owned companies in post-communist countries. Most enterprises are overstaffed and require significant degrees of restructuring that will almost inevitably lead to layoffs. Workers of such enterprises are primarily concerned about job security and will be reluctant to vote themselves out of a job. At least during the next few years, enterprises with majority employee ownership will be burdened by excessive numbers of workers. For this reason, labor-owned firms in transitional economies are unlikely to have lower levels of employment than other privatized or newly created companies.

Other potential problems identified by the Ward-Vanek-Meade model, however, are directly applicable to labor-owned firms in Eastern Europe, Russia, and Ukraine. First, in cases of monopoly power, labor-owned firms have an incentive to restrict output even more than capitalist firms, because they are maximizing profit per worker rather than total profit.

Second, labor-owned firms are less well suited for undertaking risky ventures, because their owners (workers) are less able to diversify risk than are companies traded in stock markets.

Third, "perverse" responses of worker-owned enterprises to changes in product price, technology, and capital rental lead to inefficient allocation of labor in the short run. The rise in a product price or a decrease in capital rental leads to reduction of membership size instead of encouraging greater employment and output. When a product price falls and capital rental rises, the opposite happens, also leading to inefficiency relative to the capitalist firm.

Fourth, because of distorted project selection incentives, labor-owned firms are characterized by the inefficient use of capital.[6] Projects having a positive present value may be rejected if they lower average earnings per worker, whereas projects with negative present value that increase average earnings per worker may be accepted.

Fifth, the theoretical literature predicts that underinvestment and undercapitalization will plague employee-owned firms. Their members lack capital to invest, which often makes the companies unsuitable for operation outside labor-intensive sectors. Moreover, labor-owned firms have an anti-reinvestment bias because their members can get the benefits of the project only for the duration of their membership and may not be able to recover the principal of their investment at the time of their departure.

Finally, the internal governance costs of labor-owned firms may be large. Forms of representation must be designed when there are too many employees to rely on direct democracy. The costs of democratic decision making are likely to increase as the employees are more heterogeneous in their preferences, because of differences in skills and age. These factors suggest that labor ownership is unlikely to be efficient for large enterprises with diverse employment rolls.

The governments in post-communist countries were well aware of the alleged inefficiencies associated with majority employee ownership and have generally tried to avoid privatization methods leading to the creation of labor-owned enterprises. However, the number of such enterprises continues to grow in several countries. The three competing theories of institutional change provide different explanations of why such growth is possible.

According to the economic theory of institutional change, transition from state ownership to majority employee ownership, or any other new system of property rights, can occur only if the new forms of property rights are more efficient than the old ones.

---

[6] Consideration of contracting costs suggests that for some types of human capital, labor-owned firms may actually have more efficient levels of investment than capitalist firms (see Askildsen and Ireland, 1993). This consideration is unlikely to be important for large industrial firms.

Though labor-owned firms may be more efficient than SOEs, they are clearly inefficient in comparison with capitalist firms. Why would the governments in post-communist countries agree to forgo further gains in efficiency and pursue policies leading to widespread majority employee ownership?

An explanation that is consistent with the economic theory of institutional change may take the following form. Transforming SOEs into capitalist firms may result in the greatest possible increase in efficiency, but the cost of this transformation may be so high that majority employee ownership is Pareto improving relative to state ownership whereas capitalist ownership is not. The prohibitively high costs of establishing private property to industrial enterprises may be explained by significant workers' influence at the enterprise level coupled with politically powerful unions on the national level. It is in those countries in which labor is very strong on both levels that we might expect to see workers' ownership as a common element of a new ownership structure.

According to the public choice theory of institutional change, the government may forgo further efficiency gains or even choose less efficient forms of property rights in comparison with state ownership if it can derive more revenue from the relatively inefficient methods of ownership transformation, or if it can achieve significant electoral benefits from pursuing suboptimal privatization policies.

Majority employee ownership in post-communist countries clearly cannot result in higher revenues for the government than other forms of privatization, such as, for instance, direct sales to foreign or domestic investors. Employees of SOEs generally pay much less than the outsiders when they purchase the firms in which they work. The long-term financial benefits to the government from collected taxes on profits of privatized enterprises are also likely to be lower in the case of labor-managed firms because profitability of such firms in transitional economies is usually lower than profitability of capitalist firms.

The other possible explanation for the growing number of labor-owned firms in post-communist countries, which is consistent with the public choice theory, centers around the impact of the ownership transformation process on electoral prospects of the parties in power. If electoral concerns are the driving force, than we would expect the Left parties (on the economic scale discussed in Chapter 3), whose core constituency is blue-collar workers, to support the privatization policies that lead to majority employee ownership. Right parties, on the other hand, would have to oppose such policies and support other methods of privatization.

With respect to the distributional theory, transformation of property rights in the post-communist countries may be a consequence of the drastic weakening of state actors in comparison to societal actors, such as labor unions or emerging employers' organizations after the fall of communism. The most influential societal actors were able to readjust the institutional structure, perhaps even to the detriment of the state. Where such influential actors were trade unions, one may expect to see widespread employees' ownership even if the government in power opposes such a transformation in ownership form.

Thus, if we believe that majority employee ownership is a more efficient form of property rights than state ownership, the economic and distributional theories of institutional change have compatible, if not identical implications with respect to the proliferation of labor-managed firms. Both theories imply that this form of ownership will not appear in countries where labor is weak and would be frequently encountered in those countries in which trade unions are able to strengthen their position vis-à-vis other actors as a result of regime transformation. Among the countries in which we are interested, Poland, Germany, Russia, and Ukraine all have relatively strong unions, whereas Hungary, the Czech Republic, and Slovakia have much weaker unions.

Germany clearly stands apart from all other post-communist countries because the distribution of resources between the state and society, and also among societal actors, was imported to its eastern part from the former West Germany. The unions that play an important role in shaping privatization policy are essentially West German unions extended into the East. Further, investors interested in acquiring the property of the former East German state also come from the western part of united Germany.

The financial power of domestic investors (a group that is politically much stronger than its counterparts in every other country we analyze), the solid financial position of the German state, and its willingness to offer substantial concessions to the unions in exchange for neutrality with respect to its privatization strategy determine unions' position on the issue of ownership transformation. The unions are not pressing for employees' ownership of the SOEs. Rather, they seek, and achieve, concessions in collective bargaining over wages, thus driving East German wages far above the level of productivity achieved, and, what is more relevant to the privatization process, they seek, and often obtain, from the government explicit employment guarantees for the workers of privatized enterprises.

The absence of employee-owned firms emerging from SOEs in the eastern part of Germany does not mean that workers are unable to realize advantages given to them by strong organizations extended from the West. They are simply better off pursuing other strategies open to them within the German political and economic system. And because they have the opportunity to realize their advantages elsewhere, transaction costs of

335

selecting a more efficient form of property rights, capitalist ownership, are not prohibitively high.

Among the remaining countries, Russia seems to be the one in which majority employee ownership has spread most widely. The Russian mass privatization program is a good example of how relatively strong labor unions, aligned with powerful SOE managers' organizations and anti-market opposition in the Russian parliament, may force the government to accept what it thinks to be a clearly inefficient method of privatization.

The Russian government first addressed the question of the employees' role in ownership transformation in "Basic Provisions of the Program for the Privatization of State and Municipal Enterprises in the Russian Federation in 1992." According to this document, members of labor collectives of privatized enterprises were entitled to receive free of charge nonvoting shares amounting to 25 percent of the joint-stock company's incorporation capital. They also gained the right to acquire another 10 percent of shares at a 30 percent discount from book value. Transfer of enterprises to workers was initially ruled out as an option because, as the chairman of the Russian State Property Committee put it in 1992, "A labor collective tends to use income not for long-term goals but for wages. Therefore no potential investor – native or foreign – will spend out on a plant whose labor collective retains a controlling block of shares" (*Central Eurasia Daily Report*, FBIS, February 27, 1992: 39).

This policy, however, had to be significantly modified because of an unambiguous threat on the part of the Russian Federation of Independent Trade Unions, an organization with approximately 60 million members, to organize mass strikes if employees were not given the right to choose a method of privatization of their enterprises. Managers supported and encouraged labor demands as a way of avoiding external control over their enterprises. The government agreed to give the work collectives the right to acquire 51 percent of all issued shares. As a result of the government's concessions and the extremely low residual value of SOEs, labor collectives in approximately 75 percent of all companies privatized by April 1994 have chosen an option leading to majority employee ownership.

It is too early to make conclusions about the prospects for majority employee ownership in Ukraine, because very little privatization has taken place in industry. Nevertheless, we can look at existing legislation and to the debates about it in the legislature and society. The Ukrainian government, like most other governments in the region, has declared repeatedly that workers should not be allowed to gain control of the enterprises in which they work, justifying the restriction not so much in terms of efficiency, but primarily on the grounds of fairness with respect to all citizens who are not employed in privatizing enterprises (Johnson and Eder, 1992). The government, however, was confronted with strong opposition from workers and managers of leased enterprises, supported by trade unions and anti-market forces in the parliament, who demanded free transfer of ownership rights over SOEs to the labor collectives. As a result of this pressure, the government agreed to concede to the workers limited priority rights in acquiring shares of their enterprises (Rudeka-vych, 1994). Employees of the leased enterprises got the best terms, including the possibility of buyouts.

In Poland, where labor unions are much stronger than in any other country of Eastern Europe, different forms of majority employee ownership may play an important part in privatization. Direct buyouts are not the most popular option. As of February 1992, only two companies had been partially privatized in this manner (Frydman et al., 1993).

A much more popular route to insider privatization has been found in the so-called privatization through liquidation. (See Chapter 8.) This method of ownership transformation has been widely applied to both viable and bankrupt companies. The most often encountered form of this method of privatization involves creating a new company owned by the employees of the liquidated enterprise that acquires a lease to the assets of the liquidated firm. The yearly rents on the leases include payments toward the principal, so that eventually the new company becomes the owner of the assets.

In countries in which unions are weak, the employees' privileges are usually limited to priority rights in acquiring shares of privatized companies. According to the Transformation Law adopted in Hungary, employees could only own 10 percent of stock that is not for sale outside the company. In 1992 Hungary adopted the Employee Co-Ownership Program, which provided favorable loans to workers for buying their firms, as an attempt to gain electoral support from skilled workers. (See Chapter 9.) In the Czech Republic, the employees of the privatized enterprises have no priority rights whatsoever.

The government of Vladimir Meciar in Slovakia, which was much farther to the left than its Czech counterpart and, therefore, much more dependent on workers for electoral support, started selling employees' shares at a discount and was even planning to start privatization through employee joint-stock companies. The government, however, lost the majority in the parliament and was voted out of office in March 1994. (See Chapter 7.) Meciar's plans to promote employee joint-stock companies were abandoned by a new cabinet.

This brief review of privatization strategies leading to majority employee ownership shows that, consistent with the predictions of a distributional theory of institutional change, power asymmetries among actors are extremely relevant in shaping privatization outcomes. One may also explain

these developments using the framework of transaction costs, if one be-
lieves that employees' ownership is more efficient than state ownership. But
is there any theoretical or empirical evidence that such beliefs are true?

Unfortunately, we do not have a body of theoretical literature on this
subject comparable to that which is available on the efficiency of state-
owned versus private-owned enterprises, or capitalist firms versus labor-
managed firms. Empirical evidence from post-communist societies is still
very inconclusive. In Russia the large-scale transfer of ownership rights
from the state to the labor collectives began less than two years ago. In
Poland, where privatization through liquidation started earlier, "very
little information is available on the performance of the privatized companies in the wake of the state's withdrawal from the position of ownership" (Frydman et al., 1993: 187).

Empirical evidence from developed capitalist economies provides at
least one interesting possibility for approaching this problem. Small
labor-managed enterprises seem to be much more viable and competitive
than larger ones. The deficiencies of cooperatives identified by the theoretical literature are partially compensated for by the effects of direct
participation of the workers in the decision-making process. In small
cooperatives such participation may be frequent and meaningful. But as
the size of the enterprise increases, opportunities for participation become rare and the benefits resulting from this participation are no longer
able to offset the basic deficiencies of this organizational form.

In the extreme case of very large enterprises in capital-intensive sectors
subject to sudden fluctuations in prices, labor-managed firms may not be
viable. As Nuti notes, "nobody expects oil tankers or steel mills to be
operated by cooperatives" (Nuti, 1992: 4). But if we look at what is
currently being transferred into employees' ownership in Russia, and
what may potentially happen in Poland and Ukraine, we find dozens of
examples of employee ownership in unexpected industries. At least in
these cases, we may have examples of privatization leading to less efficient
property rights, which is not possible in the economic theory.

The comparison of efficiency of state-owned versus employee-owned
enterprises in transitional economies is essentially an empirical question
that cannot yet be answered because of scarcity of available data. But as
time goes on, more and more information will become available, and
such a test may soon be possible. And if the size variable is indeed
relevant to the efficiency of labor-managed enterprises as we hypothesized, then both economic and distributional theories of institutional
change may offer correct predictions with respect to small and perhaps
medium-sized firms, but only the distributional theory is capable of explaining the developments in privatization of large enterprises constitut-
ing the bulk of SOEs in post-communist nations.

Privatization and theories of institutional change

As for the predictions about privatization policies leading to majority employee ownership based on the public choice theory of institutional change, they are completely refuted by the evidence. The parties in power did not choose inefficient policies in return for higher government revenues. Electoral considerations also cannot explain the choice of inefficient privatization policies. The only two countries in which the number of labor-owned firms increased drastically as a result of the process of ownership transformation (Poland and Russia) were controlled by parties or other political forces of the right at the time when the decisions about privatization were made. And these Right governments had no electoral incentives to promote majority employee ownership. Left-wing governments that did have such incentives, on the other hand, have either chosen other methods of privatization or have not yet started the process of ownership transformation on a large scale.

3.3 Privatization strategies and corporate control

Privatization in the post-communist countries consists primarily of the transformation of SOEs to corporate forms in which shares can be privately owned. As the managers of large corporations rarely own more than a small fraction of shares, the question of corporate control arises: To what extent do managers make decisions in the interests of the owners of shares? Because corporate control has implications for both efficiency and the interests of an important advantaged group (managers), and because various privatization strategies have different implications for corporate control and electoral prospects, investigation of it offers at least possibilities for refuting the theories of institutional change. Although we cannot be confident about realizing these possibilities, our efforts to do so provide relatively more support for the distributional theory.

The principal-agent problem provides a theoretical framework for considering corporate control (Jensen and Meckling, 1976). External owners of shares in firms (principals) wish managers to make decisions that maximize the present value of their holdings, which in the absence of market failures is consistent with economic efficiency. The managers of the enterprises (agents), however, may be motivated by such considerations as maximization of a "utility function that has renumeration, power, security, and status as its central elements" (Hill and Snell, 1989: 26). Because managers typically enjoy more information about the minimum achievable costs of their firms than do owners, they have an opportunity to pursue to some extent their personal interests.

Monitoring the exercise of managerial discretion to detect and reduce the deviations from the interests of owners is a costly activity. When ownership is widely dispersed, stockholders face a collective action prob-

339

lem with respect to monitoring – the monitor bears all the costs while the benefits accrue to all owners. Moreover, when ownership is widely dispersed, the ability of stockholders to organize and remove managers is similarly hindered. If, on the other hand, the ownership is highly concentrated in a smaller number of stockholders, then the collective action problem is likely to be less serious so that information asymmetries are reduced and the owners' ability to remove management teams is higher. As a result, managers are more constrained to pursue strategies that are in the owners' interests. These theoretical arguments are largely confirmed by the available empirical evidence (Hesterly, Liebeskind, and Zenger, 1990).

The corporate control issue has been prominent in the debate over the two broad privatization strategies, direct sale and free distribution. Advocates of sale argue that free distribution results in less effective corporate control, because it leads to more dispersed ownership. If this argument is sustained, then the selection of free distribution over direct sale could be interpreted as relatively inefficient institutional change and hence a possible refutation of the economic theory.

Although the argument holds in comparing the simplest form of free distribution with an ideal system of direct sales leading to ownership concentrated in the hands of outside parties, it is far from convincing in comparing real systems of direct sales with real systems of free distribution. On the one hand, direct sales can be carried out in a variety of ways, ranging from tenders, which indeed are likely to concentrate shares in the hands of investors with an incentive to use the firms' assets efficiently, to sales with preferential treatment of "insiders," which may result in managers gaining control of sufficient shares to block effective external control.

On the other hand, free distribution does not necessarily lead to dispersed ownership. For example, the Polish mass privatization program adopted by the Sejm in April 1993 concentrates enterprise shares in investment funds that serve as intermediaries between enterprises and individual investors.[7] Even without explicit design, investment funds are likely to arise to concentrate ownership after free distribution. For example, over 400 investment funds accumulated about three-fourths of all investment points distributed in the first wave of the Czechoslovakian

---

[7]The Law on National Investment Funds and Their Privatization has two major components. The first, which applies to approximately two hundred SOEs whose ownership is to be held by five to eight investment funds, involves the free distribution of participation certificates to public sector workers and pension holders. The second component, which applies to approximately four hundred SOEs to be held by fifteen national investment funds, involves the distribution of participation certificates to any adult citizen for a nominal fee of 5 percent of monthly earnings. The investment funds will hold 60 percent of the shares of privatized funds. Ten percent will go to employees, and 30 percent will be retained by the state.

mass privatization. Even in Russia, where investment funds were threatened with dissolution from the anti-reform legislature and hampered by widely publicized cases of financial fraud, they acquired significant blocks of shares to large industrial enterprises in the first voucher auctions (Djelic and Tsukanova, 1993).

Even if direct sale resulted in better corporate control than free distribution, it might not be a more efficient strategy from the perspective of the whole economy. Experience suggests that direct sales cannot be implemented as quickly as free distribution. Therefore, any efficiency gains at the level of the privatized firm may be offset by the continuing inefficiency of enterprises still under state ownership. For example, contrast the Czech Republic, which has relied most heavily on free distribution, with Hungary, which has relied most heavily on direct sales. The former has shown both greater progress in privatization of industry and better overall economic performance.

Consequently, we cannot easily rank the general strategies of direct sales and free distribution in terms of efficiency. A more promising efficiency ranking is in terms of the degree to which the insiders of privatized enterprises, managers and workers, are subjected to corporate control by the new external owners. The greater the external control, the greater the efficiency. But this ranking also suffers from the problem of the possible difference between firm- and economy-level efficiency.

In contrast to the cases of informal privatization and employee ownership of large enterprises, neither does it appear that sale, free distribution, or their variants lead to institutional forms less efficient than state ownership. Even privatized firms that are subject to little corporate control cannot be assumed to be less efficient than SOEs.[8] Consequently, we do not have a clear basis for rejecting the economic theory in terms of variation in corporate control.

Our best hope for refuting the distributional theory lies in comparisons across countries. To the extent we can rank the preferences of managers and their relative advantages across countries, we can formulate a refutable prediction: The stronger the position of managers in a country, the more the mix of privatization strategies will be consistent with their preferences for lower levels of external corporate control. A negative relationship between the strength of their relative positions and the favorableness of the privatization strategy would refute the distributional theory.

[8]Product market competition, the desire of SOE managers to establish good reputations prior to privatization, and, perhaps, "harder" budget constraints have resulted in a surprising degree of restructuring by Polish SOEs (Pinto, Belka, and Krajewski, 1993). Nevertheless, theory and empirical evidence suggest that, holding product market competition constant, privatized firms are likely to be at least as efficient as SOEs (see Boardman and Vining, 1989; Vining and Boardman, 1992).

Our first task is to formulate an independent variable by ranking countries in the study in terms of the relative strength of managers. In general, we assume that managers with greater autonomy are likely to have more political resources, because they have more opportunity to convert the resources of their SOEs to their own purposes. It is reasonable to assume that managers in Russia and Ukraine have the strongest relative position. They gained considerable autonomy with the collapse of the Soviet Union. In each country managers were well positioned to take advantage of concessions nominally given to workers. Further, Russian managers also had an organized voice in Civic Union. Hungary and Poland would rank next. In both countries, SOEs gained considerable independence prior to the fall of the communist governments. In Poland, however, workers gained a relatively stronger governance position that gives managers somewhat less autonomy than in Hungary. Finally, managers in Czechoslovakia and East Germany enjoyed the least autonomy under their communist and first post-communist governments. The greater prominence of large SOEs in Slovakia than in the Czech Republic suggests that the former had greater political resources. Therefore, we offer the following ranking of relative managerial strength: Russia, Ukraine, Hungary, Poland, Slovakia, the Czech Republic, and East Germany.

In order to construct the dependent variable, the ranking of privatization strategies from the perspective of managers, we assume that they wish to protect their positions relative to external corporate control.[9] We offer the following preference ordering: (1) management buyout at a low price, (2) free distribution with strong preferential treatment of insiders, (3) direct sale to investors selected by the managers, who can create situations favorable to their personal interests, (4) continued state ownership with state protection such as restricted competition or a soft budget constraint, (5) free distribution or public auction resulting in dispersed ownership, (6) free distribution with financial intermediaries, (7) continued state ownership without state protection, and (8) direct sale to an investor arranged by the government without management participation.

Ranking the privatization experiences of the countries in terms of these managerial preferences is far from straightforward; policies neither fit precisely into the preference categories nor have remained constant over the period of study. Nonetheless, we offer the following ranking: Russia (mainly 2), Hungary (8 abandoned, mainly 3), Ukraine (4, 2, and 5 proposed), Slovakia (4, 8, and 5), Poland (5 and 7 with 6 beginning), Czech Republic (mainly 6), and East Germany (8). We are fairly confident

---

[9]With respect to Czechoslovakian privatization, for instance, Frydman et al. (1993: 81) posit the following preference ordering for managers: first, management buyout at favorable prices; second, a sweetheart deal with a foreign buyer; third, dispersed ownership so that little effective control will be exercised over managers.

in ranking Russia at one extreme and the Czech Republic and East Germany at the other. The relative positions of Hungary, Ukraine, Slovakia, and Poland in the middle is less clear.

The general correspondence between managerial resources and outcomes is consistent with the distributional theory. The Kendall rank correlation between relative managerial strength and strategy preference is positive and statistically significant at the 5 percent level. Even eliminating East Germany from the sample, because of its different political circumstances, yields a positive Kendall rank correlation that is almost significant at the 5 percent level. Thus, rather than refuting the distributional theory, this simple test supports it.

To test the public choice theory, we return to the general distinction between direct sale and free distribution. In terms of electoral advantage, free distribution seems to dominate: It provides tangible benefits to large numbers of voters, and it moves the privatization process along quickly so as to reduce the financial burden of subsidizing ailing SOEs. Absent some particularly strong constraint that might be better met with direct sale, the public choice theory predicts that all post-communist governments adopt free distribution.

On the surface, it appears that the public choice theory is refuted, albeit by a demanding test, because, although free distribution has occurred in the Czech Republic, Russia, and Slovakia,[10] it is not planned in Germany or Hungary, it has not yet been fully implemented in Poland, and though proposed several times, it may not yet be implemented in Ukraine. We can easily exclude Germany from the test, however, because of the capacity of the West German government to use social welfare policy as an alternative means of gaining electoral support in East Germany. Ukraine can be discounted to some extent, because its adopted coupon privatization program has languished along with economic reforms generally. Yet free distribution in Poland has also moved very slowly, and the Hungarian privatization program does not involve free distribution to any significant extent. The Polish and Hungarian cases, however, are not so clear upon closer inspection.

In Poland, free distribution has been part of the privatization plan since October 1990 and was formally proposed in June 1991. Although it was not approved by the parliament until April 1993, the selection and com-

---

[10]The victory of the Movement for a Democratic Slovakia and its leader, Vladimir Meciar, in the October 1, 1994, national election brings the continuation of free distribution through "coupon privatization" into question. Parties that ran campaigns against privatization received over half of votes cast, while parties campaigning in favor of privatization received only about a quarter of votes cast, suggesting that free distribution is not electorally advantageous in the current political circumstances (*Eastern Europe Daily Report*, FBIS, November 4, 1994: 7–8).

mercialization of SOEs for inclusion in the free distribution program was under way in the Ministry of Privatization during the intervening period. This diligence suggests that free distribution, though not yet fully implemented after four years, should be viewed as more than a vague intention of the government. Despite the lack of enthusiasm on the part of Prime Minister Waldemar Pawlak and his Polish Peasant Party (Polskie Stronnictwo Ludowe) for privatization, and organized opposition from trade unions through the Nationwide Movement to Defend National Property, he approved a list of candidates for supervisory positions for the mass privatization program in late November 1994 that should now allow it to go forward. One interpretation of his decision to abandon opposition to free distribution is that he desired to shore up his coalition with the Alliance of the Democratic Left in anticipation of the 1995 elections. Another interpretation, more consistent with the public choice theory, is that it is an attempt to appeal to public sector employees who are not likely to benefit from employee buyouts.

Though the Hungarian privatization represents the most explicit choice of sale over free distribution, two factors reduce its value as refutation of the public choice theory.

First, immediate electoral advanatage probably was not the only motivation of the post-communist government. Hungary was burdened with a very high level of foreign debt – about 85 percent of annual GNP as opposed to only about 12 percent for Czechoslovakia. Attracting foreign investment was important for servicing the debt. Further, unlike most of the other post-communist countries with large foreign debts, Hungary had established a favorable reputation among actual and potential foreign investors. Hungary achieved this reputation because of its relative openness to foreign investment even during the last years of the communist government and because the new government moved quickly to remove numerous obstacles to the operation of foreign businesses. Thus, the government had both an incentive and an opportunity to sell SOEs to generate foreign exchange.

Second, the evolution of the Hungarian privatization program after the initial decision to rely on sales, which was favored by Hungarian expert opinion on efficiency grounds, appears to be consistent with the public choice theory. As described by László Urbán in Chapter 9, the first post-communist government in Hungary attempted to enhance its electoral prospects through various modifications of the basic strategy of sale. It could not easily abandon sales because of the foreign debt situation, but it could make marginal changes in an effort to gain support. We are reluctant, therefore, to use the Hungarian case to refute the public choice theory. Indeed, the modifications of the privatization program seem to support the public choice theory.

Table 12.2. *Post-communist privatization and theories
of institutional change*

Theory	Informal privatization	Employee ownership	Privatization strategies and corporate control
Economic	Refuted – requires implausible assumption of imperfect information about consequences	Probably refuted – employee ownership less efficient than state ownership for largest firms	Not refuted – relative efficiency of outcomes from various strategies not clear
Public choice	Consistent with termination but does not explain onset or pattern of termination across countries	Refuted – neither electoral nor fiscal advantage for Right governments in countries in which it occurs	Generally consistent with developments within countries over time
Distributional	Consistent with onset, termination, and pattern of termination across countries	Consistent with pattern across countries	Consistent with pattern across countries

4.0 CONCLUSION

How well have the theories of institutional change performed in light of the privatization experiences in Eastern Europe and the former Soviet Union? Table 12.2 provides a brief summary of their application to the three aspects of privatization considered in this chapter. We refute the economic theory as an explanation for informal privatization. Although its termination is consistent with both the public choice theory and the distributional theory, its onset and pattern of termination appear to be better explained by the latter. The worker ownership of large firms provides the clearest differentiation among the theories as it allows us to refute both the economic and the public choice theories and to confirm the distributional theory with predictions across countries. Issues relating to corporate control and general privatization strategies turn out to be disappointing from the perspective of refuting theory. We have no basis for refuting the economic or distributional theories, and it would be stretching the evidence to refute the public choice theory. But whereas the economic theory is silent about variation within and across countries, the changes in privatization strategies within countries seem more consistent with the public choice theory, and the pattern of variation in the initial choice of strategies across countries seems more consistent with the distributional theory.

Overall, the distributional theory best survives refutation in the three tests. The public choice theory fails in one, and the economic theory in one or two, of the tests. With the caveat that we found it easier to specify refutably testable implications for the economic and public choice theories (these theories thus have greater "empirical content" in Popperian terms), the distributional theory appears to be the most robust of the three. It should be kept in mind, however, that our assumption of relatively narrow governmental goals subjected the public choice theory to a stricter test than that applied to the distributional theory. Indeed, with respect to formal institutional change, which must be accomplished through the mechanisms of government, the broad interpretation of the public choice theory would be indistinguishable from the distributional theory if the latter treated the government in power as an explicit actor.

In this chapter we set out an ambitious goal – testing broad theories of institutional change. Although the "natural experiment" under way in Eastern Europe and the former Soviet Union offers an unusual opportunity for pursuing this goal, our results call for some modesty. Applying the theories required many judgments that might be questioned. Nevertheless, we believe that we have made at least a small contribution by filling a gap in empirical research between historical analysis on the grand scale and narrowly focused studies of particular subnational institutions. We hope that our effort will encourage others to take advantage of the post-communist experiment as it continues to unfold, or perhaps find other promising opportunities for the comparative study of institutional change.

REFERENCES

Askildsen, Jan Eric, and Norman J. Ireland, "Human Capital, Property Rights, and Labour Managed Firms," *Oxford Economic Papers* 45: 2 (1993), 229–42.

Boardman, Anthony E., and Aidan R. Vining, "Ownership and Performance in Competitive Environments: A Comparison of the Performance of Private, Mixed, and State-Owned Enterprises," *Journal of Law and Economics* 32: 1 (1989), 1–33.

Bonin, John P., Derek C. Jones, and Louis Putterman, "Theoretical and Empirical Studies of Producer Cooperatives: Will Ever the Twain Meet?" *Journal of Economic Literature* 31: 3 (1993), 1290–1320.

Bromley, Daniel W., *Economic Interests and Institutions: The Conceptual Foundations of Policy Analysis* (Oxford: Basil Blackwell, 1989).

Bruno, Michael, "Stabilization and Reform in Eastern Europe: Preliminary Evaluation," in Mario I. Blejer et al., editors, *Eastern Europe in Transition: From Recession to Growth?* (Washington, DC: World Bank, 1993), 12–38.

Demzetz, Harold, "Toward a Theory of Property Rights," *American Economic Review* 57: 2 (1967), 347–59.

Djelic, Bozidar, and Natalia Tsukanova, "Voucher Auctions: A Crucial Step Toward Privatization," *RFE/RL Research Report* 2: 30 (1993), 10–18.

Dobek, Mariusz Mark, *The Political Logic of Privatization: Lessons from Great Britain and Poland* (Westport, CT: Praeger, 1993).

Donahue, John D., *The Privatization Decision* (New York: Basic Books, 1989).

Eggertsson, Thrainn, *Economic Behavior and Institutions* (Cambridge: Cambridge University Press, 1990).

Filatochev, Igor, Trevor Buck, and Mike Wright, "Privatization and Buy-outs in the USSR," *Soviet Studies* 44: 2 (1992), 265–82.

Frydman, Roman, et al., *The Privatization Process in Central Europe* (Budapest: Central European University Press, 1993).

Hansmann, Henry, "When Does Worker Ownership Work? ESOPs, Law Firms, Codetermination, and Economic Democracy," *Yale Law Journal* 99: 8 (1990), 1749–1816.

Heckathorn, Douglas D., and Steven M. Maser, "Bargaining and the Sources of Transaction Costs: The Case of Government Regulation," *Journal of Law, Economics, and Organization* 3: 1 (1987), 69–98.

Hesterly, William S., Julia Liebeskind, and Todd R. Zenger, "Organizational Economics: An Impending Revolution in Organization Theory?" *Academy of Management Review* 15: 3 (1990), 402–20.

Hill, Charles W., and Scott A. Snell, "Effects of Ownership Structure and Control on Corporate Productivity," *Academy of Management Journal* 32: 1 (1989), 25–46.

Jensen, Michael C., and William H. Meckling, "Theory of the Firm: Managerial Behavior, Agency Costs and Ownership Structure," *Journal of Financial Economics* 3: 4 (1976), 305–60.

Johnson, Simon, and Santiago Eder, "Prospects for Privatization in Ukraine," *RFE/RL Research Report* 1: 37 (1992), 46–9.

Johnson, Simon, and Heidi Kroll, "Managerial Strategies for Spontaneous Privatization," *Soviet Economy* 7: 4 (1991), 281–316.

Knight, Jack, *Institutions and Social Conflict* (Cambridge: Cambridge University Press, 1992).

Libecap, Gary D., *Contracting for Property Rights* (Cambridge: Cambridge University Press, 1989).

McChesney, Fred S., "Government as Definer of Property Rights: Indian Lands, Ethnic Externalities, and Bureaucratic Budgets," *Journal of Legal Studies* 19: 2 (1990), 297–335.

Meade, James, "The Theory of Labor-Managed Firms and of Profit Sharing," *Economic Journal* 82 (1972), 402–28.

North, Douglass C., *Structure and Change in Economic History* (New York: W. W. Norton, 1981).

Institutions, Institutional Change and Economic Performance (Cambridge: Cambridge University Press, 1990).

"Institutions and Credible Commitment," *Journal of Institutional and Theoretical Economics* 149: 1 (1993), 11–23.

North, Douglass C., and Robert Paul Thomas, *The Rise of the Western World: A New Economic History* (Cambridge: Cambridge University Press, 1973).

Nuti, Domenico Mario, "On Traditional Cooperatives and James Meade's Labor-Capital Discriminating Partnerships," *Advances in the Economic Analysis of Participatory and Labor-Managed Firms* 4 (1992), 1–26.

Olson, Mancur, *The Logic of Collective Action* (Cambridge: Cambridge University Press, 1965).

The Rise and Decline of Nations (New Haven, CT: Yale University Press, 1982).

"The Hidden Path to a Successful Economy," in Christopher Clague and Gordon C. Rausser, editors, *The Emergence of Market Economies in Eastern Europe* (Cambridge, MA: Basil Blackwell, 1992), 55–75.

Pinto, Brian, Marek Belka, and Stefan Krajewski, "Transforming State Enterprises in Poland: Evidence on Adjustment by Manufacturing Firms," *Brookings Papers on Economic Activity* 1 (1993), 213–61.

Riker, William H., and Itai Sened, "A Political Theory of the Origin of Property Rights: Airport Slots," *American Journal of Political Science* 35: 4 (1991), 951–69.

Rudekavych, Lesia, "Privatization: Problems and Effectiveness in Practice," *Ukranian Legal and Economic Bulletin* 2: 7 (1994), 6–12.

Slay, Ben, "Poland: An Overview," *RFE/RL Research Report* 1: 17 (1992), 15–21.

Staniszkis, Jadwiga, "'Political Capitalism' in Poland," *East European Politics and Societies* 5: 1 (1991), 127–41.

Stark, David, "Privatization in Hungary: From Plan to Market or from Plan to Clan?" *East European Politics and Societies* 4: 3 (1990), 351–92.

Vanek, Jaroslav, *The General Theory of Labor-Managed Market Economies* (Ithaca, NY: Cornell University Press, 1970).

Vining, Aidan R., and Anthony E. Boardman, "Ownership Versus Competition: Efficiency in Public Enterprise," *Public Choice* 73: 2 (1992), 205–39.

Ward, Benjamin, "The Firm in Illiria: Market Syndicalism," *American Economic Review* 48: 4 (1958), 566–89.

Explaining the complexity of institutional change

JACK KNIGHT AND DOUGLASS C. NORTH

Institutional change is a complex process. Theories that identify the underlying mechanisms that drive this process are numerous, but efforts to assess the relative merits of the different theories empirically are few. The chapter by Lorene Allio, Mariusz Dobek, Nikolai Mikhailov, and David Weimer represents a kind of analysis of which we need more in the study of institutional change. Comparative analyses like this one ought to form the basis of our debates over how we can best explain questions of institutional emergence, design, and change. It is a creative and thoughtful attempt to assess the explanatory power of different theories in the context of one of the most significant instances of social change in modern times: the transition from public to private ownership of the means of production in Eastern Europe. Although we endorse the type of analysis offered in that chapter, we think future work in this area should take account of some issues it does not cover.

The authors analyze this transition in terms of three theories of institutional change, which they state as follows: The economic theory rests on the idea that "institutional changes occur as if they were the realization of opportunities for Pareto improvements."[1] The public choice theory "introduces the incumbent government as a strategic actor with interests that may not be consistent with Pareto efficiency." The distributional theory explains "institutional change as the byproduct of distributional conflict." The authors treat these theories as competing accounts of institutional change and seek to develop hypotheses that will allow them to "test" the relative explanatory powers of the theories.

They adopt the following approach to testing the theories. First, they

---

[1]The authors' formulation of the economic theory somewhat conflates the different approaches to the role of transaction costs in institutional change. They adopt a formulation that is closer to the standard Coasean account than the one offered by North (1990), who allows for the possibility that Pareto-improving institutional change will not occur when significant transaction costs are involved in that change.

349

establish hypotheses that capture the main predictions of the different theories. Second, they assess the predictions in terms of the available evidence on the direction of change in three areas of privatization in Eastern Europe. Third, they reject the theories whose predictions run counter to the direction of change. The main conclusion of their analysis is that the distributional theory is the most robust of the three; it does the best job of predicting the direction and nature of change in the privatization efforts in Eastern Europe. For reasons that we will discuss, this is the analytical result that both of us would have predicted.

Let us begin with a couple of conceptual criticisms of this present analysis. The authors posit the following refutable hypotheses. For the economic theory, they posit that "observation of institutional changes that are not Pareto improving refutes the economic theory." To control for the mistakes that the actors might make in assessing the efficiency consequences of the changes, they suggest that the changes must be recognized ex ante as inefficient to constitute a refutation of the theory. For the distributional theory, they posit that "observation of institutional changes that disadvantage the strongest organized groups refutes the distributional theory." For the public choice theory, they posit that "observation of institutional change that is neither electorally advantageous for the government in power, nor consistent with important fiscal constraints that it faces, refutes the public choice theory."

In these formulations we see some of the difficulties in creating "tests" to distinguish the three theories. On the one hand, the public choice theory is distinguished from the other two theories in terms of the actors who are primarily responsible for motivating the change. On the other hand, the economic and distributional theories are distinguished in terms of the different characteristics of the institutions that motivate the actors' efforts to change them (Pareto improvements for the economic theory and distributional advantage for the distribution theory). Interpreted broadly to ignore distinctions as to the type of actor involved in the process of change, the economic and distributional theories can capture all of the instances of change that might be attributed to the public choice account. That is, if state actors seek Pareto improvements (as the authors suggest is a possibility), then change can be explained by the economic theory; if, rather, the state seeks changes that enhance the distributional advantage for themselves or their supporters (another possibility acknowledged by the authors), then the change can be explained by the distributional theory.

If we want to focus on those changes that will most likely be initiated by public officials rather than private actors, then the question that we should be asking is: What are the particular set of conditions in which political entrepreneurs of the state will be involved in the institutional process? In the particular context of privatization in Eastern Europe, we think that the relevant public choice theory question should be: When will privatization be motivated by private actors, and when will it be motivated by public officials? And here it is important to note that the answer to this question is in part a function of the existing institutional order. Existing political institutions affect the degrees of freedom available to state actors.

If we set aside the question of who is the main actor initiating privatization, then the main focus of the analysis turns to the question of which of the two remaining theories, the economic or the distributional, does the best job of explaining the privatization of the means of production in Eastern Europe. The hypotheses that they highlight are fairly accurate statements of the types of change that would clearly refute the different theories. For instance, if the change produced a disadvantage for the strongest organized groups in a community, then the prediction of the distribution theory would be clearly refuted.

The problem for the authors is that there are many situations in which the predictions of the theories will not allow us to distinguish among them. For example, many forms of institutional change will produce both Pareto improvements and distributional advantage for the strongest organized groups. The authors are aware of this problem. In their efforts to deal with this complexity they emphasize the efficiency effects that they claim are implied by the three approaches. In doing so, they overemphasize the differences in terms of the efficiency predictions of the theories. Although the economic theory does give priority to the efficiency characteristics of property rights, neither of the other two approaches necessarily implies that change will be inefficient. Thus, the attempt by the authors (at the end of section 2.4) to cure the irrefutability problem by amending the predictions to give priority to efficiency as evidence of the superiority of the economic theory vis-à-vis the distributional theory fails.

We think that a more fruitful way to address the relative merits of the the different theories is to focus on the sets of conditions under which either the economic or the distributional theory does the best job of explaining change. That is to say that we want to investigate the conditions under which either the efficiency or the distributional effects of property rights are more prominent in explaining the development of those rights. This requires us to investigate not only the predictions offered by the theories, but also the mechanisms that the theories identify as the primary cause of these changes.

We can develop this suggestion by focusing on the issue of informal privatization. The decisions to embark on informal privatization of property rights were primarily made by the managers of state-owned enterprises. Both the economic and distributional theories would agree with

351

the following characterization of the motivations of these managers. In the process of constructing economic institutions, individual actors will be motivated by the benefits that they individually derive from the activities structured by these institutions. These individual benefits are determined in large part by the way in which the institution distributes the benefits of the joint activity structured by the institution. Thus, distributional questions will be of primary importance to an individual's preference over the institutional alternatives when the institutional alternatives actually produce asymmetries in distributional benefits. In the informal privatization case, if the SOE managers can determine that one form of privatization benefits them more than the other alternatives, then they will prefer to establish that form of property right.

But institutional choice is a strategic one, and it takes place in a context of social, economic, and political conditions that makes the choice more complex than that of merely establishing one's most individually preferred alternative. It is in the analysis of how these conditions affect choice that we can understand the relative importance of the economic and distributional theories in explanations of institutional change. Although this is a complex process involving many factors, there are two important issues that we want to emphasize here.

The first involves the time horizon of economic decision makers. What appears to be individually advantageous in the short term might not be advantageous in the long run. The economic theory is better at predicting the long-run rather than the short-run characteristics of property rights. The logic of the long-run explanation is as follows. In the short run, SOE managers may be motivated to choose property rights schemes that produce distributional advantage even if they are Pareto inefficient. But in the long run, if they persist in establishing property rights that are Pareto inefficient, then they will be replaced by the competitive pressure produced by economic actors who employ more efficient rights schemes. If the SOE managers take a long-run view of their individual interests, they will come to equate Pareto-improving change with their long-term distributional interests. Thus, on the economic theory account, the long-run conditions that determine the survivability of different forms of economic organization will cause the strongest economic actors to identify their long-run interests with Pareto efficiency.

We should note here that this long-run account of the economic theory does not distinguish it from the long-run prediction of the distribution theory. What it does is explain why the long-run effects of institutional change should be more consistent with the predictions of the economic theory than the effects discovered by the types of short-run evidence that we have about the Eastern European experience. The only way to distinguish the two theories in those cases in which they would predict the same direction of change in the long run would be to resort to an analysis of the causal mechanisms that underlie the two theories.

This calls attention to the second issue about the conditions of choice that we want to emphasize. We can assess the merits of the different theories in terms of the causal mechanisms upon which they rely. The economic theory posits contracting over transaction costs and competition, whereas the distributional theory posits asymmetries in bargaining power. Attention to these mechanisms will help us arbitrate cases in which the predictions of the two approaches identify the same direction and form of property rights change. Given that the two theories share a common assumption about the motivations of the actors, the differences in the theories reside in different claims about the context in which choice over institutional alternatives takes place.

To see this, consider again the choice of the SOE managers. An important factor affecting this choice is the possible existence of competing alternatives to the rights produced by the SOE managers. The distributional theory predicts that the SOE managers will produce property rights that give them the distributional advantage. But it relies on a particular mechanism to explain the production of those rights: asymmetries of bargaining power that allow them to establish the distributionally favorable rights. If the SOE managers were implementing private property rights schemes in an environment in which the various managers were in competition with each other for the economic benefits to be derived from these informal arrangements, then the bargaining advantage that they would otherwise enjoy would be mitigated by the existence of competition. This would call the explanation produced by the distribution theory into question. If the conditions under which the SOE managers make their decision were not characterized by such competition, then the bargaining mechanism central to the distribution theory would apply.

This is an example of how we might distinguish the two theories in a case in which the property rights are both Pareto improving and distributionally advantageous to the SOE managers. If the conditions of choice are such that the bargaining mechanism applies, this lends support to the distributional theory. If, rather, the conditions are such that the mechanism does not apply, then the plausibility of the economic theory is enhanced.

In summary, by focusing on questions of the social context in which institutional change occurs, we see how the economic and distributional theories can be treated in some ways as complementary accounts. Given a particular set of social conditions, one or the other approach will do the better job of explaining institutional change. From this perspective, we can better understand why the cases analyzed by Allio et al. are best explained by the distributional theory. The social conditions under which

353

privatization is presently taking place in Eastern Europe allow those actors who seek distributional advantage through a change in property rights to assert their relative bargaining advantage in the pursuit of those changes. Thus, it follows that the predictions derived from the distributional theory will be realized. It remains to be seen if the long-run consequences of these changes will be consistent with the present expectations of those actors.

This highlights a fundamental problem for actors who seek to change institutions: the unintended consequences of institutional change. In the process of deciding which form of an institution will maximize their own interests, social actors rely on their beliefs about the benefits that will be produced by the various institutional forms. But they will often be disappointed, as the causal theories they use to assess the consequences of social institutions will often be wrong. In such cases the beliefs and preferences on which they base their efforts at institutional change will not match the ultimate effects of those institutions. For those of us who seek to explain institutional change, the problem of unintended consequences complicates our efforts. When we seek to explain long-run trends in institutional change in terms of the preferences and expectations of the actors, and when the trends are characterized by unintended institutional effects, it becomes even more difficult to distinguish between the predictions of the economic and distributional theories.

REFERENCE

North, Douglass C., *Institutions, Institutional Change and Economic Performance* (Cambridge: Cambridge University Press, 1990).

Author index

Abreau, Dilip, 33
Akerlof, George A., 295
Alchian, Armen, 298
Aldrich, John, 122
Alesina, Alberto, 9, 27, 60, 84, 86n, 296n
Anderson, Terry L., 6
Andreff, Wladimir, 95
Andrews, Josephine, 87
Arrow, Kenneth, 9
Askildsen, Jan Eric, 333n
Austen-Smith, David, 299n

Balcerowicz, Leszek, 81
Banks, Jeffrey S., 299n, 300, 301n
Baron, David P., 300
Barro, Robert J., 296n
Barzel, Yoram, 3, 176
Bates, Robert H., 27, 50
Batt, Judy, 1
Baumol, William J., 6–7
Belka, Marek, 341n
Ben-Porath, Yoram, 153
Biersteker, Thomas J., 211
Bilous, Arthur, 55
Bim, Alexander, 91
Birdzell, L. E., Jr., 8, 12
Birman, Igor, 154
Blackburn, Keith, 12
Blanchard, Olivier, 247n
Blasi, Joseph, 91
Boardman, Anthony E., 5, 341n
Bonin, John P., 332
Borensztein, Eduardo, 247n
Borisova, Yevgenya, 171
Boycko, Maxim, 93, 97
Brada, Josef C., 81
Bresser Pereira, Luiz Carlos, 80n, 82
Bromley, Daniel W., 4, 5, 321
Bruno, Michael, 81, 329n
Buck, Trevor, 328

Calmfors, Lars, 295n
Calvert, Randall, 2–3, 20n, 114–16, 122
Calvo, Guillermo A., 21
Campbell, Robert W., 209
Capek, Ales, 200n
Carey, John M., 122n
Cheng Baorong, 267
Christensen, Michael, 12
Coase, Ronald, 4
Cohen, Gerald, 60
Comisso, Ellen, 1
Crane, George, 264
Crawford, Vincent, 299n, 303

Dabrowski, Janusz, 214, 218, 220
Davidheiser, Evelyn, 143
De Alessi, Louis, 5
Dell, Sidney, 211
Demsetz, Harold, 10, 155, 298, 322
Deng Xiaoping, 270
Dennis, Christopher, 59–60
de Soto, Hernando, 3, 176
Diermeier, Daniel, 34n
Djelic, Bozidar, 341
Dobek, Mariusz Mark, 183, 323n
Donahue, John D., 326n
Dornbusch, Rudiger, 247n
Duverger, Maurice, 57, 57n

Earle, John S., 88, 328, 337, 338, 342n
Eder, Santiago, 336–7
Edwards, Sebastian, 80
Eggertsson, Thrainn, 4, 20n, 153n, 209, 298, 322
Ellman, Michael, 100
Ericson, Richard, 161
Evans, Peter, 50

Faison, Seth, 284
Fama, Eugene, 243

Federowicz, Michal, 214, 218, 220
Fenno, Richard F., 114
Filatochev, Igor, 328
Fischer, Stanley, 247n
Frankel, Jacob A., 21
Friedman, James, 24n
Frydman, Roman, 85n, 88, 247n, 328, 337, 338, 342n
Frye, Timothy, 6, 38
Fudenberg, D., 27n
Furubotn, Eirik, 2

Gambetta, Diego, 38
Gelb, Alan, 81
Gendler, Leonid, 167
Gimpelson, Vladimir, 89
Gold, Thomas B., 261
Gorbachev, M. S., 125
Gorbatova, Larisa, 91, 95
Gordon, David B., 296n
Grossman, Gregory, 161
Grossman, Sanford, 85n
Gylfason, Thorvadur, 295n

Hagedorn, Jobst R., 305n
Hamada, Koichi, 296n
Hart, Oliver, 85n
Haspel, Moshe, 116n, 117, 123–4, 132, 144
Hausman, Henry, 332
Hayek, F. A., 297, 314
Heckathorn, Douglas D., 322n
Helliwell, John F., 9
Herles, Wolfgang, 296n
Hessenius, Helga, 295
Hesterly, William S., 340
Hibbs, Douglas A., Jr., 59–60, 296n
Hill, Charles W., 339
Holmlund, Bertil, 295n
Hopenhayn, Hugo, 316
Horn, Henrik, 295n

Inkeles, Alex, 8
Ireland, Norman J., 333n

Jackman, Richard, 295n
Jensen, Michael C., 4–5, 243, 339
Jin, Fang, 279–80
Johany, Ali D., 7
Johnson, Ronald N., 5
Johnson, Simon, 161, 328, 336–7
Jones, Anthony, 161
Jones, Derek C., 332
Jones, Eric L., 8, 12

Kahler, Miles, 50
Kalus, Adam, 223

Kaminski, Bartlomiej, 213
Kaminski, Tytus, 214, 220
Keefer, Philip, 8
Keohane, Robert, 22
Kiernan, Brendan, 119, 143
Kiewiet, D. Roderick, 116n, 117, 123–4, 132, 144
Kikeri, Sunita, 236
King, Arthur E., 81
Kirby, William C., 268
Kiss, Yudit, 93
Knack, Stephen, 8
Knight, Jack, 2, 11, 22, 182n, 259n, 324, 330–1
Konstantinov, Andrei, 157
Kopatsy, Sador, 247
Korbonski, Andrzej, 21
Kornai, Janos, 1, 5, 243n, 248n
Krajewski, Stefan, 341n
Kreps, David, 31n
Kroll, Heidi, 161, 163, 328
Krueger, Anne O., 27, 50, 237
Krugman, Paul, 247n
Kueh, Y. Y., 264
Kuhn, Philip A., 268
Kumar, Manmohan, 247n
Kuran, Timur, 14
Kutlimatov, Vladimir, 164–5
Kuzes, Irina, 93
Kydland, Finn E., 23n, 86, 296n

Laakso, Markku, 52n
Laver, Michael, 53, 300n
Layard, Richard, 247n, 295n
Leblang, David A., 8
Levine, Ross, 8
Levitas, Anthony, 213, 218
Levy, Brian, 12, 43n
Lewis, Steven, 259n, 276n
Libecap, Gary D., 5, 7, 10–11, 322
Liebskind, Julia, 340
Lijphart, Arend, 56, 57, 59n
Limongi, Fernando, 8, 21, 26
Limonov, Leonid, 168
Lin, Justin Yifu, 5
Lindbeck, Assar, 295n
Lindblom, Charles E., 9
Linz, Juan, 21, 116
Lipton, David, 247n
Liska, Tibor, 247
Litwack, John M., 7, 21, 154, 155, 161, 172
Lohmann, Susanne, 316, 317
Lott, John R., Jr., 5
Lueck, Dean, 6
Lundborg, Per, 295n
Lyons, Thomas P., 290

Author index

Machacek, Jan, 191, 192
Major, Ivan, 92
Maravall, Jose Maria, 80n, 82
Martin, Peter, 184n
Maser, Steven M., 322n
McChesney, Fred S., 6, 11, 323
McDonald, Ian M., 295n
McKelvey, Richard D., 9–10
McKinnon, Ronald, 44
Meade, James, 332
Meckling, William H., 4–5, 243, 339
Meyerson, Roger, 32n
Milgrom, Paul, 31n
Mizsei, Kalman, 240n, 241–2
Montinola, Gabriella, 44, 47, 275
Moore, John H., 5, 154
Moscoff, William, 161
Mroz, Bogdan, 216
Murrell, Peter, 5
Myagkov, Mikhail, 144

Nee, Victor, 261, 275, 276, 290, 291
Nellis, John R., 236
Nelson, Joan M., 80
Nelson, Lynn, 93
Nickell, Stephen, 295n
Nordhaus, William D., 296
North, Douglass C., 2, 8, 10, 11, 12, 20, 25–6, 36, 38, 43n, 44, 86, 134, 135, 140, 150, 182n, 213n, 321–4, 349
Nuti, Domenico Mario, 332, 338

Oates, Wallace, 46
O'Donnell, G., 38
Oi, Jean C., 47, 268, 275, 289–90
Olson, Mancur, 2, 5, 27, 38, 152, 324–5
Ordeshook, Peter, 10, 34–5
Ost, David, 213
Ostrom, Elinor, 5, 22, 145
Oswald, Andrew J., 295n
Ou, Zhiwei, 279–80

Pearce, David, 33
Pehe, Jiri, 203
Pejovich, Svetozar, 3
Perkins, Dwight, 259
Persson, Torsten, 84, 86n
Pinto, Brian, 341n
Pistor, Katarina, 91
Plott, Charles, 9–10
Popkin, Samuel, 291
Powell, G. Bingham, Jr., 53
Poznanski, Kazimierz, 213
Prescott, Edward C., 23n, 86, 296n
Przeworski, Adam, 8, 21, 27, 62, 68, 74, 80–2

Putnam, Robert D., 210
Putterman, Louis, 332

Qian, Yingyi, 44, 47, 268, 271, 275

Radigin, A. D., 88
Rae, Douglas W., 57
Rapaczynski, Andrzej, 85n, 88, 247n, 328, 337, 338, 342n
Reardon, Lawrence C., 264
Remington, Thomas F., 116n, 117, 123–4, 132, 143–4, 148
Renelt, David, 8
Riker, William H., 4, 10, 11, 14, 21, 44, 46, 57, 114–15, 262, 288, 298, 323
Roberts, John, 31n
Rodrik, Dani, 9, 12, 27, 81, 85
Roeder, Philip, 87
Root, Hilton, 12, 23–5, 43n, 151
Rosati, Dariusz, 81
Rose, Andrew K., 295
Rose, Richard, 93
Rosenberg, Nathan, 8, 12
Rostowski, Jacek, 226
Roubini, Nouriel, 52, 60
Rubinfeld, Daniel, 46
Rubinstein, Ariel, 36
Rudekavych, Lesia, 337
Rutgaizer, Vladimir, 88
Rutman, Mikhail, 162, 173

Sachs, Jeffrey D., 52, 247n
Sang, Bin Xue, 264, 283
Sazama, Gerald W., 200n
Schelling, Thomas, 24n, 160
Schmitter, P., 38
Schofield, Norman, 53, 300n
Schotter, Andrew, 2–3
Schroeder, Gertrude E., 1
Scully, Gerald W., 8, 9
Selten, Reinhard, 30
Sened, Itai, 11, 122–3, 297, 323
Shafik, Nemat, 233
Shepsle, Kenneth A., 10, 114
Shirk, Susan, 47–8
Shirley, Mary M., 236
Shlapentokh, Vladimir, 154, 161
Shleifer, Andrei, 21, 93, 97
Shugart, Matthew Soberg, 56, 122n
Siebert, Horst, 304
Sinn, Gerlinde, 294, 295, 307, 309n
Sinn, Hans-Werner, 294, 295, 307, 309n
Sirowy, Larry, 8
Slay, Ben, 228, 329
Slider, Darrell, 54
Slottje, Daniel J., 8

Author index

Smith, Steven S., 116n, 117, 123–4, 132, 143–4
Smyth, Regina A., 124, 128
Snell, Scott A., 339
Sobel, Joel, 299n, 303
Sobyanin, Alexander, 87, 116n, 124n
Solinger, Dorothy J., 1, 48
Solow, Robert M., 295n
Spence, Michael, 299, 300n
Spiller, Pablo T., 12, 43
Stacchetti, Ennio, 33
Staniszkis, Jadwiga, 327
Stark, David, 94, 216, 245–6, 328, 329
Steele, Jonathan, 120
Stiglitz, Joseph, 210
Strom, Kaare, 53
Su, Sijin, 261, 275, 276
Summers, Lawrence, 247n
Svensson, Lars E. O., 84, 86n
Szomburg, Jan, 214, 220
Szumanski, Andrzej, 220

Taagerpera, Rein, 52n
Tabellini, Guido, 33n, 84, 86n
Tanzi, Vito, 74
Tardos, Marton, 247
Teltschik, Horst, 306
Thayson, Uwe, 306
Thomas, Robert Paul, 8, 10, 11, 12, 38, 322, 323
Tirole, Jean, 27n
Tool, Marc R., 115n

Torstensson, Johan, 8
Tsukanova, Natalia, 341

Umbeck, John R., 10

Vanek, Jaroslav, 332
Vining, Aidan, 5, 341n
Vinton, Louisa, 56, 61n
Vishny, Robert, 21, 93, 97

Walder, Andrew, 275, 290
Ward, Benjamin, 332
Ward, Michael Don, 9
Wasylyk, Myron, 58
Webb, W. L., 56
Weimer, David L., 4, 5, 10, 21
Weingast, Barry R., 12, 24–6, 36, 43–7, 86, 134, 150, 262, 268, 271, 275, 288, 300
Whitehead, J., 38–9
Willgerodt, Hans, 304
Williamson, Oliver, 43n, 45
Wilson, Andrew, 55
Wilson, Robert, 31n
Winiecki, Jan, 241, 247n
Wolchik, Sharon, 186
Wong, Christine, 268
Wright, Mike, 328

Yellen, Janet L., 295

Zeckhauser, Richard, 12
Zenger, Todd R., 340

Subject index

agency problem, 243, 339
arbitration and credible commitment, 151, 153

bargaining, 210, 225, 232
   decentralization in, 225
   development of, 216
   and distributional theory, 324
   at enterprise level, 212–16, 234
   and institutional relationships, 239
   at international level, 211–12, 224
   at national level, 212, 234
Bielecki, Krzystof, 219
brinkmanship, 24
Burbulis, Gennadii, 120
buyouts, worker (management), 166, 252, 342

collective action; *see* free riders
commercialization, 242
   and private transactions, 245–6
   and property rights, 243–5
compensation for confiscated property, 250
constitutional choice, 135
contract enforcement, 33
cooperatives, 161–6
corporatization, 242
cost shifting, 329–30
credibility
   and arbitration, 160
   definition of, 183
   legislation and, 190
   measuring, 96–106
   of privately supplied information, 297
   of privatization, 91–5
   problems of, 85–6
   of Russian reform, 86–7
   sources of, 260

credible commitment, 8, 12, 20–5, 131
   and arbitration, 151, 153
   assessment of, 145
   and constitutions, 34–5
   devices of, 21–4, 85
   and federalism, 35–6
   and game theory, 27–35
   and general bargaining agreements ("pacts"), 38–9
   and government competition, 289
   and identification, 145
   of interest groups, 36–7
   and marketization, 43
   and nonarbitrary enforcement, 113
   and nonconfiscatory behavior, 113, 151–2, 156, 172, 175–7
   and personal ties, 291
   and privatization, 109–12, 209
   to process of reform, 127, 132, 145
   and strategic interaction, 25, 183
Czech Republic
   and Civic Democratic Party, 185, 192
   and Civic Forum, 185
   and Civic Movement, 185
   economic transformation in, 62, 63
   and Harvard Investment Fund, 195

decentralization, 44
   in bargaining, 225
   of federalism, 262
   fiscal, 289
   of investment regulation, 263–4, 266
   of property rights, 161, 167
   of regulatory authority, 270
   of state-owned enterprises, 241
decision making, 27
   dictatorial model of, 30–3
   federalism and, 35–6
   interest groups and, 36–7

and majority rule model, 33–5
and simple model, 28–30
Deng Xiaoping, 270
Dienstbier, Jiri, 185
distributional concerns, 183, 210, 247
distributional theory
 and cross-country comparisons, 341–5
 and informal bargaining, 324
 and informal privatization, 327, 329–31
 and institutional change, 11, 239, 319–21, 324–5
 and majority employee ownership, 334–5

East Germany
 and Comecon, 294
 and Communist Party, 308
 and unification, 303
 and unification treaty, 309
economic legality, 7, 155
economic performance rating, 68–9, 74
economic theory
 and informal privatization, 327, 329
 and institutional change, 10, 239, 320–3
 and majority employee ownership, 333–4
economic transition, 50–1
 and electoral systems, 53–9
 and government policies, 51–3
 and minority governments, 51–3
 and multi-party cabinets, 51–2
 and parliamentary fragmentation, 51
 and partisan governments, 59–61
 political factors in, 67–76
 and political volatility, 50, 147–9
 roll of governments in: active vs. passive, 314–18; historical, 61–7; Left–Right position and, 51, 59–62, 70, 78, 82
economics
 neoclassical, 4, 81, 217, 225, 320, 322
 neoinstitutional, 4
electoral formula, 56–7
expectations
 and credibility, 183
 and stability in change, 319

Fedorov, Boris, 105
Filatov, Sergei, 122
fiscal dependence
 and contracts, 277
 on profit sharing, 275
 on taxation, 277–9, 292
foreign investment, 184, 190–2, 195–8, 261, 263, 264, 271–5, 278, 323
 concentration of, 292

and enterprise competitiveness, 273
and regulatory enforcement, 280
and special jurisdictions of Shanghai, 282–4
free riders, 221, 316, 324

Gaider, Yegor, 55, 85, 92, 105, 136
game theoretic analysis (*see also* decision making; games), 27, 275–6, 298
games
 bargaining, 211–16; collective, 224; at enterprise level, 212–16, 234; at international level, 211–12, 224; at national level, 212, 234
 electoral and legislative, 127
 equilibriums in, 201–2; noncooperative, 122; pooling, 301; and Russian presidency, 119–21; separating, 301–2; and transition, 319
 and institutional choice, 115
 noncooperative, 25, 114
Gorbachev, Mikhail, 116–17
 and communist reform, 125–6, 161
 and demokratizatsiia, 118–19
 and preservation of Soviet Union, 119

Hungary
 and Communist Party, 241
 economic transformation of, 62, 63
 enterprise councils of, 240
 and Laws on Transformation, 244
 and State Property Agency (SPA), 243–5, 251–2

information asymmetry, 299, 302
information transmission
 and aggregation, 314–18
 and credibility, 297, 302
 through investment, 298, 300–3; in German unification, 304–10
 signaling game of, 299–300, 314–16
institutional change, 15, 182, 288
 definition of, 239
 and distributional theory, 11, 239, 320, 324–5, 327, 329–31
 and economic theory, 10, 239, 320, 322–3, 327
 and expectations, 319
 and Pareto efficiency, 319–22
 and path dependence, 321
 and public choice theory, 11, 239, 320, 323–4, 330
institutional structure, 225, 226
 in contract enforcement, 289
 inheritance of, 232
institutions
 and communication, 122, 140

and coordination, 122–4, 140
and credible commitment, 20, 26–30,
37–40, 86, 140
and expectations, 2–3
fixed, 118–19
formal, 2, 20, 259, 268
informal, 2, 20, 259, 268–71; and credible property rights, 279–81
as outcomes of games, 114
interenterprise debt (IED) trading, 226

Jezek, Tomas, 196
Jiang Zemin, 269

Kadar, Bela, 248
Khasbulatov, Ruslan, 121, 140, 143, 148
Klaus, Vaclav, 66, 185–7, 192, 196
Kohl, Helmut, 296
Kovac, Michal, 190
Kozeny, Viktor, 195
Kupa, Mihaly, 248

Left–Right continuum, 59–61, 70, 82–3,
131–2, 144, 186
liquidation as means of privatization,
219–22, 224
local corporatist theory, 289
defined, 275
and state-centered approach, 289–90,
292
tested, 275–81

market-preserving federalism, 13, 26,
44–6
and competition between local governments, 260, 288
conditions of, 44–5
and decentralization, 44; vs. economic
advantage, 271–5
de facto, 45
definition of, 262
de jure, 45
elements of, 268
limitations of, 288–9
self-enforcing, 46–8
marketization, 43, 259
Meciar, Vladimir, 66, 185, 187, 199–201,
337

Olszewski, Jan, 219
organized labor
in East Germany, 295, 335–7
in Poland (*see also* Poland, and Solidarity), 208, 214–15, 218
in Russia, 89

pacts, 38–9
German "solidarity pact," 39
Polish "social pact," 222
Polish State Enterprise Pact, 223; and
collective bargaining, 224
Pareto efficiency, 4, 29
and improvements, 239
and institutional change, 319–23
and transaction costs, 10–11
parliamentary fragmentation, 51, 69, 73
and economic reform, 221
electoral systems and, 53–9; majoritarian, 57–8; mixed, 57–8; modified
proportional representation and, 56–
7; nonparty elections and, 54–5, 58,
69, 78; pure proportional representation and, 55–6, 78
and government cohesion, 77
Pawlak, Waldemar, 222, 344
Poland
and Act on the Privatization of State-
Owned Enterprises, 225
and Balcerowicz Plan, 82, 214
and Communist Party, 55, 213
and Conservative Party, 224
and Council for Mutual Economic Assistance (CMEA), 218
and economic transition, 62
and Ministry of Ownership Transformation, 212, 218–20, 224, 226
and National Investment Fund, 222
and organized labor, 208, 215, 222;
and Peasant Party, 82, 224
and Solidarity, 55, 62, 208, 213, 218,
222, 224, 233–5
and stabilization-cum-transformation
program, 234–5
and United Democratic Left, 224
and wage controls (*popiwek*), 218, 223
post-communist "natural experiment," 1,
15, 346
preferences, 114
changing, 147–8
government, 300
private firms
and cooperatives, 162–3
and leasing, 163–4; and worker
buyouts, 166
and legalization, 162, 184
and problems with local governments,
150–2
and registration, 162
privatization, 60, 68, 80, 208, 236, 251–3
and arbitration, 150–2
and collective action, 220
and commercialization, 242–5; and
transferability, 245

and controversy, 191–2
and corporatization, 242
and cost-free transfer, 199, 246, 340–4
in Czech Republic, 14, 182–3
and direct (capital) sales, 14, 199–201, 217, 226, 236, 246, 248–9, 340–3
and economic growth, 76
and foreign investment, 184, 190–2, 195–8, 261, 263, 264, 271–5
and free riders, 221, 316
in Hungary, 14, 239–40
"informal," 242–3, 326–31; cost-shifting and, 329–30; distributional theory and, 327, 329–31; economic theory and, 327, 329; forms and, 327–8; role of governments and, 326–7
as institutional change, 182, 239
joint-stock companies and, 199
large firms and, 192; credibility in, 208, 226; stability in, 215–16
and leasing, 152, 156, 166–72
and liquidation, 218–20, 222, 224–8
and majority employee ownership, 332; and distributional theory, 334–5, 337–8; and economic theory, 333–4; and inefficiency, 333; and public choice theory, 334, 339, 343–5
managerial, 258
"mass," 225, 247, 336
and path dependency, 245–6, 253, 321
in Poland, 14, 208, 225, 232
and recentralization, 240
via restitution; and commercial property, 188; and land, 189–90
revenues from, 294
in Russia, 84–5
in St. Petersburg, 13, 150–2
in Slovakia, 14, 182–3
and small firms, 190–2
spontaneous, 240–3, 249, 326
voucher, 14, 84, 187–8; and compensation notes, 250–1; and credibility, 94–5; and prices, 97–100, 105–6; and transferability, 92, 194; Yeltsin and, 94, 100–4
property rights, 1
and bargaining, 210, 225, 232; at enterprise level, 212–16, 234; at international level, 211–12, 224; at national level, 212, 234
clarity of allocation of, 4–5
confiscation of, 151, 168, 175–6, 250
cost of allocation of, 5–6
credibility of, 7–8, 11–12, 14, 30, 33, 34; and fiscal dependence, 277–9;

and informal institutions, 279–81; sources of, 260, 262, 275
de facto, 240
definition of, 3, 209
formal, 151–6, 220; through arbitration, 153
informal, 151–6, 220
as institutions, 2–3, 182, 210, 232, 246
and leasing, 152; and contract violations, 169; and disputes, 170–2
political implications of, 9–10
and rational choice, 114–16
and security, 6–7, 35
systems of, 1, 20
taxation and, 152, 172–5; and confiscation of profits, 172, 174–5; and credibility, 276; types of, 174
and transformation, 10–11
property types, 4–6
public choice theory
and cross-country comparisons, 343–5
and informal privatization, 326, 330
and institutional choice, 11, 239, 320–1, 323–4
and majority employee ownership, 334, 343–5

Rakowski, Mieczyslaw, 82
rational choice and property rights, 114–16
rent seeking, 241, 288
Russia
and Communist Party, 119; and apparatchiks, 119, 125
and Congress of People's Deputies (CPD), 101, 113–15, 117; coordination problems of, 122–4; and creation of presidency, 119, 124–31; history of, 119–22
and coup attempt, 119, 123, 132–3
and *democratizatsiia*, 116, 118–19
and economic transformation, 63
and Federal Assembly, 140
and Federation of Independent Trade Unions (FITUR), 89
and perestroika, 116, 118, 124–5
and Russian Federation, 139
and Russian Union of Industrialists and Entrepreneurs (RUIE), 89, 100
and State Privatization Agency (GKI), 88, 90–1, 93–5, 102, 103
and State Privatization Program, 87, 90, 92, 100
and voucher privatization, 84, 92–4, 104; and credibility, 96–103
Rutskoi, Alexander, 104, 140

Subject index

St. Petersburg
and Arbitration Court, 150, 167, 171, 174
and Gosarbitrazh (State Arbitration Court), 156–60, 163, 165
and Investment-Tender Commission (ITC), 168
and Law on Cooperatives, 165
and Law on Enterprises and Entrepreneurship, 163, 165–7
and Law on Property, 163
and Law on State Enterprises, 161, 163
and Mayor's Committee for Economic Development, 168
and Mayor's Committee for the Management of State Property (KUGI), 165, 169–70
secondary markets, 228, 250
self-interest
of business executives, 248
of government players, 117, 300; and electoral support, 253, 296–7; and institutional change, 319, 323–4; modeled, 128–31
Shanghai
and centralist planned economies (CPEs), 260
and Communist Party, 269
and Economic and Technological Development Zones (ETDZs), 264–5, 271–5
and economic development zones, 261, 263, 266–7
and Pudong New Area, 264–7, 278, 281
and special economic jurisdictions, 282–4
and Township and Village Enterprises (TVEs), 260
"shock treatment" (*see also* Yeltsin, Boris, and "shock therapy"), 217
Slovakia
and Christian Democratic Movement, 185
and economic transformation, 63
and Movement for a Democratic Slovakia, 185

and Movement for an Independent Slovakia, 186
and Public against Violence, 185
Sobchak, Anatolii, 157
stabilization, 60, 68
and Balcerowicz Plan, 216–17
and economic growth, 76
successful, 73–5, 80
stabilization-cum-transformation program, 234–5
strategic interaction, 26–30, 240
and credible commitment, 25–6, 183
and expectations, 183
and signaling, 299–300
structural adjustment, 80
Suchocka, Hanna, 222

Tambovtsev, Alexander, 173–4
taxation
and credibility, 172–5
deadweight losses from, 300
fiscal dependence on, 275, 277–9, 292
and foreign investment, 282–4, 292
transaction costs, 140, 322, 335–6

uncertainty, 104
economic, 176
as obstacle to change, 122–3, 140
of players, 141
about property rights, 180
about rules, 291

Verkhovna, Rada, 55
Volskii, Arkadii, 100

wage controls, 218, 223
Walesa, Lech, 56, 224

Yeltsin, Boris, 84, 87, 126, 155
extraordinary powers of, 87, 106, 113, 119–21, 123–4, 132, 134, 139
and "shock therapy," 109, 124, 133–4
and voucher privatization, 94, 100–4

Zhirinovski, Vladimir, 105
Zhu Rongji, 269
Zorkin, Valerii, 121

363